Rick _,

BARCELONA

CONTENTS

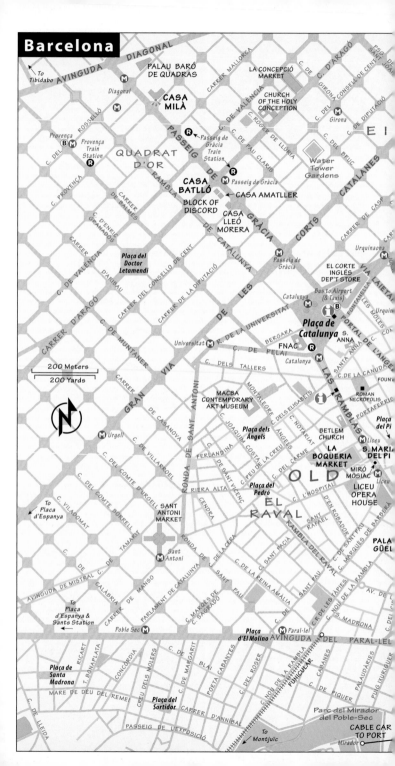

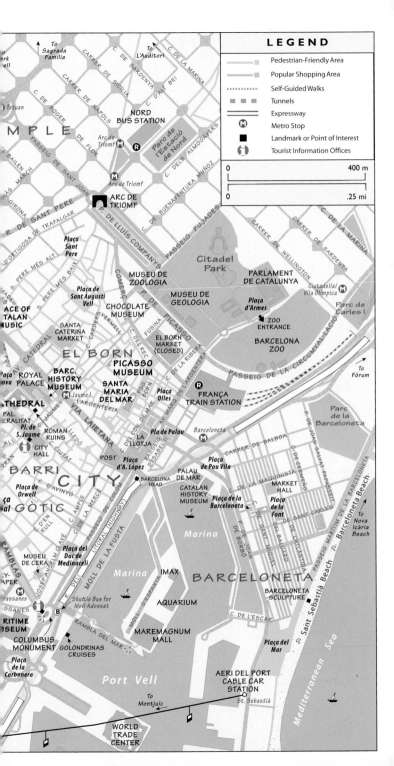

LEGEND

	Pedestrian-Friendly Area
	Popular Shopping Area
·········	Self-Guided Walks
▪ ▪ ▪	Tunnels
	Expressway
Ⓜ	Metro Stop
▪	Landmark or Point of Interest
🛈	Tourist Information Offices

0 ————————————— 400 m

0 ————————————— .25 mi

To Sagrada Familia

To L'Auditori

CARRER DE SICILIA

C. DE SARDENYA

C. DE LA MARINA

CARRER DE NAPOLS

C. D'ALI BEI

) Tetuan

DE ROGER DE FLOR

NORD BUS STATION

PASSEIG DE SANT JOAN

Arc de Triomf Ⓜ Ⓡ

Parc de l'Estació de Nord

C. DELS ALMOGÀVERS

MPLE

I BAILEN MARCH

GIRONA

Arc de Triomf Ⓜ

C. DE BUENAVENTURA MUÑOZ

R. DE SANT PERE

C. DE LLUÍS COMPANYS

ARC DE TRIOMF

PASSEIG PUJADES

CARRER DE WELLINGTON

CARRER DE LA MARINA

C. DE SARDENYA

D'ORTIGOSA DE TRAFALGAR

Plaça Sant Pere

Citadel Park

PARLAMENT DE CATALUNYA

Ciutadella/ Vila Olímpica Ⓜ

Parc de Carles I

R. PERE MÉS ALT

Plaça de Sant Agustí Vell

MUSEU DE ZOOLOGIA

MUSEU DE GEOLOGIA

Plaça d'Armes

ACE OF TALAN USIC

R. PERE MÉS BAIX

SANTA CATERINA MARKET

CHOCOLATE MUSEUM

P. DE PICASSO

↘ ZOO ENTRANCE

BARCELONA ZOO

EL BORN

VERMELL

C. DEL REC

EL BORN MARKET (CLOSED)

PASSEIG DE LA CIRCUMVAL·LACIÓ

To Fòrum

aça ova

ROYAL PALACE

BARC. HISTORY MUSEUM

PICASSO MUSEUM

SANTA MARIA DEL MAR

C. DE LA RIBERA

CARDERS

Ⓜ Jaume I

L'ARGENTERIA

Plaça Olles

Ⓡ

FRANÇA TRAIN STATION

Parc de la Barceloneta

THEDRAL

PAL ERALITAT

Pl. de S. Jaume

🛈 ROMAN RUINS

CITY HALL

VIA LAIETANA

C. DE JAUME I

LLEDÓ

C. DE L'ARGENTERIA

DE LA BÒRIA

C. DE LA PRINCESA

C. DE LA MAR

P.G. BORN

C. DE MONTCADA

Pla de Palau

Barceloneta Ⓜ

P. DE JOAN SALVAT-PAPASSEIT

BARRI CITY

Plaça de Orwell

C. D'AVINYO

C. AMPLE

C. DE LA MERCÈ

PASSEIG DE COLOM

POST

LA LLOTJA

Plaça d'A. López

BARCELONA HEAD

PALAU DE MAR

CATALAN HISTORY MUSEUM

Plaça de Pau Vila

CARRER DE BALBOA

MARKET HALL

CARRER DE CERMEÑO

ça al

GÒTIC

C. D'EN RULL

C. D'EN CARABASSA

C. DE LA MERCÈ

LITORAL HIGHWAY

Plaça de la Barceloneta

Plaça de la Font

C. DE SANT CARLES

To Nova Icària Beach

Marina

Barceloneta Beach

MUSEU DE CERA

Y-PER

rassanes

Plaça del Duc de Medinaceli

JOSEP ANSELM CLAVÉ

MOLL DE LA FUSTA

R. DEL DELS

Marina

IMAX

BARCELONETA

SANT SEBASTIÀ Beach

PASSEIG MARÍTIM DE LA BARCELONETA

SSANES

Shuttle Bus for Moll Adossat

Ⓑ

BARCELONETA SCULPTURE

RITIME SEUM

🛈

RAMBLA DEL MAR

AQUARIUM

C. DE L'ESCAR

Mediterranean Sea

COLUMBUS MONUMENT

GOLONDRINAS CRUISES

MAREMAGNUM MALL

Plaça del Mar

Plaça de la Carbonera

Port Vell

AERI DEL PORT CABLE CAR STATION

To Montjuïc

St. Sebastià

WORLD TRADE CENTER

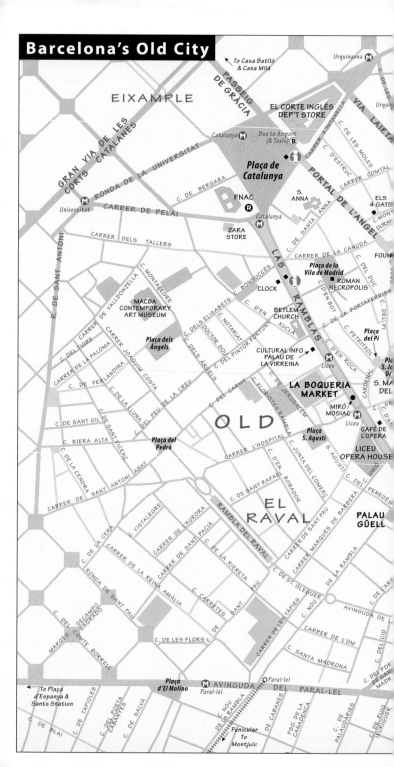

Barcelona's Old City

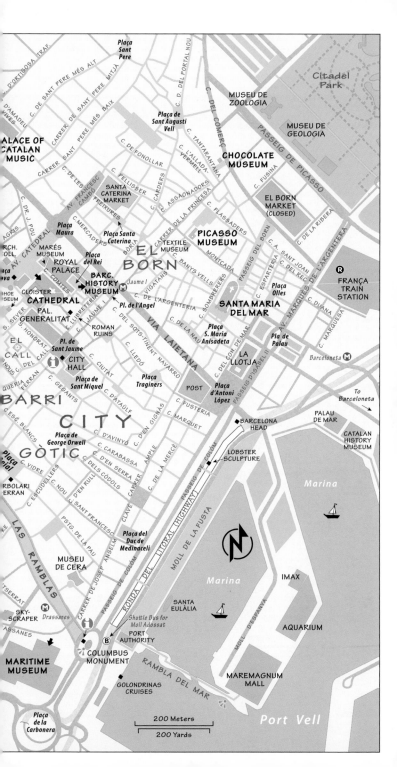

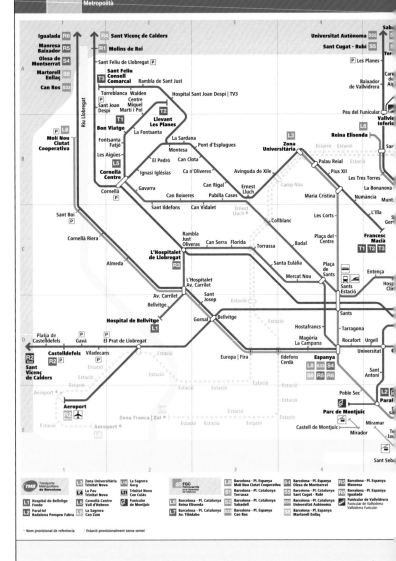

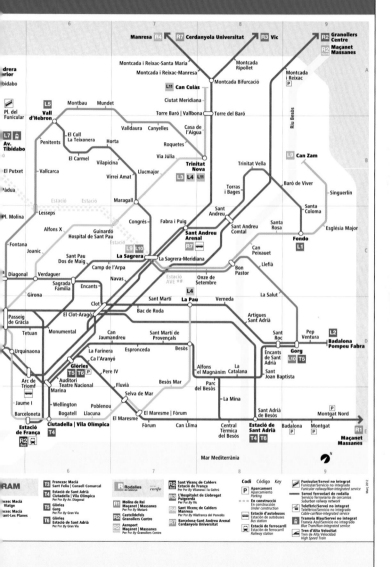

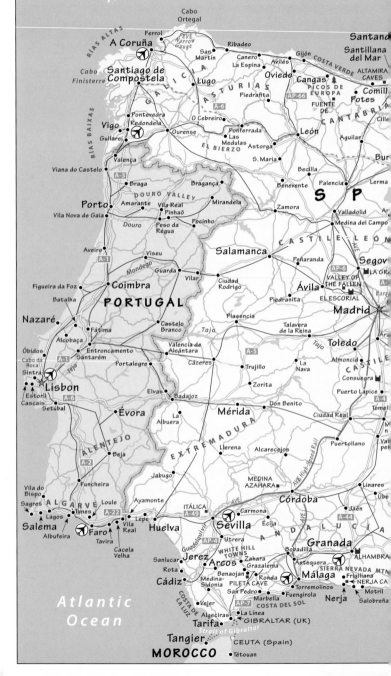

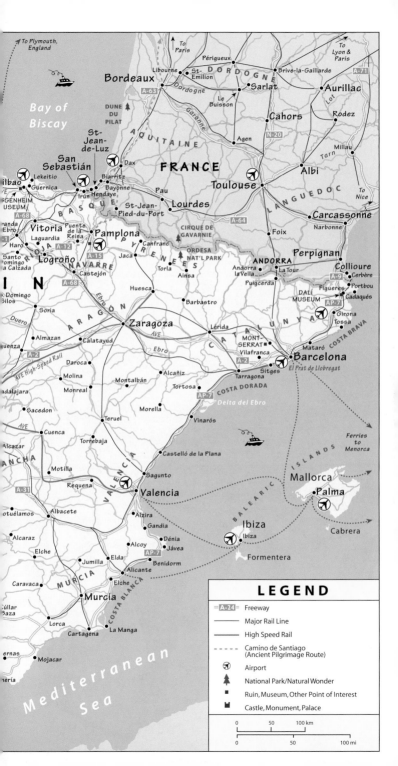

Rick Steves'®

BARCELONA

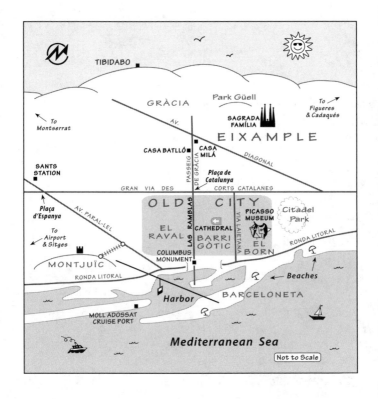

AVALON
TRAVEL

INTRODUCTION

If you're in the mood to surrender to a city's charms, let it be in Barcelona. Spain's second city bubbles with life in its narrow Barri Gòtic alleys, along the pedestrian boulevard called the Ramblas, in the funky bohemian quarter of El Born, and throughout the chic, grid-planned new part of town called the Eixample. Its Old City is made for seeing on foot, full of winding lanes that emerge into secluded squares dotted with palm trees and ringed with cafés and boutiques. The waterfront bristles with life, overlooked by the park-like setting of Montjuïc. Everywhere you go, you'll find the city's architecture to be colorful, playful, and unique. Rows of symmetrical ironwork balconies are punctuated with fanciful details: bay windows, turrets, painted tiles, hanging lanterns, flower boxes, and carved reliefs.

As the capital of the Catalan people, Barcelona is full of history. You'll see Roman ruins, a medieval cathedral, twisty Gothic lanes, and traces of Columbus and the sea trade. By the late 19th century, the city had boomed into an industrial powerhouse and a cradle of Modernism. A teenage Picasso lived in Barcelona right when he was on the verge of reinventing painting; his legacy is today's Picasso Museum. Catalan architects, including Antoni Gaudí, Lluís Domènech i Montaner, and Josep Puig i Cadafalch, forged the Modernista style and remade the city's skyline with curvy, playful fantasy buildings—culminating in Gaudí's over-the-top Sagrada Família, a church still under construction. Salvador Dalí and Joan Miró join the long list of world-changing 20th-century artists with ties to this city.

Today's Barcelona is as vibrant as ever. Locals still join hands and dance the everyone's-welcome *sardana* in front of the cathedral every weekend. Neighborhood festivals jam the events calendar. The cafés are filled by day, and people crowd the streets at night, pausing

Map Legend

⅃.	Viewpoint	✈	Airport	)▭(	Tunnel
↑	Entrance	Ⓣ	Taxi Stand		Pedestrian Zone
❶	Tourist Info	▆	Tram Stop		
WC	Restroom	Ⓑ	Bus Stop	- - - - -	Railway
⬛	Castle	Ⓜ	Metro Stop	....	Ferry/Boat Route
⬆	Church	Ⓡ	Rodalies Rail Stop	⊢——⊣	Tram
✿	Synagogue	Ⓟ	Parking	⅏⅏⅏⅏	Stairs
▪	Statue/Point of Interest	)(	Mountain Pass	- - - - -	Walk/Tour Route
		⬚	Park		
⊠	Elevator	◉	Fountain	- - - - - -	Trail

Use this legend to help you navigate the maps in this book.

to fortify themselves with a perfectly composed bite of seafood and a drink at a tapas bar. Barcelona's lively culture is on an unstoppable roll in Spain's most cosmopolitan and European corner.

About This Book

Rick Steves' Barcelona is a tour guide in your pocket. In this book, you'll find the following chapters:

Orientation to Barcelona includes specifics on public transportation, helpful hints, local tour options, easy-to-read maps, and tourist information. The "Planning Your Time" section suggests a schedule for how to best use your limited time.

Sights in Barcelona describes the top attractions and includes their cost and hours.

Four **Self-Guided Walks** cover Barcelona's most enjoyable neighborhoods: the Ramblas promenade, historic Barri Gòtic, trendy El Born, and a Modernista paradise, the Eixample.

The **Self-Guided Tours** lead you through Barcelona's most fascinating museums and sights: the Cathedral of Barcelona, the Picasso Museum, and two architectural gems, Gaudí's Sagrada Família and Park Güell.

Sleeping in Barcelona describes my favorite hotels, from good-value deals to cushy splurges.

Eating in Barcelona serves up a range of options, from inexpensive tapas bars to fancy restaurants.

Barcelona with Children includes my top recommendations for keeping your kids (and you) happy in Barcelona.

Shopping in Barcelona gives you tips for shopping painlessly and enjoyably, without letting it overwhelm your vacation or ruin your budget.

INTRODUCTION

Key to This Book

Updates

This book is updated regularly—but things change. For the latest, visit www.ricksteves.com/update, and for a valuable list of reports and experiences—good and bad—from fellow travelers, check www.ricksteves.com/feedback.

Abbreviations and Times

I use the following symbols and abbreviations in this book:

Sights are rated:

▲▲▲	Don't miss
▲▲	Try hard to see
▲	Worthwhile if you can make it
No rating	Worth knowing about

Tourist information offices are abbreviated as **TI,** and bathrooms are **WCs.** To categorize accommodations, I use a **Sleep Code** (described on page 172).

Like Europe, this book uses the **24-hour clock.** It's the same as ours through 12:00 noon, then keeps going: 13:00, 14:00, and so on. For anything over 12, subtract 12 and add p.m. (14:00 is 2:00 p.m.).

When giving **opening times,** I include both peak-season and off-season hours if they differ. So, if a museum is listed as "May-Oct daily 9:00-16:00," it should be open from 9 a.m. until 4 p.m. from the first day of May until the last day of October (but expect exceptions).

If you see a ✪ symbol near a sight listing, it means that sight is described in far greater detail elsewhere—either with its own self-guided tour, or as part of a self-guided walk.

For **transit** or **tour departures,** I first list the frequency, then the duration. So, a train connection listed as "2/hour, 1.5 hours" departs twice each hour, and the journey lasts an hour and a half.

Nightlife in Barcelona is your guide to fun, including classical concerts, nightclubs and after-hours hangouts, flamenco performances, and jazz clubs.

Barcelona Connections lays the groundwork for your smooth arrival and departure, covering transportation by train, plane, and bus (with detailed information on Barcelona's Sants train station and El Prat de Llobregat airport), plus the basics on the city's cruise ship docks.

Day Trips from Barcelona covers nearby sights: Figueres, Cadaqués, Sitges, and Montserrat.

Barcelona: Past and Present gives the background of this city and its region, including a timeline of Barcelona history, information about famous Catalans, and a rundown of contemporary events.

The **appendix** is a traveler's tool kit, with telephone tips, useful phone numbers, recommended books and films, a festival list, a climate chart, a handy packing checklist, a hotel reservation form, and Spanish and Catalan survival phrases.

Browse through this book and select your favorite sights. Then have a *meravellós* trip! Traveling like a temporary local, you'll get the absolute most out of every mile, minute, and dollar. As you visit places I know and love, I'm happy you'll be meeting my favorite Catalans.

Planning

This section will help you get started on planning your trip—with advice on trip costs, when to go, and what you should know before you take off.

Travel Smart

Your trip to Barcelona is like a complex play: It's easier to follow and really appreciate on a second viewing. While no one does the same trip twice to gain that advantage, reading this book in its entirety before your trip accomplishes much the same thing.

Design an itinerary that enables you to visit sights at the best possible times. Note holidays and specifics on sights, such as days they are closed or most crowded (all covered in this book). You can wait in line at the Sagrada Família, or get advance reservations and bypass the queue without breaking a sweat. Day-tripping to the Dalí Theater-Museum in Figueres on Monday during the off-season is a waste, since it's closed. Be careful on the first Sunday of the month; some sights such as Palau Güell and the Catalan Art Museum are jammed because they're free. A smart trip is a puzzle—a fun, doable, and worthwhile challenge.

Be sure to mix intense and relaxed periods in your itinerary. Every trip—and every traveler—needs slack time (laundry, picnics, people-watching, and so on). Pace yourself. Assume you will return.

Get online at Internet cafés or your hotel, and buy a phone card or carry a mobile phone: You can find tourist information, learn the latest on sights (special events, tour schedule, etc.), book tickets and tours, make reservations, reconfirm hotels, research transportation connections, and keep in touch with your loved ones.

Enjoy the friendliness of the Spanish people. Connect with the culture. Set up your own quest for the best square, cloister, tapas bar, or whatever. Ask questions—most locals are eager to point you in their idea of the right direction. Slow down and be open to unexpected experiences. Keep a notepad in your pocket for confirming prices, noting directions, and organizing your thoughts. Wear your money belt, learn the currency, and figure out how to estimate prices in dollars. Those who expect to travel smart, do.

Trip Costs

Five components make up your trip costs: airfare, surface transportation, room and board, sightseeing and entertainment, and shopping and miscellany.

Airfare: A basic round-trip flight from the US to Barcelona can cost, on average, about $1,000-1,800 total, depending on where you fly from and when (cheaper in winter).

Surface Transportation: A 10-ride Metro card costs about $12. For round-trip train rides to day-trip destinations, allow about $10 for Sitges, $24 for Montserrat, and $40 for Figueres. To travel between El Prat airport and Barcelona, figure (one-way) $4 by train, $8 by bus, or $40 by taxi.

Room and Board: You can manage comfortably in Barcelona on $130 a day per person for room and board. This allows $5 for breakfast, $15 for lunch, $25 for dinner, and $85 for lodging (based on two people splitting the cost of a $170 double room). Students and tightwads can do it for as little as $80 a day ($45 for a bed, $35 for meals and snacks).

Sightseeing and Entertainment: It's worth considering the $40 Articket BCN sightseeing pass, which admits you to six museums, including the recommended Picasso Museum, Catalan Art Museum, and Fundació Joan Miró (for more information, see page 31). Otherwise, figure about $17 per major sight (Picasso Museum-$14, Casa Milà-$20, Sagrada Família-$17), and $10 for others. An evening concert at the Palace of Catalan Music costs about $30-40 per person. An overall average of $30 a day works for most people. Don't skimp here. After all, this category is the driving force behind your trip—you came to sightsee, enjoy, and experience Barcelona.

Shopping and Miscellany: Figure roughly $3 per coffee, ice-cream cone, or soft drink. Shopping can vary in cost from nearly nothing to a small fortune. Good budget travelers find that this category has little to do with assembling a trip full of lifelong and wonderful memories.

When to Go

Sea breezes off the Mediterranean and a generally warm climate make Barcelona pleasant for much of the year. Late spring and early fall offer the best combination of good weather, light crowds, long days, and plenty of tourist and cultural activities. You'll encounter hot, humid weather and the biggest crowds in July and August,

"You're Not in Spain, You're in Catalunya!"

This is a popular nationalistic refrain you might see on T-shirts or stickers around town. Catalunya is *not* the land of bullfighting and flamenco that many visi- tors envision when they think of Spain (best to visit Madrid or Sevilla for those).

The region of Catalunya, with Barcelona as its capital, has its own language, history, and culture. Its people—10 mil- lion strong—have a proud, independent spirit. Historically, Catalunya ("Cataluña" in Span- ish, sometimes spelled "Catalonia" in English) has often been at odds with the central Spanish government in Madrid. The Catalan language and culture were discouraged or even out- lawed at various times in history, as Catalunya often chose the wrong side in wars and rebellions against the kings in Madrid. In the Spanish Civil War (1936-1939), Catalunya was one of the last pockets of democratic resistance against the military coup of the fascist dictator Francisco Franco, who punished the region with four decades of repression. During that time, the Catalan flag was banned—but locals vented their national spirit by flying their football team's flag instead.

Three of Barcelona's monuments are reminders of royal and Franco-era suppression. Citadel Park (Parc de la Ciutadella) was originally a much-despised military citadel, constructed in the 18th century to keep locals in line. The Castle of Montjuïc, built for similar reasons, has been the site of numerous political exe- cutions, including hundreds during the Franco era. The Sacred Heart Church atop Tibidabo, completed under Franco, was meant to atone for the sins of Barcelonans during the Spanish Civil War—the main sin being opposition to Franco. Although rivalry between Barcelona and Madrid has calmed down in recent times, it rages any time the two cities' main football clubs meet.

To see real Catalan culture, look for the *sardana* dance or an exhibition of *castellers* (both described on page 50). The main symbol of Catalunya is the dragon, which was slain by St.

and some shops and restaurants close down in August. Winter temperatures are far from freezing, but rainfall is abundant.

Know Before You Go

Your trip is more likely to go smoothly if you plan ahead. Check this list of things to arrange while you're still at home.

You need a **passport**—but no visa or shots—to travel in

George ("Jordi" in Catalan)—the region's patron saint. You'll find dragons all over Barcelona, along with the Catalan flag—called the Senyera—with four horizontal red stripes on a gold field. Nineteenth-century Catalan Romantics embraced a vivid story about the origins of their flag: In the ninth century, Wilfred the Hairy—a count of Barcelona and one of the founding fathers of Catalunya—was wounded in battle. A grateful neighboring king rewarded Wilfred's bravery with a copper shield and ran Wilfred's four bloody fingers across its surface, leaving four red stripes. While almost certainly false, this legend hints at the nostalgic mood in 19th-century Barcelona, when the Renaixença (Catalan cultural revival) prodded historians to dig deeply into their medieval past to revive obscure historical figures and lend legitimacy to the resurgent Catalan nation.

The Catalan language is irrevocably tied to the history and spirit of the people here. After the end of the Franco era in the mid-1970s, the language made a huge comeback. Schools are now required by law to conduct all classes in Catalan; most school-age children learn Catalan first and Spanish second. While all Barcelonans still speak Spanish, nearly all understand Catalan, three-quarters speak Catalan, and half can write it.

Most place names in this book are listed in Catalan. Here's how to pronounce the city's major landmarks:

Plaça de Catalunya	PLAS-sah duh kah-tah-LOON-yah
Eixample	eye-SHAM-plah
Passeig de Gràcia	PAH-sage duh GRAH-see-ah
Catedral	KAH-tah-dral
Barri Gòtic	BAH-ree GOH-teek
El Born	el BORN
Montjuïc	mohn-jew-EEK

When finding your way, these terms will come in useful:

exit	*sortida*	sor-TEE-dah
square	*plaça*	PLAS-sah
street	*carrer*	kah-REHR
boulevard	*passeig*	PAH-sage
avenue	*avinguda*	ah-veen-GOO-dah

For more Catalan words, see the survival phrases on page 309.

Spain. You may be denied entry into certain European countries if your passport is due to expire within three to six months of your ticketed date of return. Get it renewed if you'll be cutting it close. It can take up to six weeks to get or renew a passport (for more on passports, see www.travel.state.gov). Pack a photocopy of your passport in your luggage in case the original is lost or stolen.

Book rooms well in advance if you'll be traveling during peak season (July-Sept) or on any major holidays (see page 300).

You'll also need **reservations** if you want to visit the Salvador Dalí House near Cadaqués (see page 249). It's a good idea to reserve ahead for the Picasso Museum and Sagrada Família, especially in the busy summer months (see listings in Sights in Barcelona chapter).

Call your **debit- and credit-card companies** to let them know the countries you'll be visiting, to ask about fees, request your PIN (it will be mailed to you), and more. See page 12 for details.

Do your homework if you want to buy **travel insurance.** Compare the cost of the insurance to the likelihood of your using it and your potential loss if something goes wrong. Also, check whether your existing insurance (health, homeowners, or renters) covers you and your possessions overseas. For more tips, see www.ricksteves.com/insurance.

All **high-speed trains** (AVE) in Spain require a seat reservation, but it's usually possible to make arrangements in Spain just a few days ahead unless it's a holiday weekend. (For more on train travel, see page 283 and www.ricksteves.com/rail.)

If you're planning on **renting a car** for travels beyond Barcelona, you'll need your driver's license and an International Driving Permit (see page 290).

If you plan to hire a **local guide,** reserve ahead by email. Popular guides can get booked up.

If you're bringing a **mobile device,** download any apps you might want to use on the road, such as translators, maps, and transit schedules. Check out **Rick Steves Audio Europe,** featuring hours of free travel interviews and other audio content about Spain (via www.ricksteves.com/audioeurope, iTunes, Google Play, or the Rick Steves Audio Europe smartphone app; for details, see page 295).

Check the **Rick Steves guidebook updates** page for any recent changes to this book (www.ricksteves.com/update).

Because **airline carry-on restrictions** are always changing, visit the Transportation Security Administration's website (www.tsa.gov/travelers) for an up-to-date list of what you can bring on the plane with you, and what you must check.

Practicalities

Emergency and Medical Help: In **Spain,** dial 091 or 092 for police help and 112 in any emergency (medical or otherwise). If you get sick, do as the Spanish do and go to a pharmacist for advice. Or ask at your hotel for help; the desk staff knows where to find the nearest medical and emergency services.

Theft or Loss: To replace a passport, you'll need to go in per-

Barcelona Almanac

Population: Approximately 1.6 million.

Languages: Spanish and Catalan are the two official languages of Catalunya, but Catalan is the preferred language in schools and offices. Catalan is not a dialect of Spanish, but an independent language.

Currency: Euro (€)

City Layout: The tangled Gothic Quarter (Barri Gòtic) lies at the heart of the city, edged by the connected boulevards of the Ramblas. The more orderly Eixample district spreads north of the old city, while unassuming Barceloneta spills along the seafront. Looking down over it all is the big Montjuïc hill.

Tourist Tracks: Every year, 7.4 million people visit Barcelona. The bustling center for tourists and locals is the Ramblas, which sees more than 150,000 people daily. Avinguda del Portal de l'Angel is Spain's most walked street, trod upon by 3,500 pairs of feet every hour.

Architecture: Barcelona is home to the Modernista style championed by Catalan architect Antoni Gaudí, whose most famous work is the Sagrada Família church. Nearly 30 of his buildings are scattered throughout the greater Barcelona area.

Fun in the Sun: Until 1992, when the city hosted the Olympic Games, Barcelona had only one small beachfront area, in Barceloneta. Other waterfront property was taken up by industrial purposes. For the Olympics, the seaside was reconstructed, and the city shoreline is now spanned by nine beaches along a three-mile stretch.

Soccer: Futbol Club (FC) Barcelona has the largest privately owned stadium in the world, with a seating capacity of 100,000.

The Average Jordi: The average Barcelonan is 41 years old, will live to age 81, and is likely Catholic. The majority (62 percent) of Barcelona's residents were born in Catalunya.

son to an embassy or consulate office (see page 281). If your credit and debit cards disappear, cancel and replace them (see "Damage Control for Lost Cards" on page 13). File a police report either on the spot or within a day or two; it's required if you submit an insurance claim for lost or stolen railpasses or travel gear, and it can help with replacing your passport or credit and debit cards. For more information, see www.ricksteves.com/help.

Thieves target tourists throughout Spain, especially in Barcelona. While hotel rooms are generally safe, thieves break into cars, snatch purses, and pick pockets. Thieves zipping by on motor-bikes grab handbags from pedestrians or even from cars in traffic (by reaching through open car windows at stoplights). A fight or commotion is created to enable pickpockets to work unnoticed. Be on guard, use a money belt, and treat any disturbance around you as a smoke screen for theft. Don't believe any "police officers" look-ing for counterfeit bills. Precautionary measures can minimize the effects of loss—back up your photos and other files frequently.

Time Zones: Spain, like most of continental Europe, is gen-erally six/nine hours ahead of the East/West Coasts of the US. The exceptions are the beginning and end of Daylight Saving Time: Europe "springs forward" the last Sunday in March (two weeks after most of North America), and "falls back" the last Sunday in October (one week before North America). For a handy online time converter, try www.timeanddate.com/worldclock.

Business Hours: For visitors, Spain is a land of strange and frustrating schedules. Many businesses respect the afternoon siesta. When it's 100 degrees in the shade, you'll understand why. The biggest museums stay open all day. Smaller ones often close for a siesta. From Monday through Friday, shops generally open at 9:00 or 10:00, close at lunchtime (around 13:00 or 14:00), reopen at 16:30 or 17:00, then close at 20:00 or 21:00. On Saturdays, many shops are open only in the morning. On Sundays, many shops are closed, including La Boqueria and Santa Caterina markets, but sightseeing attractions are generally open. Banking hours are gen-erally Monday through Friday from 9:00 to 14:00.

Watt's Up? Europe's electrical system is 220 volts, instead of North America's 110 volts. Most newer electronics (such as laptops, battery chargers, and hair dryers) convert automatically, so you won't need a converter plug, but you will need an adapter plug with two round prongs, sold inexpensively at travel stores in the US. Avoid bringing older appliances that don't automatically convert voltage; instead, buy a cheap replacement at a Barcelona depart-ment store (see the Shopping in Barcelona chapter).

Discounts: Discounts are not listed in this book. However, many sights offer discounts for youths (up to age 18), students (with proper identification cards, www.isic.org), families, seniors (loosely defined as retirees or those willing to call themselves seniors), and groups of 10 or more. Always ask. Some discounts are available only for European Union (EU) citizens.

Money

This section offers advice on how to pay for purchases on your trip (including getting cash from ATMs and paying with plastic), deal-ing with lost or stolen cards, VAT (sales tax) refunds, and tipping.

Exchange Rate

1 euro (€) = about $1.30

To convert prices in euros to dollars, add about 30 percent: €20 = about $26, €50 = about $65. (Check www.oanda.com for the latest exchange rates.) Just like the dollar, one euro is broken down into 100 cents. Coins ranging from €0.01 to €2, and bills ranging from €5 to €500.

What to Bring

Bring both a credit card and a debit card. You'll use the debit card at cash machines (ATMs) to withdraw euros for most purchases, and the credit card to pay for larger items. Some travelers carry a third card, in case one gets demagnetized or eaten by a temperamental machine.

As an emergency backup, bring several hundred dollars in hard cash in easy-to-exchange $20 bills. Avoid using currency exchange booths (because of their lousy rates and/or outrageous fees).

Cash

Cash is just as desirable in Spain as it is at home. Small European businesses (hotels, restaurants, shops, etc.) prefer that you pay your bills with cash. Some vendors will charge you extra for using a credit card, and some won't take credit cards at all. Cash is the best—and sometimes only—way to pay for bus fares, taxis, and local guides.

Throughout Europe, ATMs are the standard way for travelers to get cash. Stay away from "independent" ATMs such as Travelex, Euronet, and Forex, which charge huge commissions and have terrible exchange rates.

To withdraw money from an ATM (called a *cajero automático* in Spain), you'll need a debit card (ideally with a Visa or MasterCard logo for maximum usability), plus a PIN code. Know your PIN code in numbers; there are only numbers—no letters—on European keypads. For security, it's best to shield the keypad when entering your PIN at an ATM. If the ATM gives you the option of converting your withdrawal amount from euros into dollars, decline (see "Dynamic Currency Conversion," later).

Although you can use a credit card for ATM transactions, it's generally more expensive (and only makes sense in an emergency) because it's considered a cash advance rather than a withdrawal. Try to withdraw large sums of money to reduce the number of per-transaction bank fees you'll pay.

Pickpockets target tourists. To safeguard your cash, wear a money belt—a pouch with a strap that you buckle around your waist like a belt and tuck under your clothes. Keep your cash, credit cards, and passport secure in your money belt, and carry only a day's spending money in your front pocket.

Credit and Debit Cards

For purchases, Visa and MasterCard are more commonly accepted than American Express. Just like at home, credit or debit cards work easily at larger hotels, restaurants, and shops. I typically use my debit card to withdraw cash to pay for most purchases. I use my credit card only in a few specific situations: to book hotel reservations by phone, to make major purchases (such as car rentals, plane tickets, and hotel stays), and to pay for things near the end of my trip (to avoid another visit to the ATM). While you could use a debit card to make most large purchases, using a credit card offers a greater degree of fraud protection (because debit cards draw funds directly from your account).

Ask Your Credit- or Debit-Card Company: Before your trip, contact the company that issued your debit or credit cards.

• Confirm that your **card will work overseas,** and alert them that you'll be using it in Europe; otherwise, they may deny transactions if they perceive unusual spending patterns.

• Ask for the specifics on transaction **fees.** When you use your credit or debit card—either for purchases or ATM withdrawals—you'll often be charged additional "international transaction" fees of up to 3 percent (1 percent is normal) plus $5 per transaction. If your card's fees seem high, consider getting a different card just for your trip: Capital One (www.capitalone.com) and most credit unions have low-to-no international transaction fees.

• If you plan to take out cash from ATMs, confirm your daily **withdrawal limit,** and if necessary, ask your bank to adjust it. Some travelers prefer a high limit that allows them to take out more cash at each ATM stop (saving on bank fees), while others prefer to set a lower limit in case their card is stolen. Note that foreign banks also set maximum withdrawal amounts for their ATMs.

• Get your bank's emergency **phone number** in the US (but not its 800 number, which isn't accessible from overseas) to call collect if you have a problem.

• Ask for your credit card's **PIN** in case you need to make an emergency cash withdrawal or encounter Europe's "chip-and-

PIN" system; the bank won't tell you your PIN over the phone, so allow time for it to be mailed to you.

Chip and PIN: If your card is declined for a purchase in Europe, it may be because Europeans are increasingly using chip-and-PIN cards, which are embedded with an electronic chip (rather than the magnetic stripe used on our American-style cards). While chip and PIN is not yet common in Spain, much of Europe is adopting it. You're most likely to encounter chip-and-PIN problems at automated payment machines, such as those at train and subway stations, toll roads, parking garages, luggage lockers, and self-serve gas pumps. If a machine won't take your card, find a cashier who can make your card work (they can print a receipt for you to sign), or find a machine that takes cash.

But don't panic. Most travelers who are carrying only magnetic-stripe cards never encounter any problems. Still, it pays to carry plenty of euros (you can always use an ATM with your magnetic-stripe debit card). Memorizing the PIN lets you use your credit card at some chip-and-PIN machines—just enter your PIN when prompted. If you're still concerned, you can apply for a chip card in the US (though I think it's overkill). While big US banks offer these cards with high annual fees, a better option is the no-annual-fee GlobeTrek Visa, offered by Andrews Federal Credit Union in Maryland (open to all US residents; see www.andrewsfcu.org).

Dynamic Currency Conversion: If merchants or ATMs offer to convert your purchase price or withdrawal into dollars (called dynamic currency conversion, or DCC), refuse this "service." You'll pay even more in fees for the expensive convenience of seeing the amount in dollars.

Damage Control for Lost Cards

If you lose your credit, debit, or ATM card, you can stop people from using your card by reporting the loss immediately to the respective global customer-assistance centers. Call these 24-hour US numbers collect: Visa (tel. 303/967-1096, toll-free number in Spain is 900-991-124); MasterCard (tel. 636/722-7111); and American Express (tel. 336/393-1111).

At a minimum, you'll need to know the name of the financial institution that issued the card, along with the type of card (classic, platinum, or whatever). Providing the following information will allow for a quicker cancellation of your missing card: full card number, whether you are the primary or secondary cardholder, the cardholder's name exactly as printed on the card, billing address, home phone number, circumstances of the loss or theft, and identification verification (your birth date, your mother's maiden name, or your Social Security number—memorize this, don't carry a copy). If you are the secondary cardholder, you'll also need to provide the primary cardholder's identification-verification details. You can generally receive a temporary card within two or three business days in Europe (see www.ricksteves.com/help for more).

If you report your loss within two days, you typically won't be responsible for any unauthorized transactions on your account, although many banks charge a liability fee of $50.

Tipping

Tipping in Spain isn't as automatic and generous as it is in the US, but for special service, tips are appreciated, if not expected. As in the US, the proper amount depends on your resources, tipping philosophy, and the circumstances, but some general guidelines apply.

Restaurants: If you order a meal at a counter—as you often will when sampling tapas at a bar—there's no need to tip (though if you buy a few tapas, you can round up the bill a few small coins). At restaurants with table service, most Spaniards tip nothing or next to nothing; a service charge is generally included in the bill (*servei inclós* in Catalan, or *servicio incluido* in Spanish). If you like to tip for good service, give up to 5 percent extra. If service is not included (*servei no inclós* in Catalan, or *servicio no incluido* in Spanish), you could tip up to 10 percent. At most places, you can leave the tip on the table. But if you're eating at an outdoor café, hand the tip to your server to avoid having it swiped by a passerby. Also, it's best to tip in cash even if you pay with your credit card. Otherwise the tip may never reach your server.

Taxis: To tip the cabbie, round up. Spanish people rarely give tips in taxis, unless it's to round up to the next full euro (if the fare is €4.85, they'll give €5). If the cabbie hauls your bags and zips you to the airport to help you catch your flight, you might want to toss in a little more. But if you feel like you're being driven in circles or otherwise ripped off, skip the tip.

Services: In general, if someone in the service industry does a super job for you, a small tip of a euro or two is appropriate...but not required. If you're not sure whether (or how much) to tip for a service, ask your hotelier or at the TI.

Getting a VAT Refund

Wrapped into the purchase price of your Spanish souvenirs is a Value-Added Tax (VAT) of 21 percent (in Spain, it's called IVA—*Impuesto sobre el Valor Añadido*). You're entitled to get most of that tax back if you purchase more than €90.15 (about $117) worth of goods at a store that participates in the VAT-refund scheme (confirm the minimum purchase amount with the clerk before you buy). Typically, you must ring up the minimum at a single retailer—you can't add up your purchases from various shops to reach the

#100 01-04-2017 12:00AM
Item(s) checked out to GREEN, LINDSAY NI

TITLE: Switched on : a memoir of brain c
CALL #: 616.858832 R6664s
BARCODE: 35192043245756
DUE DATE: 01-25-17

TITLE: Career of evil
CALL #: Fiction Galbrai
BARCODE: 35192047755230
DUE DATE: 01-25-17

TITLE: Sun, sand, murder
CALL #: Fiction Keyse
BARCODE: 35192046946598
DUE DATE: 01-25-17

TITLE: Rick Steves' Barcelona
CALL #: 914.672 S8489r 2013
BARCODE: 35192045415488
DUE DATE: 01-25-17

For Renewal, please call 862-5890 or go to http://www.library.nashville.org/

required amount.

Getting your refund is usually straightforward and, if you buy a substantial amount of souvenirs, well worth the hassle. If you're lucky, the merchant will subtract the tax when you make your purchase. (This is more likely to occur if the store ships the goods to your home.) Otherwise, you'll need to:

Get the paperwork. Have the merchant completely fill out the necessary refund document. You'll have to present your passport at the store. Get the paperwork done before you leave the store to ensure you'll have everything you need (including your original sales receipt).

Get your stamp at the border or airport. Process your VAT document at your last stop in the EU (for instance, at the airport) with the customs agent who deals with VAT refunds. Before checking in for your flight, find the local customs office, and be prepared to stand in line. Keep your purchases readily available for viewing by the customs agent (ideally in your carry-on bag—don't make the mistake of checking the bag with your purchases before you've seen the agent). You're not supposed to use your purchased goods before you leave. If you show up at customs wearing your new flamenco outfit, officials might look the other way—or deny you a refund.

Collect your refund. You'll need to return your stamped document to the retailer or its representative. Many merchants work with services, such as Global Blue or Premier Tax Free, which have offices at major airports, ports, or border crossings (either before or after security, probably strategically located near a duty-free shop). These services, which extract a 4 percent fee, can refund your money immediately in cash or credit your card (within two billing cycles). If the retailer handles VAT refunds directly, it's up to you to contact the merchant for your refund. You can mail the documents from home or, more quickly, from your point of departure (using an envelope you've prepared in advance or one that's been provided by the merchant). You'll then have to wait—it can take months.

Customs for American Shoppers

You are allowed to take home $800 worth of items per person duty-free, once every 30 days. You can also bring in duty-free a liter of alcohol. As for food, you can take home many processed and packaged foods: vacuum-packed cheeses, dried herbs, jams, baked goods, candy, chocolate, oil, vinegar, and honey. However, fresh fruits and vegetables and most meats are not allowed. Any liquid-containing foods must be packed in checked luggage, a potential recipe for disaster. To check customs rules and duty rates, visit www.cbp.gov.

Sightseeing

Sightseeing can be hard work. Use these tips to make your visits to Barcelona's finest sights meaningful, fun, efficient, and painless.

Plan Ahead

Set up an itinerary that allows you to fit in all your must-see sights. For a one-stop look at opening hours, see "Barcelona at a Glance" (page 42). Most sights keep stable hours, but you can easily confirm the latest by checking with the TI or visiting museum websites.

Don't put off visiting a must-see sight—you never know when a place will close unexpectedly for a holiday, a strike, or restoration. On holidays (see list on page 300), expect reduced hours or closures. In summer, some sights may stay open late. Off-season, many museums have shorter hours.

Going at the right time helps avoid crowds. This book offers tips on the best times to see specific sights. Try visiting popular sights very early or very late. Evening visits are usually peaceful, with fewer crowds. The Picasso Museum keeps evening hours year-round, and the Sagrada Família and Casa Milà stay open late in peak season (for an overview, see "Sights Open Late" on page 231).

Study up. To get the most out of the sight descriptions in this book, read them before you visit. Gaudí seems less gaudy if you understand his artistic vision.

At Sights

Here's what you can typically expect:

Some important sights require you to check daypacks and coats. To avoid checking a small backpack, carry it under your arm like a purse as you enter. From a guard's point of view, a backpack is generally a problem whereas a purse is not.

At churches—which generally offer interesting art (usually free) and a cool, welcome seat—a modest dress code (no bare shoulders or shorts) is encouraged.

Flash photography is often banned, but taking photos without a flash is usually allowed. Flashes damage oil paintings and distract others in the room. Even without a flash, a handheld camera will take a decent picture (or you can buy postcards or posters at the museum bookstore). Museums may have special exhibits in addition to their permanent collection. Some exhibits are included in the entry price, while others come at an extra cost (which you may have to pay even if you don't want to see the exhibit).

Expect changes—artwork can be on tour, on loan, out sick, or shifted at the whim of the curator. To adapt, pick up any available free floor plans as you enter, and ask the museum staff if you can't

How Was Your Trip?

Were your travels fun, smooth, and meaningful? If you'd like to share your tips, concerns, and discoveries, please fill out the survey at www.ricksteves.com/feedback. I value your feedback. Thanks in advance—it helps a lot.

find a particular item. Say the title or artist's name, or point to the photograph in this book, and ask, "Where is?" by saying "*¿Dónde está?*" (dohn-day ay-stah).

Many sights rent audioguides, which generally offer dry-but-useful recorded descriptions in English (about €3-4). If you bring along your own earbuds, you can enjoy better sound and avoid holding the device to your ear. To save money, bring a Y-jack and share one audioguide with your travel partner.

Important sights may have an on-site café or cafeteria (usually a handy place to rejuvenate during a long visit). The WCs at sights are free and generally clean.

Many sights sell postcards and guidebooks that highlight their attractions. Before you leave, scan the postcards and thumb through the biggest guidebook (or skim its index) to be sure you haven't overlooked something that you'd like to see.

Most sights stop admitting people 30 to 60 minutes before closing time, and some rooms may close early (often about 45 minutes before the actual closing time). Guards usher people out, so don't save the best for last.

Every sight or museum offers more than what is covered in this book. Use the information in this book as an introduction—not the final word.

Traveling as a Temporary Local

We travel all the way to Spain to enjoy differences—to become temporary locals. You'll experience frustrations. Certain truths that we find "God-given" or "self-evident," such as cold beer, ice in drinks, bottomless cups of coffee, hot showers, and bigger being better, are suddenly not so true. One of the benefits of travel is the eye-opening realization that there are logical, civil, and even better alternatives. A willingness to go local ensures that you'll enjoy a full dose of Spanish hospitality.

Europeans generally like Americans. But if there is a negative aspect to the image the Spanish have of Americans, it's that we are loud, wasteful, ethnocentric, too informal (which can seem disrespectful), and a bit naive.

While Spaniards look bemusedly at some of our Yankee

excesses—and worriedly at others—they nearly always afford us individual travelers all the warmth we deserve.

Judging from all the happy feedback I receive from travelers who have used this book, it's safe to assume you'll enjoy a great, affordable vacation—with the finesse of an independent, experienced traveler.

Thanks, and *bon viatge!*

Back Door Travel Philosophy
From *Rick Steves' Europe Through the Back Door*

Travel is intensified living—maximum thrills per minute and one of the last great sources of legal adventure. Travel is freedom. It's recess, and we need it.

Experiencing the real Europe requires catching it by surprise, going casual..."Through the Back Door."

Affording travel is a matter of priorities. (Make do with the old car.) You can eat and sleep—simply, safely, and enjoyably— anywhere in Europe for $120 a day plus transportation costs. In many ways, spending more money only builds a thicker wall between you and what you traveled so far to see. Europe is a cultural carnival, and time after time, you'll find that its best acts are free and the best seats are the cheap ones.

A tight budget forces you to travel close to the ground, meeting and communicating with the people. Never sacrifice sleep, nutrition, safety, or cleanliness to save money. Simply enjoy the local-style alternatives to expensive hotels and restaurants.

Connecting with people carbonates your experience. Extroverts have more fun. If your trip is low on magic moments, kick yourself and make things happen. If you don't enjoy a place, maybe you don't know enough about it. Seek the truth. Recognize tourist traps. Give a culture the benefit of your open mind. See things as different, but not better or worse. Any culture has plenty to share.

Of course, travel, like the world, is a series of hills and valleys. Be fanatically positive and militantly optimistic. If something's not to your liking, change your liking.

Travel can make you a happier American, as well as a citizen of the world. Our Earth is home to seven billion equally precious people. It's humbling to travel and find that other people don't have the "American Dream"—they have their own dreams. Europeans like us, but with all due respect, they wouldn't trade passports.

Thoughtful travel engages us with the world. In tough economic times, it reminds us what is truly important. By broadening perspectives, travel teaches new ways to measure quality of life.

Globetrotting destroys ethnocentricity, helping us understand and appreciate other cultures. Rather than fear the diversity on this planet, celebrate it. Among your most prized souvenirs will be the strands of different cultures you choose to knit into your own character. The world is a cultural yarn shop, and Back Door travelers are weaving the ultimate tapestry. Join in!

ORIENTATION TO BARCELONA

Bustling Barcelona is geographically big and culturally complex. Plan your time carefully, carving up the metropolis into manageable sightseeing neighborhoods. Use my day plans to help prioritize your time, and make advance reservations for sights (or get a sightseeing pass) to save time waiting in lines. For efficiency, learn how to navigate Barcelona by Metro, bus, and taxi. Armed with good information and a thoughtful game plan, you're ready to go. Then you can relax, enjoy, and let yourself be surprised by all that Barcelona has to offer.

Barcelona: A Verbal Map

Like Los Angeles, Barcelona is a basically flat city that sprawls out under the sun between the sea and the mountains. It's huge (1.6 million people, with about 5 million people in greater Barcelona), but travelers need only focus on four areas: the Old City, the harbor/Barceloneta, the Eixample, and Montjuïc.

A large square, **Plaça de Catalunya,** sits at the center of Barcelona, dividing the older and newer parts of town. Sloping downhill from Plaça de Catalunya is the Old City, with the boulevard called the Ramblas running down to the harbor. North of Plaça de Catalunya is the modern residential area called the Eixample. The Montjuïc hill overlooks the harbor. Outside the Old City, Barcelona's sights are widely scattered, but with a map and a willingness to figure out public transit (or take taxis), all is manageable.

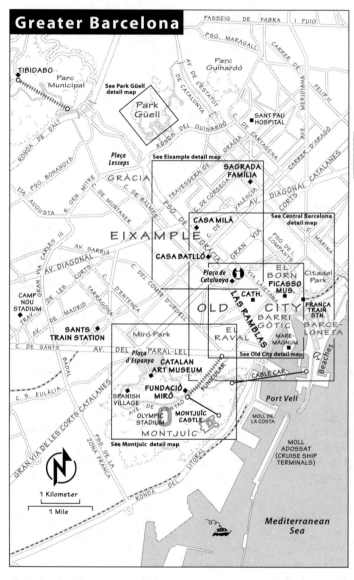

Greater Barcelona

PASSEIG DE FABRA I PUIG

PSG. MARAGALL

TIBIDABO

Parc Municipal

Parc Guinardó

See Park Güell detail map

Park Güell

Plaça Lesseps

GRÀCIA

See Eixample detail map

SAGRADA FAMÍLIA

SANT PAU HOSPITAL

CASA MILÀ

EIXAMPLE

See Central Barcelona detail map

CASA BATLLÓ

Plaça de Catalunya

EL BORN

PICASSO MUS.

Citadel Park

CAMP NOU STADIUM

AV. DIAGONAL

OLD CITY

CATH.

LAS RAMBLAS

BARRI GÒTIC

FRANÇA TRAIN STN.

BARCE-LONETA

SANTS TRAIN STATION

Miró Park

EL RAVAL

MARE-MAGNUM

Plaça d'Espanya

CATALAN ART MUSEUM

See Old City detail map

Beaches

SPANISH VILLAGE

FUNDACIÓ MIRÓ

FUNICULAR

CABLE CAR

Port Vell

OLYMPIC STADIUM

MONTJUÏC CASTLE

MOLL DE LA COSTA

MONTJUÏC

See Montjuïc detail map

MOLL ADOSSAT (CRUISE SHIP TERMINALS)

1 Kilometer

1 Mile

Mediterranean Sea

ORIENTATION

Here are overviews of the major neighborhoods:

Old City (Ciutat Vella): This is the compact core of Barcelona—ideal for strolling, shopping, and people-watching—where you'll probably spend most of your time. It's a labyrinth of narrow streets that once were confined by the medieval walls. The lively pedestrian drag called the **Ramblas**—one of Europe's most entertaining streets—goes through the heart of the Old City

ORIENTATION

Barcelona Neighborhood Overview

GRÀCIA

Park Güell

EIXAMPLE

CASA MILÀ

SAGRADA FAMÍLIA

PASSEIG DE GRÀCIA

CASA BATLLÓ

Plaça de Catalunya

OLD CITY

EL BORN

Citadel Park

VIA LAIETANA

CATHEDRAL

PICASSO MUSEUM

LAS RAMBLAS

BARRI GÒTIC

EL RAVAL

SANTS STATION

BARCELONETA

Plaça d'Espanya

FUNDACIÓ JOAN MIRÓ

MONTJUÏC

Port Vell

Not to Scale

← To Airport

CRUISE PORT

Mediterranean Sea

from Plaça de Catalunya to the harbor. The Old City is divided into thirds by the Ramblas and another major thoroughfare (running roughly parallel to the Ramblas), Via Laietana. Between the Ramblas and Via Laietana is the characteristic **Barri Gòtic** (BAH-ree GOH-teek, Gothic Quarter), with the cathedral as its navel. Locals call it simply "El Gòtic" for short. To the east of Via Laietana is the trendy **El Born** district (a.k.a. "La Ribera"), a shopping, dining, and nightlife mecca centered on the Picasso Museum and the Church of Santa Maria del Mar. To the west of the Ramblas is the **Raval** (rah-VAHL), enlivened by its university and modern-art museum. The Raval is of least interest to tourists (and, in fact, some parts of it are quite dodgy and should be avoided).

Harborfront: This area has been energized since the 1992 Olympics. A pedestrian bridge links the Ramblas with the modern Maremagnum shopping/aquarium/entertainment complex. On the peninsula across the quaint sailboat harbor is **Barceloneta,** a traditional fishing neighborhood with gritty charm and some good seafood restaurants. Beyond Barceloneta, a gorgeous man-made **beach** several miles long leads east to the commercial and convention district called the **Fòrum.**

Eixample: North of the Old City, beyond the bustling hub of Plaça de Catalunya, is the elegant Eixample (eye-SHAM-plah) district, its grid plan softened by cut-off corners. Much of Barcelona's Modernista architecture is found here—especially

Barcelona: From Small to Sprawl

The city of Barcelona has grown with its history. The original Roman town from the time of Christ was contained inside the knot of streets clustered around today's cathedral and enclosed by an oval-shaped ring of Roman walls (stretching basically southeast from the square in front of the cathedral).

When Rome fell (around A.D. 476), the Christian Visigoths made the cathedral the center of town, and the populace remained huddled inside the Roman walls. During the Dark Ages, the city was ruled briefly by Moors (714-801) and Franks (ninth century). When the Counts of Barcelona unified Catalunya (10th century), the city began expanding. They built churches outside the Roman walls (or *extra muro*), each a magnet gathering a small community. By 1250, they needed to build a larger wall to contain these new settlers. This medieval wall stretched from Plaça de Catalunya to the sea, embracing the whole Old Town. The hilltop of Montjuïc—outside the residential area—was topped with a harbor-guarding fortress.

By 1850, the growing city was bursting at the seams. The outer wall was torn down and replaced by a series of circular boulevards (named Rondas, meaning "to go around"). The city expanded northward in a regimented grid of modern boulevards—an urban waffle known as the Eixample. In 1992, Barcelona hosted the Summer Olympics, which quickly accelerated modernization and expanded the city even more.

Today, the population sprawls beyond city maps, creating a greater metropolitan area of some five million people.

along the swanky artery Passeig de Gràcia, an area called **Quadrat d'Or** ("Golden Quarter"). To the north is the **Gràcia** district and beyond that, Antoni Gaudí's **Park Güell.**

Montjuïc: The large hill overlooking the city to the southwest is Montjuïc (mohn-jew-EEK), home to a variety of attractions, including some excellent museums (Catalan Art, Joan Miró) and the Olympic Stadium. At the base of Montjuïc, stretching toward Plaça d'Espanya, are the former **1929 World Expo Fairgrounds,** with additional fine attractions (including the CaixaForum art gallery and the bullring-turned-mall, Las Arenas).

Apart from your geographical orientation, it's smart to orient yourself linguistically to a language distinct from Spanish. Although Spanish ("Castilian"/*castellano*) is widely spoken, the native tongue in this region is Catalan—nearly as different from Spanish as Italian (see the sidebar on page 6).

Planning Your Time

Barcelona is worth at least two days and can easily fill up three or four. If you can spare only one full day for the city, it can be a scramble—but a day you'll never forget.

When planning your time, be aware that many top sights are closed on Monday—making them especially crowded on Tuesday and Sunday (for a summary of sights' opening hours throughout the week, see the "Daily Reminder," later). Some of Barcelona's major sights can have long lines (such as the Sagrada Família and Casa Milà); it's smart to make advance reservations (for tips, see page 32). If you're here on a weekend, dance (or watch) the *sardana* (see page 50).

Barcelona in 1 Day

For a relaxing day, stroll the Ramblas, see the Sagrada Família, add the Picasso Museum if you're a fan, and have dinner in the trendy El Born district.

To fit in much more, try the following ambitious but doable plan. You'll have to rush through the big sights (cathedral, Picasso Museum, Sagrada Família), having just enough time to visit each one but not to linger.

9:00   From Plaça de Catalunya (with its handy TI), follow my Barri Gòtic Walk and Cathedral of Barcelona Tour.

11:00   Circle back to Plaça de Catalunya and follow my self-guided Ramblas Ramble to the harborfront.

12:30   Walk along the harborfront to El Born, grabbing a quick lunch.

14:00   Take my Picasso Museum Tour.

16:00   Hop a taxi or the Metro to the Sagrada Família.

18:00   Taxi, bus, or walk to Passeig de Gràcia in the Eixample neighborhood to see the exteriors of Gaudí's Casa Milà and the Block of Discord. Stroll back down toward Plaça de Catalunya.

19:00   If your energy is holding out, wander back into the Barri Gòtic at prime paseo time. Enjoy an early tapas dinner along the way, or a restaurant meal later somewhere in the Old City.

Barcelona in 2, 3, or More Days

To better sample the city's ample charm, spread your visit over several days. With at least two days, divide and conquer the town geographically: Spend one day in the Old City (Ramblas, Barri Gòtic/cathedral area, Picasso Museum/El Born) and another on the Eixample and Gaudí sights (Casa Milà, Sagrada Família, Park Güell). Do Montjuïc on whichever day you're not exhausted (if any)—or, better yet, on a third day.

With extra time on any day, consider taking a hop-on, hop-off

bus tour for a sightseeing overview (for instance, the Tourist Bus'
blue route links most Gaudí sights and could work well on Day 2).

Day 1—Old City

9:00   Follow my Barri Gòtic Walk and Cathedral of
Barcelona Tour.

11:00   Head to the Ramblas using the route described in
my "Barri Gòtic Shopping Walk," then follow my
Ramblas Ramble (touring Palau Güell if you're a
Gaudí fan) down to the harborfront.

13:00   Grab lunch in El Born or the Barri Gòtic.

14:00   Tour the Palace of Catalan Music in El Born
(advance reservation required).

15:00   Follow my El Born Walk, and en route, do the
Picasso Museum Tour. Afterwards complete the El
Born Walk and shop to your heart's content.

Evening   Take your pick of evening activities: Assemble a tapas
dinner by hopping from bar to bar in El Born, and
take "A Short, Sweet Walk" (page 207) for dessert.
(Other good neighborhoods for tapas are the ritzy
Eixample or touristy Barri Gòtic.) Or wait to dine
at a restaurant when locals do, around 21:00. Visit a
sight that's open late (for a list, see page 231). Take in
a performance of Spanish guitar, flamenco, or jazz,
or a concert in a fancy setting (Casa Milà, Palace
of Catalan Music, and more). Zip up to Montjuïc
for the sunset and a drink on the Catalan Art
Museum's terrace, then head down to the illuminated
Magic Fountains (Fri-Sat, plus Sun and Thu in
summer). Head to Barceloneta and choose your
favorite *chiringuito* beach bar. For more ideas, see the
Nightlife in Barcelona chapter.

Day 2—Modernisme

9:00   Take my Eixample Walk, touring Casa Milà and/or
Casa Batlló.

12:00   Eat an early lunch in the Eixample.

13:00   Take a taxi or bus to the Sagrada Família and tour it.

15:00   Choose among these three options: Taxi or bus to
Park Güell for more Gaudí. Or take a bus ride to
Montjuïc (if you're not going to Montjuïc on Day 3)
to enjoy the city view and your pick of sights. Or head
to Plaça de Catalunya, stroll down the Ramblas again
(the scene constantly changes throughout the day),
and explore the harborfront La Rambla de Mar and

ORIENTATION

Daily Reminder

Sunday: Most sights are open, but the Boqueria and Santa Caterina markets are closed. Some sights close early today, including the Catalan Art Museum, Fundació Joan Miró, Olympic and Sports Museum, and Camp Nou Stadium (all close at 14:30), along with the Chocolate Museum (closes at 15:00). Informal performances of the *sardana* national dance take place in front of the cathedral at noon (none in Aug). Some museums are free at certain times: Catalan Art Museum and Palau Güell (free on first Sun of month); Picasso Museum and Barcelona History Museum (free on first Sun of month plus other Sun from 15:00); and the Frederic Marès Museum (free every Sun from 15:00). The Magic Fountains come alive on summer evenings (May-Sept).

Monday: Many sights are closed, including the Picasso Museum, Catalan Art Museum, Palau Güell, Barcelona History Museum, *Santa Eulàlia* schooner (at the Maritime Museum), Fundació Joan Miró, Frederic Marès Museum, Shoe Museum, Roman Temple of Augustus, and Olympic and Sports Museum. But most major Gaudí sights are open today, including the Sagrada Família, Casa Milà, Park Güell, and Casa Batlló.

Tuesday: All major sights are open.

Wednesday: All major sights are open. The CaixaForum may be open until 23:00 in July and August.

Thursday: All major sights are open. Fundació Joan Miró is open until 21:30 year-round, and the Magic Fountains spout on summer evenings (May-Sept).

Friday: All major sights are open. The Magic Fountains light up Montjuïc year-round.

Saturday: All major sights are open. Barcelonans dance the *sardana* most Saturdays at 18:00, and the Magic Fountains dance all year.

Late-Hours Sightseeing: Sights with **year-round** evening hours (19:30 or later) include the Picasso Museum, Park Güell, CaixaForum, Cathedral of Barcelona, Casa Batlló, Las Arenas, Church of Santa Maria del Mar, and Maritime Museum (only temporary exhibits open while permanent exhibits undergo restoration, likely through 2014).

Sights offering later hours only in **peak season** (roughly April-Sept) include the Sagrada Família, Casa Milà, Palau Güell, Fundació Joan Miró, Castle of Montjuïc, and Gaudí House Museum (for a rundown on specific times, see the sidebar on page 231).

              Old Port (unless you already did this on Day 1, at the
              end of the Ramblas Ramble).

Evening   Choose among the evening activities listed earlier.

Day 3—Montjuïc and Barceloneta

Morning   Tour Montjuïc from top to bottom, stopping at
              sights of interest. The top priorities are the Catalan
              Art Museum, CaixaForum art gallery, and Fundació
              Joan Miró. Shoppers like Las Arenas, the bullring
              mall.

Afternoon If the weather is good (and you haven't hit the
              beach yet), take the scenic cable-car ride down from
              Montjuïc to the port, and spend the rest of the day
              at Barceloneta—stroll the promenade and have a
              seafood dinner.

Day 4

Consider these options: Visit the markets (La Boqueria and Santa
Caterina; both closed Sun). Tour more sights (Palau Güell's
Modernista interior, Barcelona History Museum, Frederic Marès
Museum, Chocolate Museum, and more). Take a walking or bike
tour. Relax or rent a rowboat in Citadel Park.

Days 5-7

With more time, choose among several tempting day trips, including the mountaintop monastery of Montserrat, the beach resort
town of Sitges, and the Salvador Dalí sights at Figueres and
Cadaqués (see the Day Trips from Barcelona chapter).

Connecting with the Rest of Spain

Located in the far northeast corner of Spain, Barcelona makes
a good first or last stop for your trip. With the fast AVE train,
Barcelona is three hours away from Madrid—faster and more comfortable than flying. Or you could sandwich Barcelona between
flights. From the US, it's as easy to fly into Barcelona as it is to land
in Madrid, Lisbon, or Paris. Those who plan on renting a car at
some point during their trip can start here first, take the train or fly
to Madrid, and sightsee Madrid and Toledo, all before picking up
their car—cleverly saving on several days' worth of rental fees. For
more on train travel and car rentals in Spain, see the Appendix.

Overview

Tourist Information

Barcelona's TI has several branches (central tel. 932-853-834,
www.barcelonaturisme.cat). The primary one is beneath the main

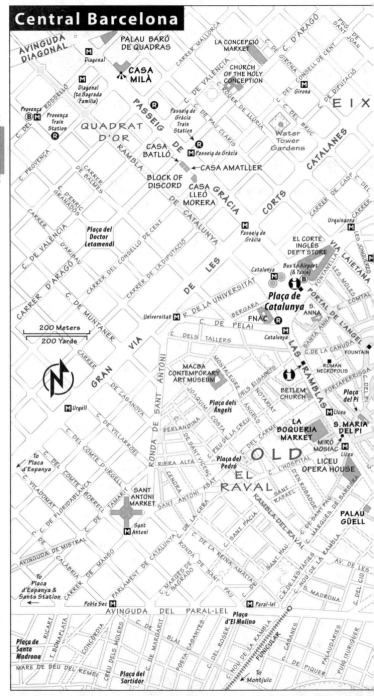

Central Barcelona

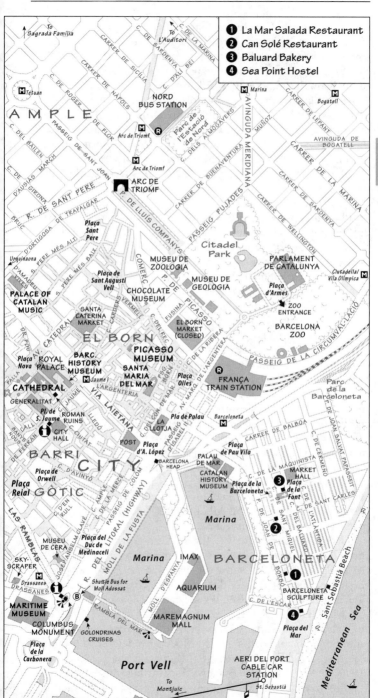

ORIENTATION

Map Legend:
1. La Mar Salada Restaurant
2. Can Solé Restaurant
3. Baluard Bakery
4. Sea Point Hostel

square, **Plaça de Catalunya** (daily 8:30-20:30, entrance along southeast side of square, across from El Corte Inglés department store—look for red sign and take stairs down, tel. 932-853-832).

Several other convenient branches include a kiosk near the top of the **Ramblas** (daily 8:30-20:30, at #115, mobile 618-783-479); on **Plaça de Sant Jaume,** just south of the cathedral (Mon-Fri 8:30-20:00, Sat 9:00-19:00, Sun 9:00-14:00, in the Barcelona City Hall at Ciutat 2); in the Catalan College of Architects building (daily 9:00-19:00); inside the base of the **Columbus Monument** at the harbor (daily 8:30-19:30); at the **airport,** in both terminals 1 and 2B (both open daily 8:30-20:30); and at **Sants train station** (daily 8:00-20:00).

You'll also find smaller info kiosks in other touristy locales: on **Plaça d'Espanya,** in the park across from the **Sagrada Família** entrance, near the **Columbus Monument** (where the shuttle bus from the cruise port arrives), at the **Nord bus station,** at the various **cruise terminals** along the port, and two on **Plaça de Catalunya.** In addition, throughout the summer, young red-jacketed tourist-info helpers appear in the most touristy parts of town; although they work for the hop-on, hop-off Tourist Bus, they are happy to answer questions.

At any TI, pick up the free city map (although the free El Corte Inglés map provided by most hotels is better), the small Metro map, the monthly *Barcelona Planning.com* guidebook (with basic tips on sightseeing, shopping, events, and restaurants), and the quarterly *See Barcelona* guide (with more in-depth practical information on museums and a neighborhood-by-neighborhood sightseeing rundown). The monthly *Time Out BCN Guide* agenda offers a concise but thorough day-by-day list of events. And the monthly *Barcelona Metropolitan* magazine has timely and substantial coverage of local topics and events. All of these are free.

TIs are handy places to buy tickets for the Tourist Bus (see "Getting Around Barcelona") or for the TI-run walking tours (see "Tours in Barcelona"). All of the TIs (except the kiosks) provide a room-booking service.

Regional Catalunya TI: The all-Catalunya TI can help with travel and sightseeing tips for the entire region, and even Madrid (Mon-Sat 10:00-19:00, Sun 10:00-14:00, in the Palau Robert near the intersection of Passeig de Gràcia and Diagonal at Passeig de Gràcia 107, tel. 932-388-091, www.catalunya.com).

Modernisme Route: Inside the Plaça de Catalunya TI is the privately run **Ruta del Modernisme** desk, which gives out a handy route map showing all 116 Modernista buildings and offers a sightseeing discount package (€12 for a great guidebook and 20-50-percent discounts to many Modernista sights—worthwhile if going beyond the biggies I cover in depth; for €18 you'll also get a guidebook to Modernista bars and restaurants; www.rutadel modernisme.com).

Sightseeing Passes: The **Articket BCN** ticket covers admission to six art museums and their temporary exhibits, letting you skip the ticket-buying lines. Sights include the recommended Picasso Museum, Catalan Art Museum, and Fundació Joan Miró (€30, valid for three months, sold at Plaça de Catalunya, Plaça de Sant Jaume, and Sants train station TIs and at participating museums, www.articketbcn.org). If you're planning to go to three or more of the museums, this ticket will save you money and time, especially at sights prone to long lines, such as the Picasso Museum. To skip the ticket-buying line at a museum, show your Articket BCN (to the ticket-taker, at the info desk, or at the group entrance), and you'll get your entrance ticket pronto.

On the other hand, I'd skip the **Barcelona Card,** which covers public transportation (buses, Metro, Montjuïc funicular, and *golondrinas* harbor tour) and includes free admission to a few minor sights and small discounts on many major sights (€37/2 days, €47/3 days, €56/4 days, €62/5 days, sold at TIs and El Corte Inglés department stores).

Arrival in Barcelona

For a comprehensive rundown on Barcelona's train station, airport, and cruise port, as well as tips on arriving or departing at each one, see the Barcelona Connections chapter.

Helpful Hints

Theft and Scam Alert: You're more likely to be pickpocketed here—especially on the Ramblas—than about anywhere else in Europe. Most of the crime is nonviolent, but muggings do occur. Leave valuables in your hotel and wear a money belt.

Street scams are easy to avoid if you recognize them. Most common is the too-friendly local who tries to engage you in conversation by asking for the time, talking sports, asking whether you speak English, and so on. If a super-friendly man acts drunk and wants to dance because his soccer team just won, he's a pickpocket. Beware of thieves posing as lost tourists who ask for your help. A typical street gambling scam is the pea-and-carrot game, a variation on the shell game. The people winning are all ringers, and you can be sure that you'll lose if you play. Also beware of groups of women aggressively selling carnations, people offering to clean off a stain from your shirt, and people picking things up in front of you on escalators. If you stop for any commotion or show on the Ramblas, put your hands in your pockets before someone else does. Assume any scuffle is simply a distraction by a team of

ORIENTATION

thieves. Crooks are inventive, so keep your guard up. Don't be intimidated...just be smart.

Some areas feel seedy and can be unsafe after dark; I'd avoid the southern part of the Barri Gòtic (basically the two or three blocks directly south and east of Plaça Reial—though the strip near the Carrer de la Mercè tapas bars is better), and I wouldn't venture too deep into the Raval (just west of the Ramblas). One block can separate a comfy tourist zone from the junkies and prostitutes.

Sight Reservations: Several of Barcelona's top sights can have long lines of up to an hour or more. To avoid needless waiting, you can buy tickets in advance by going online (or in some cases, calling). This is especially smart for the Picasso Museum (see page 53), Sagrada Família (see page 153), Casa Batlló (see page 59), and Casa Milà (a.k.a La Pedrera; see page 59). An Articket BCN (described on page 31) allows you to skip the lines at the Picasso Museum. If you want to tour the Palace of Catalan Music, you'll need to reserve it in advance (see page 53). It's also smart to reserve ahead for Park Güell (see page 64).

Festivals: Barcelona erupts with festivals all year long. For a list of the major ones, see the sidebar.

Language Barrier: In posted information throughout the city (such as museum descriptions), English plays third fiddle. You'll see Catalan first, Spanish *(castellano)* second, and English a distant third...or often not at all. Fortunately, many locals speak English.

Internet Access: The free city network, **Barcelona WiFi,** has hundreds of hotspots around town; just look for the blue diamond-shaped sign with a big "W" (for details, see www.bcn.cat/barcelonawifi). **Navega Web** has lots of computers and cheap Internet access (€2/hour); it's located across from La Boqueria market, downstairs in the bright Centre Comercial New Park (daily 10:00-24:00, Ramblas 88-94, tel. 933-179-193).

Pharmacy: A 24-hour pharmacy is across from La Boqueria Market at #98 on the Ramblas. Another is on the corner of Passeig de Gràcia and Provença, just opposite the entrance to Casa Milà.

Laundry: Several self-service launderettes are located around the Old City. **Wash 'n Dry** is centrally located just off the Ramblas, near—but not in—a scruffy neighborhood just down the street past Palau Güell (self-service-€6.50/load, full service-€14.50/load, daily 9:00-23:00, Carrer Nou de la Rambla 19—see map on page 178, tel. 934-121-953).

City of Festivals

Barcelona celebrates more festivals, markets, and street fairs than your average city. They dance the *sardana* (a circle dance), build human pyramids, parade colorful *gegants* (giant puppets), and light up the night with fireworks displays called *correfoc* (fire run). Here's a rundown of Barcelona's most lively festivals, listed roughly in chronological order.

Les Festes de Santa Eulàlia: Celebrating the patron saint of the city, this four-day festival features parades, dancing, *correfocs*, and many kid-friendly activities (mid-Feb, www .bcn.cat/santaeulalia).

El Día de Sant Jordi: This celebration of St. George, the patron saint of Catalunya, is also Barcelona's version of Valentine's Day, when lovers exchange books and flowers, and the streets are draped with the red-and-gold Catalan flag (April 23).

Corpus Christi: Barcelona's oldest festival, dating to 1320, contains traditional elements such as processions, music, and "dancing" eggs. The eggs, placed in decorated fountains, spin ("dance") atop jets of water (early June, go to http: //barcelonacultura.bcn.cat and click on "Festivals and Traditions").

Grec Festival de Barcelona: The city's premier summer arts festival has dance, theater, and music, with several events at Teatre Grec—a Greek-style amphitheater (June-July, http: //grec.bcn.cat).

Música als Parcs: Jazz and classical music fills the air in this popular series of evening concerts at city parks (June-Aug).

Montjuïc de Nit: During this dusk-to-dawn celebration of music, cinema, art, theater, and dance, many museums stay open until at least 3:00 in the morning (mid-July, www.bcn .cat/cultura/montjuicnit).

Festes de Sant Roc: Barcelona's oldest festival is also the Barri Gòtic's biggest street party, filled with *gegants*, *sardana* dancing, street games, and fireworks (mid-Aug, go to http://barcelonacultura.bcn.cat and click on "Festivals and Traditions").

Festa Major de Gràcia: For eight days and nights, this festival features live music, *sardana* dancing, human pyramids, and traditional food and drinks (mid-Aug, www.festamajorde gracia.cat).

La Mercè: Running five days, Barcelona's main street festival has fireworks, music, an air show, human pyramids, a parade, and much more (late Sept, www.bcn.cat/merce).

ORIENTATION

Bike Rental: Biking is a joy in Citadel Park, the Eixample, and along the beach (suggested route described on page 57), but it's stressful in the city center, where pedestrians and cars rule. There are bike-rental places around Citadel Park and El Born's Church of Santa Maria del Mar. The handy **Un Cotxe Menys** ("One Car Less"), near the Church of Santa Maria del Mar (50 yards behind the flame memorial), rents bikes and gives out maps and suggested biking routes (€5/hour, €10/4 hours, €18/24 hours, daily 10:00-19:00, leave €150 or photo ID for deposit, Carrer de l'Esparteria 3—see map on page 178, tel. 932-682-105, www.bicicletabarcelona.com); they also lead bike tours (see "Tours in Barcelona," later).

To rent a bike on the Barceloneta beach, consider **Biciclot** (€5/hour, €10/3 hours, €17/24 hours, daily in summer 10:00-20:00, shorter hours off-season, on the sand 300 yards from Olympic Village towers at Passeig Maritime 33, tel. 932-219-778).

Closer to downtown, **Barcelona Rent-A-Bike** is three blocks downhill from Plaça de Catalunya (€6/2 hours, €10/4 hours, €15/24 hours, includes helmet, daily 9:30-20:00, inside the courtyard at Carrer dels Tallers 45—see map on page 178, tel. 933-171-970).

You'll see racks of government-subsidized "Bicing" **borrow-a-bikes** around town, but these are only for locals, not tourists.

Updates to This Book: For any changes to this book's coverage since it was published, see www.ricksteves.com/update.

Getting Around Barcelona
By Metro

Barcelona's Metro, among Europe's best, connects just about every place you'll visit. Rides cost €2. The T10 Card is a great deal—€9.25 gives you 10 rides (cutting the per-ride cost more than in half). The card is shareable, even by companions traveling with you (insert the card in the machine per passenger). The back of your T10 card will show how many trips were taken, with the time and date of each ride. One "ride" covers you for 1.25 hours of unlimited use on all Metro and local bus lines, as well as local rides on the RENFE and Rodalies de Catalunya train lines (including rides to the airport and train station) and the suburban FGC lines (with service to Montserrat).

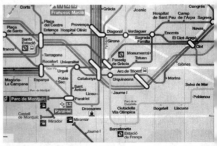

Full- and multi-day passes are also available (€7/1 day, €13/2 days, €19/3 days, €24/4 days, €27/5 days, www.tmb.cat). Automated machines at the Metro entrance have English instructions and sell all types of tickets (these can be temperamental about accepting bills, so try to have change on hand).

Study the free Metro map (available at any TI, also in the front of this book) to get familiar with the system. Barcelona has several color-coded lines, but most useful for tourists is the **L3 (green)** line. Handy city-center stops on this line include (in order):

Sants Estació—Main train station

Espanya—Plaça d'Espanya, with access to the lower part of Montjuïc and trains to Montserrat

Paral-lel—Funicular to the top of Montjuïc

Drassanes—Bottom of the Ramblas, near Maritime Museum and Maremagnum mall

Liceu—Middle of the Ramblas, near the heart of the Barri Gòtic and cathedral

Plaça de Catalunya—Top of the Ramblas and main square with TI, airport bus, and lots of transportation connections

Passeig de Gràcia—Classy Eixample street at the Block of Discord; also connection to L2 (purple) line to Sagrada Família and L4 (yellow) line (described below)

Diagonal—Gaudí's Casa Milà

The **L4 (yellow)** line, which crosses the L3 (green) line at Passeig de Gràcia, is also useful. Helpful stops include **Joanic** (bus #116 to Park Güell), **Jaume I** (between the Barri Gòtic/cathedral and El Born/Picasso Museum), and **Barceloneta** (at the south end of El Born, near the harbor action).

When you enter the Metro, first look for your line number and color, then follow signs to take that line in the direction you're going. The names of the end stops are used to indicate directions. Insert your ticket into the turnstile (with the arrow pointing in), then reclaim it. On board, most trains have handy Metro-line diagrams with dots that light up next to upcoming destinations. Because the lines cross one another multiple times, there can be several ways to make any one journey. (It's a good idea to keep a general map with you—especially if you're transferring.)

Watch your valuables. If I were a pickpocket, I'd set up shop along the made-for-tourists L3 (green) line.

By Bus

Given the excellent Metro service, it's unlikely you'll spend much time on **local buses** (also €2, covered by T10 Card, insert ticket in machine behind driver). However, buses are useful for reaching Park Güell, connecting the sights on Montjuïc, and getting to the beach.

ORIENTATION

ORIENTATION

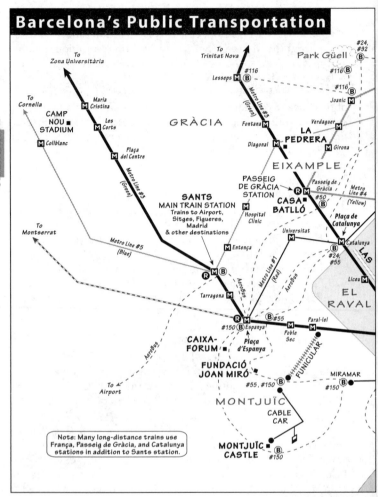

Barcelona's Public Transportation

To Zona Universitària

To Trinitat Nova

Park Güell ⓑ #24, #92

Lessops Ⓜ ⓑ #116

#116 ⓑ

To Cornella

CAMP NOU STADIUM ■

Ⓜ Collblanc

Maria Cristina Ⓜ

Les Corts Ⓜ

Plaça del Centre Ⓜ

GRÀCIA

Fontana Ⓜ

Metro Line #5 (Green)

Diagonal Ⓜ ■

LA PEDRERA

Verdaguer Ⓜ

Girona Ⓜ

Joanic Ⓜ

#116 ⓑ

EIXAMPLE

SANTS MAIN TRAIN STATION
Trains to Airport, Sitges, Figueres, Madrid & other destinations

PASSEIG DE GRÀCIA STATION

CASA BATLLÓ ■

Passeig de Gràcia ⓑ #50

Metro Line #4 (Yellow)

To Montserrat

Metro Line #5 (Blue)

Hospital Clinic

Ⓜ Entença

Universitat Ⓜ

Metro Line #1 (Red)

AeroBus

Plaça de Catalunya

Ⓜ Catalunya #24 #55

LAS

Ⓡ Ⓜ ⓑ

Tarragona Ⓜ

Liceu Ⓜ

EL RAVAL

AeroBus

ⓑ #55 Paral·lel Ⓜ

Ⓡ Ⓜ ⓑ #150 ⓑ Espanya

CAIXA-FORUM ■

Plaça d'Espanya

Poble Sec Ⓜ

FUNICULAR

To Airport

FUNDACIÓ JOAN MIRÓ ■

#55, #150 ⓑ ●

MIRAMAR ⓑ ● #150

MONTJUÏC

CABLE CAR

MONTJUÏC ■ CASTLE ⓑ ● #150

Note: Many long-distance trains use França, Passeig de Gràcia, and Catalunya stations in addition to Sants station.

The handy **hop-on, hop-off Tourist Bus** (Bus Turístic) offers three multi-stop circuits in colorful double-decker buses that go topless in sunny weather. The two-hour blue route covers north Barcelona (most Gaudí sights); the two-hour red route covers south Barcelona (Barri Gòtic and Montjuïc); and the shorter, 40-minute green route covers the beaches and modern Fòrum complex (this route runs April-Oct only). All have headphone commentary (daily

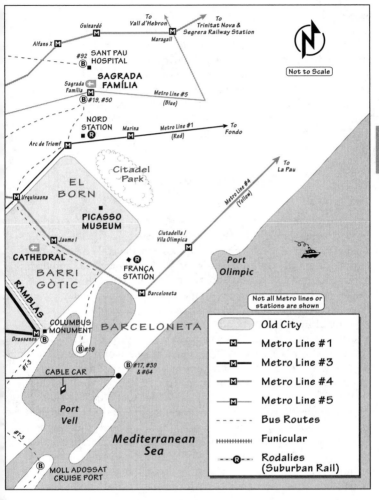

ORIENTATION

Map labels:
- To Vall d'Hebron
- To Trinitat Nova & Segrera Railway Station
- Guinardó
- Maragall
- Alfans X
- #92 SANT PAU HOSPITAL
- Sagrada Família
- SAGRADA FAMÍLIA
- #19, #50
- Metro Line #5 (Blue)
- NORD STATION
- Marina
- Metro Line #1 (Red)
- To Fondo
- Arc de Triomf
- Citadel Park
- Urquinaona
- EL BORN
- To La Pau
- Metro Line #4 (Yellow)
- PICASSO MUSEUM
- Jaume I
- Ciutadella / Vila Olimpica
- CATHEDRAL
- BARRI GÒTIC
- FRANÇA STATION
- Port Olimpic
- RAMBLAS
- Barceloneta
- Not all Metro lines or stations are shown
- COLUMBUS MONUMENT
- BARCELONETA
- Drassenes
- #19
- #17, #39 & #64
- #T-3
- CABLE CAR
- Port Vell
- Mediterranean Sea
- MOLL ADOSSAT CRUISE PORT
- #T-3

Legend:
- Old City
- Metro Line #1
- Metro Line #3
- Metro Line #4
- Metro Line #5
- Bus Routes
- Funicular
- Rodalies (Suburban Rail)

Not to Scale

9:00-20:00 in summer, 9:00-19:00 in winter, buses run every 5-25 minutes, most frequent in summer, www.barcelonabusturistic.cat). Ask for a brochure (includes city map) at the TI or at a pickup point. One-day (€24) and two-day (€31) tickets, which you can buy on the bus or at the TI, offer 10 to 20 percent discounts on the city's major sights and walking tours, which will likely save you about the equivalent of half the cost of the Tourist Bus. From Plaça de Catalunya, the blue northern route leaves from El Corte Inglés; the red southern route leaves from the west—Ramblas—side of the square. A different company, **Barcelona City Tour**, offers a nearly identical service (same price and discounts, two loops instead of three, www.barcelonacitytour.cat).

By Taxi

Barcelona is one of Europe's best taxi towns. Taxis are plentiful (there are more than 10,000) and honest, whether they like it or not. The light on top shows which tariff they're charging; a green light on the roof indicates that a taxi is available. Cab rates are reasonable (€2.50 drop charge, €1/kilometer, these *"Tarif 2"* rates are in effect 7:00-21:00, pay higher *"Tarif 1"* rates off-hours, luggage-€1/piece, €2.10 surcharge to/from train station or cruise port, €3.10 surcharge for airport, other fees posted in window). Save time by hopping a cab (figure €10 from Ramblas to Sants Station).

Tours in Barcelona

On Foot

Walking Tours—The TI at Plaça de Sant Jaume offers great guided walks through the **Barri Gòtic** in English. You'll learn the medieval story of the city as you walk from Plaça de Sant Jaume through the cathedral neighborhood (€14, daily at 9:30, 2 hours, groups limited to 35, buy your ticket 15 minutes early at the TI desk—not from the guide, in summer stop by the office a day ahead to reserve, tel. 932-853-832, www.barcelonaturisme.cat).

The TI at Plaça de Catalunya offers a **Picasso** walk, taking you through the streets of his youth and early career and finishing in the Picasso Museum (€20, includes museum admission; Tue, Thu, and Sat at 15:00; 2 hours plus museum visit). There are also **gourmet** walks (€20, Fri and Sat at 10:00, 2 hours), **Modernisme** walks (€14, Fri and Sat June-Sept at 18:00, Oct-May at 16:00, 2 hours), and a **Maritime** tour that includes a *golondrinas* boat trip on the harbor (€18, Fri and Sat at 10:00, 2 hours). Other themes include Bohemian Barcelona, the Civil War, movie locations, and a literary tour (drop by the office for a full list). These tours depart from the TI at Plaça de Catalunya (except the Maritime tour, which begins at the Columbus Monument); it's always smart to reserve in advance.

"Free" Walking Tours—Several companies offer "free" walks that rely on—and expect—tips to stay in business. Though led by young people who've basically memorized a clever script (rather than trained historians), these walks can be a fun, casual way to get your bearings.

I like **Runner Bean Tours,** run by Gorka, Ann-Marie, and a handful of local guides. They offer 2.5-hour, English-only walks covering the Old City and Gaudí (both tours depart from Plaça Reial daily at 11:00 year-round, plus daily at 16:30 in April-Oct, mobile 636-108-776, www.runnerbeantours.com). They also do night tours, family walks, and more. Groups can range from just a couple of people up to 30.

Discover Walks does similar tours, with three different two-hour itineraries: Gaudí (daily at 10:00, meet in front of Casa Batlló); Ramblas and Barri Gòtic (daily at 15:00, meet in front of Liceu Opera House on the Ramblas); and Trendy Barcelona, covering the El Born neighborhood (daily at 17:00, meet at Plaça de l'Angel next to Jaume I Metro stop). This company distinguishes itself by using exclusively native-born guides—no expats (suggested tips: €5/person for a bad guide, €10 for a good one, €15 for a great one, tel. 931-816-810, www.discoverwalks.com).

Local Guides—The **Barcelona Guide Bureau** is a co-op with about 20 local guides who give personalized four-hour tours (weekdays-€216, per-person price drops as group gets bigger; weekends and holidays-€256, no price break with size of group); **Joana Wilhelm** and **Carles Picazo** are excellent (Via Laietana 54, tel. 932-682-422 or 933-107-778, www.bgb.es).

José Soler is a great and fun-to-be-with local guide who enjoys tailoring a walk through his hometown to your interests (€195/half-day per group, mobile 615-059-326, www.pepitotours .com, info@pepitotours.com).

Cristina Sanjuán of Live Barcelona is another good, professional guide who leads walking tours and can also arrange cruise excursions. It's best to reserve by email (€155/2 hours, €20/each additional hour; €195 extra for a car for up to 2 people, €220 extra for up to 6, can combine with airport transfer; tel. 936-327-259, mobile 609-205-844, www.livebarcelona.com, info@livebarcelona .com).

On Wheels

Guided Bus Tours—The **Barcelona Guide Bureau** offers several sightseeing tours leaving from Plaça de Catalunya. Departure times can change. Tours are designed to end at a major sight in case you'd like to spend more time there. The Gaudí tour visits the facades of Casa Batlló and Casa Milà, as well as Park Güell and the Sagrada Família (€50, includes Sagrada Família admission, daily at 9:00, also mid-April-Oct Mon-Sat at 15:15, 3.5 hours). Other tours offered year-round include Montjuïc (€30, includes Spanish Village admission, daily at 12:30, 3 hours); the All Barcelona Highlights tour (€66, includes Sagrada Família and Spanish Village admissions, daily at 9:00, 6 hours); and Montserrat (€45, Mon-Sat at 15:00, 4 hours), which offers a convenient way to get to this mountaintop monastery if you don't want to deal with public transportation (see the Day Trips from Barcelona chapter). During peak season, a Gaudí Plus tour combines the standard Gaudí tour with some "off-the-beaten-path masterpieces" (€55, mid-April-Oct Mon-Sat at 9:00, 4 hours). You can get detailed information and book tickets at a TI, on their website, or simply by showing up at their departure point on Plaça de Catalunya in front of the Hard Rock Café—look for the guides holding orange umbrellas. Buying tickets online can save you about 10 percent. You can purchase tickets at many hotels for no extra charge (tel. 933-152-261, www .barcelonaguidebureau.com).

Catalunya Tourist Bus also runs excursions to nearby destinations, including some that are difficult to reach by public transportation. Trips include Montserrat (€59, 8 hours, includes Gaudí's unfinished Colònia Güell development) and Salvador Dalí sights in Figueres and Girona (€71, 11 hours). Both itineraries depart Tuesday through Sunday at 8:30 from Plaça de Catalunya (€8 discount for groups of 4 or more—team up with other travelers to save; live trilingual commentary in Catalan, Spanish, and English; €5 extra for a more in-depth English audioguide; book at TIs, by phone, or online; tel. 932-853-832, www.catalunyabusturistic .com).

For information on **hop-on, hop-off bus tours,** see "Getting Around Barcelona," earlier.

Bike Tours—Several companies run bike tours around Barcelona. **Un Cotxe Menys** ("One Car Less") offers three-hour English-only bike tours daily at 11:00 year-round (April-mid-Sept also Fri-Mon at 16:30; rents bikes, too—see "Helpful Hints," earlier). Your guide leads you from sight to sight, mostly on bike paths and through parks, with a stop-and-go commentary (€22 includes bike rental and drink, no reservations needed, tours meet just outside TI on Plaça Sant Jaume in Barri Gòtic—or, 10 minutes later, at their bike shop in El Born near the Church of Santa Maria del Mar; Carrer de l'Esparteria 3—see map on page 178, tel. 932-682-105, www .bicicletabarcelona.com).

Barcelona CicloTour runs a similar itinerary, but also adds an evening tour on peak-season weekends (€22, departs from Hard Rock Café on Plaça de Catalunya daily at 11:00, mid-April-Oct also at 16:30; night tour departs June-Sept Thu-Sun at 19:30, Oct Fri-Sat at 19:30; tel. 933-171-970, www.barcelonaciclotour.com).

Weekend Tour Packages for Students

Andy Steves (my son) runs Weekend Student Adventures, offering active and experiential three-day weekend tours from €199, designed for American students studying abroad (www.wsaeurope .com for details on tours of Barcelona and other great cities).

SIGHTS IN BARCELONA

The sights listed in this chapter are primarily arranged by neighborhood for handy sightseeing. When you see a ✪ in a listing, it means the sight is covered in much more depth in one of my walks or self-guided tours.

For tips on sightseeing, see page 16 in the Introduction. For some sights, it's either required or highly recommended that you make advance reservations (see page 32). Also, be sure to check www.ricksteves.com/update for any significant changes that may have occurred since this book was printed.

▲▲▲The Ramblas

Meandering through the heart of the Old City is the Ramblas, Barcelona's most famous boulevard. Named for the long-gone stream *(rambla)* whose course it followed, the Ramblas flows from Plaça de Catalunya, past the core of the Barri Gòtic, to the harborfront Columbus Monument. Boasting a generous pedestrian strip down the middle, the Ramblas features vibrant flower vendors, exuberantly costumed "human statues" that spring to life for a coin, and the booming **La Boqueria Market,** rife with fine people-watching opportunities (described on page 44).

For a self-guided tour of this pedestrian boulevard, see ✪ The Ramblas Ramble chapter.

Barcelona at a Glance

▲▲▲**Ramblas** Barcelona's colorful, gritty, tourist-filled pedestrian thoroughfare. **Hours:** Always open. See page 41.

▲▲▲**Picasso Museum** Extensive collection offering insight into the brilliant Spanish artist's early years. **Hours:** Tue-Sun 10:00-19:50, closed Mon. See page 53.

▲▲▲**Sagrada Família** Gaudí's remarkable, unfinished church—a masterpiece in progress. **Hours:** Daily April-Sept 9:00-20:30, Oct-March 9:00-18:30. See page 63.

▲▲**Palace of Catalan Music** Best Modernista interior in Barcelona. **Hours:** Fifty-minute English tours daily every hour 10:00-15:00, plus frequent concerts. See page 53.

▲▲**Casa Milà** Barcelona's quintessential Modernista building and Gaudí creation (a.k.a La Pedrera). **Hours:** Daily March-Oct 9:00-20:00, Nov-Feb 9:00-18:30. See page 59.

▲▲**Park Güell** Colorful Gaudí-designed park. **Hours:** Daily April-Oct 8:00-21:30, Nov-March 8:30-18:00. See page 64.

▲▲**Catalan Art Museum** World-class showcase of this region's art, including a substantial Romanesque collection. **Hours:** Tue-Sat 10:00-19:00, Sun 10:00-14:30, closed Mon. See page 73.

▲▲**CaixaForum** Modernista brick factory now occupied by cutting-edge cultural center featuring excellent temporary art exhibits. **Hours:** Mon-Fri 10:00-20:00, Sat-Sun 10:00-21:00, July-Aug open late on some days—likely Wed until 23:00. See page 75.

▲**La Boqueria Market** Colorful but touristy produce market, just off the Ramblas. **Hours:** Mon-Sat 8:00-20:00, best mornings after 9:00, closed Sun. See page 44.

▲**Palau Güell** Exquisitely curvy Gaudí interior and fantasy rooftop. **Hours:** April-Sept Tue-Sun 10:00-20:00, Oct-March Tue-Sun 10:00-17:30, closed Mon year-round. See page 44.

▲**Plaça Reial** Stately square near the Ramblas, with palm trees, Gaudí-designed lampposts, and a fine slice-of-life look at Barcelona. **Hours:** Always open. See page 45.

▲**Avinguda del Portal de l'Angel** Main boulevard leading into medieval Barcelona, now a pedestrian-only shopping street with big-name chain stores. **Hours:** Always open. See page 49.

▲**Maritime Museum** A sailor's delight, housed in a medieval shipyard (but permanent collection likely closed through 2014). **Hours:** Temporary exhibits daily 10:00-20:00. See page 45.

▲**Cathedral of Barcelona** Colossal Gothic cathedral ringed by distinctive chapels. **Hours:** Generally open to visitors Mon-Fri 8:00-19:30, Sat-Sun 8:00-20:00. See page 49.

▲*Sardana* **Dances** Patriotic dance in which proud Catalans join hands in a circle, often held outdoors. **Hours:** Every Sun at 12:00, usually also Sat at 18:00, no dances in Aug. See page 49.

▲**Barcelona History Museum** One-stop trip through town history, from Roman times to today. **Hours:** Tue-Sat 10:00-19:00, Sun 10:00-20:00, closed Mon. See page 52.

▲**Santa Caterina Market** Fine market hall built on the site of an old monastery and updated with a wavy Gaudí-inspired roof. **Hours:** Mon 7:30-14:00, Tue-Wed and Sat 7:30-15:30, Thu-Fri 7:30-20:30, closed Sun. See page 54.

▲**Church of Santa Maria del Mar** Catalan Gothic church in El Born, built by wealthy medieval shippers. **Hours:** Daily 9:00-13:30 & 16:30-20:00. See page 54.

▲**Barcelona's Beach** Fun-filled, man-made beach reaching from the harbor to the Fòrum. **Hours:** Always open. See page 55.

▲**Block of Discord** Noisy block of competing Modernista facades by Gaudí and his rivals. **Hours:** Always viewable. See page 58.

▲**Casa Batlló** Gaudí-designed home topped with fanciful dragon-inspired roof. **Hours:** Daily 9:00-20:00. See page 59.

▲**Fundació Joan Miró** World's best collection of works by Catalan modern artist Joan Miró and his contemporaries. **Hours:** July-Sept Tue-Sat 10:00-20:00, Thu until 21:30, Sun 10:00-14:30; Oct-June Tue-Sat 10:00-19:00, Thu until 21:30, Sun 10:00-14:30; closed Mon year-round. See page 69.

▲**1929 World Expo Fairgrounds** Expo site at the base of Montjuïc, featuring playful Magic Fountains, the impressive CaixaForum art gallery, cheesy Spanish Village, and Las Arenas, a mall converted from a bullring. **Hours:** Grounds always open. See page 75.

▲**Magic Fountains** Lively fountain spectacle. **Hours:** Almost always May-Sept Thu-Sun 21:00-23:00, no shows Mon-Wed; Oct-April Fri-Sat 19:00-20:30, no shows Sun-Thu. See page 75.

SIGHTS

On or near the Ramblas

▲La Boqueria Market—Barcelona has many characteristic market halls, but this is the most central—and the most crowded. Housed in a cool glass-and-steel structure, La Boqueria features a wide variety of produce and Catalan edibles that you'll pay a premium for. For less touristy markets, consider Santa Caterina in El Born (with avant-garde architecture; see page 117) or La Concepció in the Eixample (with a neighborhood vibe; see page 137). Still, La Boqueria's handy location right in the heart of the Old City makes it well worth a visit.

Cost and Hours: Free, Mon-Sat 8:00-20:00, best on mornings after 9:00, closed Sun, Rambla 91, tel. 933-192-584, www.boqueria.info.

For a self-guided walk through the market, see page 87 in ✪ The Ramblas Ramble chapter.

▲Palau Güell—Just as the Picasso Museum reveals a young genius on the verge of a breakthrough, this early building by Antoni Gaudí (completed in 1890) shows the architect taking his first tentative steps toward what would become his trademark curvy style. Dark and masculine, with its castle-like rooms, Palau Güell (Catalans pronounce it "gway") was custom-built to house the Güell clan and gives an insight into Gaudí's artistic genius. Despite the eye-catching roof (visible from the street if you crane your neck), I'd skip Palau Güell if you plan to see the more interesting Casa Milà (see page 59).

Cost and Hours: €10, includes audioguide, free first Sun of the month, open April-Sept Tue-Sun 10:00-20:00, Oct-March Tue-Sun 10:00-17:30, closed Mon year-round, last entry one hour before closing, a half-block off the Ramblas at Carrer Nou de la Rambla 3-5, Metro: Liceu or Drassanes, tel. 933-173-974, www.palauguell.cat.

Buying Tickets: As with any Gaudí sight, you may encounter lines. Since it's not possible to reserve tickets in advance, you'll have to buy them at the ticket window to the left of the entryway, then line up to the right. Each ticket has an entry time, so at busy times you may have to return later, even after buying your ticket.

Visiting the House: The parabolic-arch **entryways,** viewable from the outside, are the first clue that this is not a typical townhouse. For inspiration, Gaudí hung a chain to create a U-shape, then flipped it upside-down. The wrought-iron doors were cleverly designed so that those inside could see out, and light from the outside could get in—but not vice versa.

Once inside, an engaging 24-stop audioguide, included with your admission, fills in the details. The Neo-Gothic **cellar,** with its mushroom pillars, was used as a stable—notice the big carriage doors in the back and the rings on some of the posts used to tie up the horses.

A grand staircase leads to the **living space,** including a family room, dining room, and so on. Photos  show how the Güell family—with their textile wealth—originally furnished the place. The intricacy of Gaudí's design work evokes the impossibly complex patterns that decorate great Moorish palaces. Step onto the terrace out back, and take a look at the elaborately decorated (and unmistakably organic-looking) bay window.

The tall, skinny, atrium-like **central hall** fills several floors under a parabolic dome. Behind the grand, gilded doors is a personal chapel, which made it easy to instantly convert the hall from a secular space to a religious one.

Upstairs are the Güells' his-and-hers bedrooms, along with a **film** telling the story of the two men behind this building: Gaudí and his patron, the building's resident and namesake, Eusebi Güell. At a time when most wealthy urbanites were moving to the Eixample, Güell decided to stay in the Old City.

The most dramatic space is the **rooftop;** Gaudí slathered the 20 chimneys and ventilation towers with bits of stained glass, ceramic tile, and marble to create a forest of giant upside-down ice-cream cones.

▲**Plaça Reial**—This genteel-feeling square, with palm trees and a pair of Gaudí-designed lampposts, is a welcoming open space in the otherwise claustrophobic Old City. You can sit down for a drink at one of the touristy bars, or just lean up against the fountain and take it all in.

For more details on Plaça Reial, see page 90 in ❍ The Ramblas Ramble chapter. For food and drink recommendations nearby, see pages 199 and 233.

At the Bottom of the Ramblas, on the Harborfront

▲**Maritime Museum (Museu Marítim)**—Barcelona's medieval shipyard, the best preserved in the entire Mediterranean, is home

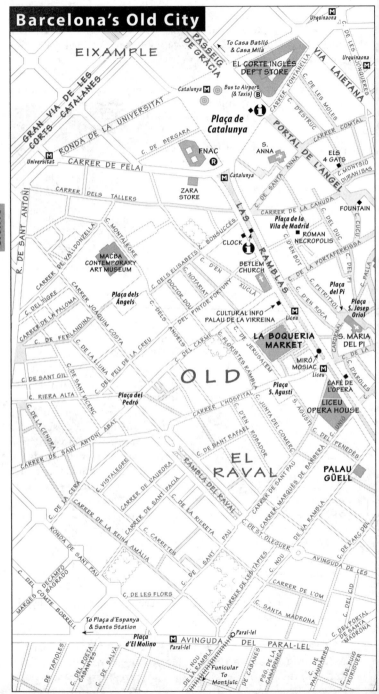

Barcelona's Old City

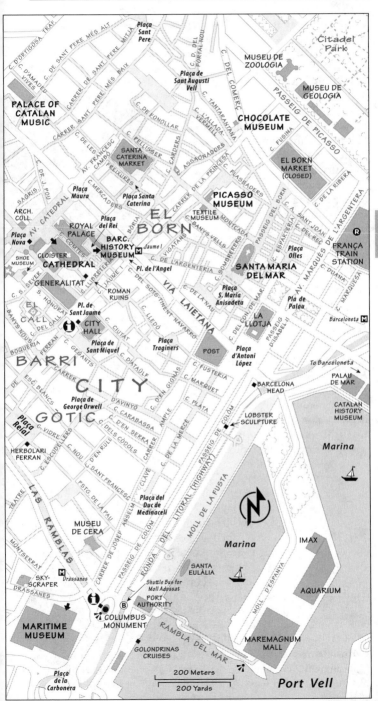

to an excellent museum. Its permanent collection is closed for renovation, likely through 2014, during which time the museum will host temporary exhibits in various sections.

The building's cavernous halls evoke the 14th-century days when Catalunya was a naval and shipbuilding power, cranking out 30 huge galleys a winter. As in the US today, military and commercial ventures mixed and mingled as Catalunya built its trading empire. When the permanent collection reopens, it'll cover the salty history of ships and navigation from the 13th to the 20th centuries. Riveting for nautical types and interesting for anyone, its modern and beautifully presented exhibits will put you in a seafaring mood. The helpful, included audioguide tells the story well

and explains the various seafaring vessels displayed—including an impressively huge and richly decorated royal galley.

Your ticket also includes entrance to the *Santa Eulàlia*, an early 20th-century schooner docked just a short walk from the Columbus Monument (on the Moll de la Fusta quay).

Cost and Hours: Museum—price depends on exhibits, daily 10:00-20:00, last entry 30 minutes before closing; *Santa Eulàlia*—€1 for entry without museum visit, Tue-Fri and Sun 10:00-19:30, Sat 14:00-19:30, closes at 17:30 in Nov-March, closed Mon year-round; breezy café in museum courtyard, Avinguda de la Drassanes, Metro: Drassanes, tel. 933-429-920, www.mmb.cat.

Columbus Monument (Monument a Colóm)—Located

where the Ramblas hits the harbor, this 200-foot-tall monument was built for the 1888 Universal Exposition (World's Fair) and commemorates Columbus' stop in Barcelona following his first trip to America. The tight four-person elevator takes you to the glassed-in observation area at the top for congested but sweeping views (elevator may be closed during your visit). A small TI is inside the base of the monument.

Cost and Hours: €4, daily May-Oct 8:30-20:30, Nov-April 8:00-20:00, Plaça del Portal de la Pau, tel. 933-025-224.

For more details on the monument, see page 92 of ✪ The Ramblas Ramble chapter.

***Golondrinas* Cruises**—At the harbor near the foot of the Columbus Monument, tourist boats called *golondrinas* offer two different unguided trips. As Barcelona's skyline isn't all that striking from the water, these trips are pretty pointless unless you'd just like to go for a boat ride. The shorter version goes around the harbor in 35 minutes (€6.90, daily on the hour 11:30-19:00, every 30 minutes mid-June-mid-Sept, might not run Nov-April—call ahead, tel. 934-423-106). The longer 1.5-hour trip goes up the coast to the Fòrum complex and back (€14.50, can disembark at Fòrum in summer only, about 7/day, daily 11:30-19:30, shorter hours in winter).

In the Barri Gòtic

For more details on this area and several of the following sights, see my ✪ Barri Gòtic Walk.

▲**Avinguda del Portal de l'Angel**—This broad, traffic-free boulevard connects Barcelona's modern Plaça de Catalunya to its historic cathedral district. It's lined with just about every type of Spanish and international chain store you can imagine—and yet, its circa-1888 remodel has left it with a certain dignified air. Just off this drag, you'll discover humble old churches and the famous bar called Els Quatre Gats, where a young Picasso got his start. For tips on shopping along this street, see page 227.

▲**Cathedral of Barcelona**—The city's 14th-century, Gothic-style cathedral (with a Neo-Gothic facade) has played a signifi-

cant role in Barcelona's history—but as far as grand cathedrals go, this one is relatively unexciting. Still, it's worth a visit to see its richly decorated chapels, finely carved choir, tomb of St. Eulàlia, and restful cloister with gurgling fountains and resident geese.

Cost and Hours: Generally open to visitors Mon-Fri 8:00-19:30, Sat-Sun 8:00-20:00. Free to enter Mon-Sat before 12:45, Sun before 13:45, and daily after 17:15, but you must pay to enter the cathedral's three minor sights (museum-€2, terrace-€2.50, choir-€2.50). The church is officially "closed" for a few hours each afternoon (Mon-Sat 13:00-17:00, Sun 14:00-17:00), but you can get in to see the interior sights by paying €6. Tel. 933-151-554, www.catedralbcn.org.

✪ See the Cathedral of Barcelona Tour chapter.

▲*Sardana* **Dances**—If you're in town on a weekend, be sure to see the *sardana*, a patriotic dance in which Barcelonans link hands and dance in a circle (see sidebar on the next page).

Cost and Hours: Free, Sun at 12:00, usually also Sat at 18:00, no dances in Aug, event lasts 1-2 hours, in the square in front of the cathedral.

SIGHTS

Circle Dances in Squares and Castles in the Air

From group circle dancing to human towers, Catalans have some interesting and unique traditions. A memorable Barcelona experience is watching (or participating in) the patriotic **sardana** dances. Locals of all ages seem to spontaneously appear. For some it's a highly symbolic, politically charged action representing Catalan unity—but for most it's just a fun chance to kick up their heels. Participants gather in circles after putting their things in the center—symbolic of community and sharing (and the ever-present risk of theft). All are welcome, even tourists cursed with two left feet. The dances are held in the square in front of the cathedral on Sundays at noon and usually also on Saturdays at 18:00 (none in Aug).

Holding hands, dancers raise their arms—slow-motion, *Zorba the Greek*-style—as they hop and sway gracefully to the music. The band *(cobla)* consists of a long flute, tenor and soprano oboes, strange-looking brass instruments, and a tiny bongo-like drum *(tambori)*. The rest of Spain mocks this lazy circle dance, but considering what it takes for a culture to survive within another culture's country, it is a stirring display of local pride and patriotism. During 36 years of Franco dictatorship, the *sardana* was forbidden.

Another Catalan tradition is the **castell,** a tower erected solely of people. *Castells* pop up on special occasions, such as the Festa Major de Gràcia in mid-August and La Mercè festival in late September. Towers can be up to 10 humans high. Imagine balancing 50 or 60 feet in the air, with nothing but a pile of flesh and bone between you and the ground. The base is formed by burly supports called *baixos*; above them are the *manilles* ("handles"), which help haul up the people to the top. The *castell* is capped with a human steeple—usually a child—who extends four fingers into the air, representing the four red stripes of the Catalan flag. A scrum of spotters (called *pinyas*) cluster around the base in case anyone falls. *Castelleres* are judged both on how quickly they erect their human towers and how fast they can take them down. Besides during festivals, you may also see people forming these towers in front of the cathedral on summer Saturdays around 19:00 (confirm locally before showing up).

One thing that these two traditions have in common is their communal nature. Perhaps it's no coincidence, as Catalunya is known for its community spirit, team building, and socialistic bent.

Frederic Marès Museum (Museu Frederic Marès)—This museum, with the eclectic collection of local sculptor and pack-rat Frederic Marès (1893-1991),

sprawls around a peaceful courtyard through several old Barri Gòtic buildings. The biggest part of the collection, on the ground and first floors, consists of sculpture—from ancient works to beautiful, evocative Gothic pieces to items from the early 20th century. Even more interesting is the extensive "Collector's Cabinet," consisting of items Marès found representative of everyday life in the 19th century. Lovingly displayed on the second and third floors are rooms upon rooms of scissors, keys, irons, fans, nutcrackers, stamps, pipes, snuff boxes, opera glasses, pocket watches, bicycles, toy soldiers, dolls, and other bric-a-brac. And in Marès' study are several sculptures by the artist himself. The tranquil courtyard café offers a pleasant break, even when the museum is closed (café open in summer only, until 22:00).

Cost and Hours: €4.20, free Sun from 15:00, 1.5-hour audioguide-€1; open Tue-Sat 10:00-19:00, Sun 11:00-20:00, closed Mon; Plaça de Sant Iu 5-6, Metro: Jaume I, tel. 932-563-500, www.museumares.bcn.cat.

Shoe Museum (Museu del Calçat)—Shoe lovers enjoy this small museum of footwear in glass display cases, watched over by an earnest attendant. You'll see shoes from the 1700s to today: fancy ladies' boots, Tibetan moccasins, big clown shoes, and shoes of minor celebrities such as the president of Catalunya. The huge shoes at the entry are designed to fit the feet of the statue atop the Columbus Monument.

Cost and Hours: €2.50, Tue-Sun 11:00-14:00, closed Mon, Plaça Sant Felip Neri 5, Metro: Jaume I, tel. 933-014-533.

Plaça de Sant Jaume—This open-feeling square (a rarity in the tight Barri Gòtic) is flanked by the two most important administrative buildings in Catalunya: the Palau de la Generalitat (home of the autonomous Catalan government) and the Barcelona City Hall.

For more details, see page 105 of the ✪ Barri Gòtic Walk chapter.

Roman Temple of Augustus (Temple Roma d'August)—Tucked inside a small medieval courtyard, four columns from an ancient temple of Augustus are a reminder of Barcelona's Roman origins. The temple, dating from the late first century B.C., stood at one corner of the ancient forum quarter.

Cost and Hours: Free; April-Sept Tue-Sun 10:00-20:00;

Oct-March Tue-Sat 10:00-14:00 & 16:00-19:00, Sun 10:00-20:00; closed Mon year-round; Carrer del Paradís 10, tel. 933-152-311.

For more on the temple, see page 106 of the ✪ Barri Gòtic Walk chapter.

Plaça del Rei—Perhaps the best place in town to get a feel for Barcelona's faint connection to Old World royalty, this "Square of the Monarch" offers a good view of the Royal Palace, where both Spanish kings and Catalan counts once resided. Although the palace complex is mostly closed to tourists, parts of the building are used for exhibits for the Barcelona History Museum.

▲Barcelona History Museum (Museu d'Història de Barcelona: Plaça del Rei)—At this main branch of the city history museum (MUHBA for short), you can literally walk through the history of Barcelona, including an underground labyrinth of excavated Roman ruins.

Cost and Hours: €7; ticket includes English audioguide and other MUHBA branches, including La Casa del Guarda in Park Güell; free all day first Sun of month and other Sun from 15:00—but no audioguide during free times; open Tue-Sat 10:00-19:00, Sun 10:00-20:00, closed Mon; last entry 30 minutes before closing, Plaça del Rei, enter on Vageur street, Metro: Jaume I, tel. 932-562-122.

Visiting the Museum: Though the museum is housed in part of the former Royal Palace complex, you'll see only a bit of that grand space. Instead, the focus is on the exhibits in the cellar. While posted information is only in Catalan and Spanish, the included English audioguide provides informative, if dry, descriptions of the exhibits.

Start by watching the nine-minute introductory video in the small theater (at the end of the first floor); it plays alternately in Catalan, Spanish, and English, but it's worth viewing in any language. Then take an elevator down 65 feet (and 2,000 years—see the date spin back as you descend) to stroll the streets of Roman Barcino.

This was a working-class part of town, so you'll see models of domestic life, sewers, areas used for laundry and dyeing, the remains of a factory that processed fish and created garum (a fish-derived sauce used extensively in ancient Roman cooking), wine-making facilities, and bits of a seventh-century early-Christian church. An exhibit in the 11th-century count's palace shows you Barcelona through its glory days in the Middle Ages.

Finally, head upstairs (or ride the elevator to floor 0) to see a model of the city from the early 16th century. From here, you can also enter **Tinell Hall** (part of the Royal Palace), with its long, graceful, rounded vaults. Nearby, step into the 14th-century **Chapel of St. Agatha** if it's hosting a free temporary exhibit.

In El Born

Despite being home to the top-notch Picasso Museum, El Born (also known as "La Ribera") feels wonderfully local, with a higher ratio of Barcelonans to tourists than most other city-center zones (Metro: Jaume I). Narrow lanes sprout from the neighborhood's main artery, Passeig del Born—the perfect springboard for exploring artsy boutiques, inviting cafés and restaurants, funky shops, and rollicking nightlife. For a tour of this neighborhood with more information on its sights, see the ✪ El Born Walk. For tips on shopping, see page 223 of the Shopping in Barcelona chapter.

▲▲▲**Picasso Museum (Museu Picasso)**—Pablo Picasso may have made his career in Paris, but the years he spent in Barcelona—from ages 14 through 23—were among the most formative of his life. It was here that young Pablo mastered the realistic painting style of his artistic forebears—and it was also here that he first felt the freedom that allowed him to leave that all behind and give in to his creative, experimental urges. When he left Barcelona, Picasso headed for Paris...and revolutionized art forever.

The pieces in this excellent museum capture that priceless moment just before this bold young thinker changed the world. While you won't find Picasso's famous later Cubist works here, you will enjoy a representative sweep of his early years, from art-school prodigy to the gloomy hues of his Blue Period to the revitalized cheer of his Rose Period. You'll also see works from his twilight years, including dozens of wild improvisations inspired by Diego Velázquez's seminal *Las Meninas,* as well as a roomful of works that reflect the childlike exuberance of an old man playing like a young kid on the French Riviera. It's undoubtedly the top collection of Picassos here in his native country and the best anywhere of his early years.

Cost and Hours: €11, free all day first Sun of month and other Sun from 15:00, audioguide-€3; Tue-Sun 10:00-19:50, closed Mon, last entry 20 minutes before closing; good café, Carrer de Montcada 15-23, ticket office at #21, Metro: Jaume I, tel. 932-563-000, www.museupicasso.bcn.cat.

Avoiding Lines: You can skip the line either with an Articket BCN or with a ticket bought in advance from the museum's website. If you just show up, expect to wait in line, sometimes for more than an hour. For more information and other crowd-beating tips, see page 127.

✪ See the Picasso Museum Tour chapter.

▲▲**Palace of Catalan Music (Palau de la Música Catalana)**—This concert hall, built in just three years and finished in 1908, features an unexceptional exterior but boasts my favorite Modernista interior in town (by Lluís Domènech i Montaner). Its inviting arches lead you into the 2,138-seat hall (accessible only with a

SIGHTS

tour). A kaleidoscopic skylight features a choir singing around the sun, while playful carvings and mosaics celebrate music and Catalan culture. If you're interested in Modernisme, taking this tour (which starts with a relaxing 12-minute video) is one of the best experiences in town—

and helps balance the hard-to-avoid over-focus on Gaudí as "Mr. Modernisme."

Cost and Hours: €15, 50-minute tours in English run daily every hour 10:00-15:00, tour times may change based on performance schedule, about 6 blocks northeast of cathedral, Carrer Palau de la Música 4-6, Metro: Urquinaona, tel. 902-442-882, www.palaumusica.cat.

Advance Reservations Required: You must buy your ticket in advance to get a spot on an English guided tour (tickets available up to 4 months in advance—purchase yours at least 2 days before, though they're sometimes available the same day or day before—especially Oct-March). You can buy the ticket in person at the concert hall box office (open daily 9:30-15:30, less than a 10-minute walk from the cathedral or Picasso Museum); by phone with your credit card (for no extra charge, tel. 902-475-485); or online at the concert hall website (€1 fee, www.palaumusica.cat).

Concerts: Music lovers see the hall's interior while attending a concert (300 per year, €22-49 tickets, see website for schedule, box office tel. 902-442-882).

▲**Santa Caterina Market**—This eye-catching market hall's colorful, rippling roof covers a delightful shopping zone that caters more to locals than to tourists. Come for the outlandish architecture, but stay for a chance to shop for a picnic without the tourist logjam of La Boqueria Market on the Ramblas.

Cost and Hours: Free, Mon 7:30-14:00, Tue-Wed and Sat 7:30-15:30, Thu-Fri 7:30-20:30, closed Sun, Avinguda de Francesc Cambó 16, www.mercatsantacaterina.net.

For more on the market, see page 120 of the ✪ El Born Walk chapter.

▲**Church of Santa Maria del Mar**—This so-called "Cathedral of the Sea" was built entirely with local funds and labor, in the heart of the wealthy merchant El Born quarter. Proudly independent, the church features a purely Catalan Gothic interior that was forcibly uncluttered of its Baroque decor by Civil War belligerents.

Cost and Hours: Free, daily 9:00-13:30 & 16:30-20:00, Plaça Santa Maria, Metro: Jaume I, tel. 933-102-390.

For more information on the church, see page 124 of the ✪ El

Born Walk chapter.

Chocolate Museum (Museu de la Xocolata)—This museum, only a couple of blocks from the Picasso Museum (and near Citadel Park—see next listing), is fun for chocolate lovers. Operated by the local confectioners' guild, it tells the story of chocolate from Aztecs to Europeans via the port of Barcelona, where it was first unloaded and processed. But the history lesson is just an excuse to show off a series of remarkably ornate candy sculptures. These works of edible art—which change every year but often include such themes as Don Quixote or the roofs of Barcelona—begin as store-window displays for Easter or Christmas. Once the holiday passes, the confectioners bring the sculptures here to be enjoyed.

Cost and Hours: €4.30, Mon-Sat 10:00-19:00, Sun 10:00-15:00, Carrer del Comerç 36, Metro: Jaume I, tel. 932-687-878, www.museuxocolata.cat.

Near the Waterfront

Citadel Park (Parc de la Ciutadella)—In 1888, Barcelona's biggest, greenest park, originally the site of a much-hated military citadel, was transformed for a Universal Exhibition (World's Fair). The stately Triumphal Arch at the top of the park, celebrating the removal of the citadel, was built as the main entrance. Inside you'll find wide pathways, plenty of trees and grass, a zoo, and museums of geology and zoology. Barcelona, one of Europe's most densely populated cities, suffers from a lack of real green space. This park is a haven and is especially enjoyable on weekends, when it teems with happy families (for more on the zoo and on kids' activities in Citadel Park, see the Barcelona with Children chapter). Enjoy the ornamental fountain that the young Antoni Gaudí helped design, and consider a jaunt in a rental rowboat on the lake in the center of the park. Check out the tropical Umbracle greenhouse and the Hivernacle winter garden, which has a pleasant café-bar (Mon-Sat 10:00-14:00 & 17:00-20:30, Sun 10:30-14:00, shorter hours off-season).

Cost and Hours: Park—free, daily 10:00 until dusk, north of França train station, Metro: Arc de Triomf, Barceloneta, or Ciutadella-Vila Olímpica.

▲**Barcelona's Beaches**—Barcelona has created a summer tourist trade by building a huge stretch of beaches east of the town center. From Barceloneta, an uninterrupted band of sand tumbles three miles northeast to the Fòrum. Before the 1992 Olympics, this area was an industrial wasteland nicknamed the "Catalan Manchester." Not anymore. The industrial zone was demolished and dumped into the sea, while sand was dredged out of the sea bed to make the pristine beaches locals enjoy today. Looking out to sea, you can't miss the W Hotel, shaped like a windblown sail,

SIGHTS

Barcelona's Best Views

Barcelona's delightful architecture is best seen up close, but to fully appreciate the city's scenic beauty, take advantage of one of many panoramic viewpoints scattered across town. For some viewpoints, you'll need to pay admission, but many are free, including the view terrace at Park Güell and the castle at Montjuïc. When deciding between viewpoints, target the ones that are already on your sightseeing route.

Cable Car: Although it's pricey and slow to load, the Aeri del Port cable car between Montjuïc and Barceloneta (in either direction) offers a dramatic moving panorama of the city. See page 65.

Park Güell: Inviting, curvy benches along a spectacular terrace offer free, sweeping views of Barcelona from this foothills park. Climb even higher to the Calvary for a bird's-eye view of the park and city below. See the Park Güell Tour chapter.

Sagrada Família Towers: Two different €3 elevators, one followed by dizzying stairs, take you up to the towers for a good view of the city and a unique angle on this fascinating church. See the Sagrada Família Tour chapter.

Montjuïc: Overlooking the port, this hilltop affords free city views from its castle ramparts and Miramar viewpoint park, as well as from the Catalan Art Museum's terrace and stylish restaurant. See page 64.

El Corte Inglés: The gigantic department store on Plaça de Catalunya has a great view cafeteria on its ninth floor. See page 227.

Casa Milà: The rooftop of this Gaudí masterpiece offers up-close views of fairytale chimneys plus a vista of the Eixample and the distant spires of the Sagrada Família. See page 59.

Las Arenas: Take a €1 glass elevator or escalate for free to the restaurant-ringed roof terrace at this former bullring (now a mall) for some of the best views of the World Expo Fairgrounds and Montjuïc.

Tibidabo: The city's highest peak offers almost limitless (but distant) city and Mediterranean views—if the weather and air quality cooperate. See page 77.

Cathedral of Barcelona: An elevator (€2.50) takes you up to a view terrace for an expansive city view from the heart of the Barri Gòtic.

dominating a small penin-
sula—controversial among
locals for displacing a popular nude beach.

The overall scene is
great for sunbathing and
for an evening paseo before
dinner. It's like a resort
island—complete with
lounge chairs, volleyball, showers, WCs, bike paths, and inviting beach bars called *chiringuitos*. Each beach segment has its own
vibe: Sant Sebastià (closest, popular with older beachgoers and
families), Barceloneta (considered the "pearl of Barcelona," near
many seafood restaurants), Nova Icària (pleasant family beach),
and Mar Bella (attracts a younger crowd, clothing-optional).

Biking the Beach: For a break from the city, rent a bike (in El
Born or Citadel Park—for details, see page 34) and take the following little ride: Explore Citadel Park, filled with families enjoying
a day out. Then roll through Barceloneta. This artificial peninsula
was once the home of working-class sailors and shippers. From the
Barceloneta beach, head north to the Olympic Village, where the
former apartments for 13,000 visiting athletes now house permanent residents. The village's symbol, Frank Gehry's striking "fish,"
shines brightly in the sun. A bustling night scene keeps this stretch
of harborfront busy until the wee hours. From here you'll come to
a series of man-made crescent-shaped beaches, each with trendy
bars and cafés. If you're careless or curious—down by Platja de la
Mar Bella—you'll pedal past people working on an all-over tan. In
the distance is the huge solar panel marking the site of the Fòrum
shopping and convention center.

The Fòrum—The original 1860 vision for Barcelona's enlarge-
ment would have extended the boulevard called Diagonal right to
the sea. Developers finally realized this goal nearly a century and
a half later, with the opening of the Fòrum. Go here for a taste of
today's Barcelona: nothing Gothic, nothing quaint, just big and
modern—a mall and a convention center. The Fòrum also tries to
be an inspiration for environmental engineering. Waste is burned
to produce heat. The giant solar panel creates perfectly clean and
sustainable energy.

In 2004, Barcelona hosted the "Forum of the Cultures," an
attempt to create a world's fair that recognized not states, but
peoples. Roma (Gypsies), Basques, Māoris, Native Americans,
and Catalans all assembled here in a global celebration of cultural
diversity, multiculturalism, peace, and sustainability. The bash
for this planet's "nations without states" was a moderate success,
with triennial follow-ups in Mexico in 2007 and Chile in 2010

(next up: Naples, Italy in 2013 and Amman, Jordan in 2016). Local government officials hoped the event—like the city's many other "expos"—would goose development...and it did. Barcelona now has a modern part of town.

Getting There: You can get out to the Fòrum by bike, bus, or taxi via the long and impressive beach. Or the Metro zips you there in just a few minutes from the center (Metro: Fòrum).

In the Eixample

For many visitors, Modernista architecture is Barcelona's main draw. And one name tops them all: Antoni Gaudí (1852-1926). Barcelona is an architectural scrapbook of Gaudí's galloping gables and organic curves. A devoted Catalan and Catholic, he immersed himself in each project, often living on-site. At various times, he called Park Güell, Casa Milà, and the Sagrada Família home. For more on Gaudí and some of his contemporaries, see the sidebar on page 146. For details on Modernisme, see page 142.

At the heart of the Modernista movement was the Eixample, a carefully planned "new town," just north of the Old City, with wide sidewalks, hardy shade trees, and a rigid grid plan cropped at the corners to create space and lightness at each intersection. Conveniently, all of this new construction provided a generation of Modernista architects with a blank canvas for creating boldly experimental designs. At the edge of the Eixample is Gaudí's greatest piece of work, the yet-to-be-finished Sagrada Família.

In this section, I've focused on the big Modernista sights in the Eixample, starting at the center of this neighborhood before winding up at the Sagrada Família. On the outskirts, just beyond the Eixample, is Park Güell, where Gaudí put his colorful stamp on 30 acres of greenery.

Even though Modernisme revolved around the Eixample, traces of this style can also be found elsewhere. Other Modernista highlights include Gaudí's Palau Güell, just off the Ramblas (see page 44); Lluís Domènech i Montaner's Palace of Catalan Music in El Born (see page 53); and Josep Puig i Cadafalch's CaixaForum, at the base of Montjuïc (page 75). For information on more Modernista sights, you can visit the main TI, where you'll find a special desk set aside just for Modernisme seekers (see page 30). For a tour of the Eixample, including a route that connects some of these sights, see my ✪ Eixample Walk.

▲**Block of Discord**—Three colorful Modernista facades jockey for your attention along a single block: Antoni Gaudí's Casa Batlló (the only one of the three that you can really get inside), Josep Puig i Cadafalch's Casa Amatller, and Lluís Domènech i Montaner's Casa Lleó Morera. Because the mansions look as though they are trying to outdo each other in creative twists, locals nicknamed

the noisy block the "Block of Discord." By the way, if you're tempted to snap photos from the middle of the street, be careful—Gaudí died after being struck by a streetcar.

Getting There: It's on Passeig de Gràcia (at the Metro stop of the same name), between Carrer del Consell de Cent and Carrer d'Aragó—three blocks from either Plaça de Catalunya or Casa Milà.

▲**Casa Batlló**—While the highlight is the roof, the interior of this Gaudí house is also interesting—and even more over-the-top than Casa Milà's (described next). Paid for with textile industry

money, the house features a funky mushroom-shaped fireplace nook on the main floor, a blue-and-white-ceramic-slathered atrium, and an attic (with more parabolic arches). There's barely a straight line in the house. You can also get a close-up look at the dragon-inspired rooftop. Because preservation of the place is privately funded, the entrance fee is steep—but it includes a good audioguide.

Cost and Hours: €18.15, daily 9:00-20:00, may close early for special events—closings posted in advance at entrance, tel. 932-160-306, www.casabatllo.cat. Purchase a ticket online to avoid lines, which are especially fierce in the morning. Your eticket isn't a timed reservation (it's good any time), but it will let you skip to the front of the queue.

▲▲**Casa Milà (La Pedrera)**—One of Gaudí's trademark works, this corner house—nicknamed "The Quarry" and located three blocks northwest of the Block of Discord—is an icon of Modernisme. While it's fun to ogle from the outside, it's also worth going inside, as it's arguably the purest Gaudí interior in town—executed at the height

of his abilities (unlike his earlier Palau Güell)—and still contains original furnishings. While Casa Batlló has a Gaudí facade and rooftop, these were appended to an existing building; Casa Milà, on the other hand, was built from the ground up according to

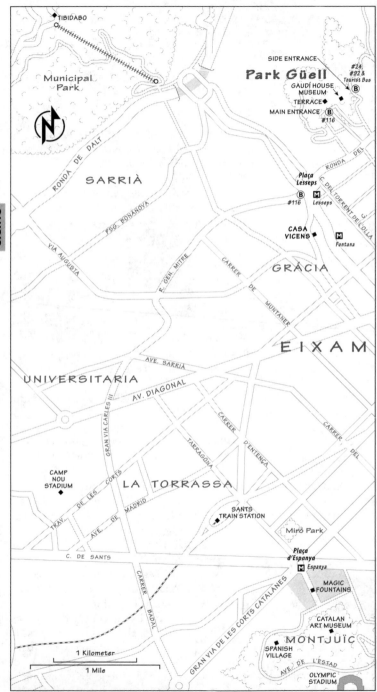

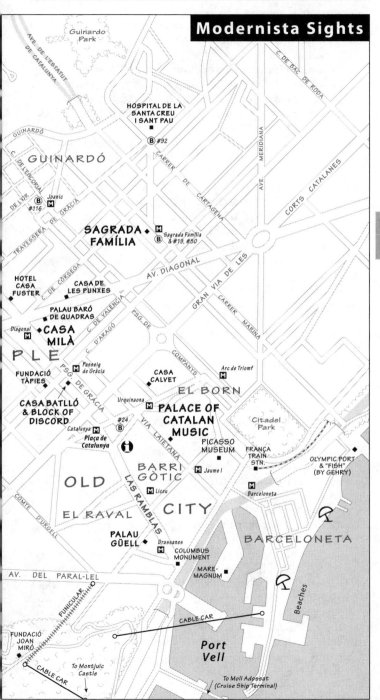

SIGHTS

Modernista Sights

Guinardo Park

AVE. DE L'ESTATUT DE CATALUNYA

C. DE BAC DE RODA

HOSPITAL DE LA SANTA CREU I SANT PAU

(B) #92

AVE. MERIDIANA

GUINARDÓ

C. DE L'ESCORIAL

C. DE L'OR

(B) #116 Joanic M

TRAVESSERA DE GRÀCIA

CARRER DE CARTAGENA

CORTS CATALANES

SAGRADA FAMÍLIA

M Sagrada Família (B) & #19, #50

HOTEL CASA FUSTER

C. DE CORSEGA

CASA DE LES PUNXES

AV. DIAGONAL

GRAN VIA DE LES

PALAU BARÓ DE QUADRAS

C. DE VALÈNCIA

Diagonal M

CASA MILÀ

C. D'ARAGÓ

PSG. DE

CARRER MARINA

PLE

FUNDACIÓ TÀPIES

PSG. DE GRÀCIA

Passeig de Gràcia M

COMPANYS

CASA CALVET

Arc de Triomf

EL BORN

CASA BATLLÓ & BLOCK OF DISCORD

Urquinaona M

#24 (B)

Catalunya M

Plaça de Catalunya

PALACE OF CATALAN MUSIC

VIA LAIETANA

Citadel Park

ℹ

PICASSO MUSEUM

FRANÇA TRAIN STN.

OLYMPIC PORT & "FISH" (BY GEHRY)

OLD

BARRI GÒTIC

M Jaume I

Barceloneta M

EL RAVAL

LAS RAMBLAS

M Liceu

CITY

COMTE D'URGELL

PALAU GÜELL

Drassanes M

BARCELONETA

COLUMBUS MONUMENT

AV. DEL PARAL·LEL

FUNICULAR

MARE-MAGNUM

Beaches

CABLE CAR

FUNDACIÓ JOAN MIRÓ

CABLE CAR

To Montjuïc Castle

Port Vell

To Moll Adossat (Cruise Ship Terminal)

Gaudí's plans. Besides entry to the interior, a ticket also gets you access to the delightful rooftop, with its forest of colorfully tiled chimneys.

Cost and Hours: €15, good audioguide-€4, daily March-Oct 9:00-20:00, Nov-Feb 9:00-18:30, last entry 30 minutes before closing, at the corner of Passeig de Gràcia and Provença (visitor entrance at Provença 261-265), Metro: Diagonal, info tel. 902-400-973, www.lapedrera.com.

Avoiding Lines: As lines can be long (up to a 1.5-hour wait to get in), it's best to reserve ahead at www.lapedrera.com (tickets come with an assigned entry time). If you come without a ticket, the best time to arrive is right when the ticket office opens. If the line stretches all the way to the corner, figure about an hour wait.

Free Entrance to Atrium: For a peek at the interior without paying for a ticket, find the door directly on the corner, which leads to the main atrium. Upstairs on the first floor are temporary exhibits (generally free, daily 10:00-20:00, may be closed between exhibitions).

Cuisine Art: A café on the mezzanine level serves Catalan-style snacks and meals (daily 8:30-24:00).

Nighttime Visits: The building hosts guided after-hour visits dubbed "The Secret Pedrera." On this pricey visit, you'll tour the building with the lights turned down low (€30; English tour offered daily March-Oct at 21:15, but check changeable schedule and offerings online).

Concerts: On summer weekends, Casa Milà hosts a rooftop concert series, "Summer Nights at La Pedrera." In addition to hearing live jazz, you can see the rooftop illuminated (€25, late June-early Sept Thu-Sat 20:30-23:00, book advance tickets online or by phone, tel. 902-101-212, www.lapedrera.com).

Visiting the House: A visit to Casa Milà covers three sections—the apartment, the attic, and the rooftop. Enter and head upstairs to the apartment. If it's near closing time, continue up to see the attic and rooftop first, to make sure you have enough time to enjoy Gaudí's works and the views (note that the roof may close when it rains).

The typical bourgeois **apartment** is decorated as it might have been when the building was first occupied by middle-class urbanites (a seven-minute video explains Barcelona society at the time). Notice Gaudí's clever use of the atrium to maximize daylight in all of the apartments.

The **attic** houses a sprawling multimedia exhibit tracing the history of the architect's career, with models, photos, and videos of his work. It's all displayed under distinctive parabola-shaped arches. While evocative of Gaudí's style in themselves, the arches are formed this way partly to support the multilevel roof above. This area was also used for ventilation, helping to keep things cool in summer and warm in winter. Tenants had storage spaces and did their laundry up here.

From the attic, a stairway leads to the undulating, jaw-dropping **rooftop,** where 30 chimneys and ventilation towers play volleyball with the clouds.

Back at the **ground level** of Casa Milà, poke into the dreamily painted original entrance courtyard.

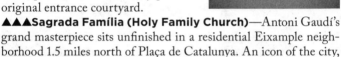

▲▲▲Sagrada Família (Holy Family Church)—Antoni Gaudí's grand masterpiece sits unfinished in a residential Eixample neighborhood 1.5 miles north of Plaça de Catalunya. An icon of the city, the Sagrada Família boasts bold, wildly creative, unmistakably organic architecture and decor inside and out—from its melting Glory Facade to its skull-like Passion Facade to its rainforest-esque interior. Begun under Gaudí's careful watch in 1883, the project saw some setbacks in the mid-20th century, but lately the progress has been remarkable. The city has set a goal of finishing by 2026, the centennial of Gaudí's death. For now, visitors get a close-up view of the dramatic exterior flourishes, the chance to walk through the otherworldly interior, and access to a fine museum detailing the design and engineering behind this one-of-a-kind architectural marvel.

Cost and Hours: €13, €16.50 combo-ticket also includes Gaudí House Museum at Park Güell (described next), elevators-€3 each, daily April-Sept 9:00-20:30, Oct-March 9:00-18:30, last entry 30 minutes before closing, guided tours and audioguides available, Carrer de Mallorca 401, Metro: Sagrada Família, exit toward Plaça de la Sagrada Família, tel. 932-073-031, www.sagradafamilia.cat.

Avoiding Lines: Lines of up to 45 minutes are not uncommon. To walk right in, buy tickets in advance for a specific entry time, either online or from ATMs at many La Caixa bank branches throughout the city. For details on these options, see page 153.

Connecting with Park Güell: For information on getting to Park Güell from the Sagrada Família, see page 153.

○ See the Sagrada Família Tour chapter.

Beyond the Eixample

▲▲**Park Güell**—Gaudí fans enjoy the artist's magic in this colorful park, located on the outskirts of town. While it takes a bit of effort to

get here, Park Güell (Catalans pronounce it "gway") offers a unique look at Gaudí's style in a natural rather than urban context. Designed as an upscale housing development for early-20th-century urbanites, the park is home to some of Barcelona's most famous symbols, including a whimsical staircase guarded by a dragon and a wavy bench—all of it covered with fragments of vivid tile—that encircles a panoramic view terrace supported by a wonderland of columns. Much of the park is free, but the part visitors want to see, the so-called Monumental Zone—with all the iconic Gaudí features—has an entry fee and time-limited admission. Also in the park is the **Gaudí House Museum,** where Gaudí lived for a time. Although he did not design the house, you can see a few examples of his furniture here (the house is within the free portion of the park, but charges admission). Even without its Gaudí connection, Park Güell is simply a fine place to enjoy a break from a busy city, where green space is relatively rare.

Cost and Hours: Monumental Zone—€8 at the gate or €7 online, it's smart to reserve tickets in advance, daily April-Oct 8:00-21:30, Nov-March 8:30-18:00, www.parkguell.cat. Gaudí House Museum—€5.50, €16.50 combo-ticket also includes Sagrada Família, daily April-Sept 10:00-20:00, until 18:00 Oct-March, www.casamuseugaudi.org.

Getting There: To reach Park Güell—about 2.5 miles north of Plaça de Catalunya—it's easiest to take a **taxi** from downtown, though you can also get there by **bus.** For details, see page 164. For instructions on linking the Sagrada Família to Park Güell, check page 163.

♻ See the Park Güell Tour chapter.

Montjuïc

Montjuïc (mohn-jew-EEK, "Mount of the Jews"), overlooking Barcelona's hazy port, has always been a show-off. Ages ago, it was capped by an impressive castle. When the Spanish enforced their rule, they built the imposing fortress that you'll see the shell of today. The hill has also played an integral role in the construction of Barcelona's great structures—significant parts of the historic city, the cathedral, the Sagrada Família, and much more were all built with stones quarried from Montjuïc.

Montjuïc has also been prominent during the last century. In

1929, it hosted an international fair, from which many of today's sights originated. And in 1992, the Summer Olympics directed the world's attention to this pincushion of attractions once again. While Montjuïc lacks any single knockout, must-see sight, it is home to a variety of very good ones, and most visitors should find one or two attractions here to suit their interests. For art lovers, the most worthwhile sights are the Fundació Joan Miró, Catalan Art Museum, and CaixaForum.

Sightseeing Strategies: I've listed these sights by altitude, from highest to lowest—from the hill-topping castle down to the 1929 World Expo Fairgrounds at the base of Montjuïc (described in the next section). If you're visiting all of my listed sights, ride to the top by bus, funicular, or taxi, then visit them in this order so that most of your walking is downhill. However, if you want to visit only the Catalan Art Museum and/or CaixaForum, you can just take the Metro to Plaça d'Espanya and ride the escalators up (with some stair-climbing as well) to those sights.

Getting to Montjuïc: You have several options. The simplest is to take a **taxi** directly to your destination (about €7 from downtown).

Buses can also take you up to Montjuïc. From Plaça de Catalunya, **bus #55** rides as far as Montjuïc's cable-car station/funicular. If you want to get higher (to the castle), ride the Metro or bus #9 or #50 from Plaça de Catalunya to Plaça d'Espanya, then make the easy transfer to **bus #150** to ride all the way up the hill. Alternatively, the red Tourist Bus will get you to the Montjuïc sights.

A **funicular** takes visitors from the Paral·lel Metro stop up to Montjuïc (covered by Metro ticket, every 10 minutes, 7:30-22:00, from 9:00 on Sat-Sun). To reach the funicular, take the Metro to the Paral·lel stop, then follow signs for *Parc Montjuïc* and the little funicular icon—you can enter the funicular directly without using another ticket (next departure posted at start of entry tunnel). From the top of the funicular, turn left and walk gently downhill two minutes to the Joan Miró museum, six minutes to the Olympic Stadium, or ten minutes to the Catalan Art Museum.

If you're heading all the way up to the castle, you can catch a bus or cable car from the top of the funicular (see castle listing, later.)

For a scenic (if very slow) approach to Montjuïc, you could ride the fun circa-1929 Aeri del Port **cable car** *(telefèric)* from the tip of the Barceloneta peninsula

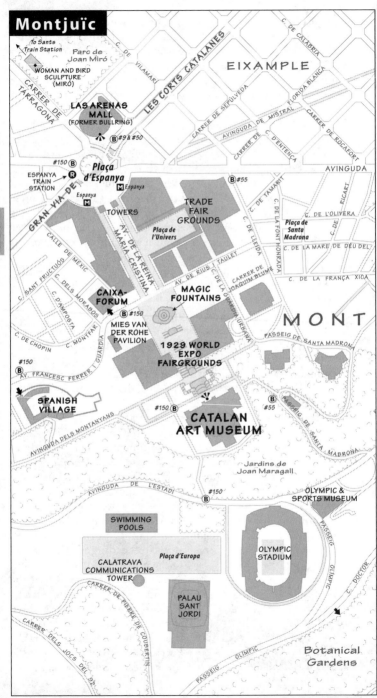

Montjuïc

SIGHTS

- To Sants Train Station
- Parc de Joan Miró
- WOMAN AND BIRD SCULPTURE (MIRÓ)
- C. DE VILAMARI
- C. DE CALABRIA
- EIXAMPLE
- LES CORTS CATALANES
- CARRER DE SEPULVEDA
- FLORIDA BLANCA
- CARRER DE ROCAFORT
- CARRER DE
- AVINGUDA DE MISTRAL
- C. D'ENTENÇA
- LAS ARENAS MALL (FORMER BULLRING)
- CARRER DE TARRAGONA
- #9 & #50
- #150 B
- ESPANYA TRAIN STATION
- Plaça d'Espanya
- Espanya M
- GRAN VIA DE
- Espanya M
- TOWERS
- AVINGUDA
- B #55
- C. DE TAMARIT
- C. DE LA FONT HONRADA
- C. DE L'OLIVERA
- RICART
- Plaça de Santa Madrona
- TRADE FAIR GROUNDS
- Plaça de l'Univers
- AV. DE LA REINA MARIA CRISTINA
- C. DE LLEIDA
- C. DE LA MARE DE DÉU DEL
- CALLE DE MEXIC
- C. SANT FRUCTUÓS
- C. DELS MORABOS
- C. D'AMPOSTA
- C. DE CHOPIN
- C. MONTJAR
- AV. DE RIUS I TAULET
- CARRER DE JOAQUIM BLUME
- C. DE LA FRANÇA XICA
- CAIXA-FORUM
- B #150
- MIES VAN DER ROHE PAVILION
- MAGIC FOUNTAINS
- CARRER DE LA GUARDIA URBANA
- M O N T
- PASSEIG DE SANTA MADRONA
- 1929 WORLD EXPO FAIRGROUNDS
- #150 B
- AV. FRANCESC FERRER I GUARDIA
- SPANISH VILLAGE
- AVINGUDA DELS MONTANYANS
- #150 B
- CATALAN ART MUSEUM
- B #55
- PASSEIG DE SANTA MADRONA
- Jardins de Joan Maragall
- AVINGUDA DE L'ESTADI
- #150 B
- OLYMPIC & SPORTS MUSEUM
- SWIMMING POOLS
- Plaça d'Europa
- CALATRAVA COMMUNICATIONS TOWER
- CARRER DE PIERRE DE COUBERTIN
- PALAU SANT JORDI
- OLYMPIC STADIUM
- PASSEIG OLIMPIC
- C. DOCTOR
- CARRER DELS JOCS DEL 92
- PASSEIG OLIMPIC
- Botanical Gardens

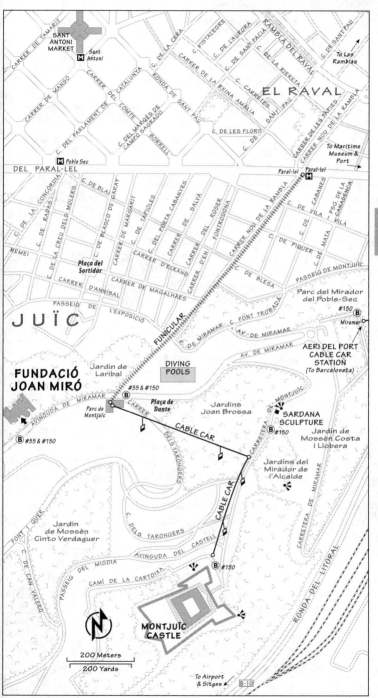

(across the harbor, near the beach) to the Miramar viewpoint park in Montjuïc. (Another station, near the port and Columbus Monument, is currently closed.) Since the cable car is expensive and goes between two relatively remote parts of town, it's only worthwhile for its sweeping views—or if you'd like to cap off your Montjuïc day with some beach time near Barceloneta (€10 one-way, €15 round-trip, 3/hour, daily 11:00-19:00, until 20:00 in June-Sept, closed in high wind, tel. 934-414-820, www.teleferi-cobarcelona.com). From the Barceloneta cable-car station, public buses (#17, #39, or #64) connect with the Barceloneta Metro stop.

Getting Around Montjuïc: Up top, it's fun to walk between the sights—especially if you're heading downhill. Otherwise, it can be easier and faster to connect the sights using the red Tourist Bus or one of the public buses that runs from different points in the city. Each bus has a slightly different route. **Bus #150** does a loop around the hilltop to link most of Montjuïc's sights, and it is the only bus that goes all the way to the castle. On the way up, it stops at or passes near CaixaForum, the Spanish Village, the Catalan Art Museum, Olympic Stadium, Fundació Joan Miró, and the lower castle cable-car station/top of the funicular before finally reaching the castle. On the downhill run, it makes a detour to loop by Miramar, the cable-car station for Barceloneta. **Bus #55** takes a shorter route up the hill, connecting only the funicular/cable-car stations, Fundació Joan Miró, and the Catalan Art Museum.

Castle of Montjuïc

The castle, while just an empty brick-and-concrete shell today, offers great city views from its ramparts...and some poignant history. It was built in the 18th century with a Vauban-type star fortress design by the central Spanish government to keep an eye on Barcelona and stifle citizen revolt. Until the late 20th century, the place functioned more to repress the people of Barcelona than to defend them. Being "taken to Montjuïc" meant you likely wouldn't be seen again. When the 20th-century dictator Franco was in power, the castle was the site of hundreds of political executions. But in 2010, Spain's Prime Minister José Luis Rodríguez Zapatero, keeping a campaign promise, turned over the control of the castle from Spain's national government to the city of Barcelona. These days it serves as a park, jogging destination, and host to a popular summer open-air cinema.

Beefy Civil War-vintage cannon point visitors to grand Mediterranean vistas. Survey the boats in the harbor: Ships belonging to Grimaldi Lines, an Italian company, sail off to Genoa, Rome, and Sardinia; Mallorca ferries make the eight-hour trip to

Barcelonans' big party escape; and the cruise-ship terminal busily hosts 800 ships a year (Barcelona is one of the main ports of embarkation for Mediterranean cruises). The seafront stretching far to the left was part of an Olympics project that turned a derelict industrial zone into a swanky stretch of promenades, beaches, and fancy condos. At the far right is Spain's leading port; you'll see containers stretching all the way to the airport.

Cost and Hours: Free, daily April-Sept 9:00-21:00, Oct-March 9:00-19:00.

Getting There: To spare yourself the hike up to the castle and to see some great views of the city, you can ride bus #150 to the base of the castle, catching it from Plaça d'Espanya, the top of the Montjuïc funicular, or various other points on Montjuïc. Or you can spring for the much pricier **cable car,** which departs from near the upper station of the Montjuïc funicular (€7 one-way, €10 round-trip, daily June-Sept 10:00-21:00, March-May and Oct 10:00-19:00, Nov-Feb 10:00-18:00).

SIGHTS

▲Fundació Joan Miró

Showcasing the talents of yet another Catalan artist, this museum has the best collection anywhere of art by Joan Miró (ZHOO-ahn mee-ROH, 1893-1983). Born in Barcelona, Miró divided his

time between Paris and Catalunya (including Barcelona and his favorite village, Mont-roig del Camp). This building—designed in 1975 by Josep Lluís Sert, a friend of Miró and a student of Le Corbusier—was purpose-built to show off Miró's art.

The museum displays an always-changing, loosely chronological overview of Miró's oeuvre (as well as generally excellent temporary exhibits of 20th- and 21st-century artists). Consider renting the wonderful audioguide, well worth the extra charge.

If you don't like abstract art, you'll leave here scratching your

Joan Miró: The Freedom of Simplicity

Miró believed that everything in the cosmos is linked—colors, sky, stars, love, time, music, dogs, men, women, dirt, and the void. He mixed childlike symbols of these things creatively, as a poet uses words. It's as liberating for the visual artist to be abstract as it is for the poet: Both can use metaphors rather than being confined to concrete explanations. Miró would listen to music and paint. It's interactive, free interpretation. He said, "For me, simplicity is freedom."

COPA DEL MUNDO DE FÚTBOL 🏆 ESPAÑA 82

Here are some tips to help you enjoy and appreciate Miró's art: First meditate on it, then read the title (for example, *The Smile of a Tear*), then meditate on it again. Repeat the process until you have an epiphany. There's no correct answer—it's pure poetry. Devotees of Miró say they fly with him and don't even need drugs. Psychoanalysts liken Miró's free-for-all canvases to Rorschach tests. Is that a cigar in that star's mouth?

head. But those who love this place are not faking it...they understand the genius of Miró and the fun of abstract art.

Cost and Hours: €10, great audioguide-€4; July-Sept Tue-Sat 10:00-20:00, Thu until 21:30, Sun 10:00-14:30; Oct-June Tue-Sat 10:00-19:00, Thu until 21:30, Sun 10:00-14:30; closed Mon year-round, 200 yards from top of funicular, Parc de Montjuïc, tel. 934-439-470, www.fundaciomiro-bcn.org. The museum has a cafeteria, a café, and a bookshop.

◑ Self-Guided Tour: From the entrance, pass through the temporary exhibits to reach the permanent collection, starting on the main floor.

Room 11: The massive 400-square-foot *Tapestry of the Foundation*, which Miró designed for this space in 1979, has real texture—like a painting with thick brushstrokes. Notice Miró's trademark star and moon high above. (A different tapestry, which Miró custom-made for New York City's World Trade Center around this same period, was lost in the 9/11 terrorist attacks.)

In the hallway to the next room, look through the window to find the *Mercury Fountain*, by American sculptor Alexander Calder. This piece was created for the same 1937 exhibition at which Picasso premiered his seminal *Guernica*. Like Picasso's canvas, Calder's fountain was created to honor victims of the Spanish

Civil War—in this case, the residents of Almadén, a mercury-mining town. Watch the liquid do its unpredictable thing as it drips and drops.

• *Now drift into...*

Room 12 (Sculpture Gallery): This gallery features several small ceramics by Miró. Ascend the ramp for a different angle. Nearby, find the stairs down to a room of pieces by other artists paying homage to Miró, a 15-minute film about Miró, and the Espai 13 installation space.

• *Make your way back to the main floor, where you'll find...*

Room 16 (Sala Joan Prats): The collection in this room loosely traces Miró's artistic development. Young Miró is a sponge of different styles—Fauvism, Cubism, Catalan folk art, Impressionism (see the canvases of beaches and countryside), Orientalism *(Portrait of a Young Girl)*—and whatever else he is exposed to. In 1920, he goes to Paris, dabbles in Dada, and socializes with Surrealists. Is Miró himself a Surrealist? Sort of. They share the same goal: circumventing the viewer's preconceptions about art and reality by juxtaposing unlikely items in order to short-circuit the brain.

Miró's early work does resemble Dalí's. But as his own idiosyncratic style evolves, Miró adds more and more abstraction to the mix. In his Green Paintings series (1925-1927), instead of placing photorealistic items against an otherworldly background (as Dalí would have), Miró arranges highly abstract symbols against a flat background. By 1925, Miró has left the figurative world behind and leaps wholeheartedly into the abyss—pushing the boundaries of abstraction. He paints a completely uninterpretable canvas...and then, just to be cheeky, titles it *Painting*.

• *Head upstairs to the...*

Second Floor: With the 1930s and the advent of the Civil War, Miró temporarily becomes more figurative with his Wind Paintings. Recognizable monsters lurk threateningly. In the early 1940s, Miró flees the Nazi takeover of France and retreats to Spain. He becomes fixated on the heavens and produces his Constellations series—23 paintings of stars, moons, and other brightly colorful items cast against bright backgrounds.

By the late 1940s, Miró is becoming internationally appreciated and within a few years, begins to do more public commissions. But corporatization doesn't tame Miró, as the Sixties Gallery demonstrates. If anything, he continues to refine his trademark style and strip everything down to basics. Star. Moon. Bird. Woman. Increasingly, Miró's works are intended as something to meditate on. Some of his best-known and most appreciated works date from this period and can't be found in any museum, but are scattered around the streets of Barcelona—in the middle of the Ramblas (see page 89), in the park behind the nearby Las Arenas bullring

SIGHTS

mall (see page 77), and elsewhere.

• *With extra time, enjoy...*

The Rest of the Museum: Gallery K contains works from the 1960s and 1970s. Return to earth with a visit to the terrace, where you'll find a modern sculpture gallery and views of the surrounding area.

Olympic Sights on Montjuïc

Olympic and Sports Museum (Museu Olímpic i de l'Esport)—This museum rides the coattails of the stadium across the street. You'll twist down a timeline-ramp that traces the history of the Olympic Games, interspersed with random exhibits about various sports. Downstairs you'll find exhibits designed to test your athleticism, a play-by-play rehash of the '92 Barcelona Olympiad, a commemoration of Juan Antonio Samaranch (the influential Catalan president of the IOC for two decades), a sports media exhibit, and a schmaltzy movie collage. High-tech but hokey, the museum is worth the time and money only for those nostalgic for the '92 Games.

Cost and Hours: €4.50; April-Sept Tue-Sat 10:00-20:00, Sun 10:00-14:30; Oct-March Tue-Sat 10:00-18:00, Sun 10:00-14:30; closed Mon year-round, Avinguda de l'Estadi 60, tel. 932-925-379, www.fundaciobarcelonaolimpica.es.

Olympic Stadium (Estadi Olímpic)—Aside from the memories of the medals, Barcelona's Olympic Stadium offers little to see today. But if the doors are open, you're welcome to step inside. History panels along the railings overlooking the playing field tell the stadium's dynamic story and show the place in happier times— filled with fans as Bon Jovi, the Rolling Stones, and Madonna pack the place.

The stadium was originally built for the 1929 World Expo, but soon thereafter, played a big part in Barcelona's plan to host the "People's Olympiad." These were to take place in July of 1936 as an alternative to Hitler's Fascist Olympics, which were scheduled for that same summer in Berlin (and which Spain had planned to boycott). But just days before the Barcelona games were to begin, civil war broke out in Spain, and the event was cancelled.

Fifty-something years later, the stadium was updated and expanded in preparation for the 1992 Summer Olympics. It was officially named for Catalan patriot Lluís Companys i Jover, the left-wing leader who was president when Spain's Civil War began. Companys had pushed for the democratic alternative to Hitler's games; he was later arrested and executed by Franco.

The XXV Olympiad, which kicked off here on July 25, 1992, was memorable for several reasons. At the opening ceremonies, an archer dramatically lit the Olympic torch—which still stands high at the end of the stadium overlooking the city skyline—with a flaming arrow. Over the next two weeks, Barcelona played host to the thrill of victory—most notably at the hands of Michael Jordan, Magic Johnson, Larry Bird, and the rest of the US basketball "Dream Team"—and the agony of defeat (i.e., the nightmares of the Dream Team's opponents). These Olympics also coincided with several turning points in global geopolitics. It was the first Olympiad after the fall of the Soviet Union (and the first since 1972 without boycotts). Twelve newly independent states sent their athletes as one big Unified Team. These were also the first Games in which the post-Apartheid South African team was invited to participate; the first Games after the breakup of Yugoslavia (with four teams from that region instead of one); and the first to feature a reunified German team.

Nearby: Hovering over the stadium is the futuristic **Montjuïc Communications Tower** (designed by prominent Spanish architect Santiago Calatrava), originally used to transmit Olympic highlights and lowlights around the world.

▲▲Catalan Art Museum
(Museu Nacional d'Art de Catalunya)

The big vision for this wonderful museum is to showcase Catalan art from the 10th century through about the mid-20th century.

Often called "the Prado of Romanesque art" (and "MNAC" for short), it holds Europe's best collection of Romanesque frescoes. It also offers a particularly good sweep of modern Catalan art—fitting, given Catalunya's astonishing contribution to the Modern. While some may find it "another boring museum," art aficionados are sure to find some surprises in this diverse collection.

Cost and Hours: €10, includes temporary exhibits, ticket valid for two days within one month, free first Sun of month; audioguide-€3.10; Tue-Sat 10:00-19:00, Sun 10:00-14:30, closed Mon, last entry 30 minutes before closing; in massive National Palace building above Magic Fountains, near Plaça d'Espanya—take escalators up; tel. 936-220-376, www.mnac.cat.

Visiting the Museum: As you enter, pick up a map (helpful for such a big and confusing building). The left wing is Romanesque, and the right wing is Gothic, exquisite Renaissance, and Baroque. Upstairs is more Baroque, plus modern art, photography, coins, and more.

The MNAC's rare, world-class collection of **Romanesque** (Romànic) art came mostly from remote Catalan village churches (most of the pieces were moved to the museum in the early 1920s to save them from scavenging art dealers). The Romanesque wing features a remarkable array of 11th- to 13th-century frescoes, painted wooden altar fronts, and ornate statuary. This classic Romanesque art—with flat 2-D scenes, each saint holding his symbol, and Jesus (easy to identify by the cross in his halo)—is impressively displayed on replicas of the original church ceilings and apses.

Across the way, in the **Gothic** wing, fresco murals give way to vivid 14th-century wood-panel paintings of Bible stories. A roomful of paintings (Room 26) by the Catalan master Jaume Huguet (1412-1492) deserves a look, particularly his *Consecration of St. Agustí Vell.*

For a break, glide under the huge **dome,** which once housed an ice-skating rink. This was the prime ceremony room and dance hall for the 1929 World Expo.

From the big ballroom, you can ride the glass elevator upstairs to the **Renaissance and Baroque** section, covering Spain's Golden Age (Zurbarán, heavy religious scenes, Spanish royals with their endearing underbites) and Romanticism (dewy-eyed Catalan landscapes). Down on the ground floor are minor works by major—if not necessarily Catalan—names (Velázquez, El Greco, Tintoretto, Rubens, and so on).

Another museum highlight is the **Modern** section, which takes you on an enjoyable walk from the late 1800s to about 1950. It's kind of a Catalan Musée d'Orsay, offering a big chronological clockwise circle covering Symbolism, Modernisme, *fin de siècle* fun, Art Deco, and more. Find the early 20th-century paintings by Catalan artists Santiago Rusiñol and Ramon Casas, both of whom had a profound impact on a young Picasso (and, through him, on all of modern art). Casas was also one of the financiers of Els Quatre Gats, the hangout of Modernista artists (see page 100); his fun Toulouse-Lautrec-esque works, including a whimsical self-portrait on a tandem bicycle, are crowd-pleasers. Crossing over to the "Modern 2" section, you'll find furniture (pieces that complement the empty spaces you likely saw in Gaudí's buildings—including a Gaudí wooden sofa), Impressionism, the shimmering landscapes of Joaquim Mir, and several distinctly Picasso portraits of women.

The museum also has a coin collection, seductive sofas scattered about, and the chic Oleum restaurant, with vast city views (and €28 fixed-price lunches).

▲1929 World Expo Fairgrounds

With the World Expo in 1929, Montjuïc morphed into an extravagant center for fairs, museums, and festivals. Except for the factory

(now housing the CaixaForum) and the bullring, everything you see here dates from 1929. The expo's theme was to demonstrate how electricity was about more than lightbulbs: Electricity powered the funicular, the glorious expo fountains, the many pavilion displays, and even the flame atop the fountain marking the center of Plaça d'Espanya (and celebrating the electric company that sponsored the show). If Barcelona is known for growing through big events, this certainly is a good example.

Standing at Plaça d'Espanya (or, better yet, on the rooftop terrace of the bullring mall—described later), look through the double-brick-tower gate, down the grand esplanade, and imagine it alive with fountains and lined by proud national pavilions showing off all that was modern in 1929. Today it's home to the Fira de Barcelona convention center. The Neo-Baroque fountain provides a brilliant centerpiece for Plaça d'Espanya.

Getting There: The fairgrounds sprawl at the base of Montjuïc, from the Catalan Art Museum's doorstep to Plaça d'Espanya. The easiest option is to see these sights on your way down from Montjuïc. Otherwise, ride the Metro to Espanya, then use the series of stairs and escalators to climb up through the heart of the fairgrounds (eventually reaching the Catalan Art Museum).

▲Magic Fountains (Font Màgica)—Music, colored lights, and huge amounts of water make an artistic and coordinated splash in the evening near Plaça d'Espanya.

Cost and Hours: Free, 20-minute shows start on the half-hour; almost always May-Sept Thu-Sun 21:00-23:00, no shows Mon-Wed; Oct-April Fri-Sat 19:00-20:30, no shows Sun-Thu; these are first and last show times; from the Espanya Metro stop, walk toward the towering National Palace.

▲▲CaixaForum—The CaixaForum Social and Cultural Center (sponsored by the leading Catalan bank) is housed in one of Barcelona's most important Art Nouveau buildings. In 1912, Josep Puig i Cadafalch (a top architect often overshadowed by Gaudí)

designed the Casaramona textile factory, which showed off
Modernista design in an industrial rather than a residential
context. It functioned as a factory
for less than a decade, then later
served a long stint as a police station under Franco. Beautifully
refurbished, the facility reopened
in 2002 as a great center for bringing culture and art to the people
of Barcelona for free.

Cost and Hours: Free, Mon-Fri 10:00-20:00, Sat-Sun 10:00-
21:00, July-Aug open late on some days—likely Wed until 23:00,
Avinguda de Francesc Ferrer i Guàrdia 6-8, tel. 934-768-600,
http://obrasocial.lacaixa.es—click on "CaixaForum Barcelona."

Visiting the Center: From the lobby, signs point to *Sala 2, 3,
4,* and *5*; each hosts different (and typically outstanding) temporary exhibitions. Ride the escalator to the first floor, which features
a modest but interesting exhibit about the history and renovation
of the building, including a model and photos. Then head into the
appealing red-brick courtyard, from which you can access the various exhibition halls. (The sight features generally limited English
descriptions.)

Take the stairs or elevator up to the Modernista Terrace, boasting a wavy floor, bristling with fanciful brick towers, and offering
views over the complex and to Montjuïc. Enjoy the genius of Puig
i Cadafalch's Modernista design, which provided state-of-the-art
working conditions—natural light, good ventilation, and even two
trademark towers filled with water (which could be broken to put
out any factory fires). The various buildings (designed to be separate
from each other to reduce the risk of fire) were built on terraces to
level out the Montjuïc slope. Notice that there's no smokestack.
This was one of the first electric-powered factories in town.

**Mies van der Rohe Pavilion (Pabellón Mies van der
Rohe)**—Architecture pilgrims flock to the pavilion that Ludwig
Mies van der Rohe designed for the German exhibits at the 1929
Expo. Even though it was dismantled at the end of the fair, the
building was heralded as a seminal example of modern architecture, and in the 1980s, the city of Barcelona reconstructed it on the
original site. It's small and stripped-down—a strictly functional
structure. Inside are examples of the Barcelona Chair, a tubular
steel and leather-cushioned chair that's an icon of 20th-century
furniture design.

Cost and Hours: €5, daily 10:00-20:00, Avinguda de Francesc
Ferrer i Guàrdia 7, tel. 934-234-016, www.miesbcn.com.

Spanish Village (Poble Espanyol)—This tacky and overpriced five-acre model village (a long hike up from the main World Expo esplanade) was built as part of the expo to show off the cultural and architectural diversity in Spain. Using fake traditional architecture from all over the country, the village was mostly a shell to contain gift shops—and today it still serves the same purpose. Craftspeople do their clichéd thing (mostly in the morning), and friendly shopkeepers offer plenty of tasty samples of traditional and local edibles. This is popular with cruise groups and people who consider Disney World's Epcot Center a history lesson.

Cost and Hours: €9.50, €3 audioguide explains all the buildings, daily 9:00-20:00 or later, closes earlier off-season, www.poble-espanyol.com.

Las Arenas (Bullring Mall)—What do you do with a big arena that's been sitting empty for decades? Make a mall. Catalunya

recently made the brutal Spanish sport (or art form, depending on your perspective) illegal. (This was done as much for Catalan national pride as it was out of concern over the barbarity of the very Spanish spectacle.) The grand Neo-Moorish Modernista *plaça de toros* functioned as an arena for bullfights from around 1900 to 1977, then reopened in 2011 as a mall. It now hosts everything you'd expect in a modern shopping center: lots of famous shops, a food-circus basement, a 12-screen cinema complex, and a rock-and-roll museum.

The **terrace,** ringed with eateries, has stupendous views of Plaça d'Espanya and Montjuïc (reachable by external glass elevator for €1 or from inside for free). From here you get a bird's-eye perspective of the fairgrounds. In the opposite direction, the park at your feet (called Parc de Joan Miró) includes the giant Miró sculpture *Woman and Bird (Dona i Ocell).* This was one of three works (along with the mosaic on the Ramblas—see page 89) that the city commissioned Miró to create in order to welcome visitors. Miró's sense of humor is evident—if the sculpture seems phallic, keep in mind that the Catalan word for "bird" is also slang for "penis."

Cost and Hours: €1 for elevator to roof terrace (free from inside), daily 10:00-22:00, Gran Via de les Corts Catalanes 373-385, Metro: Espanya, www.arenasdebarcelona.com.

Away from the Center

Tibidabo—Tibidabo comes from the Latin for "to thee I shall give," the words the devil used when he was tempting Christ. It's still an enticing offer: At the top of Barcelona's highest

SIGHTS

peak, you're offered the city's oldest fun-fair (great for kids), the Neo-Gothic Sacred Heart Church, and—if the weather and air quality are good—an almost limitless view of the city and the Mediterranean.

Cost and Hours: €25.20, hours depend on season—generally Wed-Sun in July-Aug, weekends only off-season, tel. 932-117-942, www.tibidabo.cat.

Getting There: From the Plaça de Catalunya Metro station (under Café Zürich), take the L7 (brown) line to the Tibidabo stop (the blue Tourist Bus also goes to the Tibidabo stop). Then take Barcelona's only remaining tram—Tramvía Blau—from Plaça John F. Kennedy to Plaça Dr. Andreu (€4 one-way, buy tickets on board, 2-4/hour). From there, take the funicular to the top (€7.70, €4.10 if you're also paying park admission, tel. 906-427-017). A special "Tibibus" (#T2A) runs at 10:30 from Plaça de Catalunya to the park every day that it's open (€2.95, board in front of Caja Madrid bank).

Camp Nou Stadium—The home turf of FC Barcelona is a mecca for soccer fans. A tour takes you into the press room, by the box seats, through the trophy room, and past the warm-up bench, ending in a ground-level view of the field and, of course, a big shop to buy all of your official "Barça" gear. You'll also get to tour a museum tracing the highlights of Barça history, with lots of interactive touch screens and the six championship cups that the team won in a single season ("the sextuple," 2009-2010)—a feat, they say, that will never be repeated. For more on this team and its significance to Barcelona and Catalunya, see page 84.

Cost and Hours: €23 for Camp Nou Experience (includes tour and museum); mid-April-early Oct Mon-Sat 10:00-20:00, Sun 10:00-14:30; early-Oct-mid-April Mon-Sat 10:00-18:30, Sun 10:00-14:30; shorter hours on game days, Metro: Maria Cristina or Collblanc, toll tel. 902-189-900, www.fcbarcelona.cat.

THE RAMBLAS RAMBLE

*From Plaça de Catalunya
to the Waterfront*

For more than a century, this walk down Barcelona's main boulevard has drawn locals and visitors alike. While its former elegance has been tackified somewhat by tourist shops and fast-food joints, this promenade still has the best people-watching in town. Walk the Ramblas at least once to get the lay of the land, then venture farther afield. It's a one-hour, downhill stroll, with an easy way to get back by Metro.

The word "Ramblas" is plural; the street is actually a succession of five separately named segments. But street signs and addresses treat it as a single long street—"La Rambla," singular. This pedestrian-only Champs-Elysées takes you from rich (at the top) to rough (at the port). You'll raft the river of Barcelonese life past a grand opera house, elegant cafés, flower stands, retread prostitutes, brazen pickpockets, power-dressing con men, artists, street mimes, an outdoor bird market, great shopping, and people looking to charge more for a shoeshine than you paid for the shoes.

Orientation

Length of This Walk: Allow an hour, or a bit longer if you make a pass through La Boqueria Market.

With Limited Time: Focus on the stretch between the Fountain of Canaletes and the Miró mosaic at Liceu; with a bit more time, dip into La Boqueria Market.

When to Go: The Ramblas is two different streets by day and by night. To fully experience its yin and yang, walk it once in the evening and again in the morning, grabbing breakfast on a stool in a market café.

Getting There: This walk begins at the Plaça de Catalunya end of

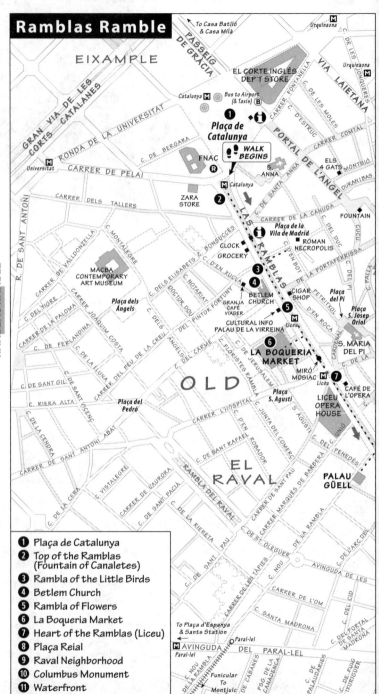

Ramblas Ramble

RAMBLAS RAMBLE

EIXAMPLE

PASSEIG DE GRACIA

To Casa Batlló & Casa Milà

Urquinaona M

EL CORTE INGLÉS DEP'T STORE

Catalunya M

Bus to Airport (& Taxis) B

1 Plaça de Catalunya

WALK BEGINS

FNAC

GRAN VIA DE LES CORTS CATALANES

RONDA DE LA UNIVERSITAT

Universitat M

CARRER DE PELAI

2 Catalunya M

ZARA STORE

CARRER DELS TALLERS

R. DE SANT ANTONI

CARRER DE VALLDONZELLA

CARRER DE MONTALEGRE

MACBA CONTEMPORARY ART MUSEUM

Plaça dels Àngels

BONSUCCÉS

CLOCK

GROCERY

3

4 BETLEM CHURCH

GRANJA CAFÉ VIADER

CULTURAL INFO PALAU DE LA VIRREINA

6 LA BOQUERIA MARKET

5

Liceu M

MIRÓ MOSIAC

7

LICEU OPERA HOUSE

CAFÉ DE L'OPERA

CARRER DE SANTA ANNA

CARRER DE LA CANUDA

Plaça de la Vila de Madrid

ROMAN NECROPOLIS

CIGAR SHOP

Plaça del Pi

Plaça S. Josep Oriol

S. MARIA DEL PI

Plaça S. Agustí

OLD

CARRER L'HOSPITAL

CARRER DE SANT RAFAEL

EL RAVAL

RAMBLA DEL RAVAL

PALAU GÜELL

To Plaça d'Espanya & Sants Station

M AVINGUDA   DEL PARAL-LEL

Paral-lel

Funicular To Montjuïc

VIA LAIETANA

Urquinaona M

PORTAL DE L'ANGEL

ELS 4 GATS

FOUNTAIN

1 Plaça de Catalunya
2 Top of the Ramblas (Fountain of Canaletes)
3 Rambla of the Little Birds
4 Betlem Church
5 Rambla of Flowers
6 La Boqueria Market
7 Heart of the Ramblas (Liceu)
8 Plaça Reial
9 Raval Neighborhood
10 Columbus Monument
11 Waterfront

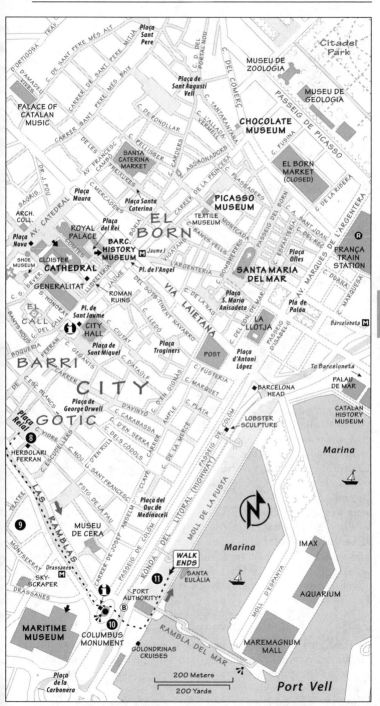

200 Meters

200 Yards

the Ramblas, across the square from El Corte Inglés department store (Metro: Plaça de Catalunya).

La Boqueria Market: Free, Mon-Sat 8:00-20:00, best mornings after 9:00, closed Sun, Rambla 91.

Palau Güell: €10, includes audioguide, free first Sun of the month, open April-Sept Tue-Sun 10:00-20:00, Oct-March Tue-Sun 10:00-17:30, closed Mon year-round, Carrer Nou de la Rambla 3-5.

Columbus Monument: €4, though may be closed; if open, daily May-Oct 8:30-20:30, Nov-April 8:00-20:00, Plaça del Portal de la Pau.

Santa Eulália: €1, Tue-Fri and Sun 10:00-19:30, Sat 14:00-19:30, closes at 17:30 Nov-March, closed Mon year-round, Moll de la Fusta quay.

Eating: Touristy places are the norm here, but you'll find a few handy lunch spots, and the stalls of La Boqueria Market invite grazing. For details, see page 199.

The Walk Begins

• *Start your ramble at the top of the Ramblas, where it connects with Plaça de Catalunya.*

❶ Plaça de Catalunya

Dotted with fountains, statues, and pigeons, and ringed by grand Art Deco buildings, this plaza is Barcelona's center. The square's stern, straight lines are a reaction to the curves of Modernisme (which predominates in the Eixample district, just to the north). Plaça de Catalunya is the hub for the Metro, bus, airport shuttle, and Tourist Bus. It's where Barcelona congregates to watch soccer matches on the big screen, to demonstrate, to celebrate, and to enjoy outdoor concerts and festivals. It's the center of the world for the 10 million Catalan inhabitants of this proud region.

Geographically, the 12-acre square links old Barcelona (the narrow streets to the south) with the new (the broad boulevards to the north). Four great thoroughfares radiate from here. The Ramblas is the popular pedestrian promenade. Passeig de Gràcia has fashionable shops and cafés (and noisy traffic). Rambla de Catalunya is equally fashionable but cozier and more pedestrian-friendly. Avinguda del Portal de l'Angel (shopper-friendly and traffic-free) leads to the Barri Gòtic.

Historically, Plaça de Catalunya links the modern city with its past. In the 1850s, when Barcelona tore down its medieval walls to expand the city, this square on the edge of the walls was one of the first places to be developed.

The inverted-staircase **monument** at the Ramblas end of the square, representing the shape of Catalunya, honors its former president, Francesc Macià i Llussà, who declared independence for the breakaway region in 1931. (It didn't quite stick.) The sculptor Josep Maria Subirachs, whose work you'll see at the Sagrada Família (see page 158), designed this memorial.

The venerable Café Zürich, just across the street from the monument, is a popular downtown rendezvous spot for locals. Homesick Americans might prefer the nearby Hard Rock Café.

• *Cross the street and start rambling down the Ramblas.*

❷ Top of the Ramblas (Fountain of Canaletes)

• *To get oriented, pause 20 yards down, at the ornate lamppost with a fountain as its base (on the right, near #129).*

The black-and-gold **fountain** has been a local favorite for more than a century. When Barcelona tore down its medieval wall and transformed the Ramblas from a drainage ditch into an elegant promenade, this fountain was one of its early attractions. Legend says that a drink from the fountain ensures that you'll come back to Barcelona one day. Watch the tourists—eager to guarantee a return trip—struggle with the awkwardly high water pressure. It's still a popular let's-meet-at-the-fountain rendezvous spot and a gathering place for celebrations and demonstrations. Fans of the Barcelona soccer team rally here before a big match—some touch their hand to their lips, then "kiss" the fountain with their hand for good luck. It's also a good spot to fill up your water bottle.

As you survey the Ramblas action, get your bearings for our upcoming stroll. You'll see the following features here and all along the way:

The wavy **tile work** represents the stream that once flowed here. *Rambla* means "stream" in Arabic, and this used to be a drainage ditch along the medieval wall of the Barri Gòtic. Many Catalan towns, established where rivers approach the sea, have streets called "Ramblas." Today Barcelona's "stream" has become a river of humanity.

Look up to see the city's characteristic shallow **balconies.** They're functional as well as decorative, with windows opening from floor to ceiling to allow more light and air into the tight, dark spaces of these cramped old buildings. The **plane trees** lining the boulevard are known for their peeling bark and hardiness in urban settings. These deciduous trees are ideal for the climate, letting in maximum sun in the  winter and providing maximum shade in the summer. Nowadays, fewer residents live around here—they've been supplanted by businesses and tourism. This shapes what's sold along the Ramblas: There are fewer flower shops and more market stalls catering to tourists.

Nearby, notice the **chairs** fixed to the sidewalk at jaunty angles. It used to be that you'd pay to rent a chair here to look at the constant parade of passersby. Seats are now free, and it's still the best people-watching in town. Enjoy these chairs while you can—you'll find virtually no public benches or other seating farther down the Ramblas, only cafés that serve beer and sangria in just one (expensive) size: *gigante.*

Across from the fountain and a few steps down, notice the first of many **ONCE booths** along this walk (pronounced OHN-thay, the Spanish "11"). These sell lottery tickets that support Spain's organization of the blind, a powerful advocate for the needs of people with disabilities.

• *Continue strolling downhill.*

All along the Ramblas are **newsstands** (open 24 hours). Among their souvenirs, you'll see soccer paraphernalia, especially the scarlet-and-blue of FC Barcelona (known as "Barça"). The team is owned by its more than 170,000 "members"—fans who buy season tickets, which come with a share of ownership (the team's healthy payroll guarantees that they're always in contention). Their motto, "More than a club" *(Mes que un club),* suggests that Barça represents not only athletic prowess but also Catalan cultural identity. This comes to a head during a match nicknamed "El Clásico," in which they face their bitter rivals, Real Madrid (whom many Barça fans view as stand-ins for Castilian cultural chauvinism).

Walk 100 yards downhill to #115, where the **Royal Academy of Science**'s clock marks official Barcelona time—synchronize. Notice the **TI** kiosk right on the Ramblas—a handy stop for any questions. The **Carrefour** supermarket just behind it has cheap groceries (at #113, Mon-Sat 10:00-22:00, closed Sun).

• *You're now standing at the...*

❸ Rambla of the Little Birds

Traditionally, kids brought their parents here to buy pets, especially on Sundays. Today, only a couple of these traditional pet stalls survive. For Barcelona's apartment-dwellers, birds, turtles, fish, hamsters, and rabbits are easier to handle than dogs and cats. But animal-rights groups started lobbying to cut back on these stalls because so many families were making impulse buys with no serious interest in taking care of the cute little critters—and many ended up being flushed. Still, if you're walking by at night, you may hear the sad sounds of little tweety birds locked up in their collapsed kiosks.

At about this part of the Ramblas, you'll see the first of the drag's surreal and goofy **human statues.** These performers—with creative and elaborate costumes—must audition and register with the city government; to avoid overcrowding, only 15 can work along the Ramblas at any one time. To enliven your Ramblas ramble, stroll with a pocketful of small change. As you wander downhill, drop coins into their cans (the money often kicks them into entertaining gear). Warning: Wherever people stop to gawk, pickpockets are at work.

At #122 (the big, modern Citadines Hotel on the left, just behind the first bird kiosk), a 100-yard detour through the passageway leads to a recently discovered **Roman necropolis.** Look down and imagine a 2,000-year-old

tomb-lined road. In Roman cities, tombs (outside the walls) typically lined the roads leading into town. Emperor Augustus spent a lot of time in modern-day Spain conquering new land, so the Romans were sure to incorporate Hispania into the empire's infrastructure. This road, Via Augusta, led into the Roman port of Barcino (today's highway to France still follows the route laid out by this Roman thoroughfare). Looking down at these ruins, you can see how Roman Barcino was about 10 feet lower than today's street level.

• *Return to the Ramblas and continue downhill 100 yards or so to the next street. At Carrer de la Portaferrissa (across from the big church),* *turn left a few steps and look right to see the **decorative tile** over the fountain. The scene shows the original city wall with the gate that once stood here and the action on what is today's Ramblas. Cross the boulevard to the front of the big church.*

❹ Betlem Church

This 17th-century church is dedicated to Bethlehem, and for centuries locals have flocked here at Christmastime to see Nativity scenes.

The church's sloping roofline, ball-topped pinnacles, corkscrew columns, and scrolls above the entrance all identify it as Baroque. But compared to the rest of Baroque-crazy Spain, that style is relatively unusual in Barcelona. That's because the city effectively skipped several centuries of architectural development between its two heydays (the medieval period and the turn of the 20th century). From about 1500 until 1850, the city's importance dropped—and consequently, there's not much Renaissance or Baroque for a city of its stature.

For a sweet treat, head down the narrow lane behind the church (going uphill parallel to the Ramblas about 30 yards) to the recommended **Café Granja Viader,** which has specialized in baked and dairy delights since 1870. Step inside to see Viader family photos and early posters advertising Cacaolat—the local chocolate milk Barcelonans love. (For more sugary treats nearby, follow "A Short, Sweet Walk" on page 207.)

• *Continue down the boulevard, through the stretch called the...*

❺ Rambla of Flowers

This colorful block, lined with flower stands, is the Rambla of

Flowers. On the left, at #100, **Gimeno** sells cigars. Step inside and appreciate the dying art of cigar boxes. Go ahead, do something forbidden in America but perfectly legal here...buy a Cuban (little singles for €1). Tobacco shops sell stamps and phone cards, plus bongs and marijuana gear—the Spanish approach to pot is very casual. While people can't legally sell marijuana, they're allowed to grow it for personal use and consume it. (You'll smell its sweet smoke all over the city.)

• *Continue to the Metro stop marked by the*

red M. At #91 (on the right) is the arcaded entrance to Barcelona's great covered market, La Boqueria. If this main entry is choked with visitors (as it often is), you can skirt around to a side entrance, one block in either direction (look for the round arches that mark passages into the market colonnade).

❻ La Boqueria Market

This lively market hall is an explosion of chicken legs, bags of live snails, stiff fish, delicious oranges, odd odors, and sleeping dogs.

The best day for a visit is Saturday, when the market is thriving. It's closed on Sundays, and locals avoid it on Mondays, when it's open but (they believe) vendors are selling items that aren't necessarily fresh—especially seafood, since fishermen stay home on Sundays.

Since as far back as 1200, Barcelonans have bought their animal parts here. The market was originally located by the walled city's entrance, as many medieval markets were (since it was more expensive to trade within the walls). It later expanded into the colonnaded courtyard of a now-gone monastery before being topped with a colorful arcade in 1850.

While tourists are drawn like moths to a flame to the area around the main entry (below the colorful stained-glass sign), locals know that the stalls up front pay the highest rent—and therefore have to inflate their prices and cater to out-of-towners. For example, the juices along the main drag just inside the entrance are tempting, but if you venture to the right a couple of aisles, the clientele gets more local and the prices drop dramatically.

Stop by the recommended **Pinotxo Bar**—it's just inside the market, under the sign—and snap a photo of Juan. Animated Juan and his family are always busy feeding shoppers. Getting Juan to crack a huge smile and a thumbs-up for your camera makes a great shot...and he loves it. The stools nearby are a fine perch for enjoying both your coffee and the people-watching.

The market and lanes nearby are busy with tempting little eateries (several are listed on page 203). Drop by a café for an *espresso con leche* or breakfast *tortilla española* (potato omelet). Once you get

RAMBLAS RAMBLE

past the initial gauntlet, do some exploring. The small square on the north side of the market hosts a farmers market in the mornings. Wander around—as local architect Antoni Gaudí used to—and gain inspiration. Go on a scavenger hunt for some of these items:

Produce stands show off seasonal fruits and vegetables that you'll see on local menus. ("Market cuisine" is big at Barcelona restaurants—chefs come to markets like this each morning to rustle up ingredients.) The tubs of little green peppers that look like jalapenos are lightly fried for the dish called *pimientos de Padrón*. In a culinary form of Russian roulette, a few of these mild peppers sometimes turn out to be hot— greeting the eater with a fiery jolt. In the fall, you'll see lots of mushrooms; in the winter, artichokes.

Full legs of *jamón* (ham) abound. The many varieties of *jamón serrano* are distinguished by the type of pig it comes from and what that pig ate. Top quality are *ibérico* (Iberian type) and *bellota* (acorn eaters)—even by the slice these are very expensive, but gourmets pay €200 or more to go whole hock (see the "Sampling *Jamón*" sidebar on page 188). You'll see many types of *chorizo*, the red Spanish sausage that's often spicy (a rare bit of heat in an otherwise tame cuisine). Also keep an eye out for a few meats that are uncommon in American dishes—rabbit and suckling pig. Beware: *Huevos del toro* means bull testicles—surprisingly inexpensive...and oh so good.

The **fishmonger** stalls could double as a marine biology lab; in this Mediterranean city, people have come up with endless ways to harvest the sea. Notice that fish is sold whole, not filleted—local shoppers like to look their dinner in the eye to be sure it's fresh. Count the many different types of shrimp (*gamba, scampi, langostino,* clawed *cigala*). One of the weirdest Spanish edibles is the tubular razor clam *(navaja de almeja),* with something oozing out of each end.

Some stalls specialize in dried **salt cod** *(bacalao).* Historically, codfish—preserved in salt and dried—provided desperately needed protein on long sea voyages and was critical in allowing seafaring cultures like that of Catalunya to venture farther from their home ports. Before it can be eaten, salt cod must be rehydrated. Fish stalls sell it either covered in salt or submerged in water, to hasten the time between market and plate.

Certain food items are associated with a particular town—for example, anchovies from L'Escala, shrimp from Palamos, and so on. Among Catalans, this is a sort of code designating quality (like

"Idaho potatoes" or "Washington apples" in the US).

Olives are a keystone of the Spanish diet. Take a look at the 25 kinds offered at Graus Olives i Conserves shop (straight in, near the back).

• *Head back out to the street and continue down the Ramblas.*

You're skirting the western boundary of the old Barri Gòtic neighborhood. As you walk, glance to the left through a modern cutaway arch for a glimpse of the medieval church tower of **Santa Maria del Pi,** a popular venue for guitar concerts (see the Nightlife in Barcelona chapter). This also marks Plaça del Pi and a great shopping street, Carrer Petritxol, which runs parallel to the Ramblas (see the Shopping in Barcelona chapter).

At the corner directly opposite the modern archway, find the highly regarded **Escribà** bakery (look for the *Antigua Casa Figueras* sign arching over the doorway), with its fine Modernista facade and interior. Notice the beautiful mosaics, stained glass, and woodwork. On the sidewalk in front of the door, a commemorative plaque notes the business's establishment in 1902 (plaques like these identify historic shops all over town).

• *After another block, you reach the Liceu Metro station, marking the...*

❼ Heart of the Ramblas

At the Liceu Metro station's elevators, the Ramblas widens a bit

into a small, lively square (Plaça de la Boqueria). Liceu marks the midpoint of the Ramblas, halfway between Plaça de Catalunya and the waterfront.

Underfoot in the center of the Ramblas, find the much-trodupon red-white-yellow-and-blue **mosaic** by homegrown abstract artist Joan Miró. The mosaic's black arrow represents an anchor, a reminder of the city's attachment to the sea. Miró's stripped-down designs are found all over the city, from murals to mobiles to the La Caixa bank logo. The best place in Barcelona to see his work is in the Fundació Joan Miró at Montjuïc (see page 69).

The surrounding buildings have playful ornamentation typical of the city. The **Chinese dragon** holding a lantern (at #82) decorates a former umbrella shop (notice the fun umbrella mosaics high up). While the dragon may seem purely decorative, it's actually an important symbol of Catalan pride for its connection to the local patron saint, St. George (Jordi).

Hungry? The recommended **Taverna Basca Irati** tapas bar is a block up Carrer del Cardenal Casanyes (find the street around the back side of the former umbrella shop). This is one of many user-friendly, Basque-style tapas bars in town; instead of ordering, you can just grab or point to what looks good on the display platters, then pay per piece.

Back on the Ramblas, a few steps down (on the right) is the **Liceu Opera House** (Gran Teatre del Liceu), which hosts world-class opera, dance, and theater (box office around the right side, open Mon-Fri 13:30-20:00). Opposite the opera house is Café de l'Opera (#74), an elegant stop for an expensive beverage. This bustling café, with Modernista decor and a historic atmosphere, boasts that it's been open since 1929, even during the Spanish Civil War.

• *We've seen the best stretch of the Ramblas; from here, it's downhill (in every sense, when it comes to the Raval neighborhood) to the port. To cut this walk short, you could catch the Metro back to Plaça de Catalunya.*

Otherwise, continue down the Ramblas. In about 30 yards, the wide, straight street on the left (Carrer de Ferran) leads to Plaça de Sant Jaume, the government center.

Stay on the Ramblas for another 50 yards (to #46), and turn left down an arcaded lane (Correr de Colom) to the square called...

❽ Plaça Reial

Dotted with palm trees, surrounded by an arcade, and ringed by yellow buildings with white Neoclassical trim, this elegant square has a colonial ambience. It comes complete with old-fashioned taverns, modern bars with patio seating, and a Sunday coin-and-stamp market (10:00-14:00). Completing the picture are Gaudí's first public works (the two colorful helmeted lampposts). While this used to be a seedy and dangerous part of

town, recent gentrification efforts have given it new life, making it inviting and accessible. (The small streets stretching toward the water from the square remain a bit sketchier.) It's a lively hangout by day or by night (see page 233). Big spaces like this (as well as the site of La Boqueria Market) often originated as monasteries. When these were dissolved in the 19th century, their fine colonnaded squares were incorporated into useful public spaces.

• *Head back out to the Ramblas.*

Across the boulevard, a half-block detour down Carrer Nou de la Rambla brings you to **Palau Güell,** designed by Antoni Gaudí (on the left, at #3-5). Even from the outside, you get a sense of this innovative apartment, the first of Gaudí's Modernista buildings. As this is early Gaudí (built 1886-1890), it's darker and more Neo-Gothic than his more famous later work. The two parabolic-arch doorways and elaborate wrought-iron work signal his emerging nonlinear style. Recently renovated, Palau Güell

offers an informative look at a Gaudí interior (see listing on page 44). Pablo Picasso had a studio at #10 (though there's nothing to see there today).

• *Retrace your steps and continue downhill on the Ramblas.*

❾ Raval Neighborhood

The neighborhood on the right-hand side of this stretch of the Ramblas is El Raval. Its nickname was Barri Xines—the world's only Chinatown with nothing even remotely Chinese in or near it. Named for the prejudiced notion that Chinese immigrants went hand-in-hand with poverty, prostitution, and drug dealing, the neighborhood's actual inhabitants were poor Spanish, North African, and Roma (Gypsy) people. At night, the Barri Xines was frequented by prostitutes, many of them transvestites, who catered to sailors wandering up from the port. Today, it's becoming gentri-fied, but it's still a pretty rough neighborhood.

The seedy zone attracts plenty of characters who don't need the palm trees to be shady. You're likely to see some good old-fashioned shell games. Stand back and observe these nervous no-necks at work. They swish around their little boxes, making sure to show you the pea. Their shills play and win. Then, in hopes of making easy money, fools lose big time.

Near the bottom of the Ramblas, take note of the Drassanes Metro stop (close to the Museo de Cera—wax museum), which can take you back to Plaça de Catalunya when this walk is over. The skyscraper to the right of the Ramblas is the Edificio Colón. When it was built in 1970, the 28-story structure was Barcelona's first high-rise. Near the skyscraper is the Maritime Museum, housed in what were the city's giant medieval shipyards (permanent collection likely closed through 2014; see listing on page 45).

• *Up ahead is the...*

❿ Columbus Monument

The 200-foot **column** honors Christopher Columbus, who came to Barcelona in 1493 after journeying to America. This Catalan

answer to Nelson's Column on London's Trafalgar Square (right down to the lions perfect for posing with at the base) was erected for the 1888 Universal Exposition, an international fair that helped vault a surging Barcelona onto the world stage.

The base of the monument, ringed with four winged victories (taking flight to the four corners of the earth), is loaded with symbolism: statues and reliefs of mapmakers, navigators, early explorers preach-

ing to subservient Native Americans, and (enthroned just below the winged victories) the four regions of Spain. The reliefs near the bottom illustrate scenes from Columbus' fateful voyage. It's ironic that Barcelona celebrates this explorer; the discoveries of Columbus started 300 years of decline for the city, as Europe began to face West (the Atlantic and the New World) rather than East (the Mediterranean and the Orient). Within a few decades of Columbus, Barcelona had become a depressed backwater, and didn't rebound until events like the 1888 Expo cemented its status as a comeback city. A tiny elevator ascends to the top of the monument (though it may be closed during your visit). If open, it lifts visitors to an observation area for fine panoramas over the city (entrance/ticket desk in TI inside the base of the monument).

• Scoot across the busy traffic circle to survey the...

⓫ Waterfront

Stand on the boardwalk (between the modern bridge and the kiosks selling harbor cruises), and survey Barcelona's bustling maritime zone. Although the city is one of Europe's top 10 ports, with many busy industrial harbors and several cruise terminals, this low-impact stretch of seafront is clean, fresh, and people-friendly.

As you face the water, the frilly yellow building to your left is the fanciful Modernista-style port-authority building. The wooden pedestrian **bridge** jutting straight out into the harbor is a modern extension of the Ramblas. Called La Rambla de

Mar ("Rambla of the Sea"), the bridge swings out to allow boat traffic into the marina; when closed, the footpath leads to an entertainment and shopping complex. Just to your right are the *golondrinas* **harbor cruise** boats, which can be fun if you'd love to get out on the water (though the views from the harbor aren't great; for details, see page 48).

• *Turn left and walk 100 yards along the promenade between the port authority and the harbor.*

This delightful promenade is part of Barcelona's **Old Port** (Port Vell), stretching from the Columbus Monument to the Barceloneta neighborhood. The port's pleasant sailboat marina is completely enclosed by La Rambla del Mar's shopping and entertainment zone (notice that La Rambla del Mar connects back around to the mainland at the far end of the port, creating a handy pedestrian loop). Its attractions include the Maremagnum shopping mall, an IMAX cinema, a huge aquarium, restaurants, and piles of people. Along the promenade is a permanently moored historic schooner, the *Santa Eulália* (part of the Maritime Museum—see page 45).

Imagine: A little more than two decades ago, this was a gloomy, depressed warehouse zone. But to spiff up its front door for the 1992 Olympics, city leaders refurbished the port area, routing a busy highway underground to create this fine walkway sprinkled with palm trees and eye-pleasing public art. On a sunny day, it's fun to walk the length of the promenade to the iconic *Barcelona Head* sculpture (by American Pop artist Roy Lichtenstein, not quite visible from here), which puts you right at the edge of El Born, one of the city's most enjoyable shopping and restaurant areas. (For details, see the ✪ El Born Walk chapter.)

From here, you can also pick out some of Barcelona's more distant charms. The triangular spit of land across the harbor is **Barceloneta.** This densely populated community was custom-built to house fishermen and sailors whose traditional neighborhood in El Born was razed so Philip V could build a military citadel there in the 18th century. Today's Barceloneta is a little gritty but charming, popular for its relatively low real-estate prices (given its handy proximity to the town center) and its easy access to a gorgeous and inviting stretch of broad, sandy beaches (on the other side of the Barceloneta peninsula). From Barceloneta, beaches and boardwalks lead all the way to the modern Fòrum development (see page 57).

Looking back toward the Columbus Monument, you'll see in the distance the majestic, 570-foot bluff of **Montjuïc,** a park-like setting dotted with a number of sights and museums (see page 64; to get there, ride the Metro from Drassanes one stop to the Parallel stop, then take the funicular up).

• *Your ramble is over. If it's a nice day, consider strolling the promenade and looping back around on La Rambla del Mar. Or maybe dip into El Born. If you're truly on vacation, walk through Barceloneta to the beach.*

To get to other points in town, your best bet is to backtrack to the Drassanes Metro stop, at the bottom of the Ramblas. Alternatively, you can catch buses #14 or #59 from along the top of the promenade back to Plaça de Catalunya.

BARRI GÒTIC WALK

*From Plaça de Catalunya
to Plaça del Rei*

Barcelona's Barri Gòtic (Gothic Quarter) is a bustling world of shops, bars, and nightlife packed into narrow, winding lanes and undiscovered courtyards. This is Barcelona's birthplace—where the ancient Romans built a city, where medieval Christians built their cathedral, and where Barcelonans lived within a ring of protective walls until the 1850s, when the city expanded.

Today, this area of atmospheric tight lanes—nicknamed simply "El Gòtic"—is Barcelona's most historic neighborhood. It's a tangled-yet-inviting grab bag of grand squares, schoolyards, Art Nouveau storefronts, baby flea markets (open Thu, closed Aug), musty junk shops, classy antiques shops (on Carrer de la Palla), street musicians strumming Catalan folk songs, and balconies with domestic jungles behind wrought-iron bars.

Treat this self-guided walk as a historical scavenger hunt. You'll focus on the earliest chunk of Roman Barcelona, right around the cathedral, and explore some legacy sights from the city's medieval era. For a more contemporary flavor, explore the shopping streets nearby (see page 224) or head to El Born (see the El Born Walk chapter).

Orientation

Length of This Walk: Figure 1.5 hours, not including entering sights such as the cathedral.

With Limited Time: Skip the former Jewish Quarter and Plaça de Sant Jaume.

When to Go: If you want to go inside the cathedral, take this walk in the morning or late afternoon, when admission is free. If you'd like to enter the museums mentioned on this walk, avoid Monday, when some sights are closed.

Barri Gòtic Walk

EL CORTE INGLÉS DEP'T STORE

ⓑ Bus to Airport (& Taxis)

To Casa Batlló & Casa Milà

100 Meters

100 Yards

👣 WALK BEGINS

C. FONTANELLA

CARRER DE LES MOLES

CARRER D'ESTRUC

❶

PLANELLES DONAT

CARRER COMTAL

AVINGUDA DEL PORTAL DE L'ANGEL

SANTA ANNA

CONDOM SHOP

❷

ELS QUATRE GATS

❸

CARRER DE MONTSIÓ

DURAN I BAS

LOANER BIKES

C. DELS

❹

ATM

ROYAL ART CIRCLE OF BARCELONA

CARRER DE SANTA ANNA

BARRI

CARRER DE LA CANUDA

CARRER DEL DUC

CARRER CUCURULLA

Plaça de la Vila de Madrid

ROMAN NECROPOLIS

CARRER D'EN BOT

GÒTIC

FARGAS CHOCOLATES

CARRER DEL PI

LAS RAMBLAS

CARRER DE LA PORTAFERRISSA

LIBRERÍA ANGEL BATLLE POSTERS

CARRER DE LA PALLA

BETLEM CHURCH

CASA COLOMINA SWEETS

CARRER

VICENS SWEETS

GRANJA LA PALLARESA (CHURROS CON CHOCOLATE)

ORO LÍQUIDO OLIVE OILS

CAELUM CAFÉ

CULTURAL INFO PALAU DE LA VIRREINA

CARRER D'EN ROCA

PETRITXOL

JOSEP ROCA CUTLERY

Plaça S. Josep Oriol

Ⓜ Liceu

VAHO SHOP

Plaça del Pi

BARRI GÒTIC WALK

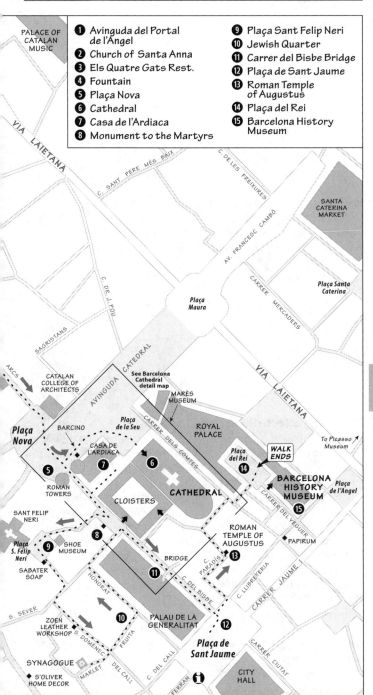

1. Avinguda del Portal de l'Àngel
2. Church of Santa Anna
3. Els Quatre Gats Rest.
4. Fountain
5. Plaça Nova
6. Cathedral
7. Casa de l'Ardiaca
8. Monument to the Martyrs
9. Plaça Sant Felip Neri
10. Jewish Quarter
11. Carrer del Bisbe Bridge
12. Plaça de Sant Jaume
13. Roman Temple of Augustus
14. Plaça del Rei
15. Barcelona History Museum

PALACE OF CATALAN MUSIC

VIA LAIETANA

C. SANT PERE MÉS BAIX

C. DE LES FREIXURES

SANTA CATERINA MARKET

AV. FRANCESC CAMBÓ

C. DE J. POU

Plaça Maura

CARRER MERCADERS

Plaça Santa Caterina

SAGRISTANS

CATALAN COLLEGE OF ARCHITECTS

AVINGUDA CATEDRAL

See Barcelona Cathedral detail map

MARÈS MUSEUM

ROYAL PALACE

VIA LAIETANA

ARCS

Plaça Nova

BARCINO

Plaça de la Seu

CARRER DELS COMTES

CASA DE L'ARDIACA

ROMAN TOWERS

CLOISTERS

CATHEDRAL

Plaça del Rei

WALK ENDS

To Picasso Museum

BARCELONA HISTORY MUSEUM

Plaça de l'Àngel

CARRER DEL VEGUER

SANT FELIP NERI

Plaça S. Felip Neri

SHOE MUSEUM

SABATER SOAP

S. SEVER

ROMAN TEMPLE OF AUGUSTUS

PAPIRUM

BRIDGE

C. PARADÍS

C. LLIBRETERIA

CARRER JAUME

HONORAT

ZOEN LEATHER WORKSHOP

S. DOMÈNEC

DEL CALL

FRUITA

PALAU DE LA GENERALITAT

C. DEL BISBE

Plaça de Sant Jaume

CARRER CIUTAT

SYNAGOGUE

S'OLIVER HOME DECOR

MARLET

C. DEL CALL

FERRAN

CITY HALL

BARRI GÒTIC WALK

Getting There: Push off from the southeast corner of the Plaça de Catalunya, near El Corte Inglés department store (Metro: Plaça de Catalunya).

Church of Santa Anna: Free, hours vary but usually Mon-Sat 9:30-13:00 & 18:00-20:00, Sun 9:30-14:00, Plazoleta de Santa Anna.

Cathedral of Barcelona: Generally free except in afternoon, open Mon-Fri 8:00-19:30, Sat-Sun 8:00-20:00, €6 to enter Mon-Sat 13:00-17:00 and Sun 14:00-17:00, Plaça de la Seu.

Old Main Synagogue: €2.50, Mon-Fri 10:30-18:30, Sat-Sun 10:30-15:00, Carrer Marlet 5, tel. 933-170-790, www.callde barcelona.org.

Roman Temple of Augustus: Free; April-Sept Tue-Sun 10:00-20:00; Oct-March Tue-Sat 10:00-14:00 & 16:00-19:00, Sun 10:00-20:00; closed Mon year-round; Carrer del Paradís 10.

Barcelona History Museum: €7, Tue-Sat 10:00-19:00, Sun 10:00-20:00, closed Mon, off Plaça del Rei.

Eating: For restaurants and tapas bars along the way, see page 204.

The Walk Begins

• *Start on Barcelona's grand main square,* **Plaça de Catalunya** *(described on page 82 of The Ramblas Ramble chapter). From the southeast corner (between the giant El Corte Inglés department store and the Banco de España), head downhill along the broad pedestrian boulevard called...*

❶ Avinguda del Portal de l'Angel

For much of Barcelona's history, this was one of the main boulevards leading into town. A medieval wall enclosed the city, and there was an entrance here—the "Gate of the Angel" that gives the street its name. An angel statue atop the gate purportedly kept the city safe from plagues and bid voyagers safe journey as they left the security of the city. Imagine the fascinating scene here at the Gate of the Angel, where Barcelona stopped and the wilds began.

Much later, this same boulevard (and much of the city) got a facelift in preparation for the 1888 Universal Exposition, the first international fair held in Spain. (The same event prompted the construction of the Columbus Monument at the bottom of the Ramblas.) The improvements to the Gate of the Angel are a good example of Barcelona's habit of spiffing itself up for big events. The city dressed up for another exposition in 1929 (Plaça d'Espanya fairgrounds) and again for the 1992 Olympic Games (sports facilities on Montjuïc and rejuvenated waterfront).

Picture the traffic congestion here in the 1980s, before this street was closed to most motorized vehicles. Today, you're elbow to elbow with shoppers cruising through the most expensive retail space in town. It's pretty globalized and sanitized, with lots of high-end Spanish and international chains (for a rundown, see page 227 in the Shopping in Barcelona chapter), but a handful of local businesses survive. For example, on the right at the first corner (at #21), a green sign marks **Planelles Donat**—long appreciated for its ice cream, sweet *turró* (or *turrón*, almond-and-honey candy), refreshing *orxata* (or *horchata*, almond-flavored drink),

and *granissat (or granizado,* ice slush).

• *A block farther down, pause at Carrer de Santa Anna to admire the Art Nouveau awning at another El Corte Inglés department store. (If you're keeping track, this is the third El Corte Inglés within a two-block radius.) Take a half-block detour down Carrer de Santa Anna to the doorway at #29 (on the right), which leads to the...*

❷ Church of Santa Anna

This 12th-century gem, with a pleasant, flower-fragrant courtyard, was an *extra muro* ("outside the walls") church; look for its marker cross still standing outside. Because it was part of a convent, the church has a fine cloister—an arcaded walk-way around a leafy courtyard (viewable through the gate to the left of the church). If the church is open, you'll see a bare Romanesque interior and Greek-cross floor plan, topped with an octagonal wooden roof. The recumbent-knight tomb is that of Miguel de Boera, renowned admiral under Emperor Charles V. The door at the far end of the nave leads to the cloister.

As you head back to the main drag, you'll pass—a few doors down—a **condom shop** on your left. It advertises (to men with ample self-esteem): *Para los pequeños placeres de la vida* ("For the little pleasures in life"). This sign is in Spanish, because the letter *ñ* doesn't exist in Catalan. Instead, Catalans write "ny" for this sound (as in "Catalunya"—which elsewhere in Spain is written "Cataluña").

• *Return to Avinguda del Portal de l'Angel, turn right, and continue for another block. At Carrer de Montsió (on the left), side-trip half a block to...*

❸ Els Quatre Gats

This restaurant ("The Four Cats"), established in 1897, is a historic monument, tourist attraction, nightspot, and one of my recommended eateries. It's famous for being the bohemian-artist hangout where Picasso nursed drinks with friends and first publicly hung his art (in 1900, at age 19). The building itself, by the prominent Catalan architect Josep Puig i Cadafalch, is a Modernista landmark. Stepping inside, you feel the turn-of-the-20th-century vibe. Rich Barcelona elites and would-be avant-garde artists looked to Paris, not Madrid, for cultural inspiration. Consequently, this place was clearly inspired by the Paris scene, especially Le Chat Noir cabaret/café, the hangout of Montmartre intellectuals. Like Le Chat Noir, Els Quatre Gats even published its own artsy magazine for a while. The story of the name? When the proprietor told his friends that he'd stay open 24 hours a day, they said, "No one will come. It'll just be you and four cats" (Catalan slang for "a few crazy people"). While you can have a snack, meal, or drink here, if you just want to look around, ask, *"Solo mirar, por favor?"*

• *Return to and continue down Avinguda del Portal de l'Angel. In a square on the left, notice the rack of* **city loaner bikes,** *part of the popular and successful "Bicing" program designed to reduce car traffic (available only to Barcelona residents). You'll soon reach a fork in the road and a building with a...*

❹ Fountain

The blue-and-yellow tilework, a circa-1918 addition to this even-older fountain, depicts ladies carrying jugs of water. In the 17th century, this was the last watering stop for horses before leaving town. As recently as 1940, one in nine Barcelonans got their water from fountains like this. It's still used today.

• *Take the left fork, down Carrer dels Arcs.*

Pause after a few steps at the yellow La Caixa ATM (on the right, under the terrace). Watch as various international languages pop up on the screen—in addition to English, French, and German, you'll see the **four languages of Spain** and their flags: Català (Catalan; thin red-and-gold stripes), Galego (Galicia, in northwest Spain; blue with a diagonal white slash), Español (Spanish; broad red, yellow, and red bands), and Euskaraz (Basque; red,

BARRI GÒTIC WALK

green, and white). As a would-be breakaway nation fiercely proud of its own customs and language, Catalunya is particularly careful to respect linguistic variation.

Just past the ATM, you'll pass the **Royal Art Circle of Barcelona,** a private collection of Dalí sculptures (Reial Cercle Artístic de Barcelona, some temporary exhibits).

• *Enter the large square called...*

❺ Plaça Nova

Two bold **Roman towers** flank the main street. These once guarded the entrance gate of the ancient Roman city of Barcino.

The big stones that make up the base of the (reconstructed) towers are actually Roman. Near the base of the left tower, **modern bronze letters** spell out "BARCINO." The city's name may have come from Barca, one of Hannibal's generals, who is said to have passed through during Hannibal's roundabout invasion of Italy. At Barcino's peak, the **Roman wall** (see the section stretching to the left of the towers) was 25 feet high and a mile around, with 74 towers. It enclosed an area of 30 acres and a population of 4,000.

One of the towers has a section of **Roman aqueduct** (a modern reconstruction). These bridges of stone carried fresh water from the distant hillsides into the walled city. Here the water supply split into two channels, one to feed Roman industry, the other for the general populace. The Roman aqueducts would be the best water system Barcelona would have until the 20th century.

Opposite the towers is the modern **Catalan College of Architects** building (Collegi d'Arquitectes de Barcelona), which

is, ironically for a city with so much great architecture, quite ugly. The frieze was designed by Picasso (1960) in his distinctive childlike style, showing Catalan traditions: shipping, music, the *sardana* dance, bullfighting, and branch-waving kings and children celebrating a local festival. Picasso spent his formative years (1895-1904, ages 14-23) in the Barri Gòtic. He had a studio a block from here (where the big CaixaCatalunya building stands today). He drank with fellow bohemians at Els Quatre Gats (which we just passed) and frequented brothels a few blocks from here on Carrer d'Avinyó ("Avignon")—which inspired his influential Cubist painting *Les Demoiselles d'Avignon*. Picasso's Barri Gòtic was a hotbed of trend-setting art, propelling him forward just before he moved to Paris and remade modern art.

• *Immediately to the left as you face the Picasso frieze,* **Carrer de la Palla** *is an inviting shopping street (and the starting point of my "Barri Gòtic Shopping Walk"; see page 224). But let's head left through Plaça Nova and take in the mighty facade of the...*

❻ Cathedral of Barcelona (Catedral de Barcelona)

This location has been a center of Christian worship since the fourth century, and this particular building dates (mainly) from the 14th century. The facade is a virtual catalog of Gothic motifs: a pointed arch over the entrance, robed statues, tracery in windows, gargoyles, and bell towers with winged angels. This Gothic variation is called French Flamboyant (meaning "flame-like"), and the roofline sports the prickly spires meant to give the impression of a church flickering with spiritual fires. The facade is typically Gothic...

but not from medieval times. It's a Neo-Gothic reinterpretation from the 19th century. The area in front of the cathedral is where Barcelonans dance the *sardana* (see page 50).

The cathedral's interior—with its vast size, peaceful cloister, and many ornate chapels—is worth a visit. ❍ See the Cathedral Tour chapter.

• *The* **Frederic Marès Museum**—*an eccentric artist's eclectic collection of 19th-century slice-of-life items—is just to the left of the cathedral (see listing on page 51).*

As you stand in the square facing the cathedral, look far to your left to see the multicolored, wavy canopy marking the roofline of the **Santa Caterina Market**. *The busy street between here and the market—called Via Laietana—is the boundary between the Barri Gòtic and the funkier, edgier* **El Born** *neighborhood.*

For now, return to the Roman towers. Pass between the towers to head up Carrer del Bisbe, and take an immediate left, up the ramp to the entrance of the...

❼ Casa de l'Ardiaca

It's free to enter this mansion, which was once the archdeacon's residence and today functions as the city archives. The elaborately carved doorway is Renaissance. To the right of the doorway is a carved mail slot by 19th-century Modernista architect Lluís Domènech i Montaner. Enter a small courtyard with a fountain. Notice how the century-old palm  tree seems to be held captive by urban man. Next, step inside the lobby of the city archives. You can't tour the archives, but there are often temporary exhibits in the lobby. At the left end of the lobby, go through the archway and look down into the stairwell—this is the back side of the ancient Roman wall. Back in the courtyard, head up to the balcony for views of the cathedral steeple and gargoyles. Note the small Romanesque chapel on the right, the only surviving 12th-century bit of the cathedral.

• *Return to Carrer del Bisbe and turn left. After a few steps, you reach a small square with a bronze statue ensemble.*

❽ Monument to the Martyrs of Independence

Five Barcelona patriots calmly receive their last rites before being garroted (strangled) for resisting Napoleon's occupation of Spain in  the early 19th century. They'd been outraged by French atrocities in Madrid (depicted in Goya's famous *Third of May* painting in Madrid's Prado Museum). According to the plaque marking their mortal remains, these martyrs to independence gave their lives in 1809 *"por Dios, por la Patria, y por el Rey"*—for God, country, and king.

The plaza offers interesting views of the cathedral's towers. Opposite the square is the "back door" entrance to the cathedral (through the cloister; relatively uncrowded but open only sporadically).

On this square (and throughout the Barri Gòtic), you're likely to see groups of hippies. Nicknamed the "dog-and-flute people," they squat together in abandoned buildings, living in communes, and spend their days begging, entertaining, and bringing chaos to otherwise peaceful demonstrations. Attracted by Barcelona's easygoing laws, they congregate here.

• *Exit the square down tiny Carrer de Montjuïc del Bisbe (to the right as you face the martyrs). This leads to the cute...*

❾ Plaça Sant Felip Neri

This square serves as the playground of an elementary school and is often bursting with energetic kids speaking Catalan (just

a generation ago, they would have had to speak Spanish). The Church of Sant Felip Neri, which Gaudí attended, is still pocked with bomb damage from the Civil War. As a stronghold of democratic, anti-Franco forces, Barcelona saw a lot of fighting. The shrapnel that damaged this church was meant for the nearby Catalan government building (Palau de la Generalitat, which we'll see later on this walk).

Study the carved reliefs on nearby buildings, paid for by the guilds that powered the local economy. It's clear that the building on the far right must have housed the shoemakers. In fact, just next door is the entertaining little **Shoe Museum** (described on page 51). Also fronting the square is the fun **Sabater Hermonos** artisanal soap shop (see page 225).

• *Exit the square down Carrer de Sant Felip Neri. At the T-intersection, you have a choice: Turn left to return to the square with the martyrs monument and Carrer del Bisbe, where you'll find an ornate bridge (described later).*

Or, if you're curious about the Jewish chapter of Barcelona's story, turn right at the T-intersection onto Carrer de Sant Sever, then immediately left on Carrer de Sant Domènec del Call. You've entered the...

❿ Jewish Quarter (El Call)

In Catalan, a Jewish quarter goes by the name El Call—literally "narrow passage," for the tight lanes where medieval Jews were forced to live, under the watchful eye of the nearby cathedral. At the peak of Barcelona's El Call, some 4,000 Jews were crammed into just a few alleys.

Walk down Carrer de Sant Domènec del Call, passing the **Zoen leather workshop and showroom,** where everything is made on the spot (on the right, at #15). After passing a charming square, also on the right, take the next lane to the right (Carrer de Marlet). On the right is the low-profile entrance to what was likely Barcelona's **main synagogue** (Antigua Sinagoga Mayor) during the Middle Ages. The structure dates from the third century, but it was destroyed during a brutal pogrom in 1391. The city's remaining Jews were expelled in 1492, and artifacts of their culture—including this synagogue—were forgotten for centuries. In the 1980s, a historian tracked down the synagogue using old tax-collection records. Another clue that this was the main synagogue: In accordance with Jewish traditions, it stubbornly faces east (toward Jerusalem), putting it at an angle at odds with surrounding structures. The sparse interior includes access to two small subterranean rooms with Roman walls topped by a medieval Catalan vault. Look through the glass floor to see dyeing vats used for a later shop on this site (run by former Jews who had been forcibly converted to Christianity).

• *At the synagogue, start back the way you came, continuing straight as the street becomes Carrer de la Fruita. At the T-intersection, turn left, then right, to find your way back to the martyrs monument. From here, turn right down Carrer del Bisbe to the...*

⓫ Carrer del Bisbe Bridge

This structure—reminiscent of Venice's Bridge of Sighs—connects the Catalan government building (on the right) with the Catalan

president's ceremonial residence (on the left). Though the bridge looks medieval, it was constructed in the 1920s by Catalan architect Joan Rubió, who also did the carved ornamentation on the buildings.

It's a photographer's dream. Check out the jutting angels on the bridge, the basket-carrying maidens on the president's house, the gargoyle-like faces on the government building. Zoom in even closer. Find monsters, skulls, goddesses, old men with beards, climbing vines, and coats of arms—a Gothic museum in stone.

• *Continue along Carrer del Bisbe to...*

⓬ Plaça de Sant Jaume

This stately central square of the Barri Gòtic takes its name from the Church of St. James (in Catalan: Jaume, jow-mah) that once stood here. After the church was torn down in 1823, the square was fixed up and rechristened "Plaça de la Constitució" in honor of the then decade-old Spanish constitution. But the plucky Catalans never embraced the name, and after Franco, they went back to the original title—even though the namesake church is long gone.

Set at the intersection of ancient Barcino's main thoroughfares, this square was once a Roman forum. In that sense, it's been the seat of city government for 2,000 years. Today it's home to the two top governmental buildings in Catalunya: Palau de la Generalitat and, across from it, the Barcelona City Hall.

For more than six centuries, the **Palau de la Generalitat** (to your immediate right as you enter the square) has housed the offices of the autonomous government of Catalunya. It always flies the Catalan flag next to the obligatory Spanish one. Above the building's doorway is Catalunya's patron saint—St. George (Jordi), slaying the dragon. The dragon (which you'll see all over town) is an important Catalan symbol—both feared and respected, as is the bull in the rest of Spain. From these balconies, the nation's leaders (and soccer heroes) greet the people on momentous days. The square is often the site of demonstrations, from a single aggrieved citizen with a megaphone to riotous thousands.

Facing the Generalitat across the square is the **Barcelona City Hall** (Casa de la Ciutat). It sports a statue (in the niche to the left of the door) of a different  James—"Jaume el Conqueridor." The 13th-century King Jaume I is credited with freeing Barcelona from French control, granting self-government, and setting it on a course to become a major city. He was the driving force behind construction of the Royal Palace (which we'll see shortly).

Locals treasure the independence these two government buildings represent. In the 20th century, Barcelona opposed the dictator Francisco Franco (who ruled from 1939 to 1975), and Franco retaliated. He abolished the regional government and (effectively) outlawed the Catalan language and customs. Two years after Franco's death, joyous citizens packed this square to celebrate the return of self-rule.

Look left and right down the main streets branching off the square; they're lined with ironwork streetlamps and balconies draped with plants. Carrer de Ferran, which leads to the Ramblas, is classic Barcelona.

In ancient Roman days, when Plaça de Sant Jaume was the town's central square, two main streets converged here— the Decumanus (Carrer del Bisbe) and the Cardus (Carrer de la Llibreteria/Carrer del Call). The forum's biggest building was a massive temple of Augustus, which we'll see next.

• *Facing the Generalitat, exit the square to the right of the building, heading uphill on tiny Carrer del Paradís. Follow this street as it turns right. When it swings left, pause at #10, the entrance to the...*

⓭ Roman Temple of Augustus

You're standing at the summit of Mont Tàber, the Barri Gòtic's highest spot. A plaque on the wall reads: "Mont Tàber, 16.9 meters" (elevation 55 feet). A millstone inlaid in the pavement at the doorstep of #10 also marks the spot. It was here that the ancient Romans founded the town of Barcino around 15 B.C. They built a *castrum* (fort) on the hilltop, protecting the harbor.

Go inside for a peek at the last vestiges of an imposing Roman temple (Temple Roma d'August). All that's left now are four columns and some fragments of the tran-  sept and its plinth (good English info on-site). The huge columns, dating from the late first century B.C., are as old as Barcelona itself. They were part of the ancient town's biggest structure, a temple dedicated to the Emperor Augustus, who was worshipped as a god. These Corinthian columns (with deep fluting and topped with leafy capitals) were the back corner of a 120-foot-long temple that extended from here to Barcino's forum.

• *Continue down Carrer del Paridís one block. When you bump into the back end of the cathedral, take a right, and go downhill a block (down Carrer de la Pietat/Baixada de Santa Clara) until you emerge into a square called...*

⓮ Plaça del Rei

The buildings enclosing this square exemplify Barcelona's medieval past. The central section (topped by a five-story addition) was the core of the **Royal Palace** (Palau Reial Major). A vast hall on its ground floor once served as the throne room and reception room. From the 13th to the 15th century, the Royal Palace housed Barcelona's counts as well as the resident kings of Aragon. In 1493, a triumphant Christopher Columbus, accompanied by six New World natives (whom he called *"indios"*) and several pure-gold statues, entered the Royal Palace. King Ferdinand and Queen Isabella rose to welcome him home and honored him with the title "Admiral of the Oceans."

To the right is the palace's church, the 14th-century **Chapel of Saint Agatha,** which sits atop the foundations of a Roman wall.

If the church is hosting a temporary exhibit, you can see it for free (climb up the stairs and head inside).

To the left is the **Viceroy's Palace** (Palau del Lloctinent, for the ruler's right-hand man). This 16th-century building currently serves as the archives of the Crown of Aragon. After Catalunya became part of Spain in the 15th century, the Royal Palace became a small regional residence, and the Viceroy's Palace became the headquarters of the local Inquisition. Step inside to see the impressive Renaissance courtyard, a staircase with coffered wood ceilings, and a temporary exhibit space. Among the archive's treasures (though it's rarely on display) is the 1491 Santa Fe Capitulations, a contract between Columbus and the monarchs about his upcoming sea voyage. (See the poster of the yellowed document on the wall.)

Ironically, Columbus' discovery of new trade routes made Barcelona's port less important, and soon the royals moved elsewhere.

• *From the square, go around the corner onto Carrer del Veguer, where you'll find the entrance to the...*

⓯ Barcelona History Museum

This museum contains primarily objects from archaeological digs around Barcelona, but the real highlight is underground, where

you can examine excavated Roman ruins. (And if you're curious about the interior of the palace, this is the only place you'll get a glimpse of what little there is to see of it—basically just one hall.)

Visiting the museum is a fine way to retrace all the history we've seen on this walk—from the city's medieval days back to the Roman foundations of Barcino—with exhibits that portray day-to-day life (for details on the museum, see page 52).

• *Your walk is over. It's easy to get your bearings by backtracking to either Plaça de Sant Jaume or the cathedral (where you can follow my "Barri Gòtic Shopping Walk," described on page 224). The Jaume I Metro stop is two blocks away (head downhill and turn left). From here, you could head over to the El Born neighborhood to browse for lunch at the Santa Caterina Market, tour the Picasso Museum (❂ see the Picasso Museum Tour chapter), or follow my ❂ El Born Walk. Or simply wander and enjoy Barcelona at its Gothic best.*

CATHEDRAL OF BARCELONA TOUR

Although Barcelona's cathedral doesn't rank among Europe's finest (and frankly, barely cracks the Top 20), it's important, easy to visit, and—most of the time—free to see. This quick tour introduces you to the cathedral's highlights: its vast nave, rich chapels, tomb of St. Eulàlia, and the oasis-like setting of the cloister. Other sights inside (which you'll pay separately for) are the elaborately carved choir, the elevator up to the view terrace, and the altarpiece museum.

Orientation

Cost: Free in the morning (Mon-Sat before 12:45, Sun before 13:45) and late afternoon (after 17:15), but you have to pay for the cathedral's three minor sights—museum, terrace, and choir (see "Other Cathedral Sights," later). Even though the church claims to be "closed" for several hours in the afternoon (Mon-Sat 13:00-17:00, Sun 14:00-17:00), you can still get in by paying €6 (which covers admission to the three interior sights). In other words, one way or another you'll pay around €6 to thoroughly tour the place; however, since the three extras inside are skippable, I'd aim to visit the church when it's free.

Hours: It's generally open to visitors Mon-Fri 8:00-19:30, Sat-Sun 8:00-20:00.

Getting There: The huge, can't-miss-it cathedral is in the center of the Barri Gòtic on Plaça de la Seu (Metro: Jaume I). For an interesting way to reach the cathedral from Plaça de Catalunya, and some commentary on the surrounding neighborhood, ✪ see the Barri Gòtic Walk chapter.

Getting In: The main, front door is open most of the time. While

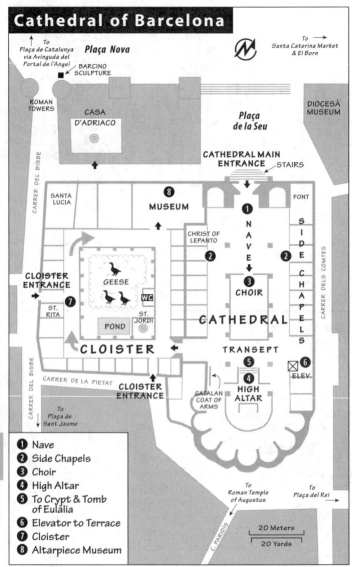

Cathedral of Barcelona

To Plaça de Catalunya via Avinguda del Portal de l'Angel

Plaça Nova

To → Santa Caterina Market & El Born

BARCINO SCULPTURE

ROMAN TOWERS

CASA D'ADRIACO

DIOCESÀ MUSEUM

Plaça de la Seu

CARRER DEL BISBE

CATHEDRAL MAIN ENTRANCE — STAIRS

SANTA LUCIA

❽ MUSEUM

FONT

❶ NAVE

CHRIST OF LEPANTO

❷

S I D E   C H A P E L S

❷

CARRER DELS COMTES

CLOISTER ENTRANCE

GEESE

WC

❼

ST. RITA

ST. JORDI

POND

❸ CHOIR

CATHEDRAL

CLOISTER

TRANSEPT

❺

❻ ELEV.

CARRER DEL BISBE

CARRER DE LA PIETAT

CLOISTER ENTRANCE

CATALAN COAT OF ARMS

❹ HIGH ALTAR

To Plaça de Sant Jaume

❶ Nave
❷ Side Chapels
❸ Choir
❹ High Altar
❺ To Crypt & Tomb of Eulàlia
❻ Elevator to Terrace
❼ Cloister
❽ Altarpiece Museum

To Roman Temple of Augustus

To Plaça del Rei →

20 Meters
20 Yards

C. PARIDIS

CATHEDRAL OF BARCELONA

it can be crowded, the line generally moves fast. Sometimes you can also enter directly into the cloister around back (through the door facing the Martyrs Statue on the small square along Carrer del Bisbe).

Information: Tel. 933-151-554, www.catedralbcn.org.

Length of This Tour: Allow 30 minutes, not counting the optional sights (choir, view terrace, museum).

With Limited Time: Zip past the many side chapels, but be sure to linger in the cloister.

Dress Code: The dress code is strictly enforced; don't wear tank tops, shorts, or skirts above the knee.

WCs: A tiny, semi-private WC is in the cloister.

Other Cathedral Sights: The three extra sights have separate fees (except during the afternoon church "closure," when €6 covers all three) and slightly shorter hours than the church itself: **Choir**—€2.50, Mon-Sat 9:00-19:00; **View Terrace**—€2.50, Mon-Sat 9:00-18:00, closed Sun; **Altarpiece Museum**—€2, daily 10:00-19:00, accessed from cloister. The extra sights can close even earlier on slow days.

Photography: Allowed without a flash.

Background

This has been Barcelona's holiest spot for 2,000 years. The Romans built their Temple of Jupiter here. In A.D. 343, the pagan temple was replaced with a Christian cathedral. That building was supplanted by a Romanesque-style church (11th century). The current Gothic structure was started in 1298 and finished in 1450, during the medieval glory days of the Catalan nation. The facade was humble, so in the 19th century the proud local bourgeoisie (enjoying a second golden age) redid it in a more ornate, Neo-Gothic style. Construction was capped in 1913 with the central spire, 230 feet tall.

The Tour Begins

• *Enter the main door and look up, letting your eyes adjust to the low light. (If you're entering through the back door, loop around the cloister and enter the church to start in the nave.)*

❶ The Nave

The spacious church is 300 feet long and 130 feet wide. Tall pillars made of stone blocks support the crisscross vaults. Each round  keystone where the arches cross features a different saint. Typical of many Spanish churches, there's a choir—an enclosed area of wooden seats in the middle of the nave, creating a more intimate space for worship. The Gothic church also has fine stained glass, ironwork chandeliers, a 16th-century organ (left transept), tombstones in the pavement, and an "ambulatory" floor plan, allowing worshippers to amble around to the chapel of their choice.

❷ Side Chapels

The nave is ringed with 28 chapels. Besides being worship spaces, these serve as interior buttresses supporting the roof (which is why

the exterior walls are smooth, without the normal Gothic buttresses outside). Barcelona—the city of 32 official public holidays—honors many of the home-grown saints found in these chapels.

From the 13th to 15th centuries, these side chapels were simply money-makers for the church. After the Black Death ravaged the population and the economy as well, the church needed money and rented chapels to guilds to function as private offices, which came with the medieval equivalent of safety-deposit boxes and notary public (documents signed here came with the force of God). Notice how the iron gates are more than decorative—they were protective. The rich ornamentation was sponsored by local guilds. Think of it: The church was the community's most high-profile space, and these chapels were a kind of advertising to illiterate worshippers.

The Church is still fund-raising. Candles, which aren't free, power your prayers. As you visit the chapels, employ one or more electronic candles. Pop in a coin and you'll get a candle for every €0.10 you donate. Try it—€0.50 turns on five candles.

• *We'll walk past a few of these chapels, just to get a sense of them. Begin by heading to the back-left corner (over your left shoulder as you enter the main door).*

The chapel at the back corner of the nave has an old **baptismal font** that once stood in the original fourth-century church. The Native Americans that Columbus brought to town were supposedly baptized here.

• *Work your way down the left aisle.*

The first chapel along the left wall is dedicated to **St. Severus,** the bishop here way back in A.D. 290.

The second chapel was by, for, and of the local **shoe guild.** Notice the two painted doors that lead to the back office. As the patron of shoemakers was St. Mark, there are plenty of winged lions in this chapel.

• *Backtrack a bit, to the large chapel in the back-right corner.*

This chapel (reserved for worship) features the beloved **"Christ of Lepanto"** crucifix. They say the angular wooden figure of Christ leaned to dodge a cannonball during the history-changing Battle of Lepanto (1571), which stopped the Ottomans (and Islam) from advancing into Europe.

• *Now head down the right aisle.*

The second chapel has a statue of **St. Anthony** holding the Baby Jesus. His feast day (January 17) is one of many celebrated in the city with an appearance by the *gegants* (giant puppets), a street fair, horse races, and a blessing of pets.

The third chapel honors a 20th-century bishop who survived an assassination attempt in the cathedral cloister.

The golden fourth chapel is for **St. Roch** (at the top, pointing to his leg wound, above St. Pancraç), whose feast day is celebrated joyously in the Barri Gòtic in mid-August.

The fifth chapel has a black-and-white sideways statue of **St. Ramon (Raymond) of Penyafort** (1190-1275), the Dominican Bishop of Barcelona who heard Pope Gregory IX's sins and is the patron saint of lawyers (and, therefore, extremely busy). Ramon figures into the city's biggest festival, La Mercè, since he had a miraculous vision of the Virgin of Mercy.

The eighth chapel is worth a look for its over-the-top golden altarpiece decor nearly crowding out **Bishop Pacià**—considered one of the Church fathers (c. A.D. 310-391).

• *If you want to visit the interior of the choir (described next), pay €2.50 or show your ticket at the choir entrance (straight ahead from the church's main doors). Otherwise, you can circle around to the far end and peer through the barrier.*

❸ Choir

The 15th-century choir *(coro)* features ornately carved stalls. During the standing parts of the Mass, the chairs were folded up, but

VIPs still had those little wooden ledges to lean on. Each was creatively carved and—since you couldn't sit on sacred things—the artists were free to enjoy some secular and naughty fun here. In 1518, the stalls were painted with the coats of arms of Europe's nobility. They gathered here as members of the Knights of the Golden Fleece to honor Charles V, King of Spain, who was making his first trip to the country he ruled. Find Charles' two-headed eagle, with the dangling lamb of the Golden Fleece. Next to Charles is the emblem (red and blue shield with lions and fleur-de-lis) of another invited guest, Henry VIII of England—who was a no-show. Check out the detail work on the impressive wood-carved pulpit near the altar, supported by flying angels.

• *At the front of the church stands the...*

❹ High Altar

Look behind the altar (beneath the crucifix) to find the archbishop's chair, or *cathedra*. As a cathedral, this church is the archbishop's seat—hence its Catalan nickname of *La Seu*. To the left of the altar is the organ and the elevator up to the terrace. To the right of the altar, the wall is decorated with Catalunya's yellow-and-red coat of arms. The two wooden coffins on the wall are of two powerful Counts of Barcelona (Ramon Berenguer I and his third wife, Almodis), who ordered the construction of the 11th-century Romanesque cathedral that preceded this structure.

• *Descend the steps beneath the altar, into the crypt, to see the...*

❺ Tomb of Eulàlia

The marble-and-alabaster sarcophagus (1327-1339) contains the remains of St. Eulàlia. The cathedral is dedicated to this saint. Thirteen-year-old Eulàlia, daughter of a prominent Barcelona

family, was martyred by the Romans for her faith in A.D. 304. Murky legends say she was subjected to 13 tortures. First she was stripped naked and had her head shaved, though a miraculous snowfall hid her nakedness. Then she was rolled down the street in a barrel full of sharp objects. After further torments failed to kill her, she was crucified on an X-shaped cross—a symbol you'll find carved into pews and seen throughout the church.

The relief on the coffin's side tells her story in three episodes: she preaches Christianity to the pagan Roman ruler; he orders her to die (while she pleads for mercy); and she's crucified on the X-shaped cross. As one of Barcelona's patron saints, Eulàlia is honored with a festival (with *gegants*—giant puppets, fireworks, and human towers) in mid-February.

• *The ❻ elevator in the left transept takes you up to the rooftop terrace for an expansive city view (€2.50).*

Otherwise, head to the right transept and go through the door to enter the...

❼ Cloister

Exit through the right transept and into the circa-1450 cloister— the arcaded walkway surrounding a lush courtyard. Ahhhh. It's a tropical atmosphere of palm, orange, and magnolia trees; a fish pond; trickling fountains; and squawking geese.

From within the cloister, look back at the **arch** you just came through, an impressive mix of Romanesque (arches with chevrons, from the earlier church) and Gothic (pointy top).

The nearby **fountain** has a tiny statue of St. Jordi (George) slaying the dragon. Jordi is one of the patron saints of Catalunya and by far the most popular boy's name here. During the Corpus Christi festival in June, kids come here to watch a hollow egg dance atop the fountain's spray.

As you wander the cloister (clockwise), check out the **coats of arms** as well as the **tombs** in the pavement. These were rich merchants who paid good money to be buried as close to the altar as possible. Notice the symbols of their trades: scissors, shoes, bakers, and so on. The cloister had a practical, economic purpose. The church sold out its chapel space, and this opened up an entire new wing to donors. A second floor was planned (look up) but not finished.

The resident **geese** have been here for at least 500 years. There are always 13, in memory of Eulàlia's 13 years and 13 torments. Other legends say they're white as a symbol of her virginity. Before modern security systems, they acted as alarms. Any commotion would get them honking, alerting the monk in charge. Faithful to tradition, they honk to this very day.

Farther along the cloister, next to the back door, the **Chapel of Santa Rita** (patron saint of impossible causes) usually has the most candles. In the next corner of the cloister is the dark, barrel-vaulted **Chapel of Santa Lucía,** a small 13th-century remnant of the earlier Romanesque cathedral. People hoping for good eyesight (Santa Lucía's specialty) pray here. Notice the nice eyes in the modern restoration of the altar painting.

• *At the far end of the cloister, you'll find the...*

❽ Altarpiece Museum (Museu Capitular)

The little museum (€2 entry) has the six-foot-tall 14th-century Great Monstrance, a ceremonial display case for the communion wafer. Made of gold and studded with jewels, it's really three separate parts: a church-like central section, topped with a crown canopy, standing on a golden chair. This huge monstrance with its wafer is paraded through the streets during the Corpus Christi festival. Nearby is a gold-plated silver statue of St. Eulàlia, carrying the X-shaped cross she was crucified on. An 11th-century baptismal font from the Romanesque church is also on view.

The next room, the Sala Capitular, has several altarpieces, including a *pietá* (a.k.a. *Desplà*) by Bartolomé Bermejo (1490). An anguished Mary cradles a twisted Christ against a bleak, stormy landscape. It's unique in Spanish art for its Italianesque, Renaissance 3-D. Rather than your basic gold backdrop, this has a strong foreground (the mourners), middle distance (the cross), and background (the city and distant hills). The kneeling donors who paid for the painting are photorealistic, complete with reading glasses and five o'clock shadows.

• *Our tour is over. May peace be with you.*

EL BORN WALK

*From Via Laietana to
the Waterfront*

The neighborhood called El Born (a.k.a. "La Ribera") is a bohemian-chic paradise, with funky shops, upscale cafés and wine bars, a colorful market hall, unique boutiques, gritty bars and nightclubs, and one of Barcelona's top museums (celebrating the early works of Picasso). Anchored by the Church of Santa Maria del Mar and just a short stroll from the waterfront, El Born is a rewarding neighborhood to explore and a welcome escape from the sightseeing grind.

Back when Barcelona was Barcino—a walled Roman town—this area was farmland. As the city sprawled beyond its walls, El Born was "born" into a neighborhood with a main square that, over the years, hosted jousting tournaments, festivals, Inquisition-era heretic-burnings, and other public spectacles. Later, during the medieval city's trading heyday, El Born housed the wealthiest shippers and merchants. Its streets are lined with their grand mansions—which, like the much-appreciated Church of Santa Maria del Mar, were built with shipping wealth. All of that came crashing down in 1714, when the Spanish crown crushed Catalan hopes and razed a big chunk of this district to erect an imposing citadel (now a delightful park). The focus of the city shifted west, to the Barri Gòtic, and El Born became a largely forgotten backwater.

But in recent years, as the Barri Gòtic has become overrun by tourism, El Born has retained its pleasantly rough-around-the-edges appeal. While it's gentrifying and becoming one of the city's most in-demand residential areas, its tight lanes are lined—not with chain stores—but with innovative one-off shops that, more often than not, make what they sell. Although we'll cover some history, this walk is designed to take you past some enticing boutique streets and provide a route for you to venture off and make your own discoveries.

Orientation

Length of This Walk: About one hour, not including shopping stops.

With Limited Time: Focus on the core of El Born, where these places and sights cluster: Passeig del Born, the Monument of Catalan Independence, Church of Santa Maria del Mar, and the characteristic shopping lanes.

Getting There: This walk begins at Plaça d'Antoni Maura, where the pedestrian area in front of the Cathedral of Barcelona meets Via Laietana. The closest Metro stop is Jaume I.

Name Game: This neighborhood (between the Barri Gòtic to the west and Citadel Park to the east) goes by several names. The traditional name, **La Ribera,** generally implies the entire area. **El Born,** the name locals tend to use, technically refers to the southern half of this area (below Carrer de la Princesa—basically the zone covered by this walk), although it's sometimes also used to describe the entire neighborhood. Complicating matters, the city's official title for this district is "Sant Pere, Santa Caterina i la Ribera."

Santa Caterina Market: Free, Mon 7:30-14:00, Tue-Wed and Sat 7:30-15:30, Thu-Fri 7:30-20:30, closed Sun, Avinguda de Francesc Cambó 16.

Picasso Museum: €11, free all day first Sun of month and other Sun from 15:00; Tue-Sun 10:00-19:50, closed Mon; Carrer de Montcada 15-23.

Church of Santa Maria del Mar: Free, daily 9:00-13:30 & 16:30-20:00, Plaça Santa Maria.

The Walk Begins

• *Our walk starts at Plaça d'Antoni Maura, which is at the east end of the square in front of the Cathedral of Barcelona. As you stand facing the cathedral, look left to see the undulating roof of the market hall in the distance. To get there, you'll cross...*

❶ Via Laietana

This traffic-choked street slices through Barcelona's Old City. It marks the boundary between the Barri Gòtic (behind you) and El Born (in front of you). When the road was built in 1908, Barcelona was turning its back on its Gothic past and racing into its Modernista future—and hundreds of historic buildings were torn up to create this new artery.

When you cross the street, you're in the neighborhood called Sant Pere. While less colorful and gentrified than El Born, just to the south, Sant Pere is home to a thriving residential population

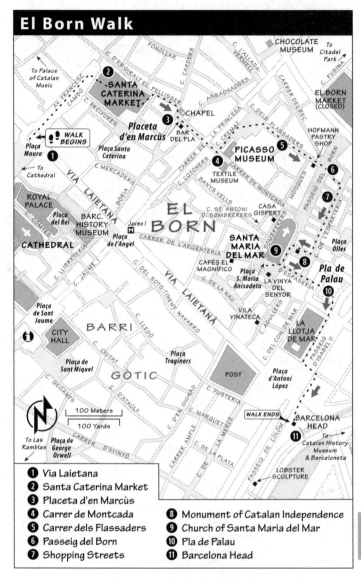

El Born Walk

❶ Via Laietana
❷ Santa Caterina Market
❸ Placeta d'en Marcùs
❹ Carrer de Montcada
❺ Carrer dels Flassaders
❻ Passeig del Born
❼ Shopping Streets
❽ Monument of Catalan Independence
❾ Church of Santa Maria del Mar
❿ Pla de Palau
⓫ Barcelona Head

of mostly immigrants. A few short blocks to your left is one of the city's architectural treasures—Lluís Domènech i Montaner's Modernista-style **Palace of Catalan Music** (see listing on page 53).

• *Across Via Laietana and on the right, you can't miss the...*

❷ Santa Caterina Market

While tourists swarm the more famous La Boqueria Market on the Ramblas, Santa Caterina Market is a lively dose of local color, still primarily serving its neighborhood. This is the place to buy *jamón* and cheese without the crowds or tourist mark-up.

The market, built on the ruins of an old monastery (see the exhibit at the far corner for a view of the foundations with English explanations), was finally renovated in 2006 with a swooping, Gaudí-inspired roof and shell built around its original white walls. The much-delayed construction took so long that locals began calling the site the "Hole of Shame." Its Catalan architect, Enric Miralles, is best known for designing the Scottish Parliament Building in Edinburgh—an unlikely connection that's also oddly fitting, since both the Catalans and the Scots consider themselves "nations without states."

Inside are beautifully lit produce stalls with mouthwatering presentations and surprising variety (one stall displays 20 different kinds of tomatoes). There are lots of tempting eateries—locals eat before shopping so as not to overbuy. For tips on exploring the market, see the description on page 44 for La Boqueria, which offers similar products.

• *Walk through the market from one end to the other—keeping an eye out for those monastery ruins. (If the market is closed, you can simply loop around the left side to the far end.) Exiting through the back of the market, angle left to the corner of the square and find the tiny Carrer d'en Giralt el Pellisser. Going down this lane, you'll pop out facing a chapel and the cute little square called...*

❸ Placeta d'en Marcùs

On this square is a humble Romanesque chapel from the 1100s, supposedly the oldest church in town. In medieval times, this is where locals would pause to share the news. Across the street from the chapel's front door, above the plaque for #1, notice the sign with the horse and the word *entrada* (entrance). This is an old-fashioned way of marking the direction of one-way streets in this tight tangle of lanes. Circling behind the chapel, find the sign's

EL BORN WALK

twin, *salida* (exit), above the
street sign for Carrer dels
Assaonadors. You'll spot
signs like these all over El
Born and the Barri Gòtic.
• *Passing between the chapel
and the recommended Bar del
Pla, continue straight down
the lane called...*

❹ Carrer de Montcada

Follow this street one block until you reach the busy, bar-lined
Carrer de la Princesa. If you turned right here, you'd go to the
Jaume I Metro stop, Barri Gòtic, and cathedral area. Instead, cross
Princesa and continue straight, noticing that Carrer de Montcada
has suddenly become the most touristy street in El Born—thanks
to the Picasso Museum, which lies just ahead. The street is named
for the Montcada family, who owned the buildings that now house
the museum (which consists of five mansions laced together).
Because it connected the wealthy merchant district right near the
waterfront with the tradesmen's quarter farther north, this drag
attracted an elite class of homeowner during its 15th-century
heyday.

A block down is the **Picasso Museum,** focused on the artist's early, formative works. You could visit the museum now if
the line's not too long (❂ see the Picasso Museum Tour chapter),
or you could come back after finishing this walk. In addition to
the museum, Carrer de Montcada is lined with other art galleries,
cafés, shops, and restaurants. While some are good (such as the
recommended El Xampanyet bar, just down the street and on the
right), most cater decidedly to tourist tastes. But a less-discovered
corner of El Born awaits just a few steps away.
• *At the corner of the Picasso Museum complex (closest to Carrer de la
Princesa), look for the covered passage next to the* salida *horse sign,
marked* Carrer de Cremat Gran i Xic. *Head down this atmospheric
little lane. You'll emerge at a leafy square behind the Picasso Museum
complex. Walk to the far end of this square, then turn right and head
down...*

❺ Carrer dels Flassaders

Like most streets in El Born, this is named for a craft of workers and merchants—in this case, "Blanket-Makers." Follow this
street, passing the first of many characteristic El Born shops we'll
see on this walk. As you explore, be sure to peek down the many
shop-lined side streets. Many stores have workshops where the
goods being sold are actually produced. Creating usable items out

of recycled materials is trendy.

Near the end of the street, about 30 yards before the next square, pause at the tiny, gated lane (on the right) called **Carrer de les Mosques.** Traditionally waste from the nearby market was tossed out in this alley, attracting flies *(mosques).* And even after the market closed down, the street—so conveniently close to the main square's cancan of bars, yet just far enough away—was a popular (if unofficial) public urinal. To keep the smells and flies at bay, this strip is now sealed off with a gate. High up on the left is a man's head with a moustache—medieval code indicating that a brothel was nearby.

The next storefront (also on the right) is the *patisseria* (pastry shop) for **Hofmann,** Barcelona's best-regarded culinary school (Mon-Wed 9:00-14:00 & 15:30-20:00, Thu-Sat 9:00-14:00 & 15:30-20:30, Sun 9:00-14:30, Flassaders 44, tel. 932-688-221).
• *At the end of the street, you'll pop out onto...*

❻ Passeig del Born

This long boulevard is the neighborhood center. Formerly a jousting square (as its Roman circus-esque shape indicates), it got its name, "El Born," from an old Catalan word for "tournament" (the name was eventually given to the entire neighborhood).

These days, Passeig del Born is a popular springboard for exploring tapas bars, fun restaurants, and nightspots in the narrow streets all around. Wandering around here at night, you'll find piles of inviting and intriguing little restaurants (I've listed my favorites on page 208).

At the far end of Passeig del Born is the vast-but-vacant, steel-frame, 19th-century **El Born Market,** which served as the city's main produce market hall up until 1971, when it was relocated to the suburbs. The loss of the market led to the neighborhood's steep decline; only in the last decade or so has El Born become rejuvenated. The large hall has stood vacant since the market closed, but recent construction work revealed medieval foundations that are now being excavated. Plans are under way to convert the market hall into a cultural center and museum.
• *From Carrer del Flassaders, continue straight across Passeig del Born and head down the arcaded Carrer del Rec. This part of El Born has a high concentration of...*

❼ Shopping Streets

Fashion boutiques populate the area around **Carrer del Rec.** And on the side streets, you can see local "fashions" flapping in the breeze from characteristic wrought-iron balconies. While strict building codes prohibit people from drying laundry outside their homes in most of the city, an exception is made for El Born—since this medieval quarter lacks interior courtyards.

Feel free to browse around now (or come back later), but eventually you'll want to take the first right turn, down **Carrer de l'Esparteria**—another great shopping street. As elsewhere in El Born, most street names are tied to a particular craft or product; for example, the third street on the right, Carrer de la Formatgeria, was home to the cheesemakers—and still today, it faces a fondue shop.

Stick with the street as it jogs slightly left, pausing at **Carrer del Malcuinat** (on the right), literally "Badly Cooked Street." Looking left, you'll notice you're just a block off the port. In the Middle Ages, this lane was home to unpretentious eateries serving fill-the-tank meals to undiscerning sailors who were fresh off the boat. These days, no self-respecting restaurateur has the nerve to open an eatery along here (except, strangely, an Irish pub).

• *Turn right down the short Carrer del Malcuinat, emerging at a big square with the...*

❽ Monument of Catalan Independence

The square is called Plaça del Fossar de les Moreres ("The Burial Place of the Mulberry Trees"). The lone mulberry tree and modern monument honor a 300-year-old massacre that's still fresh in the Catalan consciousness. On September 11, 1714, the Bourbon King Philip V, ruling from Madrid, completed a successful 14-month siege of Barcelona (the "Catalan Alamo"). In retaliation for the local resistance to Bourbon rule, he massacred Catalan patriots. From that day on, the king outlawed Catalan language, culture, and institutions, kicking off more than two centuries of cultural suppression. For example, no university was allowed in Barcelona from 1720 to 1850. To establish his hold, the king demolished 20 percent of the homes in the nearby fishermen's quarter in order to build a gigantic citadel. These suddenly homeless seafarers were moved to the tightly grid-planned Barceloneta quarter, designed by a military architect, jutting out into the harbor just east of here.

Meanwhile, the loss of a huge chunk of El Born contributed to this neighborhood's decline, as shipping shifted farther west, to the Barri Gòtic's harbor at Port Vell.

This square marks the site of a mass grave of the massacred Catalan patriots. The **eternal flame** burns atop this monument, and 9/11 remains a sobering anniversary for the Catalans, who still harbor a grudge. They say when heading to the toilet, "I'm going to Philip's house."

Here or elsewhere in El Born (which

is a particularly feisty neighborhood), you may see displayed the *estelada* **flag,** the symbol of Catalan separatists: It features the typical red-and-gold horizontal stripes of the Catalunya flag, but with a blue triangle and white star on the hoist side. This design comes from the flag of a former Spanish colony that fought hard for its independence—Cuba. It's a provocative image to Spaniards who want to keep Catalunya in their country.

• *The hulking building dominating this square is the Church of Santa Maria del Mar. To reach its entrance, turn left and walk alongside it, until you get to the small square in front of the church.*

❾ Church of Santa Maria del Mar

This 14th-century church is the proud centerpiece of El Born. "Del Mar" means "of the sea," and that's where the money came from. The proud shippers built this church in less than 60 years, so it

has a harmonious style that is considered pure Catalan Gothic. Located outside the city walls, this was a defiantly independent symbol of neighborhood pride; to this day, it's fully supported not by the Church or the city, but by the community.

On the big **front doors,** notice the figures of workers who donated their time and sweat to build the church. The stone for the church was quarried at Montjuïc and had to be carried across town on the backs of porters called *bastaixos.* Although they've always been celebrated by residents, their work is now more widely appreciated, following the release of the 2006 novel *Cathedral of the Sea,* which tells the story of the church's construction from the perspective of an ambitious *bastaixo.*

Step inside the church. The largely unadorned **Gothic interior** used to be more highly decorated with Baroque frills, up until the Spanish Civil War (1936-1939). During the war, the Catholic Church sided with the conservative forces of Franco against leftists supporting the Spanish Republic. In retaliation, the working class took their anger out on this church, burning all of its wood furnishings and decor (carbon still blackens the ceiling). Today the church remains stripped down—naked in all its Gothic glory. The tree-like columns inspired Gaudí (their influence on the columns inside his Sagrada Família church is obvious). Sixteenth-century sailors left models of their ships at the foot of the altar for Mary's protection. Even today, a classic old Catalan ship remains at Mary's feet. As within the Cathedral of Barcelona, here you can see the characteristic Catalan Gothic buttresses flying inward, defining

Indulgences near the Church

Barcelona's most colorful bohemian quarter—this neighborhood around the Church of Santa Maria del Mar—offers plenty of inviting places to eat, drink, and shop. Explore!

The recommended **La Vinya del Senyor** wine bar, good for a drink or a meal, faces the front door of the church, and several other recommended eateries are nearby (see page 208 of Eating in Barcelona). For liquid souvenirs, try **Vila Vinateca,** a wine shop with (they claim) the widest selection in Barcelona (Mon-Sat 8:30-20:30, closed Sun, Carrer des Agullers 7—as you face the church it's buried in the streets over your right shoulder, tel. 902-327-777).

A caffeine jolt awaits at **Cafés El Magnífico,** selling what's reputed to be the city's best coffee (Mon-Sat 10:00-14:00 & 16:00-20:00, closed Sun, one block up Carrer de l'Argenteria at #64—immediately to the left as you face the church's front door, tel. 933-196-081). For a fragrant snack, head to **Casa Gispert,** which has been roasting nuts in the same wood-fired oven since 1851. Drop in to enjoy the aroma of fire-roasted nuts and pick up a snack (Tue-Fri 9:30-14:00 & 16:00-20:30, Sat 10:00-14:00 & 17:00-20:30, closed Sun-Mon; facing front door of church, circle around left side and walk almost all the way to the end—store is on the left at Carrer dels Sombrerers 23, tel. 933-197-535).

Near Casa Gispert is the start of an excellent **shopping area.** Head up the little lane just to the right of Gispert, Carrer de Sant Antoni dels Sombrerers. Follow this street as it jogs left, then (at the dead-end), turn right onto Carrer dels Banys Vells. Follow this all the way up to Princesa—a bunch of great shops hide along the lanes branching off to the left. The streets wedged between here and Carrer de l'Argenteria are particularly interesting and an easy place to score some cool finds.

the chapels that ring the nave. The colorful windows come with modern themes.

Around the right side of the church is a poignant memorial to the "Catalan Alamo" of September 11, 1714 (described earlier, under "Monument of Catalan Independence").

• *If you've seen enough, you could end our walk now and give in to El Born's many buyable and edible temptations (see sidebar for ideas). To continue on to the **waterfront**, face the cathedral, and turn right up Carrer d'Espaseria. You'll pop out at the square...*

❿ Pla de Palau

The hulking building on your right, at the end of the square, is **La Llotja de Mar,** or fish exchange. Back when Barcelona was a major shipping center and El Born was its ritziest neighborhood, this was one of Europe's first stock exchanges. From the late 17th through the late 20th centuries, the building also housed the prestigious Barcelona Arts and Crafts School. The oldest design school in Spain (from 1715), this local institution has provided state-subsidized instruction to budding artists—including Pablo Picasso and Joan Miró.

The stone on the pillar in the middle of the busy street is a popular ending point for demonstrations.

• *Walk along the front of La Llotja de Mar, cross the wide street, and turn right to walk under the shaded arches of the big arcaded building. At the busy intersection, turn left around the corner and come face-to-face with the...*

⓫ *Barcelona Head*

This sculpture, created for the 1992 Summer Olympics by American Pop artist Roy Lichtenstein, instantly became an icon of the city. It brings together the colors of Miró, the tiles of Gaudí, the Cubism of Picasso, and the comic-newsprint trademark of Lichtenstein. The grand Main Post Office stands just behind it.

Down the promenade from the head, look for the canopy with a giant, whimsical **lobster sculpture** waving from on top. This was designed by Javier Mariscal, best known for creating the Catalan sheepdog Cobi, the lovable cartoon mascot for the 1992 Olympics (also the star of a much-loved cartoon show still fondly remembered by Spaniards). While the restaurant that commissioned this work is long gone, the cheery lobster survives—one more piece of invigorating public art on Barcelona's fine waterfront, a veritable open-air art museum.

• *Barcelona's inviting waterfront beckons. From here, you can walk left, past the Catalan History Museum, to reach* **Barceloneta** *and the beach (or consider renting a bike at the recommended Un Cotxe Menys shop for a pedal down the beach promenade to the Fòrum—described on page 34). Going right takes you along the delightful art-lined* **promenade** *next to the Old Port (bristling with sailboats) to the Columbus Monument at the bottom of the Ramblas. Another option is to head up busy* **Via Laietana,** *which we crossed at the beginning of this walk. Or you can backtrack to the* **Picasso Museum** *and take my self-guided tour (see next chapter). Finally, if you haven't yet explored El Born's shopping streets (see sidebar on previous page), what better time than now?*

PICASSO MUSEUM TOUR

Museu Picasso

This is the best collection in the country of the work of Spaniard Pablo Picasso (1881-1973). And, since Picasso spent his formative years (from the ages of 14 to 23) in Barcelona, it's the best collection of his early works anywhere. The museum is sparse on later, better-known works from his time of international celebrity; visit this museum not to see famous canvases but to get an intimate portrait of the young man finding his way as an artist. By experiencing his youthful, realistic art, you can better understand his later, more challenging art and more fully appreciate his genius.

Picasso's personal secretary amassed many examples of his work and bequeathed them to Barcelona. The artist, happy to have a museum showing off his work in the city of his youth, added to the collection throughout his life. The artworks are scattered through several connected Gothic palaces.

Orientation

Cost: €11, free all day first Sun of month and other Sun from 15:00.

Hours: Tue-Sun 10:00-19:50, closed Mon, last entry 20 minutes before closing.

Crowd-Beating Tips: There's almost always a line, sometimes with waits of more than an hour. The busiest times are mornings before 13:00, all day Tuesday, and during the free entry times on Sundays (see above). If you have an Articket BCN (see page 31), skip the line by going to the "Meeting Point" entrance (30 yards to the right of the main entrance). You can also skip the line by buying your ticket online at www.museu picasso.bcn.cat (no additional booking fee). Stuck in line without a ticket? Figure that about 25 people are admitted every 10 minutes.

Getting There: It's at Carrer de Montcada 15-23; the ticket office is at #21. From the Jaume I Metro stop, it's a quick five-minute walk. Just head down Carrer de la Princesa (across the busy Via Laietana from the Barri Gòtic), turning right on Carrer de Montcada. It's a 10-minute walk from the cathedral and many parts of the Barri Gòtic; for an interesting approach from the cathedral area, ○ take the El Born Walk.

Information: Tel. 932-563-000, www.museupicasso.bcn.cat.

Audioguide: The 1.5-hour audioguide costs €3 and offers ample detail about the collection.

Length of This Tour: Allow at least an hour, or more time for lingering.

With Limited Time: Focus on the first part of the collection (through the Blue Period), with Picasso's lesser-known but formative early works.

Services: The ground floor, which is free to enter, has a required bag check, as well as a handy array of other services (bookshop, WC, and cafeteria).

Photography: Strictly forbidden.

Cuisine Art: The museum itself has a good **café** (€8 sandwiches and salads). Outside the museum, right along Carrer de Montcada in either direction, are two great recommended tapas bars (both closed Mon): With your back to the museum, a few steps to the left is **El Xampanyet,** while to the right (across Carrer de la Princesa and up a block) is **Bar del Pla.** For details, see the Eating in Barcelona chapter.

The Tour Begins

The Picasso Museum's collection of nearly 300 paintings is presented more or less chronologically (though specific pieces may be out for restoration or on tour, and the rooms are sometimes rearranged). But with the help of thoughtful English descriptions for each stage (and guards who don't let you stray), it's easy to follow the evolution of Picasso's work. This tour is arranged by the stages of his life and art.

• *Begin in rooms 1 and 2.*

Boy Wonder

Pablo's earliest art is realistic and sober. The young genius gets serious about art at age 14, when his family moves to Barcelona and he enrolls in art school. Early **self-portraits** show the self-awareness of a blossoming intellect (and a kid who must have been a handful in junior high school). He seems proud—as if confident of future success.

Picasso Museum—First Floor

Not to Scale

ENTRANCE
(AT GROUND LEVEL)

CARRER DE MONTCADA

← To Santa Caterina Market
(5 min. walk)

→ To Church of Santa Maria del Mar
(5 min. walk)

↙ To Jaume 1 Ⓜ (5 min. walk)
& Cathedral (10 min. walk)

1 Self-Portraits
2 Portraits & Art-School Work
3 First Communion
4 Portrait of Artist's Mother
5 Science and Charity
6 Horta de San Joan
7 Els Quatre Gats Menu Cover
8 Velázquez Copy
9 Cancan Dancer
10 Still Life

11 Landscape
12 The Wait
13 The Forsaken
14 Rooftops of Barcelona
15 Portrait of Benedetta Bianco
16 Woman with Mantilla
17 Synthetic Cubism
18 Las Meninas Studies (3)
19 Ceramics
20 French Riviera

Even at this young age, his **portraits** of grizzled peasants demonstrate surprising psychological insight and impressive technique. You'll see portraits of Pablo's first teacher, his father—himself a curator and artist who quit painting to nurture his young prodigy. Because his dedicated father kept everything his son ever did, Picasso must have the best-documented youth of any great painter.

Displays show Pablo's **art-school work.** Every time he starts breaking rules, he's sent back to the standard classic style. The assignment: Sketch nude models to capture human anatomy accurately.

PICASSO MUSEUM

Pablo Picasso
(1881-1973)

Pablo Picasso was the most famous and—OK, I'll say it—the greatest artist of the 20th century. Always exploring, he became the master of many styles (Cubism, Surrealism, Expressionism, and so on) and of many media (painting, sculpture, prints, ceramics, and assemblages). Still, he could make anything he touched look unmistakably like "a Picasso."

Born in Málaga, Spain, Picasso was the son of an art teacher. At a very young age, he quickly advanced beyond his teachers. Picasso's teenage works are stunningly realistic and capture the inner complexities of the people he painted. As a youth in Barcelona, he fell in with a bohemian crowd that mixed wine, women, and art.

In 1900, at age 19, Picasso started making trips to Paris. Four years later, he moved to the City of Light and absorbed the styles of many painters (especially Henri de Toulouse-Lautrec) while searching for his own artist's voice. His paintings of beggars and other social outcasts show the empathy of a man who was himself a poor, homesick foreigner. When his best friend, Spanish artist Carlos Casagemas, committed suicide, Picasso plunged into a **Blue Period** (1901-1904)—so called because the dominant color in these paintings matches their melancholy mood and subject matter (emaciated beggars, hard-eyed pimps, and so on).

In 1904, Picasso got a steady girlfriend (Fernande Olivier) and suddenly saw the world through rose-colored glasses—the **Rose Period.** He was further jolted out of his Blue Period by the "flat" look of the Fauves. Not satisfied with their take on 3-D, Picasso played with the "building blocks" of line and color to find new ways to reconstruct the real world on canvas.

At his studio in Montmartre, Picasso and his neighbor Georges Braque worked together, in poverty so dire they often didn't know where their next bottle of wine was coming from. And then, at the age of 25, Picasso reinvented painting. Fascinated by the primitive power of African and Iberian tribal masks, he sketched human faces with simple outlines and almond eyes. Intrigued by the body of his girlfriend, Fernande, he sketched it from every angle, then experimented with showing several different views on the same canvas. A hundred paintings and nine months later, Picasso gave birth to a monstrous canvas of five nude, fragmented prostitutes with mask-like faces—*Les Demoiselles d'Avignon* (1907).

This bold new style was called **Cubism.** With Cubism, Picasso shattered the Old World and put it back together in a new way. The subjects are somewhat recognizable (with the help of the titles), but they're built with geometric shards (let's call them "cubes")—like viewing the world through a kaleidoscope of brown and gray. Cubism gives us several different angles of the subject at once—say, a woman seen from the front and side angles simultaneously, resulting in two eyes on the same side of the nose. This involves showing the traditional three dimensions, plus Einstein's new fourth dimension—the time it takes to walk around the subject to see other angles.

In 1918, Picasso married his first wife, Olga Kokhlova, with whom he had a son. He then traveled to Rome and entered a **Classical Period** (the 1920s) of more realistic, full-bodied women and children, inspired by the three-dimensional sturdiness of ancient statues. While he flirted with abstraction, throughout his life, Picasso always kept a grip on "reality." His favorite subject was people. The anatomy might be jumbled, but it's all there.

Though he lived in France and Italy, Picasso remained a Spaniard at heart, incorporating Spanish motifs into his work. Unrepentantly macho, he loved bullfights, seeing them as a metaphor for the timeless human interaction between the genders. The horse—clad with blinders and pummeled by the bull—has nothing to do with the fight. To Picasso, the horse symbolizes the feminine, and the bull, the masculine. Spanish imagery—bulls, screaming horses, a Madonna—appears in Picasso's most famous work, *Guernica* (1937, on display in Madrid). The monumental canvas of a bombed village summed up the pain of Spain's brutal Civil War (1936-1939) and foreshadowed the onslaught of World War II.

At war's end, Picasso left Paris and his emotional baggage behind, finding fun in the sun in the **south of France** (1948-1954). Sun! Color! Water! Spacious skies! Freedom! Sixty-five-year-old Pablo Picasso was reborn, enjoying worldwide fame and the love of a beautiful 23-year-old painter named Françoise Gilot. Dressed in rolled-up white pants and a striped sailor's shirt, bursting with pent-up creativity, Picasso often cranked out more than a painting a day. Picasso's Riviera works set the tone for the rest of his life—sunny, lighthearted, uncomplicated, experimenting in new media and using motifs of the sea, of Greek mythology (fauns, centaurs), and animals (birds, goats, and pregnant baboons). His simple sketch of a dove holding an olive branch became an international symbol of peace.

Picasso also made collages, built "statues" out of wood, wire, ceramics, papier-mâché, or whatever, and even turned everyday household objects into statues (like his famous bull's head made of a bicycle seat with handlebar horns). **Multimedia** works like these have become so standard today that we forget how revolutionary they were when Picasso invented them. His last works have the playfulness of someone much younger. As it is often said of Picasso, "When he was a child, he painted like a man. When he was old, he painted like a child."

• In room 2, you'll find more paintings relating to Pablo's...

Developing Talent

During a summer trip to Málaga in 1896, Picasso dabbles in a series of fresh, Impressionistic-style landscapes (relatively rare in Spain at the time). As a 15-year-old, Pablo dutifully enters art-school

competitions. His first big work, *First Communion* (1896)—while portraying the prescribed religious subject—is more an excuse to paint his family. Notice his sister Lola's exquisitely painted veil. This piece is heavily influenced by the academic style of local painters.

Find the **portrait of his mother** (if it's on view—this fragile 1896 pastel is sometimes out for conservation). The teenage Pablo is working on the fine details and gradients of white in her blouse and the expression in her cameo-like face. Notice the signature. Spaniards keep both parents' surnames, with the father's first, followed by the mother's: Pablo Ruiz Picasso. Pablo is closer to his mom than his dad, and eventually he keeps just her name.

• Continue into room 3.

Early Success

Science and Charity (1897), which won second prize at a fine-arts exhibition, got Picasso the chance to study in Madrid. Now Picasso

conveys real feeling. The doctor (modeled on Pablo's father) represents science. The nun represents charity and religion. From her hopeless face and lifeless hand, it seems that Picasso believes nothing will save this woman from death. Pablo painted a little perspective trick: Walk back and forth across the

room to see the bed stretch and shrink. Three small studies for this painting (on the right) show how this was an exploratory work. The frontier: light.

Picasso travels to Madrid for further study. Stifled by the stuffy fine-arts school there, Pablo hangs out instead in the Prado Museum and learns by copying the masters. (An example of his impressive mimicry is coming up later, in room 5.) Having absorbed the wisdom of the ages, in 1898 Pablo visits **Horta de San Joan,** a

rural Catalan village, and finds his artistic independence. (See the small landscapes and scenes of village life he did there.) Poor and without a love in his life, he returns to Barcelona.
• *Head to room 4.*

Barcelona Freedom

Art Nouveau is all the rage in Barcelona when Pablo returns there in 1900. Upsetting his dad, he quits art school and falls in with the avant-garde crowd. These bohe-

mians congregate daily at Els Quatre Gats ("The Four Cats," a popular restaurant to this day—see page 204). Notice the **menu cover** he did for this favorite hangout. Further establishing his artistic freedom, he paints **portraits**—no longer of his family... but of his new friends (including one of Jaume Sabartés, who later became his personal assistant and donated the works to establish this museum). Only 19 years old, Pablo puts on his first one-man show.
• *Pause in the small room 5.*

Notice young Picasso's nearly perfect **copy** of a portrait of Philip IV by an earlier Spanish master, Diego Velázquez. (Near the end of this tour, we'll see a much older Picasso riffing on another Velázquez painting.)
• *The next few pieces are displayed in rooms 6 and 7.*

Paris

In 1900 Picasso makes his first trip to Paris, a city bursting with life, light, and love. Dropping the paternal surname Ruiz, Pablo

establishes his commercial brand name: "Picasso." Here the explorer Picasso goes bohemian and befriends poets, prostitutes, and artists. He paints **cancan dancers** like Henri de Toulouse-Lautrec, **still lifes** like Paul Cézanne, brightly colored Fauvist works like Henri Matisse, and Impressionist **landscapes** like Claude Monet. In *The Wait,* the subject—with her bold outline and strong gaze—pops out from the Impressionistic background. It is Cézanne's technique of "building" a figure with "cubes" of paint that will inspire Picasso to invent Cubism—soon.

• *Turn right into the hall, then—farther along—right again, to find rooms 8 and 9.*

Blue Period

Picasso travels to Paris several times (he settles there permanently in 1904). The suicide of his best friend, his own poverty, and the influence of new ideas linking color and mood lead Picasso to his Blue Period (1901-1904). He cranks out stacks of blue art just to stay housed and fed. With blue backgrounds (the coldest color) and depressing subjects, this period was revolutionary in art history. Now the artist is painting not what he sees, but what he feels. Just off room 8, the touching 1903 portrait of a mother and child, *The Forsaken,* captures the period well. Painting misfits and street people, Picasso, like Velázquez and Toulouse-

Lautrec, sees the beauty in ugliness. Back home in Barcelona, Picasso paints his hometown at night from **rooftops** (in the main part of room 8). The painting is still blue, but here we see proto-Cubism...five years before the first real Cubist painting.

• *Just off room 8, we get a hint of Picasso's...*

Rose Period

Picasso is finally lifted out of his funk after meeting a new lady, Fernande Olivier. He moves out of the blue and into the happier Rose Period (1904-1907). For a fine example, see the portrait of a woman wearing a classic Spanish mantilla *(Portrait of Benedetta Bianco).* Its glistening pink and reddish tones are the colors of flesh and sensuality. (This is the only actual Rose Period painting in the museum, but don't be surprised if it is out on loan.)

In *Woman with Mantilla* (room 9), we see a little Post-Impressionistic Pointillism in a portrait that looks like a classical statue. Although it's a later work (from 1917), its cheery palette evokes the Rose Period.

• *Continue through room 10, into room 11.*

Cubism

Pablo's invention (roughly from 1906 to 1913, with fellow artist Georges Braque) of the shocking Cubist style is well-known—at least I hope so, since this museum has no true Cubist paintings. The Cubist pulls apart the basic elements of a subject and re-presents them all at once from multiple viewpoints. In the museum, you'll see some so-called Synthetic Cubist paintings—a later variation that flattens the various angles, as opposed to the purer, original Analytical Cubist paintings, in which you can simultaneously see several 3-D facets of the subject.

• *Remember that this museum focuses on Picasso's early years. As a result, it has very little from the most famous and prolific "middle" part of his career—basically, from Picasso's adoption of Cubism to his sunset years on the French Riviera. (To fill in these gaps in his middle career, see the "Pablo Picasso" sidebar earlier in this chapter.) Skip ahead more than 30 years and into rooms 12-14 (at the end of the main hallway, on the right).*

Picasso and Velázquez

This series of rooms relates to what many consider the greatest painting by anyone, ever: Diego Velázquez's *Las Meninas* (the

17th-century original is displayed in Madrid's Prado Museum). Heralded as the first completely realistic painting, *Las Meninas* became an obsession for Picasso centuries later.

Picasso, who had great respect for Velázquez, painted more than **40 interpretations** of this piece. Picasso seems to enjoy a relationship of equals with Velázquez. Like artistic soul mates, the two Spanish geniuses spar and tease. Picasso deconstructs Velázquez and then injects light, color, and perspective as he improvises on the earlier masterpiece. In Picasso's big black-and-white canvas, the king and queen (reflected in the mirror in the back of the room) are hardly seen, while the painter towers above everyone. The two women of the court on the right look like they're in a tomb—but they're wearing party shoes. Browse the various studies, a playground of color and perspective. See the fun Picasso had playing paddleball with Velázquez's tour de force—filtering Velázquez's realism through the kaleidoscope of Cubism.

• *Head back into the **ceramics** area (room 16), where you'll find a flock of carefree white birds, and continue into room 15.*

The French Riviera

Picasso spends the last 36 years of his life living simply in the south of France. He said many times that "Paintings are like windows open to the world." We see his sunny Riviera world: With simple black outlines and Crayola colors, Picasso paints sun-splashed nature, peaceful doves, and the joys of the beach. He dabbles in the timeless art of ceramics, shaping bowls and vases into fun animals decorated with simple, childlike designs. He now has little kids of his own and hangs out with uncomplicated (even childlike) artists like Marc Chagall.

Picasso died with brush in hand, still growing. Sadly, since Picasso vowed never to set foot in a fascist, Franco-ruled Spain, the artist never returned to his homeland...and never saw this museum (his death came in 1973—two years before Franco's). However, to the end, Picasso continued exploring and loving life through his art.

• *Our tour is finished. You're in the heart of the delightful El Born neigh-borhood. For a self-guided walk of this area,* ✪ *see my El Born Walk.*

EIXAMPLE WALK

From Plaça de Catalunya to Casa Milà (and Beyond)

Literally "The Expansion," L'Eixample is where Barcelona spread when it burst at the seams in the 19th century. Rather than allowing unchecked growth, city leaders thoughtfully funneled Barcelona's newfound wealth into creating a standardized yet refreshingly open grid plan—as if attempting to achieve the opposite of the claustrophobic Gothic lanes that had contained locals for centuries. The creation of the Eixample also coincided with a burst in architectural creativity, as great Modernista minds such as Antoni Gaudí, Lluís Domènech i Montaner, and Josep Puig i Cadafalch were given both artistic license and seemingly limitless funds to adorn the new boulevards with fanciful facades. It was a perfect storm of urban planning, unbridled architectural innovation, Industrial Age technology, ample wealth, and Catalan cultural pride.

This walk takes you through the Eixample's "Golden Quarter" (Quadrat d'Or) to see two of the city's Modernista musts—the Block of Discord and Casa Milà—as well as several other sights. The roundabout route also winds you through some pleasant, relatively untouristy residential neighborhoods that showcase modern Barcelona's unusual street plan and everyday life in this elegant quarter.

Orientation

Length of This Walk: Allow about 1.5 hours (more if you tour the Casa Milà or Casa Batlló, or detour to other Modernista buildings).

With Limited Time: Skip the first part of this walk and make a beeline for the Block of Discord and Casa Milà.

Planning Your Time: If you want to see the interiors, reservations are smart at both Casa Milà and Casa Batlló.

Getting There: This walk starts at Plaça de Catalunya (Metro: Plaça de Catalunya).

Church of the Holy Conception: Free, Mon-Sat 7:30-13:00 & 17:00-21:00, Sun 7:30-14:00 & 17:00-21:00, enter at Carrer de Roger de Llúria 70, tel. 934-576-552, www.concepciobcn .com.

La Concepció Market: Free, Mon and Sat 8:00-15:00, Tue-Fri 8:00-20:00, closed Sun, Carrer de València 317, tel. 934-575-329.

Casa Batlló: €18.15, daily 9:00-20:00; for ticketing, see page 59.

Fundació Antoni Tàpies: €7, includes audioguide, Tue-Sun 10:00-19:00, closed Mon, Carrer d'Aragó 255, tel. 934-870-315, www.fundaciotapies.org.

Casa Milà: €15, daily March-Oct 9:00-20:00, Nov-Feb 9:00-18:30, last entry 30 minutes before closing, for reservation info and crowd-beating tips, see page 62.

Eating: Several fine tapas bars and restaurants are on or near the course of this walk. For details, see page 211.

Background

Barcelona boomed in the 1800s, with its population doubling (from a half-million to a million) over the course of one century. Before its upsurge, Barcelona languished through centuries of stagnation: Columbus' discoveries had shifted trade from the Mediterranean to the Atlantic. Catalunya also suffered under the thumb of Madrid, which feared—perhaps rightfully—a Catalan uprising. Eventually, Queen Isabella II loosened Madrid's grip on Barcelona. Barcelona was allowed to trade with the Americas, bringing new wealth. And locally, this land of abundant coal deposits and many rivers flowing from the Pyrenees to the Mediterranean provided the perfect resources for powering textile mills. Industrialization brought people from all over Spain (and beyond) to find work, and Barcelona's textile magnates powered a remarkably robust economy. Barcelona was back on the map.

But the upwardly mobile city had nowhere to grow. Because of the Madrid government's centuries-old restrictions, the city was forced to stay within its medieval walls. By the mid-19th century, 200,000 residents were crammed into the Old City. It was a slum of steep and crowded tenements where disease was rampant, the air was choked with coal soot, and the quality of life was miserable. It was clear that expansion was necessary. (At around the same time, Paris, Vienna, Copenhagen, and other cities were dealing with similar growing pains.)

Finally, in 1854, Queen Isabella II allowed the growing city to tear down the medieval wall and expand northward. Because very little existed outside the Old City, urban planners had a blank slate.

Civil engineer Ildefons Cerdà (1815-1876) proposed a carefully plotted, remarkably modern, and efficient grid of streets that would surround the convoluted tangle of Barcelona's Old

City. Uptown Barcelona would be a unique variation on the common grid-plan city. By snipping off the building corners, light and spacious octagonal "squares" were created at every intersection.

Work began in 1860 on Cerdà's progressive Eixample plan, which envisioned a new town in which everything was made accessible to everyone. Each block-square district would have easy access to its own hospital, park, market, schools, and day-care centers. Restrictions on the height, width, and depth of buildings ensured that sunlight would reach every unit. The hollow space found inside each "block" of apartments would form a neighborhood park. (Cerdà was inspired by his childhood in a traditional Catalan farmstead that consisted of four buildings surrounding a protected courtyard.) Although parts of Cerdà's vision didn't quite pan out, the Eixample is an urban success.

The birth of the Eixample also coincided with two other important moments in the city's history: The revival of Catalan cultural pride (the Renaixença) and the emergence of Catalunya's own spin on Art Nouveau—Modernisme (see sidebar, later).

Rich-and-artsy big shots bought plots along the Eixample grid and hired some of the best and brightest architects in the business, including Antoni Gaudí, Lluís Domènech i Montaner, and Josep Puig i Cadafalch. It's no accident that Modernista mansions come with big bay windows and outlandish decoration: The people who paid for them wanted both to be seen, and to be recognized for their forward-thinking embrace of the new art. The wealthiest landowners built as close to the center as possible—that's why the most distinctive buildings are near Passeig de Gràcia.

Today's Eixample remains Barcelona's upscale and genteel uptown. The heart of the Eixample is the Quadrat d'Or, or "Golden Quarter," with the richest collection of Modernista facades...and the richest local residents. This remains one of the city's most desirable neighborhoods. It's also one center of the local gay community (especially a few blocks west of Passeig de Gràcia, around Carrer d'Aribau), earning it the nickname "Gayshample."

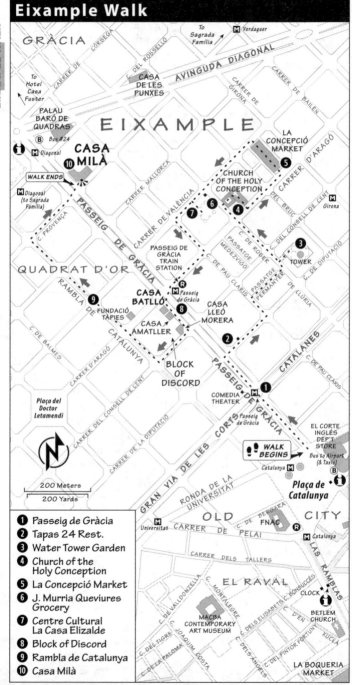

Eixample Walk

1. Passeig de Gràcia
2. Tapas 24 Rest.
3. Water Tower Garden
4. Church of the Holy Conception
5. La Concepció Market
6. J. Murria Queviures Grocery
7. Centre Cultural La Casa Elizalde
8. Block of Discord
9. Rambla de Catalunya
10. Casa Milà

The Walk Begins

• *Begin at Plaça de Catalunya. Head up the broad boulevard (Passeig de Gràcia) at the top end of the giant El Corte Inglés department store. Walk up one block (on the right side of this street) to the huge intersection with Gran Via de les Corts Catalanes; there's a big fountain in the middle.*

❶ Passeig de Gràcia

In the 500 feet between here and the Barri Gòtic, you've traveled 500 years—from the medieval Gothic vibe of the Barri Gòtic to the ambitiously modern late-19th-century Eixample.

In Catalan, *passeig* means "boulevard"—and this one leads to Gràcia, once a separate town but now a neighborhood in Barcelona. Glancing at a map, you'll see that this is just about the only street in the Eixample that doesn't follow the regular grid—it angles slightly on its way to Gràcia. As one of the first major thoroughfares of the Eixample, this was prime real estate. To this day, the boulevard remains the top street in town. Notice the extra-wide girth of this drag, the inviting park-like median strips, and the unique Modernista lampposts anchored by Gaudí-style benches slathered with broken white tile mosaics.

Originally Barcelona's wealthy class built elaborate residences along here. But within just a few decades, as the city continued to grow and real estate was at a premium, it became more lucrative to tear down those mansions and replace them with multistory townhouses. (One of the few surviving original mansions, now the Comedia theater, is kitty-corner across the

intersection—just beyond the fountain.) Notice that, despite great architectural variation in their facades, most Eixample homes share an identical design: Shops and businesses on the ground floor; above that, a large first (our "second") floor, the *piano nobile* where the wealthy family lived; and, higher up, smaller floors for tenants. Throughout the Eixample, you'll see that the first floor is usually taller and more elaborate than the other floors—often with balconies or bay windows that higher floors are lacking. (Most of these houses predate the elevator; after that convenience was

Modernisme and the Renaixença

Modernisme is Barcelona's unique contribution to the Europe-wide Art Nouveau movement. Meaning "a taste for what is modern"—things like streetcars, electric lights, and big-wheeled bicycles—this free-flowing organic style lasted from 1888 to 1906.

Broadly speaking, there were two kinds of Modernisme (Catalan Art Nouveau). Early Modernisme is a kind of Neo-Gothic, clearly inspired by medieval castles and towers—logically, since architects wanted to recall the days when Barcelona was at its peak. From that same starting point, Antoni Gaudí branched off on his own, adding the color and curves we most associate with Barcelona's Modernisme look.

The aim was to create objects that were both practical and decorative. To that end, Modernista architects experimented with new construction techniques. Their most important material was concrete, which they could use to make a hard stone building that curved and rippled like a wave. Then they sprinkled it with brightly colored glass and tile. The structure was fully modern, but the decoration was a clip-art collage of nature images, exotic Moorish or Chinese themes, and fanciful Gothic crosses and knights to celebrate Catalunya's medieval glory days.

It's ironic to think that Modernisme was a response to the Industrial Age—and that all those organic shapes were only made possible thanks to Eiffel Tower-like iron frames. As you wander through the Eixample looking at all those fanciful facades and colorful, leafy, flowing, blooming shapes in doorways, entrances, and ceilings, remember that many of these homes were built at the same time as the first skyscrapers in Chicago and New York City.

Underpinning Modernisme was the Catalan cultural revival movement, called the Renaixença. As Europe was waking up to the modern age, downtrodden peoples across Europe—from the Basques to the Irish to the Hungarians to the Finns—were throwing off the cultural domination of other nations and celebrating what made their own culture unique. Here in Catalunya, the Renaixença encouraged everyday people to get excited about all things Catalan—from their language, patriotic dances, and inspirational art to their surprising style of architecture.

invented and widely installed, penthouse living became popular.) Many houses have two doors—one for the owners and another for the upstairs tenants. Most house blocks had an interior garden courtyard for ventilation and light, although over time many of these spaces have been covered over by one-story structures or parking lots.

Because the Eixample was developed during the Renaixença, you'll spot Catalan themes, such as St. George (Jordi)—the local patron saint—slaying the dragon. See any flags? Added to Catalunya's flag of narrow red-and-gold stripes is a red cross on a white field (the same symbol is embraced by England, which also considers St. George one of its patrons).

Speaking of Catalan pride, imagine this street (and the ones around it) clogged with an estimated one million furious Catalans. It happened on July 10, 2010, after Spanish constitutional courts overturned key provisions of a Catalan statute for home rule (which had been approved by an overwhelming 73 percent of Catalan voters). These patriots of Catalunya—which considers itself a "nation without a state"—waved flags that read, *Som una nació. Nosaltres decidim.* (We are a nation. We decide.) This peaceful demonstration was a reminder that the Catalans—like the Basques and the Scots—take home rule very seriously.

Continue one more block up Passeig de Gràcia (to the intersection with Carrer de la Diputació) to appreciate the delightfully airy street plan you'll find throughout the Eixample. Notice that the four corners are cropped off, creating a wide-open pleasant space at the intersection (which can be filled by café tables, inviting benches, or public art).

• *From here, if you're tight on time or not interested in a slice of Eixample life, you can easily continue directly to the Block of Discord: Just keep going straight up the boulevard one more block. But to get a better sense of the neighborhood, turn right on* Carrer de la Diputació.

❷ Tapas 24

A few steps down on the left, you'll see the recommended Tapas

24, my favorite of the many trendy Eixample tapas bars (for listings, see page 211).

Catalunya has recently become a culinary hotspot, thanks largely to one revolutionary chef: Ferran Adrià. His restaurant El Bulli (in a small Costa Brava town) was a trendsetting laboratory of "molecular gastronomy," which experiments with the basic properties of food by deconstructing classic dishes to create wildly inventive new presentations (think liquid nitrogen and flavored foams). Adrià's trademark dish is a "liquid olive," which looks like a real olive but is actually a thin spherical membrane filled with intensely flavored essence of olive. Adrià closed El Bulli (which had been heralded as the best restaurant in the world) in 2011, but it's slated to reopen as a culinary institute in 2014. In the meantime, foodies flock to the restaurants of Adrià's many apprentices and disciples—including chef Carles Abellan, whose Tapas 24 is the least swanky of his four eateries.

Continue one block down Carrer de la Diputació, noticing the distinctive paving stones (four squares with a circle in each one). This is one of a handful of distinctive patterns on mass-produced tiles that are a symbol of Barcelona.

• *At the corner, turn left up Carrer de Pau Claris. Halfway up the block, notice the gated* **passage** *on the right (Passatge Permanyer, at #116). Cut through here for a peek at a fine residential strip buried in the middle of the block. Although such passageways were not a planned feature of the Eixample, here and there they've been carved out of the buildings' central courtyards, and make a pretty stroll. Popping out the other end, cross the street and jog 30 yards to the left, then go down the passage at #56 (on the right, marked* Jardins de Torre de les Aigües, *open daily 10:00-sunset). This leads you to a...*

❸ Water Tower Garden

This tranquil (if somewhat sterile) courtyard has trees, benches, and a pool, all watched over by a brick water tower from 1867. In the summer, a temporary "beach" is sometimes created here. Courtyards like this were part of the original vision for the Eixample. Each block was supposed to have a shared central patio, but over the last century, many of them have been converted to other purposes. More recently, as properties become available, the city of Barcelona has slowly begun restoring Cerdà's original public spaces.

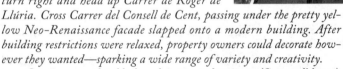

• *Exiting the garden the way you entered, turn right and head up Carrer de Roger de Llúria. Cross Carrer del Consell de Cent, passing under the pretty yellow Neo-Renaissance facade slapped onto a modern building. After building restrictions were relaxed, property owners could decorate however they wanted—sparking a wide range of variety and creativity.*

Continue another block and cross another street (Carrer d'Aragó). Go straight a half-block, entering the cloister at #70, on the right of the...

❹ Church of the Holy Conception

Work your way through the cloister to the interior of the church. This is a purely Gothic, 13th-century church with a 14th- and 15th-

century cloister that once stood in the Old City. But when the wall that once surrounded the Old City came down as part of Barcelona's expansion, a few historic churches like this one were moved, brick by brick, to new locations in the 1870s. The bell tower came from a different Gothic church.

• *Exiting the church through its front door, turn left and continue one block, passing (at the far side of the intersection) the entrance to the Seu del Districte Eixample—the Eixample's own "seat," or branch office, of city hall. Continuing straight just beyond that, you'll reach (on the left)...*

❺ La Concepció Market

While it has many of the same features as La Boqueria (on the Ramblas) and the Santa Caterina Market (in El Born), this market has virtually zero tourists. Walk through the building, from one end to the other. It's a good place to sample local cheeses, buy olives, or pick up some fruit. At the far end, you'll emerge into a delightful flower market crowding the sidewalk.

• *Turn left and stroll along...*

Carrer de València

As you walk, you'll pass many more flower stands and the turreted Municipal Conservatory of Barcelona, a city-run music academy.

Ponder the fact that in just a couple of blocks, we've passed a church, a municipal building, a market, and a school (just up the street next to the market). This is very much in keeping with the original vision for the Eixample: a series of self-sufficient neighborhood zones that give residents easy access to important services.

Continuing straight on Carrer de València, you'll pass (at the corner, on the right) an unfortunate brick monstrosity that breaks up the Eixample harmony, followed by its antidote, at #293, a fine Modernista building with wrought-iron railings and twin bay

Modernista Masters: Gaudí and Beyond

Yes, you'll hear plenty about Gaudí, but he's merely one of many great minds who contributed to the architectural revolution of Modernisme. Here's a rundown of the movement's stars. For a sense of the historical context that gave rise to these talented architects, see the "Modernisme and the Renaixença" sidebar, earlier.

The Stars of Modernisme

Antoni Gaudí (1852-1926), Barcelona's most famous Modernista artist, was descended from four generations of metalworkers—a lineage of which he was quite proud.

He incorporated ironwork into his architecture and came up with novel approaches to architectural structure and space. Gaudí's work strongly influenced his younger Catalan contemporary, Salvador Dalí. Notice the similarities: While Dalí was creating unlikely and shocking juxtapositions of photorealistic images, Gaudí did the same in architecture—using the spine of a reptile for a bannister or a turtle shell design on windows. Entire trips (and lives) are dedicated to seeing the works of Gaudí, but on a brief visit in Barcelona, the ones most worth considering are his great unfinished church, the Sagrada Família; several mansions in the town center, including Casa Milà, Casa Batlló, and Palau Güell; and Park Güell, his ambitious and never-completed housing development.

While Gaudí gets 90 percent of the tourists' attention, two other great Modernista architects were just as important: Lluís Domènech i Montaner and Josep Puig i Cadafalch. Gaudí was certainly a remarkable innovator, but these two were perhaps more purely representative of the Modernista style.

Lluís Domènech i Montaner (1850-1923), a professor and politician, was responsible for some major civic buildings, including his masterwork, the Palace of Catalan Music (described on page 53), and the Hospital de Sant Pau, a sprawling complex covering nine blocks (roughly between the Sagrada Família and Park Güell). Domènech i Montaner also designed Casa Lleó

windows. At the next intersection, cross the street to peek inside the classic Modernista grocery of ❻ **J. Murria Queviures** (Tue-Thu 9:00-14:00 & 17:00-21:00, Fri 9:00-21:00, Sat 10:00-14:00 & 17:00-21:00, closed Sun, Carrer de Roger de Llúria 85, tel. 932-155-789). This old-fashioned gourmet deli is stocked with pricey ingredients for a top-end picnic that may be a bit too classy for a park bench. Breathe deep to smell the cheese aging in the cellar. The

Morera on the Block of Discord (described later) and Casa Fuster (now a luxury hotel—see page 232), along with several works in the towns of Canet de Mar, Comillas, and others.

Josep Puig i Cadafalch (1867-1956) was a city planner who oversaw the opening up of Via Laietana (through the middle of the Old City, see page 118), the redevelopment of Montjuïc for the 1929 World Expo, and a redesign of the monastery at Santa Maria de Montserrat. Later  he flourished as a Modernista architect in his own right, best known for manor houses such as Casa de les Punxes (described on page 152) and Casa Amatller on the Block of Discord (described later). He designed the brick Casaramona factory complex, which was recently converted into the cutting-edge CaixaForum exhibition space (see page 75). Perhaps most importantly, Puig i Cadafalch designed Casa Martí, a home for the Modernista hang-out bar Els Quatre Gats, which became a cradle of sorts for the whole movement. The bar still welcomes visitors today (see page 204).

Supporting Cast

All architects worked with a team of people who, while not famous, made real contributions. For example, Gaudí's colleague **Josep Maria Jujol** (1879-1949) is primarily responsible for much of what Gaudí became known for—the broken-tile mosaic decorations (called *trencadís*) on Park Güell's benches and Casa Milà's chimneys.

Each of these architects also had deep-pocketed patrons who financed their works. Gaudí's most important benefactor was **Eusebi Güell** (1846-1918), who used his nearly $90 billion fortune to bankroll Gaudí and others, much as the Medici financed Michelangelo and Leonardo da Vinci. Güell's name still adorns two of Gaudí's most important works: Palau Güell and Park Güell (described on pages 44 and 64).

vintage ad on the corner—dubbed *La Mona y el Mono (The Classy Lady and the Monkey)*—advertised anise liquor to Modernista-era clients.

Press ahead a half-block farther to the ❼ **Centre Cultural La Casa Elizalde** (Carrer de València 302, on the left). This cultural center, a facility of the city of Barcelona, is a hive of creative and personal growth activities. Head into the passage, noticing the community bulletin board listing classes and events. Continuing down the hall, you'll pop out into an appealing park in the middle of the block with benches and WCs.

Head back out to the street and turn left (the way you were going). A couple of doors down (at #300, also on the left), the **Multiplastic** shop sells all manner of sleek, colorful, and durable Euro-housewares (closed Sun, tel. 932-155-876).

• *At the end of the block, go left down Carrer de Pau Claris. After a block, turn right on the wide Carrer d'Aragó. Walk one block, and you'll find yourself kitty-corner from the...*

❽ Block of Discord (Illa de la Discòrdia)

One block, three buildings, three astonishingly creative Modernista architects. Over a short span of time, the three big names of Catalunya's bold Art Nouveau architectural movement erected innovative facades along this one short stretch of Passeig de Gràcia. Although each of these architects has better works elsewhere in town, this is the most convenient place to see their sharply contrasting visions side by side. While these three buildings were done by famous, groundbreaking architects, the whole block is a jumble of delightful architectural whimsy. Reliefs, coats of arms, ironwork, gables, and bay windows adorn otherwise ordinary buildings.

• *Work your way down the block, beginning with the unmistakably Gaudí-style facade that's one building in from the corner.*

Casa Batlló (#43)

First and most famous is the green-blue ceramic-speckled facade of Casa Batlló, designed by Antoni Gaudí (you can tour the interior—see listing on page 59). It has tibia-like  pillars and skull-like balconies, inspired by the time-tested natural forms that Gaudí knew made the best structural supports. The tiled roof has a soft-ice-cream-cone turret topped with a cross. It's thought that Gaudí based the work on the popular legend of St. George (Jordi) slaying the dragon: The humpback roofline suggests a cresting dragon's back, and the smallest, top balcony is shaped like a rosebud (echoing the legend that a rose grew in the place where St. George spilled the dragon's blood). But some see instead a Mardi Gras theme, with mask-like balconies, a facade flecked with purple and gold confetti, and the ridge of a harlequin's hat up top. The inscrutable Gaudí preferred to leave his designs open to interpretation.

• *Next door is...*

Casa Amatller (#41)

Josep Puig i Cadafalch completely remodeled this house for the Amatller family. The facade features a creative mix of three of  Spain's historical traditions: Moorish-style pentagram-and-vine designs; Gothic-style tracery, gargoyles, and bay windows; and the step-gable roof from Spain's Habsburg connection to the Low Countries. Notice the many layers of the letter "A": The house itself (with its gable) forms an A, as does the decorative frieze over the bay window on the right side of the facade. Within that frieze, you'll see several more As sprouting from branches (*amatller* means "almond tree"). The reliefs above the smaller windows show off the hobbies of the Amatller clan: Find the cherubs holding the early box camera, the open book, and the amphora jug (which the family collected). Look through the second-floor bay window to see the corkscrew column. If you want, you can pop inside for a closer look at the elaborate entrance hall.

For another dimension of Modernisme, peek into the ground-floor windows of the Bagues Joieria jewelry shop and notice the slinky pieces by Spanish Art Nouveau jeweler Masriera.

• *Now head left, to the end of the block. There, on the corner, you'll find...*

Casa Lleó Morera (#35)

Here's another paella-like mix of styles, this one by the architect Lluís Domènech i Montaner, who also designed the Palace of Catalan Music (you'll notice similarities). The lower floors have classical columns and a Greek-temple-like bay window. Farther up are Gothic balconies of rosettes and tracery, while the upper part has faux Moorish stucco work. The whole thing is ornamented with fantastic griffins, angels, and fish. Flanking the third-story windows are figures holding the exciting inventions of the day—the camera, lightbulb, and gramophone—designed to demonstrate just how modern the homeowners were  in this age of Modernisme. Unfortunately, the wonderful interior is closed to the public.

• *From here, it's three long blocks gently uphill to Gaudí's Modernista masterpiece, Casa Milà. While the easiest route is to simply turn around and plow back up Passeig de Gràcia—passing top-end shops—you may find it more interesting to detour around the block to...*

❾ Rambla de Catalunya

As you head up Rambla de Catalunya, you'll find a narrower, more manageable street with a delightful, park-like median strip. It's lined with inviting cafés and shops—boutiques that are still upscale, but generally more local and unique than those on the main drag.

On the way up, a half-block detour (to the right) on Carrer d'Aragó gets you to the **Fundació Antoni Tàpies,** dedicated to the 20th-century abstract artist from Barcelona. The Montaner-designed building sums up the Modernist credo: modern brick, iron, and glass materials; playful decorative motifs; and a spacious, functional, and light-filled interior. The collection itself is pricey to view (€7), but fans of the artist's work will enjoy seeing his distinct mud-caked canvases. Tàpies (1923-2012) laid the canvas on the floor, covered it with wet varnish, and sprinkled in dust, dirt, and paint. Then he drew simple designs in the still-wet goop, capturing the primitive power of cavemen tracing the first art in mud with a stick.

• *When you get to Carrer de Provença, turn right and make your way to...*

❿ Casa Milà (a.k.a. La Pedrera)

This Gaudí exterior laughs down on the crowds filling Passeig de Gràcia. Casa Milà, also called La Pedrera ("The Quarry"),

has a much-photographed roller coaster of melting-ice-cream eaves. This is Barcelona's quintessential Modernista building and was Gaudí's last major work (1906-1910) before he dedicated his final years to the Sagrada Família.

The building has a steel structural skeleton to support its weight (a new construction technique at the time). Gaudí's planned statues of the Virgin Mary and archangels were vetoed by the owner. If you have time—and the line's not too long—consider touring the house's interior and rooftop (see listing on page 59).Or just take a peek inside the main atrium for free.

• *From here, you can head back to Plaça de Catalunya—it's a straight shot, seven blocks down Passeig de Gràcia. The Diagonal Metro station near Casa Milà, on the L3 (green) line, has easy connections to Plaça de Catalunya and other key stops.*

But for a finale to our walk, consider heading another two blocks up Passeig de Gràcia to the boundary of the Eixample. Just after Casa Milà, on the right, look for the fun **Vinçon** *shop with its stylish office and home furnishings (see page 227 of the Shopping in Barcelona chapter). Then continue up Passeig de Gràcia until you run into...*

Avinguda Diagonal

This aptly named boulevard slashes diagonally through the middle of the Eixample, connecting the neighborhood to the port.

Diagonal marks the end of the Eixample; just across the street begins the neighborhood of **Gràcia.** Compared to the urban, upscale street plan of the Eixample, Gràcia feels like what it is—a onetime small town that's now part of a big city, with narrower streets and more character. Gràcia is known as an upper-middle-class, intellectual part of town, with many design schools and a youthful scene (see page 235 in the Nightlife in Barcelona chapter).

Cross over to the left side of Passeig da Gràcia and find the Catalunya TI. Go through the gate to the left of the TI entrance to find your way to one of Barcelona's most enjoyable little parks—a tropical oasis in the heart of the city. Relax.

• *If you're a Modernista completist, it's just a short walk from here to three more fine buildings—"extra credit" for those fascinated by this era.*

Modernista Detour

Cross Diagonal, continuing two long blocks on Passeig de Gràcia. Where the street curves around the tree-lined median, you'll find the **Hotel Casa Fuster,** a fine Modernista building by Lluís Domènech i Montaner. This top-of-the-top luxury hotel is a favorite of Woody Allen (who has an affinity for Barcelona, featuring it in his film *Vicky Cristina Barcelona*). Seeking a place to play jazz in town, Allen prodded the hotel to sponsor jazz concerts. The hotel's Café Vienés now hosts a jazz night every Thursday (for details, see page 232).

Backtrack to Diagonal to reach two works by Josep Puig i Cadafalch. Take a left (go east) down the busy Diagonal boulevard. After a block, you reach the **Palau Baró de Quadras** (Diagonal 373, on the right). Puig i Cadafalch's plateresque (Spain's medieval "silverwork" style of intricate decoration) facade celebrates a time when Catalunya was powerful, and the statues flanking the door—of St. George defeating the dragon—make the building's Catalan pride even more evident. Today the building houses Casa Àsia, Barcelona's Asia-Pacific cultural center. As a public cultural center, it's a rare Modernista interior that's free to enter and explore (Tue-Sat 10:00-20:00, Sun 10:00-14:00, closed Mon, tel. 933-680-836, www.casaasia.eu).

Continuing another block and a half down Diagonal leads to the distinctively turreted Casa Terrades (at #416, on the left)—better known as **Casa de les Punxes** ("House of Spikes"). Here Puig i Cadafalch lassoed together what had been three separate buildings into one large complex, wrapping them in a fanciful Gothic castle cloak (no inside access). The turrets, spires, balconies, and ceramic tiles celebrate Catalan culture.

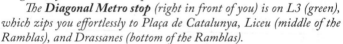

• *Back at Passeig de Gràcia (where it hits Diagonal), you have several options:*

The **Diagonal Metro stop** *(right in front of you) is on L3 (green), which zips you effortlessly to Plaça de Catalunya, Liceu (middle of the Ramblas), and Drassanes (bottom of the Ramblas).*

You can also use the Metro to reach the *pièce de résistance of Modernisme, the **Sagrada Família:** Head west one block on Carrer del Rosselló to find the entrance to the Diagonal stop for L5 (blue); take it to the Sagrada Família stop. (See the* ✪ *Sagrada Família Tour chapter.)*

*Or, to visit another great Modernista sight, hop on bus #24 to Gaudí's **Park Güell** (catch it on Passeig de Gràcia just south of Diagonal, same side of street as Casa Milà; get off at Ctra Carmel-Parc Güell stop; see the* ✪ *Park Güell Tour chapter).*

SAGRADA FAMÍLIA TOUR

Architect Antoni Gaudí's most famous and awe-inspiring work is this unfinished, super-sized church. With its cake-in-the-rain facade and otherworldly spires, the church is not only an icon of Barcelona and its trademark Modernista style, but also a symbol of this period's greatest practitioner. As an architect, Gaudí's foundations were classics, nature, and religion. The church represents all three.

Nearly a century after his death, people continue to toil to bring Gaudí's designs to life. There's something powerful about a community of committed people with a vision, working on a church that won't be finished in their lifetime—as was standard in the Gothic age. The progress of this remarkable building is a testament to the generations of architects, sculptors, stonecutters, fund-raisers, and donors who've been caught up in the audacity of Gaudí's astonishing vision. After paying the steep admission price (becoming a partner in this building project), you will actually feel good. If there's any building on earth I'd like to see, it's the Sagrada Família...finished.

Orientation

Cost: €13, €16.50 combo-ticket includes Gaudí House and Museum at Park Güell (see page 64).

Hours: Daily April-Sept 9:00-20:30, Oct-March 9:00-18:30, last entry 30 minutes before closing.

Advance Reservations: To avoid the ticket-buying line, you can reserve an entry time and buy tickets in advance (€1.30 booking fee). The easiest option is to book online at www.sagrada familia.cat (English instructions, just type in your information and credit-card number).

You can also get tickets from ATMs at many La Caixa bank branches throughout the city—including the branch to the left as you face the ticket windows and Passion Facade (at the corner, just across the street). If tickets are available, you can buy them for the same day, even for immediate entry. However, not every La Caixa ATM sells tickets (use their larger ServiCaixa machines), and the instructions may be in Spanish (though English-only users can figure it out). Start the transaction by selecting "Event Tickets/Entradas Espectáculos" at the top of the screen.

Crowd-Beating Tips: The ticket windows and entrance for individuals are on the west side of the church, at the Passion Facade. If you've pre-purchased tickets, head straight for the "online ticket office" window, to the right of the main ticket line, and show your ticket or eticket to the guard. Though the ticket-buying line can seem long (often curving around the block), it generally moves quickly; you can ask for a time estimate from the guards at the front of the line. Still, the wait can be up to 45 minutes at peak times (most crowded in the morning). To minimize waiting, arrive right at 9:00 (when the church opens) or after 16:00. To skip the line, buy advance tickets, take a tour, or hire a private guide.

Getting There: It's at Carrer de Mallorca 401. The Sagrada Família Metro stop puts you right on the doorstep: Exit toward Plaça de la Sagrada Família.

Information: Tel. 932-073-031, www.sagradafamilia.cat.

Tours: The 50-minute English tours (€4) run June-Oct daily at 11:00, 12:00, and 13:00; Nov-May Mon-Fri at 11:00 and 13:00, Sat-Sun at 11:00, 12:00, and 13:00. Or rent the good 1.5-hour audioguide (€4). Good English information is posted throughout.

Elevators: Two different elevators (€3 each, pay at main ticket office, each ticket comes with an entry time) take you partway up the towers for a great view of the city and a gargoyle's-eye perspective of the loopy church.

The easier option is the **Passion Facade elevator,** which takes you 215 feet up and down. (You can climb higher, but expect the spiral stairs to be tight, hot, and congested.)

The **Nativity Facade elevator** is more exciting and demanding. You'll get the opportunity to cross the dizzying bridge between the towers, but you'll need to take the stairs all the way down.

Length of This Tour: Allow 1.5 hours. With limited time, skip the museum and schoolhouse.

Nearby: Inviting parks flank the building, facing the two completed facades.

A Dream Made Real

For over 130 years, Barcelona has labored to bring Antoni Gaudí's vision to reality. Local craftsmen often cap off their careers by spending a couple of years on this exciting construction site. The present architect has been at it since 1985. The work is funded exclusively by private donations and entry fees, which is another reason its completion has taken so long. Your admission helps pay for the ongoing construction.

Like Gothic churches of medieval times, the design has evolved over the decades. At heart, it's Gothic, a style much admired by Gaudí. He added his own Art Nouveau/Modernisme touches, guided by nature and engineering innovations. Today the site bristles with cranking cranes, rusty forests of rebar, and scaffolding. Sagrada Família offers a fun look at a living, growing bigger-than-life building.

Sagrada Família Timeline

1882	The church is begun in Gothic-revival style (by architect Francisco de Paula del Villar).
1883	Paula del Villar quits, and Antoni Gaudí is hired—and proceeds to completely re-envision the church's design.
1892	Gaudí begins the Nativity Facade.
1914	Gaudí turns his attention exclusively to the Sagrada Família.
1925	The first bell tower is completed.
1926	Gaudí dies with the project about 20 percent complete.
1936-1939	The Spanish Civil War halts all work; the crypt is burned, along with many of Gaudí's plans.
1950s	Building resumes in earnest with the start of the Passion Facade.
1976	The four Passion spires are finished, bringing the total of completed spires to eight (out of 18 planned).
1980s	Computer technology is introduced, greatly accelerating the pace of construction.
2000	The nave roof is completed.
2005	Passion statues are completed.
2010	Crossing vaults are finished (enclosing the roof), and Pope Benedict XVI dedicates the church as a basilica.
2026?	Tentative plans are that the church will be finished in time for the 100th anniversary of Gaudí's death. Make a date to attend the dedication ceremonies with your kids...to teach them a lesson in delayed gratification.

Background

Gaudí labored on the Sagrada Família for 43 years, from 1883 until his death in 1926 (see sidebar previous page). Since then, construction has moved forward in fits and starts, though much progress was made in recent decades, thanks to Barcelona's 1992 Olympics renaissance, the ensuing rediscovery of the genius of Gaudí, and advances in technology. In 2010, the main nave was finished enough to host a consecration Mass by the pope (as a Catholic church, it is used for services, though irregularly). As I stepped inside on my last visit, the brilliance of Gaudí's vision for the interior was apparent.

The main challenges today: Ensure that construction can withstand the vibrations caused by the speedy AVE trains rumbling underfoot, construct the tallest church spire ever built, and find a way to buy out the people who own the condos in front of the planned Glory Facade so that Gaudí's vision of a grand esplanade approaching the church can be realized. The goal, which seems overly optimistic but tantalizing nonetheless, is to finish the church by the 100th anniversary of Gaudí's death, in 2026.

The Tour Begins

• *Start at the ticket entrance (at the Passion Facade) on the western side of the church. The view is best from the park across the street. Before heading to the ticket booth, take in the...*

❶ Exterior

Stand and imagine how grand this church will be when completed. The four 330-foot spires topped with crosses are just a fraction of

this mega-church. When finished, the church will have 18 spires. Four will stand at each of the three entrances. Rising above those will be four taller towers, dedicated to the four Evangelists. A tower dedicated to Mary will rise still higher—400 feet. And in the very center of the complex will stand the grand 560-foot Jesus tower, topped with a cross that will shine like a spiritual lighthouse, visible even from out at sea.

The Passion Facade that tourists enter today is only a side entrance to the church. The grand main entrance will be around to the right. That means that the nine-story apartment building will eventually have to be torn down to accommodate it. The three facades—Nativity, Passion, and

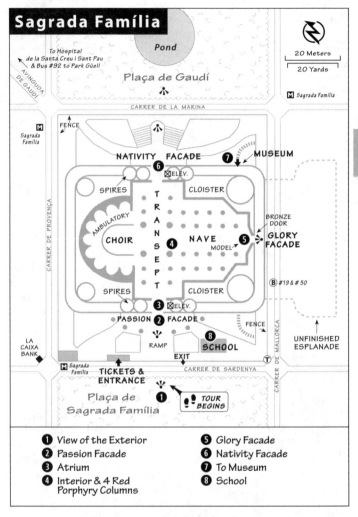

Sagrada Família

To Hospital
de la Santa Creu i Sant Pau
& Bus #92 to Park Güell

AVINGUDA DE GAUDÍ

Pond

Plaça de Gaudí

20 Meters
20 Yards

Ⓜ Sagrada Família

CARRER DE LA MARINA

SAGRADA FAMÍLIA

FENCE

Ⓜ Sagrada Família

NATIVITY FACADE ❼ → MUSEUM

❻ ⊠ELEV.

SPIRES

CLOISTER

AMBULATORY

CHOIR

T R A N S E P T

NAVE

MODEL

❹ ❺

BRONZE DOOR

GLORY FACADE

CARRER DE PROVENÇA

Ⓑ #19 & #50

SPIRES

CLOISTER

❸ ⊠ELEV.

PASSION ❷ FACADE

FENCE

RAMP

❽ SCHOOL

UNFINISHED ESPLANADE

CARRER DE MALLORCA

LA CAIXA BANK

Ⓜ Sagrada Família

TICKETS & ENTRANCE

EXIT

CARRER DE SARDENYA

Ⓣ

Plaça de Sagrada Família

❶

👣 TOUR BEGINS

❶ View of the Exterior
❷ Passion Facade
❸ Atrium
❹ Interior & 4 Red Porphyry Columns
❺ Glory Facade
❻ Nativity Facade
❼ To Museum
❽ School

Glory—will chronicle Christ's life from birth to death to resurrection. Inside and out, a goal of the church is to bring the lessons of the Bible to the world. Despite his boldly modern architectural vision, Gaudí was fundamentally traditional and deeply religious. He designed the Sagrada Família to be a bastion of solid Christian values in the midst of what was a humble workers' colony in a fast-changing city.

When Gaudí died, only one section (on the Nativity Facade—the opposite side, not visible from here) had been completed. The rest of the church has been inspired by Gaudí's long-range vision, but designed and executed by others. This artistic freedom was amplified in 1936, when Civil War shelling burned many of Gaudí's blueprints. Supporters of the ongoing work insist that Gaudí, who enjoyed saying, "My client (God) is not in a hurry," knew he wouldn't live to complete the church and recognized that later architects and artists would rely on their own muses for inspiration. Detractors maintain that the church's design is a uniquely, intensely personal one and that it's folly (if not disrespectful) for anyone to try to guess what Gaudí would have intended. Studying the various plans and models in the museum below the church, it's clear that Gaudí's plan evolved dramatically the longer he worked. Is it appropriate to keep implementing a century-old vision that can no longer be modified by its creator? Discuss.

• *Pass through the ticket entrance into the complex, approaching closer to the...*

❷ Passion Facade

Judge for yourself how well Gaudí's original vision has been carried out by later artists. The Passion Facade's four spires were designed by Gaudí and completed (quite faithfully) in 1976. But the lower part was only inspired by Gaudí's designs. The stark sculptures were interpreted freely (and controversially) by Josep Maria Subirachs (b. 1927), who completed the work in 2005.

Subirachs tells the story of Christ's torture and execution. The various scenes—Last Supper, betrayal, whipping, and so on—zigzag up from bottom to top, culminating in Christ's crucifixion over the doorway. The style is severe and unadorned, quite different from Gaudí's signature playfulness. But the bone-like archways are closely based on Gaudí's original designs. And Gaudí had made it clear that this facade should be grim and terrifying.

The facade is full of symbolism. A stylized Alpha-and-Omega is over the door (which faces the setting sun). Jesus, hanging on the cross, has hair made of an open book, symbolizing the word of God. To the left of the door is a grid of numbers, always adding up to 33—Jesus' age at the time of his death. The distinct face of the man below and just left of Christ is a memorial to Gaudí. Now look high above: The two-ton figure suspended between the towers is the soul of Jesus, ascending to heaven.

• *Enter the church. As you pass through the ❸ atrium, look down at the fine porphyry floor (with scenes of Jesus' entry into Jerusalem), and look right to see one of the elevators up to the towers. For now, continue into the...*

❹ Interior

Typical of even the most traditional Catalan and Spanish churches, the floor plan is in the shape of a Latin cross, 300 feet long and

200 feet wide. Ultimately, the church will encompass 48,000 square feet, accommodating 8,000 worshippers. The nave's roof is 150 feet high. The crisscross arches of the ceiling (the vaults) show off Gaudí's distinctive engineering. The church's roof and flooring were only completed in 2010—just in time for Pope Benedict XVI to arrive and consecrate the church.

Part of Gaudí's religious vision was a love for nature. He said, "Nothing is invented; it's written in nature." Like the trunks of trees, these **columns** (56 in all) blossom with life, complete with branches, leaves, and knot-like capitals. The columns are a variety of colors—brown clay, gray granite, dark-gray basalt. The taller columns are 72 feet tall; the shorter ones are exactly half that.

The angled columns form many **arches.** You'll see both parabolas (u-shaped) and hyperbolas (flatter, elliptical shapes). Gaudí's starting point was the Gothic pointed arch used in medieval churches. But he tweaked it after meticulous study of which arches are best at bearing weight.

Little **windows** let light filter in like the canopy of a rainforest, giving both privacy and an intimate connection with God. The clear glass is temporary and will gradually be replaced by stained glass. As more and more stained glass is installed, splashes of color will breathe even more life into this amazing space. Gaudí envisioned an awe-inspiring canopy with a symphony of colored light to encourage a contemplative mood.

High up at the back half of the church, the U-shaped **choir**—suspended above the nave—can seat 1,000. The singers will eventually be backed by four organs (there's one now).

Work your way up the grand nave, walking through this forest of massive columns. At the center of the church stand four **red porphyry columns,** each marked with an Evangelist's symbol and name in Catalan: angel (Mateu), lion (Marc), bull (Luc), and eagle (Joan). These columns support a ceiling vault that's 200 feet high—and eventually will also support the central steeple, the 560-foot Jesus tower with the shining cross. The steeple will be further supported by four underground pylons, each consisting of 8,000 tons of cement. It will be the tallest church steeple in the world, though still a few feet shorter than the city's highest point at the summit of Montjuïc hill, as Gaudí believed that a creation of man should not attempt to eclipse the creation of God.

Stroll behind the altar through the **ambulatory** to see videos of the 2010 consecration Mass, and look through windows down at the **crypt** (which holds the tomb of Gaudí). Peering down into that surprisingly traditional space, imagine how the church was started as a fairly conventional, 19th-century Neo-Gothic building until Gaudí was given the responsibility to finish it.

• *Head to the far end of the church, to what will eventually be the main entrance. Just inside the door, find the **bronze model** of the floor plan for the completed church. Facing the doors, look high up to see Subirachs' statue of one of Barcelona's patron saints, **George (Jordi)**. Go through the doors to imagine what will someday be the...*

❺ Glory Facade

As you exit, study the fine **bronze door,** emblazoned with the Lord's Prayer in Catalan, surrounded by "Give us this day our daily bread" in 50 languages. Once outside, you'll be face-to-face

with...drab, doomed apartment blocks. In the 1950s, the mayor of Barcelona, figuring this day would never really come, sold the land destined for the church project. Now the city must buy back these buildings in order to complete Gaudí's

vision: that of a grand esplanade leading to this main entry. Four towers will rise. The facade's sculpture will represent how the soul passes through death, faces the Last Judgment, avoids the pitfalls of Hell, and finds its way to eternal glory with God. Gaudí purposely left the facade's design open for later architects—stay tuned.

• *Re-enter the church, backtrack up the nave, and exit through the right transept. Once outside, back up as far as you can to take in the...*

❻ Nativity Facade

This is the only part of the church essentially finished in Gaudí's lifetime. The four spires decorated with his unmistakably non-linear sculpture mark this facade as part of his original design. Mixing Gothic-style symbolism, images from nature, and Modernista asymmetry, the Nativity Facade is the best example of Gaudí's original vision, and it established the template for future architects.

The theme of this facade, which faces the rising sun, is Christ's birth. A statue above the doorway shows Mary, Joseph,

and Baby Jesus in the manger, while curious cows peek in. It's the Holy Family—or "Sagrada Família"—for whom this church is dedicated. Flanking the doorway are the three Magi and adoring shepherds. Other statues show Jesus as a young carpenter and angels playing musical instruments. Higher up on the facade, in the arched niche, Jesus crowns Mary triumphantly.

The facade is all about birth and new life, from the dove-covered Tree of Life on top to the turtles at the base of the columns flanking the entrance. At the bottom of the Tree of Life is a white pelican. Because it was believed that this noble bird would kill itself to feed its young, it was often used in the Middle Ages as a symbol for the self-sacrifice of Jesus. The chameleon gargoyles at

the outer corners of the facade (just above door level) represent the changeability of life. It's as playful as the Passion Facade is grim. Gaudí's plans were for this facade to be painted. Cleverly, this attractive facade was built and finished first to bring in financial support for the project.

The four **spires** are dedicated to Apostles, and they repeatedly bear the word "Sanctus," or holy. Their colorful ceramic caps symbolize the miters (formal hats) of bishops. The shorter spires (to the left) symbolize the Eucharist (communion), alternating between a chalice with grapes and a communion host with wheat.

To the left of the facade is one section of the **cloister.** Whereas most medieval churches have their cloisters attached to one side of the building, the Sagrada Família's cloister will wrap around the church, more than 400 yards long.

• *Notice the second **elevator** up to the towers. But for now, head down the ramp to the left of the facade, where you'll find WCs and the entrance to the...*

❼ Museum

Housed in what will someday be the church's crypt, the museum displays Gaudí's original **models and drawings,** and chronicles the progress of construction over the last 130 years. Wander among the plaster models used for the church's construction, including a model of the nave so big you walk beneath it. The models make clear the influence of nature. The columns seem light, with branches springing forth and capitals that look like palm trees. You'll notice that the models don't always match the finished product—these are ideas, not blueprints set in stone. The Passion Facade model (near the entrance) shows Gaudí's original vision, with which Subirachs tinkered very freely (see "Passion Facade," earlier).

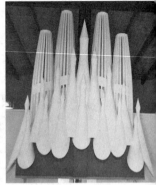

Turn up the main hallway. On the left you can peek into a busy **workshop** still used for making the same kind of plaster models Gaudí used to envision the final product in 3-D. Farther along, a small hallway on the right leads to some original Gaudí architectural **sketches** in a dimly lit room and a worthwhile 20-minute **movie** (generally shown in English at :50 past each hour).

From the end of this hall, you have another opportunity to look down into the crypt and at **Gaudí's tomb.** Gaudí lived on the site for more than a decade and is buried in the Neo-Gothic 19th-century crypt (also viewable from the apse). There's a move afoot to make Gaudí a saint. Perhaps someday his tomb will be a place of pilgrimage.

Back in the main hallway, on the right is the intriguing **"Hanging Model"** for Gaudí's unfinished Church of Colònia Güell (in a suburb of Barcelona), featuring a similar design to the Sagrada Família. The model illustrates how the architect used gravity to calculate the arches that support the church. Wires dangle like suspended chains, forming perfect hyperbolic arches. Attached to these are bags, representing the weight the arches must support. Flip these arches over, and they can bear the heavy weight of the roof. The mirror above the model shows how the right-side-up church is derived from this. Across the hall is a small exhibit commemorating **Pope Benedict XVI's** 2010 consecration visit.

After passing some original sculptures from the Glory Facade (on the right) and continuing beneath a huge plaster model, turn right to find **three different visions** for this church. Notice how the arches evolved as Gaudí tinkered, from the original, pointy Neo-Gothic arches, to parabolic ones, to the hyperbolic ones he eventually settled on. Also in this hall are replicas of the **pulpit** and **confessional** that Gaudí, the micro-manager, designed for his church. Before exiting at the far end of the hall, scan the photos (including one of the master himself) and timeline illustrating how construction work has progressed from Gaudí's day to now.

• *You'll exit near where you started, at the Passion Facade.*

❽ School and Rest of Visit

The small building outside the Passion Facade was a school Gaudí erected for the children of the workers building the church. Today it includes more exhibits about the design and engineering of the church, along with a classroom and a replica of Gaudí's desk as it was the day he died. Pause for a moment to pay homage to the man who made all this possible. Gaudí—a faithful Catholic whose medieval-style mysticism belied his Modernista architecture career—was certainly driven to greatness by his passion for God.

• *Our tour is over. From here, you have several options.*

Return to Central Barcelona: You can either hop on the Metro or take one of two handy buses (both stop on Carrer de Mallorca, directly in front of the Glory Facade). Bus #19 takes you back to the **Old City** *in 15 minutes, stopping near the cathedral and in the El Born district (with the ✪ Picasso Museum and ✪ El Born Walk). Bus #50 goes from the Sagrada Família to the heart of the* **Eixample** *(corner of Gran Via de les Corts Catalanes and Passeig de Gràcia—near the start of the ✪ Eixample Walk), then continues on through the university area and out to the Camp Nou soccer stadium (see page 219).*

Visit Park Güell: Many visitors like to combine their visit here with a trip to **Park Güell***, which sits nearly two (uphill) miles to the northwest (✪ see the Park Güell Tour). By far the easiest way to get there is to spring for a taxi (around €10-12). But if you prefer public transportation and don't mind a little walking, here's a scenic way to get there that also takes you past another, often overlooked Modernista masterpiece: With the Nativity Facade at your back, walk to the near-left corner of the park across the street. Then cross the street to reach the diagonal Avinguda de Gaudí (between the Repsol gas station and the KFC). Follow the funky lampposts four blocks gradually uphill (about 10 minutes) along Avinguda de Gaudí, a pleasantly shaded, café-lined pedestrian street. Soon you reach the striking Modernista-style* **Hospital de la Santa Creu i Sant Pau***, designed by Lluís Domènech i Montaner (for more about him, see page 146). Cross the street and go up one block (left) on Carrer de Sant Antoni Maria Claret to catch bus #92, which will take you to the side entrance of Park Güell.*

From the Sagrada Família, you could also get to Park Güell by taking the Metro to the Joanic stop, then hop on bus #116 (described on page 164)—but that involves two changes...and less scenery.

PARK GÜELL TOUR

Tucked in the foothills at the edge of Barcelona, this fanciful park—designed by Antoni Gaudí—combines playful design, inviting public spaces, and sweeping views over the rooftops of the city. Exploring this fairly compact space, you'll see a pair of gingerbread houses, a grand staircase monitored by a trademark dragon, a forest of columns supporting a spectacular view terrace, a famously undulating balcony slathered in colorful tile shards, tubular passages burrowing under never-completed roadways, a network of nature trails...and Barcelonans and tourists alike enjoying a day at the park.

The area of the park with the iconic Gaudí structures is called the Monumental Zone. For preservation purposes, the number of visitors admitted here at any one time is controlled, and there's an entrance fee (see below).

Orientation

Cost: Monumental Zone—€8 at the gate or €7 online; it's smart to reserve an entry time in advance. The rest of the park is free. Tel. 932-130-488, www.parkguell.cat.

Hours: Daily April-Oct 8:00-21:30, Nov-March 8:30-18:00.

Other Park Güell Sights: Gaudí House Museum—€5.50, €16.50 combo-ticket includes Sagrada Família church, daily April-Sept 10:00-20:00, until 18:00 Oct-March, tel. 932-193-811, www.casamuseugaudi.org.

Length of this Tour: An hour is plenty to get your bearings, but it's a pleasant place to linger longer.

Getting There: Park Güell (pronounced "Gway") is about 2.5 miles due north of Plaça de Catalunya, beyond the Gràcia neighborhood in Barcelona's foothills.

From downtown, a **taxi** (about €12) will drop you off at the main entrance; the blue Tourist Bus stops about two blocks below the entrance. From Plaça de Catalunya, **public bus** #24 travels to the park's side entrance. From elsewhere in the city, follow this **Metro-plus-bus combination:** Go by Metro to the Joanic stop and look for the Carrer de l'Escorial exit. Walk up Carrer de l'Escorial to the bus stop in front of #20. Take bus #116 directly to the park's main entrance; you'll see gate houses and a grand stairway. To get back to the city center, catch bus #116 going in the same direction; get off at Plaça de Lesseps and take the Metro from there. (It's a 15-minute downhill walk from the park's main entrance to the Lesseps Metro: Walk straight ahead down Carrer de Larrard and turn right on busy Travessera de Dalt to find the Metro.)

For tips on reaching Park Güell from Gaudí's Sagrada Família church, see page 163.

Eating in the Park: Options are limited. On the main view terrace, a **snack bar** with tables offers simple sandwiches and beverages. A few vendors hawk drinks and snacks at the side entrance. If you've packed a **picnic** (a good idea), head just above the Rosary pathway near the main terrace, where you'll find tree-shaded tables.

Overview

Funded by his frequent benefactor Eusebi Güell, Gaudí intended this 30-acre garden to be a 60-residence housing project—a kind of gated community. Work began in 1900, but progress stalled in 1914 with the outbreak of World War I and the project never resumed. Only two houses were built, neither designed by Gaudí—the structures are now home to the Gaudí House Museum and Casa Trias (not open to the public). As a high-income housing development, it flopped; but as a park, it's a delight, offering another peek into Gaudí's eccentric genius in a setting that's more natural than man-made—appropriate considering the naturalism that pervades Gaudí's work.

Many sculptures and surfaces in the park are covered with colorful *trencadís* mosaics—broken ceramic bits rearranged into new patterns. This Modernista invention, made of discarded tile, dishes, and even china dolls from local factories, was an easy, cheap, and aesthetically pleasing way to cover curvy surfaces like benches and columns. Although Gaudí promoted the technique, most of what you see was executed by his collaborator, Josep Maria Jujol.

The Tour Begins

• *This tour assumes you're arriving at the front/main entrance (by taxi or bus #116). If you instead arrive at the side entrance, walk straight ahead through the gate to find the terrace with colorful mosaic benches, then walk down to the stairway and front entrance.*

Front Entrance

Before entering the park, notice the **mosaic medallions** along the outside wall that say "park" in English—reminding folks that Park Güell was modeled on the British "garden city" concept of integrating urban communities with green space.

Entering the park, you walk through a palm-frond **gate** and pass Gaudí's gas lamps (1900-1914), both made of wrought iron. His dad was a blacksmith, and he always enjoyed this medium.

Two Hansel-and-Gretel gingerbread lodges flank the entrance, signaling to visitors that this park is a magical space. One of the buildings houses a good bookshop; the other is home to the skippable **La Casa del Guarda,** a branch of the Barcelona History Museum (MUHBA). The sparse exhibit inside features video slideshows about Gaudí's building methods and works, old black-and-white movies of the age, and no real artifacts. True Gaudí fans might want to take a close look at the structure, though, as it's one of the few built examples of his ideas for simple housing. (The Gaudí House Museum, described later, is more interesting to me.)

• *Now face the grand...*

Stairway

The **cave-like enclosures** flanking the stairs were functional: One was a garage for Eusebi Güell's newfangled automobiles, while the other was a cart shelter.

Three **fountains** are stacked in the middle of the stairway. The first, at the base of the steps, is rocky and leafy, typical of Gaudí's naturalism. Next is a red-

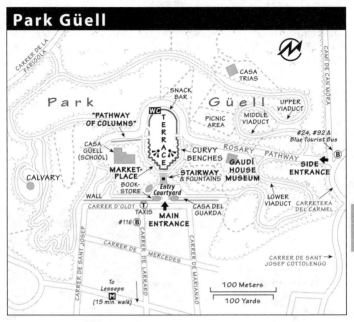

Park Güell

and-gold-striped Catalan shield with the head of a serpent poking
out. The third is a very famous dragon—an icon of the park (and of Barcelona). While the dragon—slain by Barcelona's patron saint, George (Jordi)—is a symbol of Catalan pride, this creature also evokes the crocodile mascot of Nîmes, France, where Eusebi Güell spent much of his youth. As for the ornamental brown tripod at the top of the stairs: Is it the Oracle of Delphi? The tail of the serpent whose head pokes out down below? Or something else entirely? Gaudí lets the viewer decide.

• *At the top, dip into the...*

Marketplace (Hall of 100 Columns)

This space was designed to house a **produce market** for the neighborhood's 60 mansions. The Doric columns—each lined at the base with

white ceramic shards—add to the market's vitality (despite the hall's name, there are only 86 columns). White ceramic pieces also cover the multiple domes of the ceiling, which is interrupted by colorful mosaic rosettes. Look up to find four giant sun-like decorations representing the four seasons. Notice the hook in the middle of each one, where a lantern could be hung. Arranged around these are smaller rosettes, meant to suggest the lunar cycle. Street performers and musicians like the acoustics here.

• *Continue up the left-hand staircase, looking left, down the playful...*

"Pathway of Columns"

Gaudí drew his inspiration from nature, and this arcade is like a surfer's perfect tube. This is one of many clever double-decker **via- ducts** that Gaudí designed

for the grounds: vehicles up top, pedestrians in the portico down below. Gaudí intended these walkways to remind visitors of the pilgrim routes that crisscross Spain (such as the famous Camino de Santiago). Eusebi Güell lived in the pink house (now a school) next to the terrace. This house predates the park project and was not designed by Gaudí.

• *At the top of the stairway, you pop out on the...*

Terrace

Sit on a colorful bench and enjoy one of Barcelona's best views. (Find Gaudí's Sagrada Família church in the distance.) The

360-foot-long bench is designed to fit your body ergonomically. Supposedly, Gaudí enlisted a construction worker as his guinea pig to figure out exactly where to place the lumbar support (back in a time when "ergonomics" and "lumbar support" hadn't even been invented). To Gaudí, this terrace evoked ancient Greek theaters that burrowed scenically into the sides of hills—but its primary purpose was that of the ancient Greek agora, a wide-open meeting place. Gaudí engineered a water-catchment system by which rain hitting this plaza would flow through natural filters, then through the columns of the market below to a 300,000-gallon underground cistern. The water was bottled and sold as a health cure (this location—far away from polluting city factories—had a healthy cachet); excess water powers the park's fountains. Notice the lion's-head gargoyles and the big stone droplets that cling to the outside edge of the terrace, which hint at this hidden functional purpose.

• *From here, as you face the city, the **Gaudí House Museum** is to your left, and the **Calvary** is high up on your right (both described below).*

Gaudí House Museum

This pink house with a steeple, standing in the middle of the park (near the side entrance), was Gaudí's home for 20 years. Designed not by Gaudí but by a fellow architect, it was originally built as a model home to attract prospective residents. Gaudí lived here from 1906 until 1925. His humble artifacts are mostly gone, but the house is now a museum with some quirky Gaudí furniture. Though small, it offers a good taste of what could have been.

The main drag connecting this house to the terrace, called the **Rosary Pathway,** is lined with giant stone balls that represent the beads of a rosary. During the years he lived here, the reverent Gaudí would pray the rosary while walking this path.

The Calvary

High on a wooded hill beyond the pink school building is a stubby stone tower topped with three crosses, representative of the Hill of Calvary where Jesus was crucified. Gaudí envisioned the topography of Park Güell as a metaphor for the soul's progress: starting at the low end and toiling uphill to reach spiritual enlightenment (a chapel was originally intended to occupy this spot). And indeed, the park's higher paths seem to converge to lead pilgrims to this summit. The tower rewards those who huff up here with grand views over Barcelona and its bay.

The Rest of the Park

Like any park, this one is made for aimless rambling. As you wander, imagine living here a century ago—if this gated community had succeeded and was filled with Barcelona's wealthy. When considering the failure of Park Güell as a community development, also consider that it was an idea a hundred years ahead of its time. Back then, high-society ladies didn't want to live so far from the cultural action. Today, the surrounding neighborhoods are some of the wealthiest in town, and a gated community here could be a big hit.

SLEEPING IN BARCELONA

For hassle-free efficiency, I favor hotels and restaurants that are handy to your sightseeing activities. Rather than list hotels scattered throughout Barcelona, I describe several favorite neighborhoods and recommend the best accommodations values in each, from bunk beds to fancy doubles with all the comforts.

A major feature of this book is its extensive listing of good-value rooms. I like places that are clean, central, relatively quiet at night, reasonably priced, friendly, small enough to have a hands-on owner and stable staff, run with a respect for Spanish traditions, and not listed in other guidebooks. (In Barcelona, for me, six out of these eight criteria means it's a keeper.) I'm more impressed by a handy location and a fun-loving philosophy than flat-screen TVs and shoeshine machines.

Barcelona is Spain's most expensive city. Still, it has reasonably priced rooms. Cheap places are more crowded in summer (book ahead); fancier business-class hotels fill up in winter and offer discounts on weekends and in summer. When considering relative hotel values, in summer and on weekends you can often get modern comfort in centrally located business-class hotels for about the same price (€100) as you'll pay for ramshackle charm.

Rates and Deals

I've described my recommended accommodations using a Sleep Code (see sidebar on page 172). Prices listed are for one-night stays in peak season, and assume you're booking directly (not through a TI or online hotel-booking engine). Using an online booking service costs the hotel about 20 percent and logically closes the door on special deals. Book direct.

These days, many hotels change prices from day to day according to demand. Given the economic downturn, hoteliers are often willing and eager to make a deal. In general, prices can soften if you offer to pay cash or stay at least three nights. I'd suggest emailing several hotels to ask for their best price. Comparison-shop and make your choice.

As you look over the listings, you'll notice that some accommodations promise special prices to my readers who book direct. To get these rates, you must mention this book when you reserve, and then show the book upon arrival. Rick Steves discounts apply to readers with ebooks as well as printed books. Discounts may not apply to promotional rates.

Types of Accommodations
Hotels
Spain offers some of the best accommodations values in Western Europe. Most places are government-regulated, with posted prices. Don't judge economy hotels by their bleak and dirty entryways. Landlords, stuck with rent control, often stand firmly in the way of hardworking hoteliers who'd like to brighten up their buildings.

Rooms with private bathrooms are often bigger and renovated; cheaper rooms without bathrooms often will be dingier and/or on the top floor. All rooms have sinks with hot and cold water, and any room without a bathroom has access to one in the corridor.

Spain has stringent restrictions on smoking in public places. Smoking is not permitted in common areas, but hotels can designate 10 percent of their rooms for smokers.

Some hotels don't use central heat before November 1 and after April 1 (unless it's unusually cold); prepare for cool evenings if you travel in spring and fall. Summer can be extremely hot. Consider air-conditioning, fans, and noise (since you'll want your window open). Many rooms come with mini-refrigerators.

Be aware that some hotels have centrally controlled air-conditioning—the manager chooses the temperature (with an eye on his bottom line). In some hotel rooms, air-conditioning units are mounted high on the wall. These come with control sticks (like a TV remote, sometimes requiring a deposit) that generally have similar symbols: fan icon (toggle through wind power); louver icon (choose steady air flow or waves); snowflake and sunshine icons (heat or cold); clock ("O" setting: run x hours before turning off; "I" setting: wait x hours to start); and the temperature control (20 degrees Celsius is comfortable).

If you're arriving on an early flight or an overnight train, your room probably won't be ready first thing in the morning. You can drop your bag safely at the hotel and dive right into sightseeing.

Hotel elevators, while becoming more common, are often very small, forcing you to send your bags up separately—pack light.

While many of my recommendations are on pedestrian

SLEEPING

Sleep Code

(€1 = about $1.30, country code: 34)

Price Rankings

To help you sort easily through my listings, I've divided the accommodations into three categories based on the price for a double room with bath during high season:

$$$ Higher Priced—Most rooms €150 or more.
$$ Moderately Priced—Most rooms between €100-150.
$ Lower Priced—Most rooms €100 or less.

I always rate hostels as $, whether or not they have double rooms, because they have the cheapest beds in town. Prices can change without notice; verify the hotel's current rates online or by email.

Abbreviations

To pack maximum information into minimum space, I use the following code to describe accommodations in this book. Prices listed are per room, not per person. When a price range is given for a type of room (such as double rooms listed for €100-150), it means the price fluctuates with the season, size of room, or length of stay; expect to pay the upper end for peak-season stays. In Spain, high season (*temporada alta*) is from July to September; shoulder season (*temporada media*) is roughly April through June and October; and low season (*temporada baja*) runs from November through March.

S = Single room (or price for one person in a double).
D = Double or twin. "Double beds" are often two twins sheeted together and are big enough for non-romantic couples.
T = Triple (generally a double bed with a single).
Q = Quad (usually two double beds; adding an extra child's bed to a T is usually cheaper).
b = Private bathroom with toilet and shower or tub.
s = Private shower or tub only (the toilet is down the hall).

According to this code, a couple staying at a "Db-€140" hotel would pay a total of €140 (about $182) for a double room with a private bathroom.

Unless otherwise noted, credit cards are accepted, English is spoken, and prices listed generally include the 8 percent IVA hotel tax. Many hotels charge extra for breakfast, which can range from simple spreads (either included or cheap) to pricey buffets.

There's almost always Wi-Fi and/or Internet access available, either free or for a fee.

SLEEPING

streets, night noise can be a problem (especially in cheap places, which have single-pane windows). Always ask to see your room first. If you suspect night noise will be a problem, request a quiet *(tranquilo)* room in the back or on an upper floor *(piso alto)*. In most cases, view rooms *(con vista)* come with street noise. You'll often sleep better and for less money in a room without a view.

Hoteliers can be a great help and source of advice. Most know their city well, and can assist you with everything from public transit and airport connections to finding a good restaurant, the nearest launderette, or an Internet café.

Even at the best places, mechanical breakdowns occur: Air-conditioning malfunctions, sinks leak, hot water turns cold, and toilets gurgle and smell. Report your concerns clearly and calmly at the front desk. For more complicated problems, don't expect instant results. Any legitimate place is legally required to have a complaint book *(libro de reclamaciones)*. A request for this book will generally prompt the hotelier to solve your problem to keep you from writing a complaint.

To guard against theft in your room, keep valuables out of sight. Some rooms come with a safe, and other hotels have safes at the front desk. I've never bothered using one.

Checkout can pose problems if surprise charges pop up on your bill. If you settle your bill the afternoon before you leave, you'll have time to discuss and address any points of contention (before 19:00, when the night shift usually arrives).

Above all, keep a positive attitude. Remember, you're on vacation. If your hotel is a disappointment, spend more time out enjoying the city you came to see.

Hostales and *Pensiones*

Budget hotels—called *hostales* and *pensiones*—are easy to find, inexpensive, and, when chosen properly, a fun part of the Spanish cultural experience. These places are often family-owned, and may or may not have amenities like private bathrooms and air-conditioning. Don't confuse a *hostal* with a hostel—a Spanish *hostal* is an inexpensive hotel, not a hostel with bunks in dorms.

Hostels

You'll pay about €15-18 per bed to stay at a hostel *(albergue juvenil)*. Travelers of any age are welcome if they don't mind dorm-style accommodations (usually in rooms of four to eight beds) and meeting other travelers. Cheap meals are sometimes offered, and most hostels offer kitchen facilities, Internet access, Wi-Fi, and self-service laundry. Nowadays, concerned about bedbugs, hostels are likely to provide all bedding, including sheets. Expect youth groups in spring, crowds in the summer, snoring, and variability in

Making Reservations

Given the quality of the accommodations I've found for this book, reserve your rooms several weeks in advance—or as soon as you've pinned down your travel dates—particularly if you'll be traveling during peak times. Note that some national holidays jam things up and merit your making reservations far in advance (see "Holidays and Festivals" on page 300).

Requesting a Reservation: It's usually easiest to book your room through the hotel's website; many have a reservation-request form built right in. (For the best rates, be sure to use the hotel's official site and not a booking agency's site.) Just type in your preferred dates and the website will automatically display a list of available rooms and prices. Simpler websites will generate an email to the hotelier with your request. If there's no reservation form, or for complicated requests, send an email from your personal address. Other options include calling (see "Phoning" below, and be mindful of time zones) or faxing. Most recommended hotels are accustomed to guests who speak only English.

The hotelier wants to know these key pieces of information (also included in the sample request form in the appendix):

- number and type of rooms
- number of nights
- date of arrival
- date of departure
- any special needs (such as bathroom in the room or down the hall, twin beds vs. double bed, air-conditioning, quiet, view, ground floor, etc.)

When you request a room, use the European style for writing dates: day/month/year. For example, for a two-night stay in July, I would request "1 double room for 2 nights, arrive 16/07/14, depart 18/07/14." Consider carefully how long you'll stay; don't just assume you can tack on extra days once you arrive. Make sure you mention any discounts—for Rick Steves readers or otherwise—when you make the reservation.

If you don't get a response to your email, it usually means the hotel is already fully booked—but try sending the message again or call to follow up.

Confirming a Reservation: Most places will request your credit-card number to hold the room. To confirm a room using a hotel's secure online reservation form, enter your contact information and credit-card number; the hotel will email a confirmation.

If you sent an email to request a reservation, the hotel will reply with its room availability and rates. This is not a confirmation. You must email back to say that you want the room at the given rate. While you can email your credit-card information (I do), it's safer to share that confidential info via phone call, two emails (splitting your number between them), or the hotel's secure online reservation form.

Canceling a Reservation: If you must cancel your reservation, it's courteous to do so with as much notice as possible. Simply make a quick phone call or send an email. Family-run places lose money if they turn away customers while holding a room for someone who doesn't show up. Understandably, many hoteliers bill no-shows for one night.

Cancellation policies can be strict: For example, you might lose a deposit if you cancel within two weeks of your reserved stay, or you might be billed for the entire visit if you leave early. Internet deals may require prepayment, with no refunds for cancellations. Ask about cancellation policies before you book.

If canceling via email, request confirmation that your cancellation was received to avoid being accidentally billed.

Reconfirming Your Reservation: Always call to reconfirm your room reservation a few days in advance. Smaller hotels and B&Bs appreciate knowing your estimated time of arrival. If you'll be arriving late (after 17:00), alert your hotelier. On the small chance that a hotel loses track of your reservation, bring along a hard copy of their confirmation.

Reserving Rooms as You Travel: You can make reservations as you travel, calling hotels a few days to a week before your arrival. If everything's full, don't despair. Call a day or two in advance and fill in a cancellation. If you'd rather travel without any reservations at all, you'll have greater success snaring rooms if you arrive at your destination early in the day. When you anticipate crowds (weekends are worst), call hotels at about 9:00 or 10:00 on the day you plan to arrive, when the receptionist knows who'll be checking out and which rooms will be available. If you encounter a language barrier, ask the fluent receptionist at your current hotel to call for you.

Phoning: To call Spain from the US or Canada, dial 011-34 and then the local number. (The 011 is our international access code, and 34 is Spain's country code.) If you're calling Spain from another European country, dial 00-34-local number. (The 00 is Europe's international access code.) To make calls within Spain, simply dial the nine-digit number (area codes are not used in Spain). For more tips on calling, see page 274.

quality from one hostel to the next. Family and private rooms may be available on request.

Independent hostels tend to be easygoing, colorful, and informal (no membership required); see www.hostelz.com, www.hostelseurope.com; www.hostels.com; and www.hostelbookers.com. **Official hostels** are part of Hostelling International (HI) and share an online booking site (www.hihostels.com). HI hostels typically require that you either have a membership card or pay extra per night.

Apartments

It's easy, though not necessarily cheaper than a hotel room, to rent a furnished apartment in Barcelona. Consider this option if you're traveling as a family or with friends, staying a week or longer, and planning to cook many of your own meals. For more information on apartment rentals, see the end of this chapter.

Accommodations

Near Plaça de Catalunya: Business-Class Comfort

These hotels have sliding-glass doors leading to plush reception areas, air-conditioning, and perfectly sterile modern bedrooms. Most are on big streets within two blocks of Barcelona's exuberant central square, where the Old City meets the Eixample. As business-class hotels, they have hard-to-pin-down prices that fluctuate wildly. I've listed the average rate you'll pay. But in summer and on weekends, supply often far exceeds the demand, and many of these places cut prices to around €100—always ask for a deal. Most of these are located between two Metro stops: Catalunya and Universitat; if arriving by Aerobus, note that the bus also stops at both places.

$$$ Hotel Catalonia Plaça Catalunya has four stars, an elegant old entryway with a mod new reception area, splashy public spaces, slick marble and hardwood floors, 140 comfortable but simple rooms, and a garden courtyard with a pool a world away from the big-city noise. It's a bit pricey for the quality of the rooms—you're paying for the posh lobby (Db-€200 but can drop to as low as €100, extra bed-€38, breakfast-€19, air-con, elevator, free Internet access and Wi-Fi, a half-block off Plaça de Catalunya at Carrer de Bergara 11, Metro: Catalunya, tel. 933-015-151, fax 933-173-442, www.hoteles-catalonia.com, catalunya@hoteles-catalonia.es).

$$ Hotel Denit is a small, stylish, 36-room hotel on a pedestrian street two blocks off Plaça de Catalunya. It's chic, minimalist, and fun: Guidebook tips decorate the halls, and the rooms are sized like T-shirts ("small" Sb-€109, "medium" Db-€119, "large" Db-€144, "XL" Db-€164, includes breakfast when you book direct—otherwise pay €6, air-con, elevator, free Wi-Fi, Carrer d'Estruc 24-26, Metro: Catalunya, tel. 935-454-000, fax 935-454-001, www.denit.com, info@denit.com).

$$ Hotel Inglaterra is owned by the same people as Hotel Denit (listed above) but on the other side of Plaça de Catalunya. It has 60 rooms, a more traditional style, a rooftop terrace and swimming pool, and slightly higher prices (Sb-€119, Db-€129, €30 more for bigger "deluxe" rooms, breakfast-€15, air-con, elevator, free Internet access and Wi-Fi, Carrer de Pelai 14, Metro: Universitat, tel. 935-051-100, www.hotel-inglaterra.com, recepcion@hotel-inglaterra.com).

$$ Hotel Reding, on a quiet street a 10-minute walk west of the Ramblas and Plaça de Catalunya action, is a slick and sleek place renting 44 mod rooms at a reasonable price (Db-€124—this rate includes breakfast with this book but only if you book direct—otherwise pay €14 for breakfast, prices go up during trade fairs, extra bed-€38, air-con, elevator, free Internet access and Wi-Fi, Carrer de Gravina 5-7, Metro: Universitat, tel. 934-121-097, fax 932-683-482, www.hotelreding.com, recepcion@hotelreding.com).

$$ Hotel Lleó (YEH-oh) is well-run, with 92 big, bright, and comfortable rooms; a great breakfast room; and a generous lounge (Db-€130 but flexes way up with demand, can be cheaper in summer, extra bed-about €30, breakfast-€13, air-con, elevator, free Internet access and Wi-Fi, small rooftop pool, Carrer de Pelai 22, midway between Metros: Universitat and Catalunya, tel. 933-181-312, fax 934-122-657, www.hotel-lleo.com, info@hotel-lleo.com).

$$ Hotel Atlantis is solid, with 50 big, nondescript, modern rooms and fair prices for the location (Sb-€92, Db-€120, Tb-€138, check for deals on website, breakfast-€9, air-con, elevator, free Internet access and Wi-Fi, faces busy street—request a quieter room in back, Carrer de Pelai 20, midway between Metros: Universitat and Catalunya, tel. 933-189-012, fax 934-120-914, www.hotelatlantis-bcn.com, inf@hotelatlantis-bcn.com).

On or near the Ramblas:
Affordable Hotels with "Personality"

These places are generally family-run, with ad-lib furnishings, more character, and lower prices.

$$ Hotel Continental Barcelona, in a building overlooking the top of the Ramblas, offers classic, tiny-view balcony opportunities if you don't mind the noise. Its 39 comfortable but faded rooms come with wildly clashing carpets and wallpaper, and perhaps one too many clever ideas. Choose between your own little

Barcelona's Old City Hotels

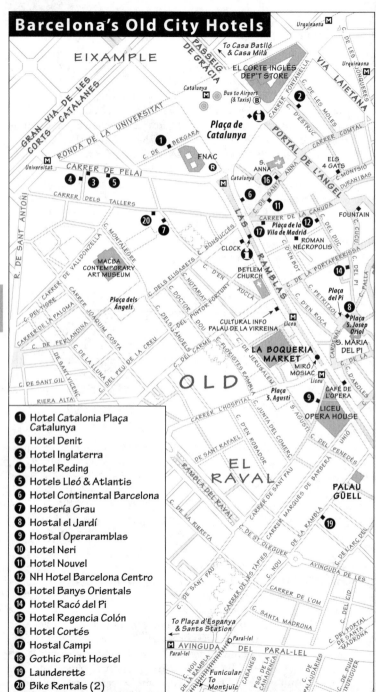

1. Hotel Catalonia Plaça Catalunya
2. Hotel Denit
3. Hotel Inglaterra
4. Hotel Reding
5. Hotels Lleó & Atlantis
6. Hotel Continental Barcelona
7. Hostería Grau
8. Hostal el Jardí
9. Hostal Operaramblas
10. Hotel Neri
11. Hotel Nouvel
12. NH Hotel Barcelona Centro
13. Hotel Banys Orientals
14. Hotel Racó del Pi
15. Hotel Regencia Colón
16. Hotel Cortés
17. Hostal Campi
18. Gothic Point Hostel
19. Launderette
20. Bike Rentals (2)

SLEEPING

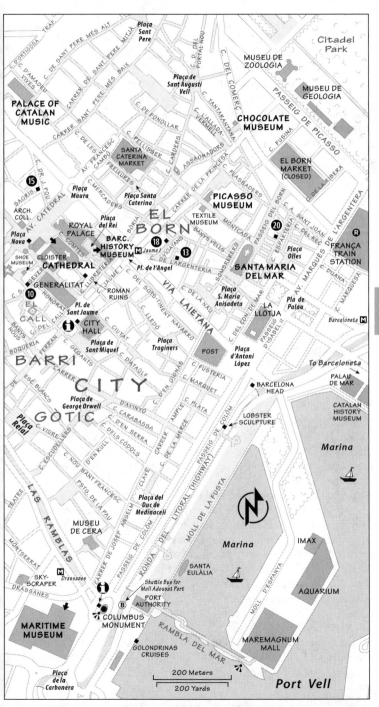

Ramblas-view balcony (where you can eat your breakfast) or a quieter back room. J. M.'s (José María's) free breakfast and all-day snack-and-drink bar are a plus (Sb-€95, Db-€105, twin Db-€115, Db with Ramblas balcony-€125, extra bed-€40, 5 percent discount off these rates with this book, includes breakfast, air-con, elevator, free Internet access and Wi-Fi, Ramblas 138, Metro: Catalunya, tel. 933-012-570, fax 933-027-360, www.hotelcontinental.com, barcelona@hotelcontinental.com).

$ **Hostería Grau** is homey, family-run, and almost alpine. Its 25 cheery, garden-pastel rooms are a few blocks off the Ramblas in the colorful university district. The first two floors have seven-foot-high ceilings, then things get tall again (S-€40, D-€75, Db-€98, extra bed-€18; 2-bedroom family suites: Db-€110, Tb-€130, Qb-€165; slippery prices jump during fairs and big events, 5 percent discount off these rates when you book direct and show this book, breakfast extra, strict cancellation policy, air-con, elevator, free Internet access and Wi-Fi, 200 yards up Carrer dels Tallers from the Ramblas at Ramelleres 27, Metro: Catalunya, tel. 933-018-135, fax 933-176-825, www.hostalgrau.com, reservas@hostal grau.com, Monica).

$ **Hostal el Jardí** offers 40 clean, remodeled rooms on a breezy square in the Barri Gòtic. Many of the tight, plain, comfy rooms come with petite balconies (for an extra charge) and enjoy an almost Parisian ambience. It's a good deal only if you value the quaint-square-with-Barri-Gòtic ambience—you're definitely paying for the location. Book well in advance, as this family-run place has an avid following (small basic interior Db-€75, nicer interior Db-€90, outer Db with balcony or twin with window-€95, large outer Db with balcony or square-view terrace-€110, extra bed-€12, breakfast-€6, air-con, elevator, some stairs, free Wi-Fi in lobby, halfway between Ramblas and cathedral at Plaça Sant Josep Oriol 1, Metro: Liceu, tel. 933-015-900, fax 933-425-733, www.eljardi -barcelona.com, reservations@eljardi-barcelona.com).

$ **Hostal Operaramblas,** with 68 stark rooms 20 yards off the Ramblas, is clean, institutional, modern, and a great value. The street can feel a bit seedy at night, but it's safe, and the hotel is very secure (Sb-€45, Db-€65, no breakfast, air-con only in summer, elevator, pay Internet access, free Wi-Fi in lobby, Carrer de Sant Pau 20, Metro: Liceu, tel. 933-188-201, www.operaramblas.com, info@operaramblas.com).

In the Old City

These accommodations are buried in Barcelona's Old City, mostly in the Barri Gòtic. The Catalunya, Liceu, and Jaume I Metro stops flank this tight tangle of lanes; I've noted which stop(s) are best for each.

SLEEPING

$$$ Hotel Neri is posh, pretentious, and sophisticated, with 22 rooms spliced into the ancient stones of the Barri Gòtic, overlooking an overlooked square (Plaça Sant Felip Neri) a block from the cathedral. It has big flat-screen TVs, pricey modern art on the bedroom walls, dressed-up people in its gourmet restaurant, and stuffy service (Db-€300, suites-€365-450, generally cheaper on weekdays, breakfast-€22, air-con, elevator, free Wi-Fi, rooftop tanning deck, Carrer de Sant Sever 5, Metro: Liceu or Jaume I, tel. 933-040-655, fax 933-040-337, www.hotelneri.com, info@hotel neri.com).

$$$ Hotel Nouvel, in an elegant, Victorian-style building just of the Ramblas on a handy pedestrian street, is less business-oriented than many of Barcelona's hotels and offers more character than the others listed here. It boasts royal lounges and 78 comfy rooms (Sb-€110, Db-€192, online deals can be much much cheaper than these rates so check their website, extra bed-€35, includes breakfast, €20 deposit for TV remote, air-con, elevator, pay Wi-Fi, Carrer de Santa Anna 20, Metro: Catalunya, tel. 933-018-274, fax 933-018-370, www.hotelnouvel.com, info@hotelnouvel.com).

$$$ NH Hotel Barcelona Centro, with 156 rooms and tasteful chain-hotel predictability, is professional yet friendly, buried in the Barri Gòtic just three blocks off the Ramblas (Db-€160, rates fluctuate with demand, bigger "superior" rooms on a corner with windows on 2 sides-€25 extra, breakfast-€15, air-con, elevator, pay Internet access, free Wi-Fi in lobby—30-minute limit, Carrer del Duc 15, Metro: Catalunya or Liceu, tel. 932-703-410, fax 934-127-747, www.nh-hotels.com, barcelonacentro@nh-hotels.com).

$$ Hotel Banys Orientals—despite being a big, modern, business-class type place—has a people-to-people ethic and refreshingly straight prices. Its 43 rooms are located in the El Born district on a pedestrianized street between the cathedral and Church of Santa Maria del Mar (Sb-€85, Db-€105, breakfast-€10, air-con, free Wi-Fi, Carrer de l'Argenteria 37, 50 yards from Metro: Jaume I, tel. 932-688-460, www.hotelbanysorientals .com, reservas@hotelbanysorientals.com). They also run the adjacent, recommended El Senyor Parellada restaurant.

$$ Hotel Racó del Pi, part of the H10 hotel chain, is a quality, professional place with generous public spaces and 37 modern, bright, quiet rooms. It's located on a wonderful pedestrian street immersed in the Barri Gòtic (Db-often around €130-145, can be as low as €100, cheaper if you book "nonrefundable" room online, breakfast-€10, air-con, free Internet access and Wi-Fi, around the corner from Plaça del Pi at Carrer del Pi 7, 3-minute walk from Metro: Liceu, tel. 933-426-190, www.h10hotels.com, h10.raco .delpi@h10.es).

$$ **Hotel Regencia Colón,** in a handy location one block in front of the cathedral, offers 50 slightly older but solid, classy, and well-priced rooms (Db-€110, more on weekends, extra bed-€33, breakfast-€13, air-con, elevator, free Wi-Fi, Carrer dels Sagristans 13-17, Metro: Jaume I, tel. 933-189-858, fax 933-172-822, www.hotelregenciacolon.com, info@hotelregenciacolon.com).

$ **Hotel Cortés** has 44 rooms on a traffic-free shopping street just off Avinguda del Portal de l'Angel (between Plaça de Catalunya and the cathedral). It's a bit sterile and scruffy, but well-priced and wonderfully located. Back rooms overlook an old *extra muro* cloister, while front rooms face the busy pedestrian drag (Sb-€70, Db-€100, includes breakfast, air-con, elevator, free Internet access and Wi-Fi, Carrer de Santa Anna 25, Metro: Catalunya, tel. 933-179-112, www.hotelcortes.com, reservas@hotelcortes.com).

$ **Hostal Campi** is big, subdued, and ramshackle, but offers simple class. This easygoing old-school spot renting 24 rooms a few doors off the top of the Ramblas is rumored to be closing sometime soon (S-€35, D-€60, Ds-€62, Db-€69, T-€78, Tb-€92, no breakfast, lots of stairs with no elevator, pay Internet access, free Wi-Fi in some rooms, Carrer de la Canuda 4, Metro: Catalunya, tel. 933-013-545, www.hostalcampi.com, reservas@hostalcampi.com).

In the Eixample

For an uptown, boulevard-like neighborhood, sleep in the Eixample, a 10-minute walk from the Ramblas action (see map on page 184). Most of these places use the Passeig de Gràcia or Catalunya Metro stops. Because these stations are so huge—especially Passeig de Gràcia, which sprawls underground for a few blocks—study the maps posted in the station to establish which exit you want before surfacing.

$$ **Hotel Granvía,** filling a palatial 1870s mansion, offers Botticelli and chandeliers in the public areas; a large, peaceful sun patio; and 54 spacious rooms—along with deliberate and sometimes quirky service. Its salon is plush and royal, making the hotel worth considering for romantics. To reduce street noise, ask for a quiet interior room or a room overlooking the courtyard in the back of the building (Sb-€75-85, Db-€125-150, Tb-€145-155, does not include 8 percent IVA tax, can be cheaper in slow times, mention Rick Steves to get best available rate, breakfast-€11, air-con, elevator, free Internet access and Wi-Fi, Gran Via de les Corts Catalanes 642, Metro: Catalunya, tel. 933-181-900, fax 933-189-997, www.hotelgranvia.com, hgranvia@nnhotels.com).

$$ **Hotel Continental Palacete,** with 19 small rooms, fills a 100-year-old chandeliered mansion. With flowery wallpaper and ornately gilded stucco, it's gaudy in the city of Gaudí, but it's also friendly, quiet, and well-located. Guests have unlimited

access to the outdoor terrace and the "cruise-inspired" fruit, veggie, and drink buffet (Sb-€105, Db-€140, €35-45 more for bigger and brighter view rooms, 5 percent discount with this book, extra bed-€55, includes breakfast, air-con, free Internet access and Wi-Fi, 2 blocks north of Plaça de Catalunya at corner of Rambla de Catalunya and Carrer de la Diputació, 30 Rambla de Catalunya, Metro: Passeig de Gràcia, tel. 934-457-657, fax 934-450-050, www.hotelcontinental.com, palacete@hotelcontinental.com).

$ Hotel Ginebra has 10 recently renovated rooms in an apartment building overlooking the main square. It's minimal, clean, and quiet considering its central location, though rooms facing the square get some noise (Sb-€75, Db-€85, Tb-€110, more for view rooms, air-con, elevator, guest computers, Wi-Fi, Rambla de Catalunya 1/3, third floor, Metro: Catalunya, tel. 932-502-017, www.barcelonahotelginebra.com, info@barcelonahotelginebra.com).

$ Hostal Oliva is a spartan, old-school place with 15 basic, high-ceilinged rooms and no breakfast or public spaces. It's on the fourth floor of a classic old Eixample building in a perfect location, just a couple of blocks above Plaça de Catalunya (S-€40, D-€69, Db-€89, elevator, free Wi-Fi, corner of Passeig de Gràcia and Carrer de la Diputació, Passeig de Gràcia 32, Metro: Passeig de Gràcia, tel. 934-880-162, www.hostaloliva.com, hostaloliva@lasguias.com).

$ BCN Fashion House B&B is a meditative place with 10 rooms, a peaceful lounge, and a leafy backyard terrace on the first floor of a nondescript old building (S-€35-55, D-€55-80, bigger "veranda" D-€70-90, Db-€90-125, 2-night minimum stay, breakfast-€6, Wi-Fi, between Carrer d'Ausiàs Marc and Ronda de Sant Pere at Carrer del Bruc 13, just steps from Metro: Urquinaona, mobile 637-904-044, www.bcnfashionhouse.com, info@bcnfashionhouse.com).

Hostels

Equity Point Hostels: Barcelona has a terrific chain of well-run and centrally located hostels (tel. 932-312-045, www.equity-point.com), providing €25-32 dorm beds (prices lower off-season) in 4- to 14-bed coed rooms with €2 sheets and towels, pay Internet access, free Wi-Fi, included breakfast, lockers (B.Y.O. lock, or buy one there), and plenty of opportunities to meet other backpackers. They're open 24 hours but aren't party hostels, so they enforce quiet after 23:00. There are three locations to choose from: the Eixample, Barri Gòtic, or near the beach. **$ Centric Point Hostel** is a huge place renting 400 cheap beds at what must be the best address in Barcelona (bar, kitchen, Passeig de Gràcia 33—see map on page 184, Metro: Passeig de Gràcia, tel. 932-151-796, fax 932-461-552, www.centricpointhostel.com). **$ Gothic Point**

Hotels & Restaurants in Barcelona's Eixample

1. Hotel Granvía
2. Hotel Continental Palacete
3. Hostal Oliva
4. BCN Fashion House B&B
5. Centric Point Hostel
6. Somnio Hostel
7. La Rita Restaurant
8. La Bodegueta
9. Restaurante la Palmera
10. La Flauta
11. Cinc Sentits
12. Tapas 24
13. La Bodegueta Provença
14. Ciutat Comtal Cerveceria
15. La Tramoia
16. Hotel Ginebra

SLEEPING

To Joanic M

CARRER DE TORRIJOS
C. RAMÓN Y CAJAL
TRAVESSERA DE GRÀCIA
PASSEIG DE GRÀCIA
PASSEIG DE SANT JOAN
CARRER
PASSEIG
CARRER DE BAILEN
CARRER DE CORSEGA
CARRER DEL ROSSELLÓ

CASA DE LES PUNXES

C. DE MOZART

HOTEL CASA FUSTER

R Gràcia

VIA AUGUSTA

PALAU BARÓ DE QUADRAS

EIX

AVINGUDA DIAGONAL

M Diagonal

LA PEDRERA

RAMBLA DE CATALUNYA

M Diagonal (To Sagrada Familia)

PASSEIG DE GRÀCIA

CARRER MALLORCA

CARRER DE PARIS

CARRER DE CORSEGA

Provença B M

CARRER DEL ROSSELLÓ

13

PROVENÇA TRAIN STATION R

8

QUADRAT D'OR

PASSEIG DE GRÀCIA TRAIN STATION 7

CASA BATLLÓ

M R Passeig de Gràcia

CARRER DE BALMES

CARRER DE PROVENÇA

CARRER D'ENRIC GRANADOS

9

FUNDACIÓ TÀPIES

CASA AMATLLER

RAMBLA DE CATALUNYA

5

N

CARRER D'ARIBAU

BLOCK OF DISCORD

2

C. DE MUNTANER

CARRER DE VALENCIA

Plaça del Doctor Letamendi

11

6

CARRER DE CASANOVA

200 Meters
200 Yards

CARRER DEL CONSELL DE CENT

CARRER DE LA DIPUTACIÓ

10

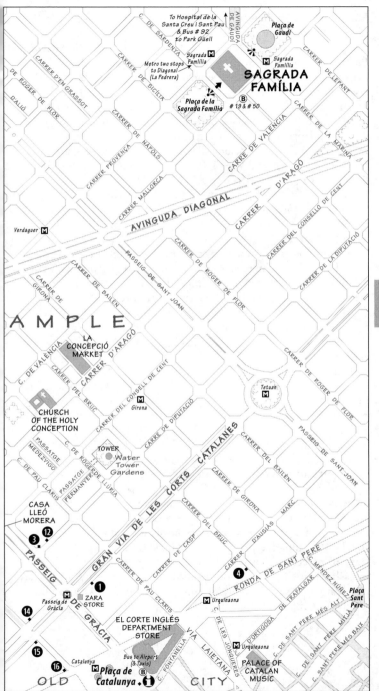

Hostel rents 130 beds a block from the Picasso Museum (roof terrace, Carrer Vigatans 5—see map on page 178, Metro: Jaume I, reception tel. 932-687-808, www.gothicpoint.com). **$ Sea Point Hostel** has 70 beds on the beach nearby (Plaça del Mar 4—see map on page 28, Metro: Barceloneta, reception tel. 932-247-075, www.seapointhostel.com).

$ Somnio Hostel, an innovative smaller place run by a pair of American expats, has 26 beds in 10 rooms. Choose between dorms and private rooms (bunk in 6-bed dorm-€26, S-€44, D-€78, Db-€87; prices include sheets, towels, and lockers; air-con, free Internet access and Wi-Fi, Carrer de la Diputació 251, second floor, Metro: Passeig de Gràcia, tel. 932-725-308, www.somnio hostels.com, info@somniohostels.com). They have a second location that's five blocks farther out.

Apartments

I recommend these two apartment-booking companies in Barcelona. Unlike huge aggregator websites like HomeAway or VRBO, these companies handpick their listings. Search their website for a listing you like, then submit your reservation online.

Cross-Pollinate is a reputable online booking agency representing B&Bs and apartments in a handful of European cities, including Barcelona. Choose a place online and submit a reservation; if the place is available, you'll be charged a small deposit and emailed the location and check-in details. Policies vary from owner to owner, but in most cases you'll pay the balance on arrival in cash. Barcelona listings range from a B&B double room near Sagrada Família for €75 per night to a three-bedroom Eixample apartment sleeping eight for €288 per night. Minimum stays vary from one to three nights (US tel. 800-270-1190, www.cross -pollinate.com, info@cross-pollinate.com).

Tournights Barcelona, run by American Frederick and his Spanish wife, rents 55 renovated apartments with kitchens. Most are near the beach in the lively Barceloneta neighborhood; others are in the Barri Gòtic or Eixample (2 people-€105 April-Oct, €85 Nov-March; prices vary with size—see photos and videos on website, €40 cleaning fee, 3-night minimum stay, discount for 7-night stay, 20 percent deposit required to reserve online, pay balance in cash when you arrive, no breakfast, arrange meeting to check in when you reserve, Frederick's mobile 620-585-594, www.tour nights.com, info@tournights.com).

EATING IN BARCELONA

Barcelona, the capital of Catalan cuisine—starring seafood—offers a tremendous variety of colorful eateries, ranging from basic and filling to chic and trendy. You can eat well in restaurants for about €15 per person—or even more cheaply if you graze on tapas in bars.

The Spanish eating schedule—lunch from 13:00 to 16:00, dinner after 21:00—frustrates many visitors. Most Spaniards eat one major meal of the day—lunch *(comida)*—around 14:00, when stores close, schools let out, and people gather with their friends and family for the siesta. Because most Spaniards work until 19:30, supper *(cena)* is usually served at about 21:00 or 22:00. And, since few people want a heavy meal that late, many Spaniards build a light dinner out of appetizer portions called tapas.

Don't buck this system. Generally, no self-respecting *casa de comidas* ("house of eating"—when you see this label, you can bet it's a good, traditional eatery) serves meals at American hours. If you're looking for the "nontouristy restaurant," remember that a popular spot is often filled with tourists at 20:00; then at 22:00 the scene is entirely different—and more authentic.

Not only are mealtimes different—the portions are, too. It's unusual to find a restaurant with "starters" and "main dishes." Instead, most restaurants (like bars) serve their dishes in portions called *raciones*, or the smaller half-servings, *media-raciones*. (The smaller tapas, and even tinier *pinchos*, are more commonly served at bars than at sit-down restaurants; for details, see later.) Enjoy this as an opportunity to explore the regional cuisine. Ordering *media-raciones* may cost a bit more per ounce, but you'll broaden your tasting experience. Two people can fill up on four *media-raciones*.

No matter where you eat, you'll encounter the cured ham

Sampling *Jamón*

The staple of Spanish cuisine, *jamón* (hah-MOHN) is pro-sciutto-like ham that's dry-cured and aged. It's generally sliced thin (right off the hock) and served raw and cold. *Jamón* can be eaten straight, served in a *bocadillo* (baguette sandwich), or mixed into a wide variety of dishes. Bars proudly hang ham hocks from the rafters as part of the decor. *Jamón* is more than a food. It's a way of life. Spaniards treasure memories of Grandpa thinly carving a *jamón*, supported in a *jamonero* (ham-hock holder), during Christmas, just as we savor the turkey carving at Thanksgiving.

Like connoisseurs of fine wine, Spaniards debate the merits of different breeds of pigs, the pig's diet, and the quality of the curing. The two major types of ham are **jamón serrano,** from white pigs whose meat is cured in the *sierras* (mountains) of Spain, and the higher-quality **jamón ibérico,** made with the back legs of black-hooved pigs (a.k.a. *pata negra,* "black foot"). Originating in Spain, these "Iberian" black pigs are said to be fatter and happier (slaughtered much later than other pigs), thereby producing particularly fine ham. Another indication of quality is **de bellota,** which means the pig was raised on acorns *(bellotas)*. **Jamón ibérico de bellota** is, to Spanish connoisseurs, as good as it gets. (Ham labeled **Jamón ibérico de recebeo** or **de cebo** is still good, but comes from pigs that are partly or entirely grain-fed rather than acorn-fed.) Additionally, there are regional variations of *jamón* indicating high quality, some of them officially controlled by EU authorities.

To sample this delicacy without the high price tag you'll find in bars and restaurants, go to the local market. Ask for 100 grams of top-quality ham (*cien gramos de jamón ibérico;* about €70/kilo, so your portion will run about €7), and enjoy it as a picnic with red wine and a baguette. To round out the perfect picnic, also pick up 100 grams each of *salchichón* (salami), chorizo (spicy sausage), and characteristic *manchego* or *cabrales* cheese, along with some olives and pickles.

called *jamón*. The cheapest meal is simply a *bocadillo de jamón* (sandwich of ham on a baguette), sold virtually everywhere.

The Spanish diet—heavy on *jamón*, weird seafood (especially in Barcelona), and deep-fried foods (usually fried in olive oil)—can be brutal on Americans more accustomed to salads, fruit, and grains. A few perfectly good vegetarian and lighter options exist, but you'll have to seek them out. The secret to getting your veggies at restaurants is to order two courses, because the first course generally has a green option. Resist the cheese-and-ham appetizers and instead choose first-course menu items such as creamed vegetable soup, *parrillada de verduras* (sautéed vegetables), or *ensalada mixta*. (Spaniards rarely eat only a salad, so salads tend to be small and simple—just iceberg lettuce, tomatoes, and maybe olives and tuna.) Main courses such as meats or fish are usually served with only a garnish, not a side of vegetables. Fruit isn't normally served for breakfast or as a snack—it's a dessert. After-meal dessert menus usually have a fruit option. For tips on tipping, see page 14.

Survival Tactics: To get by in Spain, either adapt yourself to the Spanish schedule and cuisine, or scramble to get edible food in between. Have an early light lunch at a bar. Many Spaniards have a *bocadillo* (baguette sandwich) at about 11:00 to bridge the gap between their coffee-and-roll breakfast and lunch at 14:00 (hence the popularity of fast-food *bocadillo* chains such as Pans & Company). Besides *bocadillos,* bars often have slices of *tortilla española* (potato omelet) and fresh-squeezed orange juice.

Then, either have your main meal at a restaurant at 15:00, followed by a light tapas snack for dinner later; or reverse it, having a tapas meal in the afternoon, followed by a late restaurant dinner. Either way, tapas in bars are the key (see "Tapas Bars," later).

A Note on Food Terms: Spanish and Catalan are the official languages of Barcelona, and many menus include both. Throughout this book, I've given most food terms in Spanish, but with Catalan added where helpful. For tapas and bar terms in Spanish and Catalan, consult the "Tapas Menu Decoder" and "Spanish Drinking Words" sidebars later in this chapter.

Breakfast

Hotel breakfasts are generally handy, optional, and pricey (starting at about €6). Start your day instead with a Spanish flair at a corner bar or at a colorful café in or near one of Barcelona's public markets (and pay just a few euros). Ask for the *desayunos* (breakfast special, usually only available until noon), which can include coffee, a roll (or sandwich), and juice for one price—much cheaper than ordering them separately. Sandwiches can either be on white bread (called "sandwich") or on a baguette *(bocadillo).*

A basic and standard savory breakfast item is *tostada con aceite,* toasted bread with olive oil (sometimes with tomato as well). For something more substantial, look for a *tortilla española*—an inexpensive potato omelet cooked fresh each morning and served in slices.

Those with a sweet tooth will find various sweet rolls (*bollos* or *bollería*)—the familiar *croissant, palmera* (palm-shaped, like a French *palmier* or "elephant ear"), *caracola* ("snail"-shaped, similar

EATING

to a cinnamon roll), *napolitana* (rolled pastry, usually filled with chocolate—like a French *pain au chocolat*), *rosquilla* (doughnut), and *bamba de nata* (cream puff). If you like a donut and coffee in American greasy-spoon joints, you must try the Spanish equivalent: greasy cigar-shaped fritters called *churros* (or the thicker *porras*) that you dip in warm chocolate pudding or your *café con leche*.

Here are some key words for breakfast:

café solo	shot of espresso
café con leche	espresso with hot milk
cortado	espresso with a little milk
té or *infusión*	tea
zumo	juice
zumo de naranja (natural)	orange juice (freshly squeezed)
pan (de molde/de barra)	bread (sandwich bread/baguette
tostada con aceite	toasted bread with olive oil
(y tomate)	(and tomato)
sandwich (tostado)	white bread sandwich (toasted)
bocadillo	baguette sandwich
...con jamón/queso/mixto	...with ham/cheese/both
...mixto con huevo	...with ham and cheese topped by an over-easy egg
tortilla española	potato omelet
bollos, bollería	sweet pastry
croissant (a la plancha)	croissant (grilled and slathered with butter)

Restaurants

When restaurant hunting, choose a spot filled with locals, not the place with the big neon signs boasting, "We Speak English and Accept Credit Cards." Venturing even a block or two off the main drag leads to higher-quality food for less than half the price of the tourist-oriented places. Locals eat better at lower-rent locales.

Don't expect "My name is Carlos and I'll be your waiter tonight" cheery service. Service is often *serio*—it's not friendly or unfriendly...just white-shirt-and-bow-tie proficient.

The restaurant scene in Barcelona ranges from avant-garde places and homey Catalan bistros *("cans")* to crowded tapas bars and affordable everyman eateries. In general, Barcelona's restaurants rise to a higher level than elsewhere in Spain, propelled by a contingent of talented chefs who aren't afraid to experiment and the availability of good fresh ingredients—especially fish and seafood. Cod, hake, tuna, squid, and

anchovies appear on many menus, and you'll see Catalan favorites such as *fideuà*, a thin, flavor-infused noodle served with seafood, and *arròs negre*, black rice cooked in squid ink. As everywhere in Spain, Catalan cooks love garlic and olive oil—many dishes are soaked in both.

For a budget meal in a restaurant, try a *plato combinado* (combination plate), which usually includes portions of one or two main dishes, a vegetable, and bread for a reasonable price; or the *menú del día* (menu of the day, also known as *menú turístico*), a substantial three- to four-course meal that may come with a carafe of house wine.

Sometimes the distinction between a bar and a restaurant blurs. Formal restaurants have a standard à la carte menu. Most eateries have a bar with some tables in the back or outside. And though tourists are often hot on tapas, these places are likely to serve larger *raciones* rather than bite-size tapas or restaurant entrées. Typically, couples or small groups order a few *raciones* and share the plates family-style. This can be very economical if you don't over-order.

Whether you go to a restaurant or bar, you won't be bothered by indoor smoke. Smoking is banned in closed public spaces in Spain.

Typical Desserts

In Spain, desserts are often an afterthought. Here are a few items you may see on Spanish menus:

arroz con leche	rice pudding
brazo de gitano	sponge cake filled with butter cream; literally "gypsy's hug"
flan de huevo	flan (crème caramel)
fruta de la estación	fruit in season
queso	cheese
helados (variados)	ice cream (various flavors)
torrijas	sweet fritters
ensaïmada	Mallorca-style croissant with powdered sugar

Tapas Bars

You can eat well any time of day in tapas bars. Tapas are small portions of seafood, salads, meat-filled pastries, deep-fried tasties, and on and on.

Tapas typically cost about €1.50-2 apiece and up. Most bars push larger portions called *raciones* (dinner plate-sized) rather than smaller tapas (saucer-sized). Ask for the smaller tapas portions or a *media-ración* (listed as ½ *ración* on a menu)—though some bars simply don't serve anything smaller than a *ración*.

Unlike in many Spanish cities, most Barcelona tapas bars do

not provide a free, small tapa with the purchase of a drink; if you want food, order it separately.

Eating and drinking at a bar is usually cheapest if you sit or stand at the counter *(barra)*. You may pay a little more to eat sitting at a table *(mesa* or *salón)* and still more for an outdoor table *(terraza)*. Locate the price list (often posted in fine type on a wall somewhere) to know the menu options and price tiers. (It's bad form to order food at the bar, then take it to a table. If you're standing and a table opens up, it's OK to move as long as you signal to the waiter; anything else you order will be charged at the higher *mesa/salón* price.) In the right place, a quiet snack and drink on a terrace on the town square is well worth the extra charge. But the cheapest seats sometimes get the best show. Sit at the bar and study your bartender—he's an artist.

I'll be blunt: The authentic tapas experience can be intimidating: elbowing up to a bar crowded with pushy Spaniards, squinting at a hand-scrawled monolingual chalkboard menu, and trying to communicate with the brusque bartender. Your bartender isn't a "waiter," in any sense. He's not there to patiently help you sort through your options—he wants to take your order, period. Hang back and observe before ordering. Read the posted or printed menu (likely in Spanish and/or Catalan). Use the "Tapas Menu Decoder" to sort through your options. You can also look around to see what appeals on other patrons' plates. Sometimes a few of the selections are displayed under glass at the counter. Handwritten signs that start out *"Hay _____"* mean "Today we have _____," as in *"Hay caracoles"* ("Today we have snails").

When you're ready to order, be assertive or you'll never be served. *Por favor* (please) grabs the guy's attention. Then quickly rattle off what you'd like (pointing to other people's food if necessary). Don't worry about paying until you're ready to leave (he's keeping track of your tab). To get the bill, ask: *"¿La cuenta?"* (*"El compte?"* in Catalan).

Although tapas are served all day, the real action begins late—21:00 at the earliest. But for beginners, an earlier start is easier and comes with less commotion. For less competition at the bar, go early or on Monday and Tuesday.

Chasing down a particular bar for tapas nearly defeats the purpose and spirit of tapas—they are impromptu. Just drop in at any lively place. I look for the noisy spots with piles of napkins and food debris on the floor (it's considered unsanitary to put trash back on the bar; go local and toss your napkins on the floor too),

Tapas Menu Decoder

You can often just point to what you want on the menu or in the display case, say *por favor*, and get your food, but these words will help you learn the options and fine-tune your request. Many of Barcelona's tapas bars use Catalan terms, so I've given both Spanish (first column) and Catalan (second column). When you see the same word in both columns, it's not a mistake—in some instances, a particular word (either Spanish or Catalan) is preferred.

Tapas Terms

Spanish	Catalan	
pincho	*pincho*	bite-size portion
pinchito	*pinchito*	tiny *pincho*
tapa	*tapa*	snack-size portion
½ *ración* (*media-ración*)	*mitja ració*	half portion
ración	*ració*	full portion
surtido (de ___)	*assortit* (de ___)	assortment (of ___)
frito	*fregit*	fried
a la plancha	*a la planxa*	grilled (on a flat-top griddle)
a la parrilla	*a la graella*	barbecued
brocheta	*broqueta*	shish kebab (on a stick)
¿Cuánto cuesta una tapa?	*Quant costa una tapa?*	How much per tapa?

Sandwich Words

Many tapas come in sandwich form—tasty bites perched on a baguette.

bocadillo	*entrepà*	baguette sandwich, cheap and basic—a tapa on bread
canapé	*canapè*	tiny open-faced sandwich
flauta	*flauta*	sandwich made with flute-thin baguette
montadito	*montadito*	small bun (or baguette slice) with the tapa "mounted" on top
pulga, pulguita, pepito	*pepito*	a small, closed baguette sandwich
sandwich	*sandvitx*	American-style sandwich on square bread

(continued on next page)

EATING

Typical Tapas

aceitunas	olives	olives
albóndigas	mandonguilles	spiced meatballs with sauce
almejas (a la marinera)	cloïsses (a la marinera)	clams (in paprika sauce)
almendras	ametlles	almonds (usually fried)
anchoas	anxoves	cured anchovies (salted or in oil)
atún	tonyina	tuna
bacalao	bacallà	cod
banderilla	banderilla	skewer of spicy, pickled veggies—eat all at once for the real punch
bombas	bombes	fried meat-and-potato ball
boquerones (en vinagre)	seitons (en vinagre)	fresh anchovies (marinated in olive oil, vinegar, and garlic)
cabrillas	cabrillas	snails (cheap but not as good as French escargot)
calamares fritos	calamars fregits	fried squid rings
callos	tripa	tripe
caracoles	cargols	tree snails (May-Sept)
cazón en adobo	caçó en adob	salty marinated dogfish
champiñones	xampinyons	mushrooms
charcutería	xarcuteria	cured meats
chorizo	xoriço	spicy sausage
croquetas	croquetes	croquettes—breaded and fried béchamel with various fillings (often jamón)
empanadillas	crestes	pastries stuffed with meat or seafood
ensaladilla rusa	ensalada russa	potato salad with lots of mayo, peas, and carrots
espinacas (con garbanzos)	espinacs (amb cigrons)	spinach (with garbanzo beans)
gambas (a la plancha/ al ajillo/cáscara/ peladas)	gambes (a la planxa/ al ajillo/closca/ pelades)	shrimp (grilled/ with garlic/shell/ peeled)
gazpacho	gaspatxo	cold soup made with tomato, bread, garlic, and olive oil
guiso	guisat	stew
jamón	pernil	cured ham (like prosciutto); for details, see page 188
judías (verdes)	mongeta (verda)	(green) beans
lomo	llom	pork tenderloin

mejillones	musclos	mussels
merluza	lluç	hake (whitefish)
morcilla	botifarró	blood sausage
morros	morro	pig snout
paella	paella	saffron rice dish with mix of seafood and meat
pan	pa	bread
patatas bravas	patates braves	fried potatoes with spicy tomato sauce
pescaditos fritos	peixet fregit	assortment of fried little fish
picos	bastons	little breadsticks
pimiento (relleno)	pebrot (farcit)	pepper (stuffed)
pimientos de Padrón	pebrots de Padró	lightly fried small green peppers
pinchos morunos	pinchos morunos	skewer of spicy lamb or pork
pisto	pisto	mixed sautéed vegetables
pollo (alioli)	pollastre (allioli)	chicken (with garlic and olive oil sauce)
pulpo	polp	octopus
queso	formatge	cheese
queso manchego	formatge manxec	classic Spanish sheep-milk cheese
rabas	rabas	squid tentacles
rabo de toro	cua de brau	bull's-tail stew (fatty and oh so tender)
revuelto de... ...setas	remenat de... ..bolets	scrambled eggs with... ...wild mushrooms
salchichón	salsitxó	salami-like sausage
sardinas	sardines	sardines
sesos	cervell	lamb brains
tabla serrana	taula d´embotits i formatge	hearty plate of mountain meat and cheese
tortilla española	truita de patata	potato omelet
tortilla de jamón/ queso	truita de pernil/ formatge	potato omelet with ham/ cheese
tortillitas de camarones	truita de gambes	shrimp fritters
variado fritos	variat fregits	mix of various fried fish

EATING

Spanish Drinking Words

Here are some words to help you quench your thirst—in Spanish (first column) and Catalan (second column). ¡Salud! (Cheers!)

Wine and Spirits

Spanish	Catalan	
vino	vi	wine
rojo / blanco	negre / blanc	red / white
cava	cava	sparkling wine (Spanish champagne)
un tinto / un blanco	un vi negre / un vi blanc	small glass of house red / white wine
un crianza	un criança	a glass of nicely aged, quality wine
un reserva / gran reserva	un reserva / gran reserva	much higher-quality (and pricier) wine
chato	gotet	small glass of house wine
tinto de verano	tinto de verano	red wine with lemonade (similar to sangria)
seco / dulce	sec / dolç	dry/sweet
mucho cuerpo	molt cos	full-bodied
afrutado	afruitat	fruity
vermú	vermut	vermouth
jerez	xerès	sherry (fortified wine from Jerez)
amontillado, fino, manzanilla	amontillat, fino, mançanilla	rich, dry sherries

lots of customers, and the TV blaring. Popular television-viewing includes bullfights and soccer games, American sitcoms, and Spanish interpretations of soaps and silly game shows (you'll see Vanna Blanco).

Get a fun, inexpensive sampler plate. Ask for *una tabla de canapés variados* to get a plate of various little open-faced sandwiches. Or ask for a *surtido de* (an assortment of) *charcutería* (a mixed plate of meat) or *queso* (cheese). *Un surtido de jamón y queso* means a plate of different hams and cheeses. Order bread and two glasses of red wine on the right square, and you've got a romantic (and €10) dinner for two.

Spanish Drinks

Spain is one of the world's leading producers of grapes, and that means lots of excellent wine: both red *(tinto)* and white *(blanco)*.

Beer

cerveza	cervesa	beer
caña	canya	small glass of draft beer
clara con limón / con casera	clara de llimona / de casera	shandy—small beer with lemonade / with soda
doble, tubo	tub	tall glass of beer
sidra	sidra	dry cider, a bit more alcoholic than beer

Nonalcoholic

agua con / sin gas	aigua amb / sense gas	water with / without bubbles
un vaso de agua (del grifo)	un got d'aigua (de l'aixeta)	glass of (tap) water
una jarra de agua	una gerra d'aigua	pitcher of tap water
refresco	refresc	soft drink (common brands are Coca-Cola, Fanta—limón or naranja, and Schweppes—limón or tónica)
mosto	most	nonalcoholic grape juice, red or white, served wherever wine is served
una sin	una cervesa sense alcohol	nonalcoholic beer

EATING

Major wine regions include Valdepeñas and Penedès (Cabernet-style wines from near Barcelona); Rioja (spicy, lighter reds from the *tempranillo* grape, from the high plains of northern Spain); and Ribera del Duero (northwest of Madrid). For a basic glass of red wine, you can order *un tinto*. But for quality wine, ask for *un crianza* (old), *un reserva* (older), or *un gran reserva* (oldest). The single most important tip for good, economical wine drinking is to ask for *un crianza*—for little or no more money than a basic *tinto,* you'll get a quality, aged wine.

Sherry, a fortified wine from the Jerez region, is a shock to the taste buds if you're expecting a sweet dessert drink. Named for its city of origin, *jerez* ranges from dry *(fino)* to sweet *(dulce)*—Spaniards drink the *fino* and export the *dulce*. *Cava* is Spain's answer to champagne. Sangria (a punch of red wine mixed with fruit slices) is refreshing and popular with tourists; Spaniards generally prefer *tinto de verano* (wine with lemonade).

Most places just have the standard local beer—a light lager—on tap. The brand is determined by regional pride, rather than quality. The most common beers are the locally brewed Damm (especially Estrella Damm) and Moritz, as well as San Miguel. To get a small draft beer, ask for a *caña*.

Nonalcoholic beer is quite popular and often on tap. If you say *"una sin,"* which means "one without," it's assumed you want a nonalcoholic beer. While *sin* comes with less than 1 percent alcohol, you can get totally alcohol-free brew by asking for *"zero punto zero"* (0.0). If you'd prefer a grape-juice alternative to wine, ask for *mosto* (it comes in red or white).

Spain's bars often serve fresh-squeezed orange juice *(zumo de naranja natural)*. For something completely different, try *horchata* (*orxata* in Catalan), a sweet, milky beverage extracted from *chufa* tubers (a.k.a. tigernuts or earth almonds). If ordering mineral water in a restaurant, request a *botella grande de agua* (big bottle). They push the more profitable small bottles. For a glass of tap water, specify *un vaso de agua del grifo*. The waiter may counter with *"Embotellada?"* ("Bottled?"), hoping to sell you something. Be strong and insist on tap water *(del grifo)* and you'll get it.

One challenge for tapas bar-hoppers is that you'll generally order a drink in each place. If you're visiting several different bars (as you should), this can add up. If you'd like to drink a lot without getting drunk, remember a few key terms: *caña* (small beer), *clara con limón* (small beer with lemonade) or *con casera* (with soda), *tinto de verano* (red wine with lemonade), and *una sin* (nonalcoholic beer, pronounced "seen").

Restaurants

Most of my listings are lively spots with a busy tapas scene at the bar, along with restaurant tables for *raciones*. A regional specialty is *pa amb tomàquet* (pah ahm too-MAH-kaht), toasted bread rubbed with a mix of crushed tomato and olive oil.

I've listed mostly practical, characteristic, colorful, and affordable restaurants. My recommendations are grouped by neighborhood—along the Ramblas, in the Barri Gòtic, in El Born (best for foodies), in the Eixample, and in Barceloneta. I also include some budget options scattered throughout the city and a suggested route for finding Catalan sweets. Note that many restaurants close in August (or July), when the owners take a vacation.

Remember that restaurants generally serve lunch from 13:00 to 16:00 and dinner from 20:00 or even later. It's deadly to your Barcelona experience to eat too early—if a place feels touristy, come back later and it may be a thriving local favorite.

Catalans seem to have an affinity for Basque culture, so you'll find a lot of **Basque-style tapas places** here (look for *basca* or *euskal taberna*; *euskal* means "Basque"). Enticing buffets of bite-size tapas invite you to simply take what you want. These places are particularly user-friendly,

since you don't have to look at a menu or wait to be served—just grab what looks good, order a drink, and save your toothpicks (they'll count them up at the end to tally your bill). For tips, terms, and more information, see "Tapas Bars," earlier. I've listed several of these bars (including Taverna Basca Irati, Xaloc, and Sagardi Euskal Taberna), though Barcelona has many other similar options. Throughout the city, you'll see signs both for Spanish *tapas* and Catalan *tapes* (same pronunciation and meaning).

EATING

Along the Ramblas

Within a few steps of the Ramblas, you'll find handy lunch places, an inviting market hall, and some good vegetarian options. For locations, see the map on page 200.

Lunching Simply yet Memorably near the Ramblas

Although these places are enjoyable for a lunch break during your Ramblas sightseeing, many are also open for dinner.

Taverna Basca Irati serves 40 kinds of hot and cold Basque *pintxos* for €1.80 each. These are small open-faced sandwiches—like sushi on bread. Muscle in through the hungry local crowd, get an empty plate from the waiter, and then help yourself. Every few minutes, waiters prance proudly by with a platter of new, still-warm munchies. Grab one as they pass by...it's addictive (you'll be charged by the number of toothpicks left on your plate when you're done). Wash it down with €2-3 glasses of Rioja (full-bodied red wine), Txakolí (sprightly Basque white wine), or *sidra* (apple wine)

EATING

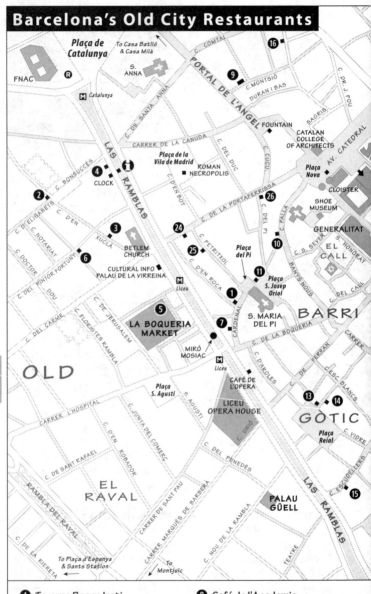

Barcelona's Old City Restaurants

1. Taverna Basca Irati
2. Restaurant Elisabets
3. Café Granja Viader
4. Carrefour Market
5. La Boqueria Market Eateries
6. Biocenter Veggie Rest.
7. Juicy Jones
8. Café de l'Academia
9. Els Quatre Gats
10. Xaloc
11. Bar del Pi
12. Restaurant Agut
13. Les Quinze Nits
14. La Crema Canela

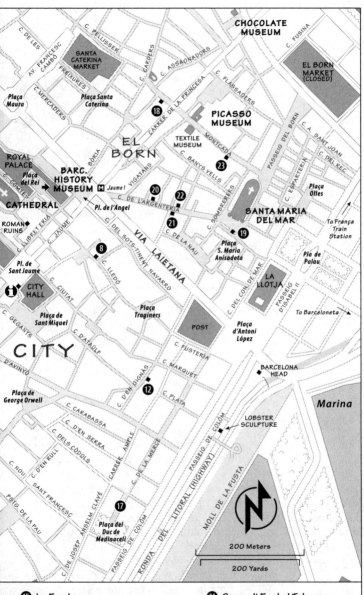

15 La Fonda

16 La Dolça Herminia

17 Carrer de la Mercè Tapas Bars

18 Bar del Pla

19 La Vinya del Senyor

20 El Senyor Parellada

21 Sagardi Euskal Taberna & Sagardi Restaurant

22 Taller de Tapas

23 El Xampanyet

24 Casa Colomina

25 Granja La Pallaresa

26 Fargas Chocolate Shop

Budget Meals Around Town

Bright, clean, and inexpensive sandwich shops proudly hold the cultural line against the fast-food invasion that has hamburgerized the rest of Europe. Catalan sandwiches are made to order with crunchy French bread. Rather than butter, locals prefer *tomàquet* (a spread of crushed tomatoes). You'll see two big local chains (Bocatta and Pans & Company) everywhere, but these serve mass-produced McBaguettes ordered from a multilingual menu. I've had better luck with hole-in-the-wall sandwich shops—virtually as numerous as the chains—where you can see exactly what you're getting. Kebab places are another good, super-cheap standby; you'll see them all over town, offering a quick and tasty meal for about €3-4.

poured from on high to add oxygen and bring out the flavor (daily 11:00-24:00, a block off the Ramblas, behind arcade at Carrer del Cardenal Casanyes 17, Metro: Liceu, tel. 933-023-084).

Restaurant Elisabets is a rough little neighborhood eatery packed with antique radios; it's popular with locals for its €12 "home-cooked" three-course lunch special. Stop by for lunch, survey what those around you are enjoying, and order what looks best. Apparently, locals put up with the service for the tasty food (Mon-Sat 7:30-23:00, closed Sun and Aug, lunch special served 13:00-16:00, otherwise only €3 tapas, 2 blocks west of Ramblas on far corner of Plaça del Bonsuccés at Carrer d'Elisabets 2, Metro: Catalunya, tel. 933-175-826, run by Pilar).

Café Granja Viader is a quaint time capsule, family-run since 1870. They boast about being the first dairy business to bottle and distribute milk in Spain. This feminine-feeling place—specializing in baked and dairy treats, toasted sandwiches, and light meals— is ideal for a traditional breakfast. Or indulge your sweet tooth: Try a glass of *orxata* (or *horchata*—*chufa*-nut milk, summer only), *llet mallorquina* (Majorca-style milk with cinnamon, lemon, and sugar), *crema Catalana* (crème brûlée, their specialty), or *suis* ("Swiss"—hot chocolate with a snowcap of whipped cream). *Mel y mató* is fresh cheese with honey...very Catalan (Tue-Sat 9:00-13:30 & 17:00-20:30, Mon 17:00-20:30 only, closed Sun, a block off the Ramblas behind Betlem Church at Xuclà 4, Metro: Liceu, tel. 933-183-486).

Cafeteria: For a quick, affordable lunch with a view, the ninth-floor cafeteria at **El Corte Inglés** can't be beat (€10 salads and sandwiches, also café with €1.50 coffee and sit-down restaurant with €20 fixed-price meals, Mon-Sat 10:00-22:00, closed Sun, Plaça de Catalunya, Metro: Catalunya, tel. 933-063-800).

Picnics: Shoestring tourists buy groceries at **El Corte Inglés** (described above, supermarket in basement), **Carrefour Market** (Mon-Sat 10:00-22:00, closed Sun, Ramblas 113, Metro: Liceu), and **La Boqueria Market** (closed Sun, described next).

In and near La Boqueria Market

Try eating at La Boqueria Market at least once (#91 on the Ramblas). Like all farmers markets in Europe, this place is ringed by colorful, good-value eateries.  Lots of stalls sell fun take-away food—especially fruit salads and fresh-squeezed juices—ideal for picnickers. There are several good bars around the market busy with shoppers munching at the counter (breakfast, tapas all day, coffee). The market, and most of the eateries listed here (unless noted), are open Monday through Saturday from 8:00 until 20:00 (though things get very quiet after about 16:00) and are closed on Sunday (nearest Metro: Liceu). For a more complete description of the market itself, see page 87 of the Ramblas Ramble.

Pinotxo Bar is just to the right as you enter the market. It's a great spot for coffee, breakfast (spinach *tortillas,* or whatever's cooking, with toast), or tapas. Fun-loving Juan and his family are La Boqueria fixtures. Grab a stool across the way to sip your drink with people-watching views. Be careful—this place can get expensive.

Kiosko Universal is popular for its great prices on wonderful fish dishes. As you enter the market from the Ramblas, it's all the way to the left in the first alley. If you see people waiting, ask who's last in line *("¿El último?").* You'll eat immersed in the spirit of the market (€14 fixed-price lunches with different fresh-fish options 12:00-16:00, always packed but better before 12:30, tel. 933-178-286).

Restaurant la Gardunya, at the back of the market, offers tasty meat and seafood meals made with fresh ingredients bought directly from the market (€13.50 fixed-price lunch includes wine

EATING

and bread, €16.50 three-course dinner specials include wine, €10-20 à la carte dishes, Mon-Sat 13:00-16:00 & 20:00-24:00, closed Sun, mod seating indoors or outside watching the market action, Carrer Jerusalem 18, tel. 933-024-323).

Vegetarian Eateries near Plaça de Catalunya and the Ramblas

Biocenter, a Catalan soup-and-salad restaurant popular with local vegetarians, takes its cooking very seriously and feels a bit more like a real restaurant than most (€8-10 weekday lunch specials include soup or salad and plate of the day, €15 dinner specials, otherwise €7-9 salads and €11-13 main dishes, Mon-Sat 13:00-23:00, Sun 13:00-16:00, 2 blocks off the Ramblas at Carrer del Pintor Fortuny 25, Metro: Liceu, tel. 933-014-583).

Juicy Jones is a tutti-frutti vegan/vegetarian eatery with colorful graffiti decor, a hip veggie menu (served downstairs), groovy laid-back staff, and a stunning array of fresh-squeezed juices served at the bar. Pop in for a quick €2.50 "juice of the day." For lunch you can get the Indian-inspired €6 *thali* plate, the €6.25 plate of the day, or an €8.50 meal including one of the two plates plus soup or salad and dessert (daily 9:00-23:30, also tapas and salads, Carrer del Cardenal Casanyes 7, Metro: Liceu, tel. 933-024-330). There's another location on the other side of the Ramblas (Carrer Hospital 74).

In the Barri Gòtic

These eateries populate Barcelona's atmospheric Gothic Quarter, near the cathedral. Choose between a sit-down meal at a restaurant or a string of tapas bars. For locations, see the map on page 200.

Restaurants in the Barri Gòtic

Café de l'Academia is a delightful place on a pretty square tucked away in the heart of the Barri Gòtic—but patronized mainly by the neighbors. They serve "honest cuisine" from the market with Catalan roots. The candlelit, air-conditioned interior is rustic yet elegant, with soft jazz, flowers, and modern art. And if you want to eat outdoors on a convivial, mellow square...this is the place. Reservations can be smart (€10-13 first courses, €12-16 second courses, fixed-price lunch for €10 at the bar or €14 at a table, Mon-Fri 13:30-16:00 & 20:30-23:30, closed Sat-Sun, near the City Hall square, off Carrer de Jaume I up Carrer de la Dagueria at Carrer dels Lledó 1, Metro: Jaume I, tel. 933-198-253).

Els Quatre Gats ("The Four Cats") was once the haunt of the Modernista greats—including a teenaged Picasso, who first publicly displayed his art here, and architect Josep Puig i Cadafalch, who designed the building. Inspired by Paris' famous Le Chat Noir café/cabaret, Els Quatre Gats celebrated all that was modern at the turn of the 20th century (for more on the illustrious history of the place, see page 100 in the Barri Gòtic Walk). You can snack or drink at the bar, or go into the back for a sit-down meal. While touristy (less so later), the food and service are good, and the prices aren't as high as you might guess (€17 three-course lunch special Mon-Fri 13:00-16:00, €12-20 plates, daily 10:00-24:00, just steps off Avinguda del Portal de l'Angel at Carrer de Montsió 3, Metro: Catalunya, tel. 933-024-140).

Xaloc is *the* place in the old center for nicely presented gourmet tapas. It's a classy, woody, modern dining room with a fun energy, good service, and reasonable prices. The walls are covered with *ibérico* hamhocks and wine bottles. They focus on homestyle Catalan classics and serve only one quality of ham—and it's tops. A gazpacho, plank of ham, *pa amb tomàquet* (toast with tomato), and nice glass of wine make a terrific light meal (€2-6 tapas, €5-12 main dishes, open daily, a block toward the cathedral from Plaça de Sant Josep Oriol at Carrer de la Palla 13, Metro: Catalunya, tel. 933-011-990).

Bar del Pi is a simple, hardworking bar serving good salads, sandwiches, and tapas. It has just a handful of tables on the most inviting little square in the Barri Gòtic (Tue-Sun 9:00-23:00, closed Mon, on Plaça de Sant Josep Oriol 1, Metro: Liceu, tel. 933-022-123).

Restaurant Agut, around since 1924, features a comfortable, wood-paneled dining room that's modern and sophisticated, but still retains a slight bohemian air. The pictures lining the walls are by Catalan artists who are said to have exchanged their canvases for a meal. The menu includes very tasty traditional Catalan food, with some seasonal specialties (€13 three-course weekday lunch special, €10-14 starters, €13-18 main dishes, Tue-Sat 13:30-16:00 & 21:00-24:00, Sun 13:30-16:00 only, closed Mon, just up from Carrer de la Mercè and the harbor at Carrer d'En Gignàs 16, Metro: Jaume I, tel. 933-151-709).

Andelana Restaurants: A local chain called Andelana has several bright, modern eateries that are wildly popular for their artfully presented Spanish and Mediterranean cuisine, crisp ambience, and unbeatable prices. Because of their three-course €10 lunches and €16-21 dinners (both with wine), all are crowded with locals and in-the-know tourists (à la carte: €7-9 starters, €8-11 main dishes, all open daily 13:00-15:45 & 20:30-23:30, unless otherwise noted; the first three are near Metro: Liceu). Warning: These places are notorious for long lines at the door—arrive 30 minutes before opening, or be prepared to wait. **Les Quinze Nits** has great seating right on atmospheric Plaça Reial (daily 11:00-16:30 & 19:00-23:00, at

#6—you'll see the line, tel. 933-173-075). Two others are within a block: **La Crema Canela,** a few steps north of Plaça Reial, feels cozier than the others and is the only one that takes reservations (opens at 20:00 for dinner, Passatge de Madoz 6, tel. 933-182-744). **La Fonda** is a block south of Plaça Reial (opens at 19:30 for dinner, Carrer dels Escudellers 10, tel. 933-017-515). Another location, **La Dolça Herminia,** is near the Palace of Catalan Music in El Born (2 blocks toward Ramblas from Palace of Catalan Music at Carrer de les Magdalenes 27, Metro: Jaume I, tel. 933-170-676); the fifth restaurant in the chain, **La Rita,** is described later, under "Restaurants in the Eixample."

Tapas on Carrer de la Mercè in the Barri Gòtic

This area lets you experience a rare, unvarnished bit of old Barcelona with great *tascas*—colorful local tapas bars. Get small plates (for maximum sampling) by asking for "tapas," not the bigger "*raciones.*" Glasses of *vino tinto* go for about €1. And though trendy uptown restaurants are safer, better-lit, and come with English menus and less grease, these places will stain your journal. The neighborhood's dark, the regulars are rough-edged, and you'll get a glimpse of a crusty Barcelona from before the affluence hit. Nowadays many new, mod restaurants are popping up in this area, but don't be seduced—you came here for something different. Try *pimientos de padrón*—Russian roulette with little green peppers that are lightly fried in oil and salted... only a few are jalapeño-spicy. At the cider bars, it's traditional to order *queso de cabrales* (a very moldy blue cheese) and spicy chorizo (sausage), ideally prepared *al diablo* ("devil-style")—soaked in wine, then flambéed at your table. Several places serve *leche de pantera* (panther milk)—liquor mixed with milk.

From the bottom of the Ramblas (near the Columbus Monument, Metro: Drassanes), hike east along Carrer de Josep Anselm Clavé. Then follow Carrer de la Mercè, the small street that runs along the right side of the church. For a montage of edible memories, wander west to east and consider these spots, stopping wherever looks most inviting. Most of these places close down around 23:00.

Bar Celta (marked *la pulpería,* at #16) has a bit less character than the others, but eases you into the scene with fried fish, octopus, and *patatas bravas,* all with Galician Ribeiro wine.

A Short, Sweet Walk

Let me propose this three-stop dessert (or, since these places close well before the traditional Barcelona dinnertime, a late-afternoon snack). Start with a chunk of *torró* or a glass of *orxata,* then munch some *churros con chocolate,* and end with a visit to a fine *xocolateria*—all within a three-minute walk of one another in the Barri Gòtic just off the Ramblas (Metro: Liceu). Start at the corner of Carrer de la Portaferrissa midway down the Ramblas. For the best atmosphere, begin your walk at about 18:00 (note that the last place is closed on Sun). For locations, see the map on page 200.

Torró **at Casa Colomina:** Walk down Carrer de la Portaferrissa to #8 (on the right). Casa Colomina, founded in 1908, specializes in homemade *torró* (or *turrón* in Spanish)—a variation of nougat made with almond, honey, and sugar, brought to Spain by the Moors 1,200 years ago. Three different kinds are sold in €8-12 slabs: *blando, duro,* and *yema*—soft, hard, and yolk (€2 pre-wrapped chunks on the counter). In the summer, the shop also sells ice cream and the refreshing *orxata* (or *horchata,* a drink made from chufa nuts—a.k.a. earth almonds or tiger nuts). Order a glass and ask to see and eat a chufa nut (Mon-Sat 10:00-20:30, Sun 12:30-20:30, tel. 933-122-511).

Churros con Chocolate **at Granja La Pallaresa:** Continue down Carrer de la Portaferrissa, taking a right at Carrer Petritxol to this fun-loving *xocolateria.* Elegant, older ladies gather here for the Spanish equivalent of tea time—dipping their greasy churros into pudding-thick cups of hot chocolate (€4.50 for five *churros con chocolate*). Or, for a more local treat, try an *ensaïmada* (a Mallorca-style croissant with powdered sugar) or the *crema Catalana,* like a crème brûlée (Mon-Fri 9:00-13:00 & 16:00-21:00, Sat-Sun 9:00-13:00 & 17:00-21:00, Carrer Petritxol 11, tel. 933-022-036).

Homemade Chocolate at Fargas: For your last stop, head for the ornate Fargas chocolate shop. Continue down Carrer Petritxol to the square, hook left through the two-part square, and then left up Carrer del Pi to the corner of Carrer de la Portaferrissa. Since the 19th century, gentlemen with walking canes have dropped by here for their chocolate fix. Founded in 1827, this is one of the oldest and most traditional chocolate shops in Barcelona. If they're not too busy, ask to see the old chocolate mill *("¿Puedo ver el molino?")* to the right of the counter. (It's still used, but nowadays it's powered by a machine rather than a donkey in the basement.) They sell even tiny quantities (one little morsel) by weight, so don't be shy. A delicious chunk of the crumbly semi-sweet house specialty costs €0.40 (glass bowl on the counter). The tempting bonbons in the window cost about €1 each (Mon-Sat 9:30-13:30 & 16:00-20:00, closed Sun).

EATING

Farther down at the corner (#28), **La Plata** keeps things wonderfully simple, serving extremely cheap plates of sardines (€2.50), little salads, and small glasses of keg wine (less than €1). **Tasca el Corral** (#17) serves mountain favorites from northern Spain by the half-*ración* (see their list), such as *queso de cabrales* and chorizo *al diablo* with *sidra* (hard cider sold by the bottle-€6). **Sidrería Tasca La Socarrena** (#21) offers hard cider from Asturias in €6.50 bottles with *queso de cabrales* and chorizo. At the end of Carrer de la Mercè, **Cerveceria Vendimia** slings tasty clams and mussels (hearty *raciones* for €4-6 a plate—they don't do smaller portions, so order sparingly). Sit at the bar and point to what looks good. Their *pulpo* (octopus) is more expensive and is the house specialty. Carrer Ample and Carrer d'En Gignàs, the streets parallel to Carrer de la Mercè inland, have more refined bar-hopping possibilities.

In El Born, near the Picasso Museum

El Born (a.k.a. La Ribera), the hottest neighborhood in town, sparkles with eclectic and trendy as well as subdued and classy little restaurants hidden in the small lanes surrounding the Church of Santa Maria del Mar. While I've listed a few well-established tapas bars that are great for light meals, to really dine, simply wander around for 15 minutes and pick the place that tickles your gastronomic fancy. I think those who say they know what's best in this area are kidding themselves—it's changing too fast and the choices are too personal. One thing's for sure: There are a lot of talented and hardworking restaurateurs with plenty to offer. Consider starting off your evening with a glass of fine wine at one of the *enotecas* on the square facing the Church of Santa Maria del Mar (such as La Vinya del Senyor). Sit back and admire the pure Catalan Gothic architecture. Most of my listings are either on Carrer de l'Argenteria (stretching from the church to the cathedral area) or on or near Carrer de Montcada (near the Picasso Museum). Many restaurants and shops in this area are, like the Picasso Museum, closed on Mondays. For locations, see the map on page 200.

Bar del Pla is a local favorite—near the Picasso Museum but far enough away from the tourist crowds. This classic diner/bar, overlooking a tiny crossroads next to Barcelona's oldest church, serves traditional Catalan dishes, *raciones,* and tapas. Prices are the same at the bar or at a table, but eating at the bar puts you in the middle of a great scene (€4-8 tapas, Tue-Sun 12:00-24:00, closed Mon; with your back to the Picasso Museum, head right 2 blocks, past Carrer de la Princesa, to Carrer de Montcada 2; Metro: Jaume I, tel. 932-683-003).

La Vinya del Senyor is recommendable only for its location—with wonderful tables on the square facing the Church of Santa Maria del Mar in the middle of a charming and lively pedestrian zone. Their wine list is extensive—7 cl gives you a few sips, while 14 cl is a standard serving. They also have good cheeses, hams, and tapas (Tue-Sun 12:00-24:00, closed Mon, Plaça de Santa Maria 5, Metro: Jaume I or Barceloneta, tel. 933-103-379).

El Senyor Parellada, filling a former cloister, is an elegant restaurant with a smart, tourist-friendly waitstaff. It serves a fun menu of Mediterranean and Catalan cuisine with a modern twist, all in a classy chandeliers-and-white-tablecloths setting (€10-15 plates, open daily, Carrer de l'Argenteria 37, 100 yards from Metro: Jaume I, tel. 933-105-094).

Sagardi Euskal Taberna offers a wonderful array of Basque goodies—tempting *pintxos* and *montaditos* at €1.80 each—along its huge bar. Ask for a plate and graze (just take whatever looks good). You can sit on the square with your plunder for 20 percent extra. Wash it down with Txakolí, a Basque white wine poured from the spout of a huge wooden barrel into a glass as you watch. When you're done, they'll count your toothpicks to tally your bill (daily 12:00-24:00, Carrer de l'Argenteria 62-64, Metro: Jaume I, tel. 933-199-993).

Sagardi, hiding behind its thriving tapas bar (described

above), is a mod, rustic, and minimalist woody restaurant committed to serving Basque T-bone steaks and grilled specialties with only the best ingredients. A big open kitchen with sizzling grills contributes to the ambience. Reservations are smart (€10-20 first courses, €20-25 second courses, plan on €45 for dinner, daily 13:00-16:00 & 20:00-24:00, Carrer de l'Argenteria 62, Metro: Jaume I, tel. 933-199-993).

Taller de Tapas ("Tapas Workshop") is an upscale, trendier tapas bar and restaurant that dishes up well-presented, sophisticated morsels and light meals in a medieval-stone-yet-mod setting. Pay 15 percent more to sit on the square. Elegant, but a bit stuffy, it's favored by local office workers who aren't into the Old World Gothic stuff. Four plates will fill a hungry diner for about €20 (daily 8:30-24:00, Carrer de l'Argenteria 51, Metro: Jaume I, tel. 932-688-559).

El Xampanyet ("The Little Champagne Bar"), a colorful family-run bar with a fun-loving staff (Juan Carlos, his mom, and the man who may be his father), specializes in tapas and anchovies. Don't be put off by the seafood from a tin: Catalans like it this way. A *sortido* (assorted plate) of *carne* (meat) or *pescado* (fish) with *pa amb tomàquet* (bread with crushed-tomato spread) makes for a fun meal. It's filled with tourists during the sightseeing day, but this is a local favorite after dark. The scene is great but—especially during busy times—it's tough without Spanish skills. When I asked about the price, Juan Carlos said, "Who cares? The ATM is just across the street." Plan on spending €20 for a meal with wine (same price at bar or table, Tue-Sat 12:00-15:30 & 19:00-23:00, Sun 12:00-16:00 only, closed Mon, a half-block beyond the Picasso Museum at Carrer de Montcada 22, Metro: Jaume I, tel. 933-197-003).

In the Eixample

The people-packed boulevards of the Eixample (Passeig de Gràcia and Rambla de Catalunya) are lined with appetizing eateries featuring breezy outdoor seating. Choose between a real restaurant or an upscale tapas bar. For locations, see the map on page 184.

Restaurants in the Eixample

La Rita is a fresh and dressy little restaurant serving Catalan cuisine near the Block of Discord. Their lunches (three courses with wine for €10, Mon-Fri 13:00-15:45) and dinners (€10 plates, €21 fixed-price dinners, Sun-Thu 20:00-23:00, Fri-Sat from 20:30) are a great value. Like most of its sister Andelana restaurants—described on page 205—it takes no reservations and its prices attract long lines, so arrive just before the doors open...or wait (near corner of Carrer de Pau Claris and Carrer d'Aragó at d'Aragó 279, a block from Metro: Passeig de Gràcia, tel. 934-872-376).

La Bodegueta is an atmospheric below-street-level bodega serving hearty wines, homemade vermouth, *anchoas* (anchovies), tapas, and *flautas*—sandwiches made with flute-thin baguettes. On a nice day, it's great to eat outside, sitting in the median of the boulevard under shady trees. Its daily €12 lunch special of three courses with wine is served 13:00-16:00. A long block from Gaudí's Casa Milà, this makes a fine sightseeing break (Mon-Sat 8:00-24:00, Sun 19:00-24:00, at intersection with Carrer de Provença, Rambla de Catalunya 100, Metro: Provença, tel. 932-154-894).

Restaurante la Palmera serves a mix of Catalan, Mediterranean, and French cuisine in an elegant room with bottle-lined walls. This untouristy place offers great food, service, and value—for me, a very special meal in Barcelona. They have three zones: the classic main room, a more forgettable adjacent room, and a few outdoor tables. I like the classic room. Reservations are smart (€12-16 plates, creative €20 six-plate *degustation* lunch—also available during dinner Mon-Thu, open Mon-Sat 13:00-15:45 & 20:30-23:15, closed Sun, Carrer d'Enric Granados 57, at the corner with Carrer Mallorca, Metro: Provença, tel. 934-532-338).

EATING

La Flauta fills two floors with enthusiastic eaters (I prefer the ground floor). It's fresh and modern, with a fun, no-stress menu featuring €5 small plates, creative €4 *flauta* sandwiches, and a €12.50 three-course lunch deal including a drink. Consider the list of *tapas del día*. Good €2.30 wines by the glass are listed on the blackboard. This is a place to order high on the menu for a satisfying, moderately priced meal (Mon-Sat 13:00-24:00, closed Sun, upbeat and helpful staff recommends the fried vegetables, no reservations, just off Carrer de la Diputació at Carrer d'Aribau 23, Metro: Universitat, tel. 933-237-038).

Cinc Sentits ("Five Senses"), with only about 30 seats, is my gourmet recommendation. At this chic, minimalist, but slightly snooty place, all the attention goes to the fine service and beautifully presented dishes. The €59 *essència menu* and the €79 *sensacions menu* are unforgettable extravaganzas. Expect *menus* only—no à la carte. It's run by Catalans who lived in Canada (so there's absolutely no language barrier) and serve avant-garde cuisine inspired by Catalan traditions and ingredients. Reservations are required (Tue-Sat 13:30-15:00 & 20:30-22:30, closed Sun-Mon, near Carrer d'Aragó at Carrer d'Aribau 58, between Metros: Universitat and Provença, tel. 933-239-490, maître d' Amelia).

Tapas Bars in the Eixample

Many trendy and touristic tapas bars in the Eixample offer a cheery welcome and slam out the appetizers. These four are particularly handy to Plaça de Catalunya and the Passeig de Gràcia artery (for all of them, the closest Metro stops are Catalunya and Passeig de Gràcia).

Tapas 24 makes eating fun. This local favorite, with a few street tables, fills a spot a few steps below street level with happy energy, funky decor (white counters and mirrors), and absolutely excellent tapas. The menu has all the typical standbys and quirky inventions (such as the McFoie burger), plus daily specials. Service is friendly, and the owner, Carles Abellan, is one of Barcelona's hot chefs. This is a chance to eat his food at reasonable prices, which are the same whether you dine at the bar, a table, or outside. Figure about €40 for lunch for two with wine (€4-10 tapas, €12-14 plates, Mon-Sat 9:00-24:00, closed Sun, just off Passeig de Gràcia at Carrer de la Diputació 269, tel. 934-880-977).

Quasi Queviures ("**Qu Qu**" for short) offers upscale tapas, sandwiches, or the whole nine yards—classic food served fast from a fun menu with modern decor and a high-energy ambience. It's bright, clean, and not too crowded. Walk through their enticing kitchen to get to the tables in back. Committed to developing a loyal following, they claim, "We fertilize our local customers

EATING

with daily specialties" (€3-5 tapas, €5 dinner salads, €9-14 plates, prices 17 percent higher on the terrace, daily 8:00-24:00, Sun from 10:30, between Gran Via de les Corts Catalanes and Carrer de la Diputació at Passeig de Gràcia 24, tel. 933-174-512).

Ciutat Comtal Cerveceria brags that it serves the best *montaditos* (€2-4 little open-faced sandwiches) and beers in Barcelona. It's an Eixample favorite, with an elegant bar and tables plus good seating out on the Rambla de Catalunya for all that people-watching action. It's classier than Qu Qu and packed 21:00-23:00, when you'll likely need to put your name on a list and wait. While it has no restaurant-type menu, the list of tapas and *montaditos* is easy, fun, and comes with a great variety (including daily specials). This place is a cut above your normal tapas bar, but with reasonable prices (most tapas around €4-10, daily 8:00-24:00, facing the intersection of Gran Via de les Corts Catalanes and Rambla de Catalunya at Rambla de Catalunya 18, tel. 933-181-997).

La Tramoia, at the opposite corner from Ciutat Comtal Cerveceria, serves piles of €1.70 *montaditos* and tapas at its ground-floor bar and at nice tables inside and out. If Ciutat Comtal Cerveceria is jammed, you're more likely to find a seat here. The brasserie-style restaurant upstairs bustles with happy local eaters enjoying grilled meats (€9-20 plates), but I'd stay downstairs for the €4-9 tapas (daily 12:00-24:00 for tapas, 13:00-16:00 & 17:30-24:00 for meals, also facing the intersection of Gran Via de les Corts Catalanes and Rambla de Catalunya at Rambla de Catalunya 15, tel. 934-123-634).

In Barceloneta

The nearest Metro stop to this former sailors' quarter is Barceloneta. For locations, see the map on page 28.

Along the Waterfront: Barceloneta's harborfront (Passeig de Joan de Borbó), facing the city, is lined with multiple, interchangeable seafood restaurants and cafés. Locals love to come here for celebrity-spotting. One of many eateries along here is **La Mar Salada,** a traditional seafood restaurant with a slight modern twist. Their à la carte menu includes seafood-and-rice dishes, fresh fish, and homemade desserts. A nice meal will run you about €30-35 per person (€15 fixed-price weekday meal, Wed-Fri and Mon 13:00-16:00 & 20:00-23:00, Sat-Sun 13:00-23:00, closed Tue, indoor and outdoor seating, Passeig de Joan de Borbó 59, tel. 932-212-127).

In the Heart of Barceloneta: **Can Solé,** serving seafood since 1903, is a splurge. Hiding on a nondescript urban lane, this venerable restaurant draws a celebrity crowd, judging by the autographed pictures of the famous and not-so-famous that line the walls. But the place is homey, with sky-blue walls and café curtains, and the charming owner couldn't be more gracious (Tue-Sat 13:30-16:00 & 20:30-23:00, Sun 13:30-16:00 only, closed Mon, Carrer de Sant Carles 4, one block off the harborfront promenade, tel. 932-215-012).

Bakery: **Baluard,** one of Barcelona's most highly regarded artisan bakeries, faces one side of the big market hall in the center of Barceloneta. Line up with the locals to get a loaf of heavenly bread, a pastry, or a slice of pizza (Mon-Sat 8:00-21:00, closed Sun, Carrer del Baluard 38, tel. 932-211-208).

BARCELONA WITH CHILDREN

Barcelona is a great place to travel with kids; it's bubbling with inexpensive, quirky sights and an infectious human spirit. Sure, there's an amusement park, a zoo, and a science museum, but your kids will have an adventure simply wandering down the city's tangled streets. And when it's time for a break, Barcelona has one of Europe's best urban beach scenes.

Trip Tips

Eating

Your kids may be surprised to find out that Catalan food is nothing like Mexican food back home. Picky eaters may have a hard time with *jamón*, deep-fried dishes, and strange seafood. Try these tips to keep your kids content throughout the day.

- Start the day with a good breakfast (at hotels, kids sometimes eat free).
- Picnic lunches or dinners work well. Try large grocery stores such as Carrefour Market, El Corte Inglés, or Bonpreu, or drop by a *panadería* (bakery). Near the beach? Head to the market—El Mercat de la Barceloneta—near the Barceloneta Metro stop (Mon-Thu and Sat 7:00-15:00, Fri 7:00-20:00, closed Sun; Plaça de la Font 1, tel. 932-216-471). Having snacks on hand can avoid meltdowns.
- Choose easy eateries. A good, safe (though not exotic) bet is the cafeteria/restaurant at the El Corte Inglés department store on Plaça de Catalunya (service all day, €7 kids menu). Quick chain restaurants such as Bocatta or Pans & Company serve reasonably priced *bocadillos* and fries—and grownups can order a beer. Tapa Tapa has booth seating just right for kids, and the pictograph menus make ordering fun (just north of

Plaça de Catalunya at Passeig de Gràcia 44, tel. 934-883-369).
- Catalans eat late—usually about 21:00 or 22:00—and dinner can take two hours. If you're eating late with your kids at a restaurant, bring something to occupy them and seek out places on squares where kids can run free while you dine.

Sightseeing

The key to a successful Barcelona family vacation is to slow down. Tackle one or two key sights each day, mix in a healthy dose of pure fun at a park or beach, and take extended breaks when needed.

- Incorporate your child's interests into each day's plans. Let your kids make some decisions: choosing lunch spots or deciding which stores to visit. Turn your kid into your personal tour guide and navigator of the Metro system. Deputize your child to lead you on my self-guided walks and museum tours.
- Since a trip is a splurge for parents, the kids should enjoy a larger allowance, too. Provide ample money and ask your kids to buy their own treats, postcards, and trinkets within that daily budget.
- Seek out kid-friendly museums, such as CosmoCaixa or the Maritime Museum. If you're visiting art museums with younger children, hit the gift shop first so you can buy postcards; then hold a scavenger hunt to find the pictured artwork.
- Even if you have the most well-behaved kids in the world, mix-ups happen. It's good to have a "what if" procedure in place in case something goes wrong, such as getting separated in the Metro. Be sure to give each child a business card from your hotel so they have local contact information.
- If your kids love playing in the sand, consider staying in an apartment near one of Barcelona's many beaches; see page 186. Easy access to the beach offers a convenient daily activity for children, and the sights and attractions of the city are easily accessible by Metro or bus.

Top Sights and Activities

Kid-Centric Attractions

Tibidabo—This 100-year-old amusement park (the city's oldest) sits atop the Tibidabo foothills above town; visiting it could easily fill an entire day. The fun starts even before you arrive, as a funicular (€7.50, €4 with park admission) can take you right to the park entrance. At the top, kids will find a mixture of 25 Disneyland-like rides appealing to both younger children and teens; older kids might like modern attractions such as a 4-D cinema show and the Tibidabo Express roller-coaster.

Cost and Hours: Kids under 3 feet tall are free; kids under 4 feet are charged €9; adults pay €25.20; hours depend on season—generally Wed-Sun 12:00-23:00 in summer, closed Mon-Tue; weekends only off-season, tel. 932-117-942, www.tibidabo.cat. For directions, see page 77.

CosmoCaixa—One of Europe's most advanced science museums, CosmoCaixa features hands-on exhibits, many of which are specifically geared toward small children. Youngsters will love *¡Toca toca!* (Touch touch!), an exhibit exploring the natural world, while the newly renovated 3-D planetarium (€2 extra) may entice older kids and teens. Other kid-focused highlights include a jungle greenhouse and a treasure hunt.

Cost and Hours: Kids under 6-free, families and kids 7 and older-€2 each, adults-€3, free on first Sun of the month; Tue-Sun 10:00-20:00, closed Mon; Metro: Tibidabo, then hop on bus #196 for one stop or about a 15-minute walk to the museum, Carrer d'Isaac Newton 26; tel. 932-126-050, www.obrasocial.lacaixa.es.

Barcelona Zoo (Zoo de Barcelona)—This enormous zoo, which gained fame in the 1960s as the home of the only known albino gorilla in the world, *Copito de Nieve* (Snowflake), is inside Citadel Park (see page 55). The zoo features all the kid-recognizable animals such as tigers, hippos, and zebras as well as oddities like Komodo dragons. Daily shows with the dolphins and sea lions in "Aquamara," the small SeaWorld-like marina arena, may impress the young and old.

Cost and Hours: Kids 3-12-€10.20, adults-€17; hours vary by season, summer hours daily 10:00-20:00; Metro: Barceloneta, Ciutadella-Vila Olímpica, Marina, or Arc de Triomf; tel. 902-457-545, www.zoobarcelona.cat.

Barcelona Aquarium at Port Vell (L'Aquàrium de Barcelona Port Vell)—Located on the waterfront not far from the Columbus Monument, the aquarium is home to more than 11,000 animals. Its star attraction is the "Oceanarium," a 262-foot underwater glass tunnel that lets you walk beneath schools of deep-sea creatures such as sharks and stingrays. The IMAX Theater next door shows movies in Spanish or Catalan, sometimes with English subtitles. The Port Vell area is an inviting mix of towering sailboats and a steady flow of people on the boardwalk in the midst of daily life; the green space offers room for a picnic or quick rest in between sightseeing.

Cost and Hours: Kids 3-12-€13, adults-€18; daily 9:30-21:00, July-Aug until 23:00; Metro: Drassanes or Barceloneta, Moll d'Espanya del Port Vell, tel. 932-217-474, www.aquariumbcn.com.

Magic Fountains (Font Màgica)—This popular, free spectacle uses classic and modern tunes—including film scores—as the soundtrack for a fanciful water show. Built for the 1929 World's Fair and renovated before the 1992 Olympics, it's part of a web of ponds and waterfalls on Avinguda Maria Cristina in Montjuïc.

Cost and Hours: Free 20-minute shows start on the half-hour; almost always May-Sept Thu-Sun 21:00-23:00, no shows Mon-Wed; Oct-April Fri-Sat 19:00-20:30, no shows Sun-Thu; these are first and last show times; Metro: Espanya; www.bcn.cat /parcsijardins/fonts, see page 75.

Museums and Exhibits

Art Museums—A short visit to some of Barcelona's modern and contemporary art museums could dazzle your kids visually. All of the following offer educational programs aimed at children and their families:

Museu d'Art Contemporani (MACBA) houses a vast collection of artwork from the past 50 years and offers lectures, video screenings, and special exhibits covering contemporary culture and art (kids under 14-free, adults-€8; late June-Sept Mon and Wed-Thu 11:00-20:00, Fri 11:00-22:00, Sat 10:00-22:00, Sun 10:00-15:00; Oct-late June Mon and Wed-Fri 11:00-19:30, Sat 10:00-20:00, Sun 10:00-15:00, closed Tue year-round; Metro: Universitat or Catalunya, Plaça dels Àngels 1, tel. 934-120-810, www.macba.cat).

The **Picasso Museum** gives kids a chance to marvel at the artist's early works (see page 53).

If you feel like venturing outside of the city for a surreal experience, a two-hour drive or train ride will take you to the **Salvador Dalí Theater-Museum** in the town of Figueres (see page 244).

Chocolate Museum (Museu de la Xocolata)—Satisfy everyone's sweet tooth while learning the history of traditional Catalan confectionery through a range of kid-friendly exhibits. You'll see chocolate statues of well-known pop-culture icons such as Minnie Mouse and SpongeBob. Family activities may even include painting with chocolate.

Cost and Hours: Kids under 7-free, adults-€4.30; Mon-Sat 10:00-19:00, Sun 10:00-15:00; Metro: Jaume I, Carrer del Comerç 36, tel. 932-687-878, www.museuxocolata.cat; see page 55.

Maritime Museum (Museu Marítim de Barcelona)—While its permanent exhibits are closed likely through 2014, the museum currently hosts temporary exhibits. When it reopens, the renovated museum will feature the history of Catalunya's rich maritime past from the 13th to the 21st century. Boat aficionados and sailors-to-be enjoy the collection of model boats and seafaring gadgets, as well as the sprawling marina.

A useful audioguide is included in the ticket price. The museum also includes the nearby *Santa Eulàlia* (docked on the Moll de la Fusta quay), a historic three-masted schooner from 1918 that was meticulously restored to its original state.

Cost and Hours: Museum—price depends on exhibits, kids under 7-free, kids 7-16-half price; daily 10:00-20:00 entrance to the temporary exhibits is free Sun starting at 15:00; *Santa Eulàlia*—€1, Tue-Fri and Sun 10:00-19:30, Sat 14:00-19:30, closes at 17:30 in Nov-March, closed Mon year-round; Metro: Drassanes, take the Portal de Santa Madrona exit; Avinguda de la Drassanes, tel. 933-429-920, www.mmb.cat; see page 45.

Blue Museum (Museu Blau)—A good choice for any kid interested in nature, this new natural history museum—home to more than three million specimens—celebrates the diversity in flora, fauna, and geology in Catalunya and beyond. Its main exhibit, Planet Earth, follows the birth of our planet and the evolution of life. A special space, the "Science Nest," has activities designed for preschoolers, but you'll need to reserve your visit in advance (closed Aug, though museum is open).

Cost and Hours: Kids under 16-free, adults-€6—free on Sun after 15:00; June-Sept Tue-Sun 10:00-20:00; Oct-May Tue-Fri 10:00-19:00, Sat-Sun 10:00-20:00; closed Mon year-round; Metro: El Maresme-Fòrum, Plaza Leonardo da Vinci 4-5, tel. 932-566-002, www.museublau.bcn.cat.

Botanical Gardens—Montjuïc is the home of the natural history museum's Botanical Gardens and its Botanical Institute as well as the recently reopened Historical Botanical Garden. A network of paths follows the natural terrain, taking visitors past 87 outdoor exhibits known as "phytoepisodes."

Cost and Hours: Kids under 16-free, adults-€3.50; daily June-Aug 10:00-20:00, April-May and Sept 10:00-19:00, Oct-March 10:00-18:00; take bus #150 from Plaça d'Espanya or the Montjuïc funicular from Paral-lel, main entrance between Olympic Stadium and castle—see map on page 66, Carrer Dr. Font i Quer 2; tel. 932-564-160, www.museublau.bcn.cat.

Olympic and Sports Museum (Museu Olímpic i de l'Esport)—Barcelona hosted the Olympics in 1992 and has never been the same since. Sports-crazed kids might enjoy this museum, as well as exploring what is left of the adjacent, anticlimactic 1992 Olympic Stadium. The mod-yet-tacky museum offers up several kid-friendly multimedia installations,  such as a virtual race against Carl Lewis, but it ultimately appeals only to Olympics fanatics.

Cost and Hours: Kids 14 and under-free, adults-€4.50; April-Sept Tue-Sat 10:00-20:00, Sun 10:00-14:30; Oct-March Tue-Sat 10:00-18:00, Sun 10:00-14:30, closed Mon year-round; Metro: Espanya, Avinguda de l'Estadi 60, tel. 932-925-379, www .museuolimpicbcn.cat; see page 72.

Camp Nou Soccer Stadium—"Barça" is to Barcelona what the Cowboys are to Dallas; the city lives and breathes for this top-ranked soccer team, as evidenced by their motto, "More Than a Club." The team's pricey visitors center has an interactive museum, features memorabilia from past seasons of glory, and includes a behind-the-scenes visit onto the soccer field. An English audio-guide helps explain the exhibits—and the city's soccer obsession. The crowded, energetic FC Barcelona superstore *(La FC Botiga)* is a cool spot for kids and teens as well (pick up a scarlet-and-blue jersey or scarf as a souvenir).

Cost and Hours: Kids under 6-free, kids 6-13-€17, adults-€23, audioguide included, mid-April-early Oct Mon-Sat 10:00-20:00, Sun 10:00-14:30; early-Oct-mid-April Mon-Sat 10:00-18:30, Sun 10:00-14:30; shorter hours on game days, Metro: Maria Cristina or Collblanc, Carrer d'Arístides Mallol 12, toll tel. 902-189-900, www.fcbarcelona.com/camp-nou.

Parks

Citadel Park (Parc de la Ciutadella)—Barcelona's most central park sprawls its grassy fields and large avenues across the grounds of an old fortress, and offers plenty for curious kids to discover. Attractions include a giant mammoth statue, a small lake with rental rowboats and duck feeding, a large Baroque fountain *(La Cascada)*, and several outdoor events held throughout the year. The Barcelona Zoo is also accessible from the park. Bikes can be rented from the bike-rental shop opposite the entrance to the park on Passeig de Picasso and Avinguda del Marquès de l'Argentera.

Cost and Hours: Free, daily 10:00 until dusk; north of França train station, Metro: Arc de Triomf, Barceloneta, or Ciutadella-Vila Olímpica; see page 55.

Horta Labyrinth Park (Parc del Laberint d'Horta)—Away from the city center in an unassuming location lies the most tranquil green space in town. With barely a tourist in sight, the park holds a handful of Neoclassical and Romantic gardens, highlighted by a small central maze that was used in the filming of Guillermo del Toro's hit, *Pan's Labyrinth* (2006) and Tom Tykwer's *Perfume* (2006). There are more than 20 water features—pools, fountains, reservoirs, canals, and an artificial waterfall—and the tricky labyrinth should provide ample entertainment as youngsters and teens attempt to figure out the puzzle.

Cost and Hours: Kids under 5-free, kids 5-14-about €1.50, adults-about €2.25, free on Wed and Sun; daily May-Sept 10:00-21:00, April 10:00-20:00, March and Oct 10:00-19:00, Nov-Feb 10:00-18:00, last entry one hour before closing; Metro: Mundet then a 15-minute walk, the park is behind a velodrome; www.bcn .cat/parcsijardins/fonts.

Beaches

Sant Sebastià and Barceloneta Beaches—These are the closest, longest, and busiest beaches (with Sant Sebastià preferred by locals). Both are near the city center, making them a good stop before or after sightseeing. A long boardwalk with food, drink, and ice-cream options lines both beaches; on the sand, you'll come upon children's play areas (including one with a cool climb-  ing frame). Expect beach sports such as ping pong, beach volleyball, and the Basque handball game, *pelota*. Look out on the waves and you'll also spot a surfer or two. Both beaches are accessible from the Old City area by bus or Metro (Metro: Barceloneta, walk along Passeig de Joan de Borbó, streets on the left cut across to the beachfront or walk all the way to Plaça del Mar to reach the start of Sant Sebastià; bus #36 runs right along the waterfront and will save some steps; for biking these beaches, see page 57).

Nova Icària Beach—If you don't care for crowds, head instead for the nearby Nova Icària beach; this more tranquil beach is frequented by families. Nova Icària is within walking distance of the 1992 Olympic Marina, a popular place for sailing and boating (Metro: Ciutadella-Vila Olímpica or Bogatel; bus #36 will get you closer than the Metro).

Other Experiences

***Sardana* Dance**—The easy-to-do *sardana* is a beloved traditional symbol of Catalan unity and pride. Kids might enjoy this

CHILDREN

spectacle of local culture—and may even be invited to join in. The dances are held in the square in front of the Cathedral of Barcelona every Sunday at 12:00 and usually also on Saturdays at 18:00 (none in Aug); the performance lasts between one and two hours; see page 50.

Cable Car (El Transbordador Aeri del Port)—This is a fun and scenic ride between the Barcelona waterfront and Montjuïc, providing spectacular views of the city. Note that the car is often crowded and very slow-moving; if there's a long line—and your child is impatient—you may regret waiting.

Cost and Hours: One-way-€10, round-trip-€15; 3/hour, daily 11:00-19:00, June-Sept until 20:00, closed in high wind; Metro: Barceloneta or Drassanes; tel. 932-252-718, see page 65.

CHILDREN

SHOPPING IN BARCELONA

Barcelona is a fantastic shopping destination, whatever your taste or budget. I've arranged most of my shopping information by neighborhood: The streets of the Barri Gòtic and El Born are bursting with characteristic hole-in-the-wall shops, while the Eixample is the upscale "uptown" shopping district. The area around Avinguda del Portal de l'Angel (at the northern edge of the Barri Gòtic) has a staggering array of department and chain stores.

Store Hours: Most shops are open Monday through Friday from about 9:00 or 10:00 until lunchtime (around 13:00 or 14:00). After the siesta, they reopen in the evening, around 16:30 or 17:00, and stay open until 20:00 or 21:00. Large stores and some smaller shops in touristy zones may remain open through the afternoon—but don't count on it. On Saturdays, many shops are open in the morning only. On Sundays, most shops are closed (though the Maremagnum complex on the harborfront is open).

Souvenir Ideas

In this very artistic city, consider picking up prints, books, posters, decorative items, or other keepsakes featuring works by your favorite **artist** (Picasso, Dalí, Miró, Gaudí, etc.). Gift shops at major museums (such as the Picasso Museum and Gaudí's Casa Milà) are a bonanza for art lovers.

Foodies might enjoy shopping for local **food items**—olive oil, wine, spices (such as saffron or sea salts), high-quality canned foods and preserves, dried beans, cheese, and so on. Remember, food items must be sealed to make it back through US customs (see page 15).

Torró (or *turrón* in Spanish) is the locally beloved nougat treat that's traditionally eaten around Christmastime, but has become popular anytime.

In this design-oriented city, **home decor** shops are abundant and fun to browse, offering a variety of Euro-housewares unavailable back home. For something more classic, look for glassware or other items with a dash of Modernista style.

Department and chain stores can be fun to explore for **clothing**—including European fashions you won't find back home.

Decorative **tile** and **pottery** can be a good keepsake. Eixample sidewalks are paved with a few different, distinctive tile patterns, which are sold in some local shops.

An *espadenya*—or *espadrille* in Spanish—is a soft-canvas, rope-soled shoe that originated as humble Catalan peasant footwear but has become trendy for its lightweight comfort in hot weather. A few shops in Barcelona (including La Manual Alpargatera, described later) still make these the traditional way.

Jewelry shops are popular here. While the city doesn't have a strictly local style, finding a piece with a Modernista flourish gives it a Barcelona vibe.

Accessories crafted from discarded materials into stylish, useful products (such as handbags) sell well in "green" Barcelona.

If you're intrigued by **Catalunya's** culture, consider a Catalan flag (gold and red stripes) or some depiction of the mascot dragon of St. Jordi.

Sports fans love jerseys, scarves, and other gear associated with the wildly popular **Barça** soccer team.

Shopping Tips

- If you need just souvenirs, find a **souvenir shop** or consult your neighborhood **supermarket** for that saffron or *torró*—perfect for tucking into your suitcase at the last minute.
- For more elaborate purchases, large **department stores** provide painless one-stop shopping.
- Barcelona—particularly its Old City—is studded with hundreds of delightful neighborhood **boutiques,** the best of which specialize in a unique item and do it well. If you're a collector of anything in particular, do some homework to find the perfect shop.
- Don't leave souvenir shopping for the **siesta** (roughly 14:00-17:00) or **Sunday,** when most stores are buttoned up tight.
- For information on **VAT refunds** and **customs regulations,** see page 14.
- For **clothing size comparisons** between the US and Europe, see page 302 of the appendix.

SHOPPING

The Old City

Within the Old City, the Barri Gòtic and El Born are the most interesting places to shop. El Raval, to the west, is seedier and has more in the way of secondhand shops. You'll find most of the Barri Gòtic shops on the "Barri Gòtic Walk" map on page 96; the El Born shops are on the "El Born Walk" map on page 119.

Barri Gòtic Shopping Walk (from the Cathedral to the Ramblas)

Most visitors going between the cathedral and the Ramblas follow the straight shot along the wide Carrer de la Portaferrissa.

This drag is lined with shops, but they're mostly international clothing stores catering to teens and young adults (H&M, Mango, etc.). For a more characteristic route—leading you through far more interesting streets lined with little local shops—plunge into some lanes just to the south. This brief, U-shaped walk is designed to lead you through some of the Barri Gòtic's most enjoyable shopping streets. Keep in mind that the walk could be disappointing during the midafternoon siesta, when many shops are closed, and it's completely dead on Sundays.

• Begin on **Plaça Nova**, the long square in front of the cathedral. At the west end of that square, stand facing the old Roman towers and the big BARCINO letters. Turn 90 degrees to the right, and just to the left of the restaurant (Bilbao Berria), head up the tight lane called…

Carrer de la Palla: This is ideal for antiques, with a half-dozen ancient-feeling shops crammed with mothballed treasures. (You'll also find, on the left, a fenced-in area with fragments of the old Roman walls.) Mixed in are a few contemporary art galleries, offbeat shops (such as **Librería Angel Batlle** at #23, selling vintage posters), and a motorcycle museum. Stay on this street until you reach the fork, marked by the building with **Caelum**—a casual but classy-feeling café that sells a wide range of nun-made pastries from convents around Spain. Peruse the boxes of sisterly goodies, and consider sticking around for a coffee—either on the main floor, or down in the cellar (Mon-Thu 10:30-20:30, Fri-Sat 10:30-23:00, Sun 11:30-21:00, Carrer de la Palla 8, tel. 933-026-993).

From here, you could detour left and head down **Carrer dels Banys Nous,** which curves gracefully south as it follows the route of the original Roman wall; while it's out of the way for this walk, it's another great shopping street. Just down this street, on the left at #10, the sprawling **S'Oliver** home-decor shop has the remains of an old Arabic bath in the back.

But to carry on toward the Ramblas, take the right fork past Caelum to another fine shop, **Oro Líquido** ("Liquid Gold"), selling a wide range of high-quality (and expensive) olive oils from around Spain (Mon-Sat 10:30-20:30, Sun 11:30-15:30, Carrer de la Palla 8, tel. 933-022-980).

• After another block, you'll pop out on the charming, café-lined Plaça de Sant Josep Oriol, facing the Church of Santa Maria del Pi (a popular venue for guitar concerts). Skirt around the right side of the church to find...

Plaça del Pi: While small, this square has some worthwhile shops. Gentlemen enjoy checking out the genteel **Josep Roca** shop, a *ganiveteria* (cutlery shop) selling knives, shaving gear, and other manly items (Mon-Fri 10:00-13:30 & 16:15-20:00, Sat 10:00-14:00 & 17:00-20:00, closed Sun, Plaça del Pi 3). Nearby, the **Vaho** shop keeps hipsters happy with "trashion bags" made of recycled fabrics (Mon-Sat 10:30-20:30, closed Sun). On the first Friday and Saturday of each month, local artisanal producers set up stalls in the middle of this square.

• Head up the street immediately left of Josep Roca...

Carrer Petritxol: This fun, narrow, characteristic lane (pronounced "peht-ree-CHUHL") runs parallel to the Ramblas. It's a fun combination of art galleries (such as Sala Parés, at #5, where Picasso had his first professional exhibition in town), fancy jewelry shops, and simple local places for hot chocolate and churros or other treats (check out **Granja La Pallaresa,** near the end of the street on the left, just after #11—described on page 207). A bit farther along, on the left (at #15), is a fancy sweets shop (specializing in *torró*) called **Vicens.**

• You'll dead-end onto touristy Carrer de la Portaferrissa. Head one block left to get to the Ramblas, or five blocks right to return to the cathedral. Or retrace your steps, this time poking into side-streets to discover more shops.

More Shops in the Barri Gòtic

The streets described in the above walk are just the beginning. While exploring the many other characteristic lanes of the Barri Gòtic, keep an eye out for these shops.

Sabater Hermonos (abbreviated "Hnos." on the sign) is a Chile-based shop selling handmade, natural, colorful soaps. The simple but fragrant shop feels like an artisanal Lush. To buy soap and call it a culturally redeemable souvenir, look for the bars shaped like characteristic Barcelona sidewalk tiles (daily 10:30-20:30, Plaça Sant Felip Neri 1, tel. 933-019-832).

Papirum is an inviting hole-in-the-wall selling craft paper, stationery, and hand-bound blank books (Mon-Fri 10:00-20:30,

Sat 10:00-12:00 & 17:00-20:30, closed Sun, Baixada de la Llibre-teria 2, tel. 933-105-242).

The street called **Carrer de Sant Domènec del Call,** which runs through the old Jewish Quarter (and is described on my Barri Gòtic Walk), is lined with some fun cafés, plus a leather workshop (Zoen, at #15, described on page 104 of the Barri Gòtic Walk) and a guitar shop.

La Manual Alpargatera is a famous *espadenya (espadrille)* store with a long tradition, dating back to the 1940s. These popular shoes are comfy, lightweight, and affordable (Mon-Fri 9:30-13:30 & 16:30-20:00, Sat 9:30-13:30, closed Sun, 7 Carrer d'Avinyó, just off of Carrer de Ferran between the Ramblas and Plaça Sant Jaume, tel. 933-010-172).

Herbolari Ferran, on Plaça Reial (to the right as you enter the square from the Ramblas), is a fine and aromatic shop of herbs, with fun souvenirs such as top-quality saffron, or *safra* (also an inviting little café inside, Mon-Fri 9:30-14:00 & 16:30-20:00, closed Sat-Sun, downstairs at Plaça Reial 18).

Carrer Ample, the street one block up from the tapas-loaded Carrer de la Mercè (in the lower part of Barri Gòtic—just above the waterfront), feels local but with little bursts of trendy energy. For example, **Papabubble** is an artisan candy shop where you can watch treats being made the old-fashioned way (daily 10:00-14:00 & 16:00-20:30, Ample 28, tel. 932-688-625).

El Born

El Born may be the most appealing place in Barcelona for bou-tique-hopping. My ✪ **El Born Walk,** designed partly as a frame-work for shoppers, suggests a route through the heart of this district, including tips on which streets in particular are worth exploring.

The Eixample

This ritzy "uptown" district is home to some of the city's top-end shops. In general, you'll find a lot of big international names along **Passeig de Gràcia,** the main boulevard that runs north from Plaça de Catalunya to the Gaudí sights—an area fittingly called the "Golden Quarter" (Quadrat d'Or). Appropriately enough, the "upper end" of Passeig de Gràcia has the fancier shops—Gucci, Luis Vuitton, Escada, Chanel, and so on—while the southern part of the street is relatively "low-end" (Zara). One block to the west, **Rambla de Catalunya** holds more local (but still expensive) options: fashion, home decor, jewelry, perfume, and so on. The streets that connect Rambla de Catalunya to Passeig da Gràcia are also home to some fine shops.

Vinçon, nearly next door to Casa Milà right on Passeig de Gràcia (at #96), is a design showroom with a lot of stylish cookware, housewares, lighting, furniture, baby gear, and so on. Combining the practical and the avant-garde, it's a fun place to take a look at Euro-housewares in a sprawling shop that feels like a trendy Spanish Ikea. At the far end of the store, find La Sala Vinçon, with temporary design exhibits and installations. Upstairs, filling the rooms of a fancy old apartment, is a showroom of various living spaces (Mon-Sat 10:00-20:30, closed Sun, Passeig de Gràcia 96, tel. 932-156-050, www.vincon.com).

Cubiñá, three blocks east and a block south, is another highly regarded furniture and home-decor shop—worth a peek for its upscale-mod collection, as well as for the Domènech i Montaner building that houses it (Mon-Sat 10:00-14:00 & 16:30-20:30, closed Sun, Carrer Mallorca 291, tel. 934-765-721).

Farther south, the street called **Consell de Cent** has a variety of art galleries (close to Plaça de Catalunya, roughly between Passeig de Gràcia and Carrer d'Enric Granados). And much farther to the west, the broad main boulevard **Diagonal** is another popular shopping zone—especially the stretch between Plaça de Francesc Macià and where it crosses Gran Via de Carles III (at the Maria Cristina Metro stop).

Department and Chain Stores

Avinguda del Portal de l'Angel

Barcelona natives do most of their shopping at big department stores. While most chains have several locations scattered around the city, you'll find the highest concentration on one convenient street, Avinguda del Portal de l'Angel, which connects Plaça de Catalunya with the cathedral. On this street, and throughout town, you'll find all of the following: **El Corte Inglés** is "Macy's-plus," the Spanish answer to one-stop shopping—everything from clothes, housewares, and furniture to electronics, bonsai trees, a travel agency, haircuts, and cheap souvenirs (get the complete list by picking up an English directory at their info desk). The chain **Zara** is focused on clothes. (Locals report that shops like Zara can vary from store to store—for example, the one in Barri Gòtic has more casual clothes, while the one along the ritzy Diagonal street emphasizes business attire.) Zara also owns several smaller clothing stores, including **Massimo Dutti** (upscale business attire, like Banana Republic), **Bershka** (teens), and **Pull and Bear** (young adults—sort of the Spanish Gap). The Barcelona-based **Mango** is another popular clothing chain, along with **Desigual** (with boldly colorful designs), the teen-oriented French chain **Pimkie,** and the more sophisticated **Podivm** and **Blanco.** Big international clothing chains include **H&M, Esprit,** and **Benetton. Kemper** is a local shoe store, and **Yamamay** and **Women's Secret** are the Spanish answer to Victoria's Secret, while **Itimissimi** and its parent company, **Calzedonia,** are Italian lingerie and swimwear stores. For Spanish fashion, simply walk down the street and dip into any of these that appeal.

At the top of Avinguda del Portal de l'Angel, Plaça de Catalunya has some large shops—including a gigantic **El Corte Inglés** (with a supermarket in the basement and a ninth-floor view café, Mon-Sat 10:00-22:00, closed Sun) and, across the square, **FNAC**—a French department store that sells electronics, music, books, and tickets for major concerts and events (Mon-Sat 10:00-22:00, closed Sun).

Las Arenas

While the shops inside it are nothing special, the Las Arenas shopping mall itself is—since it fills Barcelona's repurposed bullring. The former *plaça de toros* sat unused for decades before being converted into a modern mall. It has familiar chain stores, a food court, a view terrace, and an escalator that trundles all the way up through its wide-open atrium (daily 10:00-22:00, restaurants serve until 24:00 and later, Gran Via de les Corts Catalanes 373-385, www.arenasdebarcelona.com). Located on Plaça d'Espanya, it's convenient to combine with a visit to the Montjuic sights (see page 64).

NIGHTLIFE IN BARCELONA

Like all of Spain, Barcelona is extremely lively after hours. People head out for dinner at 22:00, then bar-hop or simply wander the streets until well after midnight. Sometimes it seems that more people are out and about at 2:00 in the morning (party time) than at 2:00 in the afternoon (siesta time). The most "local" thing you can do here after sunset is to explore neighborhood watering holes and find your favorite place to nurse a cocktail. I've described several parts of town ideally suited to doing just that. For a musical event, consider taking in a serious performance at a fancy venue (such as the Palace of Catalan Music or the Liceu Opera House), or opt for a jazz, flamenco, or classical guitar show.

Information: The TI hands out a free, monthly, user-friendly *Time Out BCN Guide* booklet (in English, with descriptions of each day's main events and websites for getting tickets). The TI's culture website is also helpful: barcelonacultura.bcn.cat. The weekly *Guía del Ocio,* sold at newsstands for €1.20 (or free in some hotel lobbies), is a Spanish-language entertainment listing (with guidelines for English speakers inside the back cover; www.guia delocio.com). Although it's in Catalan only, the *Butxaca* monthly cultural agenda includes a detailed schedule that's easy to figure out (available free around town and at Palau de la Virreina—described next, www.butxaca.com). Other resources are the monthly *Barcelona Planning.com* (www.barcelonaplanning.com), quarterly *See Barcelona,* and monthly *Barcelona Metropolitan* (all available free from the TI).

Palau de la Virreina Cultura, an arts-and-culture information office, sells tickets and provides details on Barcelona cultural events, including music, opera, and theater (daily 10:00-20:30, Ramblas 99—see map on page 80, tel. 933-161-000).

Getting Tickets: Most venues have links to booking engines on their websites. The majority of tickets for Barcelona events are booked through www.ticketmaster.es or www.telentrada.com. You can also get tickets through the box offices in the main El Corte Inglés department store or the giant FNAC electronics store (both on Plaça de Catalunya, extra booking fee), or at the ticket desk in Palau de la Virreina (listed earlier).

Music

Serious Concerts

Several classy venues host high-end performances.

The **Palace of Catalan Music** (Palau de la Música Catalana), with one of the finest Modernista interiors in town (see listing on page 53), offers a full slate of performances, ranging from symphonic to Catalan folk songs to chamber music to flamenco (€22-49 tickets, Carrer Palau de la Música 4-6, Metro: Urquinaona, box office tel. 902-442-882, www.palaumusica.cat).

The **Liceu Opera House** (Gran Teatre del Liceu), right in the heart of the Ramblas, is a pre-Modernista, sumptuous venue for opera, dance, children's theater, and concerts (tickets from €10, La Rambla 51-59, box office just around the corner at Carrer Sant Pau 1, Metro: Liceu, box office tel. 934-859-913, www.liceubarcelona .cat).

Another, much less architecturally interesting venue for classical music is **L'Auditori,** the home of the city's orchestra (boxy modern building northeast of Old City at Lepant 150; Metro: Glòries, Marina, or Monumental; tel. 932-479-300, www.auditori .cat).

Some of Barcelona's top sights host good-quality concerts. Try **Casa Milà** (described later under "Jazz"), **Fundació Joan Miró** (www.fundaciomiro-bcn.org), and **CaixaForum** (http://obra social.lacaixa.es—choose "CaixaForum Barcelona"); for details, check their websites.

Touristy Performances of Spanish Clichés

Two famously Spanish types of music—flamenco and Spanish guitar—have little to do with Barcelona or Catalunya, but are performed to keep visitors happy. If you're headed for other parts of Spain where these musical forms are more typical (such as Andalucía for flamenco), you might as well wait until you can experience the real deal. But if this is your only stop in Spain, here are some options.

Flamenco: Tarantos, on Plaça Reial in the heart of the Barri Gòtic, puts on cheap, brief (30 minutes), riveting flamenco performances several times nightly. While flamenco is foreign

Sights Open Late

Many of Barcelona's major sights are open well into the evening (and the hop-on, hop-off **Tourist Bus** runs until 20:00 daily in summer). If you like to extend your sightseeing day, here's where to do it:

Near the Ramblas

Maritime Museum: Daily until 20:00 (only temporary exhibits open while permanent exhibits undergo restoration, likely through 2014).

Palau Güell: April-Sept Tue-Sun until 20:00, closed Mon.

La Boqueria Market: Mon-Sat until 20:00, though quiet after about 16:00, closed Sun.

Barri Gòtic and El Born

Cathedral of Barcelona: Mon-Fri until 19:30, Sat-Sun until 20:00.

Picasso Museum: Tue-Sun until 19:50, closed Mon.

Church of Santa Maria del Mar: Daily until 20:00.

Eixample and Beyond

Sagrada Família: April-Sept daily until 20:30.

Casa Milà: March-Oct daily until 20:00.

Casa Batlló: Daily until 20:00.

Park Güell: Daily until 20:00 (plus Gaudí House Museum: April-Sept daily until 20:00).

Montjuïc and Vicinity

Castle of Montjuïc: April-Sept daily until 21:00.

Fundació Joan Miró: Thu until 21:30 year-round, also July-Sept Tue-Wed and Fri-Sat until 20:00.

Magic Fountains: May-Sept Thu-Sun 21:00-23:00, Oct-April Fri-Sat 19:00-20:30.

CaixaForum: Mon-Fri until 20:00, possibly Wed until 23:00 in July-Aug, Sat-Sun until 21:00.

Las Arenas (Bullring Mall): Daily until 22:00.

to Catalunya (locals say that it's like going to see country music in Boston), this is a fun and easy way to enjoy it. Performances are in a touristy little bar/theater with about 50 seats and reliably good-quality performers (€8, nightly at 20:30, 21:30, and 22:30; in July-Aug extra shows at 18:30, 19:30, and 23:30; Plaça Reial 17, tel. 933-191-789, www.masimas.com/en/tarantos). It's right on Plaça Reial, so it's easy to drop by and get tickets.

Other options include the pricey **Tablao Cordobés** on the

Ramblas (€39 includes a drink, €70 includes mediocre buffet dinner and better seats, 2-3 performances/day, La Rambla 35, tel. 933-175-711, www.tablaocordobes.com) and **Palau Dalmases** in the heart of the El Born district (€20 includes a drink, Mon-Wed and Fri-Sat at 21:00, in atmospheric old palace courtyard, Carrer de Montcada 20, tel. 933-100-673, www.palaudalmases.com).

For flamenco in a concert-hall setting, try one of the Palace of Catalan Music's regular performances (see listing earlier, under "Serious Concerts").

Spanish Guitar: "Masters of Guitar" concerts are offered nearly nightly at 21:00 in the Barri Gòtic's Church of Santa Maria del Pi (€21 at the door, €3 less if you buy at least 3 hours ahead—look for ticket-sellers in front of church and scattered around town, Plaça del Pi 7; sometimes in Sant Jaume Church instead, at Carrer de Ferran 28; tel. 647-514-513, www.maestrosdelaguitarra.com). The same company also does occasional concerts in the Palace of Catalan Music (€25-29).

Jazz

On summer weekends, a particularly classy option is the **"Summer Nights at La Pedrera"** concerts at Gaudí's Modernista masterpiece, Casa Milà, in the Eixample. This evening rooftop concert series generally features live jazz and also gives you the chance to see the rooftop illuminated (€25, late June-early Sept Thu-Sat 20:30-23:00, book advance tickets online or by phone, tel. 902-101-212, www.lapedrera.com).

Hotel Casa Fuster, a Modernista landmark designed by Lluís Domènech i Montaner, is a luxury hotel that hosts a Woody Allen-inspired jazz night each Thursday (in the basement of Café Vienés, 21:00-23:00, €15 "membership" required, reservations recommended, across Avinguda Diagonal from the Eixample at Passeig de Gràcia 132, tel. 932-553-006, cafevienesjazzclub.blogspot.com).

Jamboree jazz and dance club, right on Plaça Reial, features two jazz sets nightly, at 20:00 and 22:00, in a cellar under brick vaults (€4-10 in advance, a euro or two more at the door, check schedule online or stop by to pick one up, Plaça Reial 17, Metro: Liceu, tel. 933-191-789, www.masimas.com/en/jamboree).

Also consider the divey **Harlem Jazz Club** (€6-10, a block off Plaça Reial at Comtessa de Sobradiel 8, tel. 933-100-755, www .harlemjazzclub.es).

After-Hours Hangout Neighborhoods

Most Barcelonans' idea of "nightlife" is hopping from bar to bar with a circle of friends, while nibbling tapas and enjoying a variety of drinks (see "Spanish Drinks," page 196). The streets are jammed with people. In general, the weekend progression (Thu-Sat) goes like this: dinner at 22:00 or 23:00; a music club for cocktails and DJ music from midnight; then, at about 2:00 or 3:00 in the morning, hit the discos until dawn. To join this social ritual, here are a few neighborhoods in particular to seek out, and some tips for each one.

El Born

Passeig del Born, a broad park-like strip stretching from the Church of Santa Maria del Mar up to the old market hall, is lined with inviting bars and nightspots. The side streets also teem with options. Wander to find a place that appeals to you.

Right on Passeig del Born is **Miramelindo,** a local favorite—mellow yet convivial, with two floors of woody ambience and a minty aura from all those mojitos the bartenders are mashing up (Passeig del Born 15). **Palau Dalmases,** in the atmospheric courtyard of an old palace, slings cocktails when it's not hosting flamenco shows. **La Vinya del Senyor,** one of my recommended eateries, is a fine place for a good glass of wine out on the square in front of the Church of Santa Maria del Mar.

The **Aire de Barcelona** Arab-style thermal baths, across from Citadel Park, are open late. Recently renovated with great style, these are ideal for recovering from a busy day of sightseeing (€28 per person for 1.5 hours, massage also possible; reserve ahead—a week ahead for weeknights, a month ahead for weekends; Passeig Picasso 22, tel. 902-555-789, www.airedebarcelona.com).

Plaça Reial (in the Barri Gòtic) and Nearby

This elegant-feeling square, just off the Ramblas, has a trendy charm. It bustles with popular bars and restaurants offering inflated prices at pleasant outdoor tables. While not a great place to eat (the only one worth seriously considering for a meal is the recommended **Les Quinze Nits**), this is a great place to sip a before- or after-dinner drink. **Ocaña Bar,** at #13, has a dilapidated-mod interior, a see-through industrial kitchen, and rickety-chic second-hand tables out on the square (€3-9 tapas, reasonable drinks, open nightly). Or there's always the student option: Buy a cheap €1 beer from a convenience store (you'll find several just off the square, including a few along Carrer dels Escudellers, just south of Plaça Reial), then grab a free spot on the square, either sitting on one of the few fixed chairs, perched along the rim of the fountain, or simply leaning up against a palm tree.

Plaça Reial is also home to the **Tarantos** flamenco bar and **Jamboree** jazz club (both described earlier). You'll find a variety of nightclubs here, including the hip **Sidecar Factory Club** (at #7, often live music, www.sidecarfactoryclub.com) and the hidden, mellow, pipe-happy **Barcelona Pipa Club** (at #3—find and ring the doorbell to get inside, this member's club opens to the public around 22:00, www.bpipaclub.com).

The street running just south of Plaça Reial, **Carrer de Escudellers,** is a significantly rougher scene, with a few trendy options mixed in with several sketchy dives.

Carrer de la Mercè: This lower Barri Gòtic street, which runs parallel to the harbor one block inland, is lined with more than its share of salty local tapas bars (described on page 206 of the Eating in Barcelona chapter). But mixed in are several trendy watering holes. The next street up, **Carrer Ample,** has a similar scene.

Barceloneta

A broad beach stretches for miles from the former fishermen's quarter at Barceloneta to the Fòrum. Every 100 yards or so is a *chiringuito*—a shack selling drinks and light snacks. Originally these sold seafood, but now they keep locals and tourists well-lubricated. It's a very fun, lively scene on a balmy summer evening and a nice way to escape the claustrophobic confines of the city to enjoy some sea air and the day's final sun rays.

Barceloneta itself has a broad promenade facing the harbor, lined with interchangeable seafood restaurants. But the best beach experience is beyond the tip of Barceloneta. From here, a double-decker boardwalk runs the length of the beach, with a cool walkway up above and a series of fine seafood restaurants with romantic candlelit beachfront seating tucked down below. Pricey but well-regarded places featuring high-quality Catalan cuisine are **Agua, Ca la Nuri,** and **Arenal.** Farther along, **Carpe Diem Lounge Club** (a.k.a. CDLC) is a fun Turkish-themed chill-out bar with cozy lounging sofas—ideal for a post-dinner drink; later, it becomes an edgier disco.

Nightclubs: Around Frank Gehry's glittering fish sculpture (at the former Olympic village) are several popular discos, crowded with partying twentysomethings. These get going extremely late—the kind of place where you have to be on the list, look good, and pay upwards of €10 for a drink. One of the most famous—and exclusive—is **Opium Mar,** a haunt of Barça footballers and other celebrities (www.opiummar.com). Beyond the beach, at the Olympic port, you'll find more bars with chill-out music (which later turn into livelier discos).

Montjuïc

With a little hustle, in summer it's possible to string together a fun evening of memorable views from the Monjuïc hilltop. Start with sweeping city vistas as you ride the Aeri del Port cable car (catch it at the tip of the Barceloneta peninsula; see page 221) up to the park's Miramar viewpoint. From there, head up to Montjuïc Castle on foot for more breathtaking views. Finally, wind your way around the hilltop to the Catalan Art Museum and reward yourself with a drink at its terrace café—a prime spot for taking in the Magic Fountains show, which makes a dramatic splash every half-hour (Thu-Sun nights in summer; see page 75). For a splurge, consider dinner at the museum's Òleum Restaurant (open until 23:30), which also overlooks the fountains and the entire 1929 Expo site.

Each July the normally peaceful hill pulls an all-nighter for the Montjuïc de Nit festival. Montjuïc Castle, Fundació Joan Miró, and the park's botanic garden are among the venues hosting this night of free musical and other performances (mid-July; see page 33 for details).

The Eixample

Barcelona's upscale uptown isn't quite as lively or funky as some other neighborhoods, but a few streets have some fine watering holes. Walk along the inviting, park-like **Rambla de Catalunya,** or a couple of blocks over, along **Carrer d'Enric Granados** and **Carrer d'Aribau** (near the epicenter of the Eixample's gay community); all of these streets are speckled with cocktail bars offering breezy outdoor seating. In the opposite direction (east of Passeig de Gràcia), **Bar Dow Jones**—popular with the American expat student crowd—has a clever gimmick: Drink prices rise and fall like the stock market (Carrer del Bruc 97).

Gràcia

A bit farther flung, and more local-feeling because of it, the Gràcia neighborhood sits between the Eixample and Park Güell. Known for its design schools and its international art-house cinema (the Cines Verdi, www.cines-verdi.com/barcelona), it's the unpretentious but intellectual corner of town. Though it lacks the twisty-Gothic-lanes ambience of the Old City, Gràcia feels more like a small town (which it was, before it was swallowed up by an expanding Barcelona). It's popular with students—both local and international—and can be a bit rowdy. The district is even more vibrant in August, when it hosts the Festa Major de Gràcia, with street music everywhere (see page 33).

The most interesting stretch of Gràcia is squeezed between

NIGHTLIFE

two Metro stops: Fontana, on the L3 (green) line; and Joanic, on the L4 (yellow) line. Here's a handy bar-crawl route: From the Fontana stop, exit and turn left, heading down the shop-lined Carrer d'Astúries. After crossing the busy Carrer del Torrent de l'Olla, keep going straight two short blocks to **Carrer de Verdi.** You'll find several nightspots up and down this street, and a block over, at **Plaça de la Virreina** (where several places fill the square in front of the church with outdoor tables). From there you can head down Carrer de Torrijos, with more options— including **Café Salambo,** with an Art Deco vibe (at #51, www. cafesalambo.com). A right turn at Carrer de Ramón y Cajal leads you (in three blocks) to your grand finale, **Plaça del Sol,** the epicenter of Gràcia nightlife.

Tibidabo

Many people enjoy heading up to Tibidabo for drinks with a great view—ideal for watching the sunset. At the top of the Tramvía Blau (blue tram)—which is also the bottom of the Tibidabo funicular—you'll find two places: **Mirabé** (nightly from 19:00, Manuel Arnús 2, www.mirabe.com) and **Mirablau** (Plaça Dr. Andreu, www.mirablaubcn.com). While this probably isn't worth the long trip from downtown (unless you're a panorama seeker), it's handy to combine with a visit to Tibidabo or Park Güell. Come here for a pricey drink with a view—not for dinner.

BARCELONA CONNECTIONS

This chapter covers Barcelona's airports, main train station, cruise port, and main bus station.

I don't advise driving in Barcelona—thanks to its excellent public transportation and taxis, you won't need a car here, and the parking fees are outrageously expensive (for example, the lot behind La Boqueria Market charges upward of €25/day).

By Plane

Most flights use Barcelona's **El Prat de Llobregat Airport;** a few budget flights use a smaller airstrip 60 miles away, called **Girona–Costa Brava Airport.** Information on both airports can be found below and on the official Spanish airport website, www.aena-aeropuertos.es. For information on cheap flights, see page 238.

El Prat de Llobregat Airport

Barcelona's primary airport is eight miles southwest of town (airport code: BCN, info tel. 913-211-000). It has two large terminals, linked by shuttle buses. Terminal 1 serves Air France, Air Europa, American, British Airways, Delta, Iberia, Lufthansa, United, US Airways, Vueling, and others. EasyJet and minor airlines use the older Terminal 2, which is divided into sections A, B, and C.

Terminals 1 and 2B each have a TI—and along with 2A—also have a post office, a pharmacy, a left-luggage office, plenty of good cafeterias in the gate areas, and ATMs (at Terminal 1, avoid the gimmicky machines before the baggage carousels; instead, use the bank-affiliated ATMs at the far-left end of the arrivals hall as you face the street).

Getting Between the Airport and Downtown

To get downtown cheaply and quickly, take the bus or train (about 30 minutes on either).

By Bus: The Aerobus (#A1 and #A2, corresponding with Terminals 1 and 2) stops immediately outside the arrivals lobby of both terminals (and in each section of Terminal 2). In about 30 minutes, it takes you to downtown, where it makes several stops, including Plaça d'Espanya and Plaça de Catalunya—near many of my recommended hotels (departs every 5 minutes, from airport 6:00-1:00 in the morning, from downtown 5:30-24:15, €5.65 one-way, €9.75 round-trip, buy ticket from machine or from driver, tel. 934-156-020). The line to board the bus can be very long, but—thanks to the high frequency of buses—it moves fast.

By Train: The RENFE train (on the Rodalies R2 Sud line) leaves from Terminal 2 and involves more walking. Head down the long orange-roofed overpass between sections A and B to reach the station (2/hour at about :08 and :38 past the hour, 20 minutes to Sants Station, 25 minutes to Passeig de Gràcia Station—near Plaça de Catalunya and many recommended hotels, 30 minutes to França Station; €3 or covered by T10 Card—described on page 34—which you can purchase at automated machines at the airport train station). Long-term plans call for the RENFE train and eventually the AVE to be extended to Terminal 1, and for the Metro's L9 (orange) line to be extended to both Terminals 1 and 2. Stay tuned.

By Taxi: A taxi between the airport and downtown costs about €30—about €25 on the meter plus a €3.10 airport supplement and fee of €1 per bag. For good service, add up to a 10 percent tip.

Girona–Costa Brava Airport

Some budget airlines, including Ryanair, use this airport, located 60 miles north of Barcelona near Girona (airport code: GRO, tel. 972-186-600). Ryanair runs a **bus,** operated by Sagalés, to the Barcelona Nord bus station (€15, departs airport about 20-25 minutes after each arriving flight, 1.25 hours, tel. 902-361-550, www.sagales.com). Or you could go to Girona by Sagalés bus (hourly, 25 minutes, €2.50) or taxi (€25), then catch a train to Barcelona (at least hourly, 1.25 hours, €15-20). A taxi between the Girona airport and Barcelona costs at least €120.

Cheap Flights

Check the reasonable flights from Barcelona to Sevilla or Madrid. **Vueling** is Iberia's most popular discount airline; for example, Barcelona-Madrid flights cost as little as €40 if booked well in advance (tel. 902-333-933, www.vueling.com). These two airlines typically offer €80 flights to Madrid: **Iberia** (tel. 902-400-500, www.iberia.com) and **Air Europa** (tel. 902-401-501 or 932-983-907, www.aireuropa.com).

For flights to other parts of Europe, try **easyJet** (tel. 902-299-992, www.easyjet.com), **Ryanair** (www.ryanair.com), or **British Airways** (tel. 902-111-333, www.britishairways.com).

Search Engines: The best comparison search engine for both international and intra-European flights is www.kayak.com. For inexpensive flights within Europe, try www.skyscanner.com or www.hipmunk.com. If you're not sure who flies to your destination, check its airport's website for a list of carriers.

Buyer Beware: There are potential drawbacks to flying on the cheap—nonrefundable and nonchangeable tickets, minimal or nonexistent customer service, and stingy baggage allowances with steep overage fees. If you're traveling with lots of luggage, a cheap flight can quickly become a bad deal. To avoid unpleasant surprises, read the small print before you book.

By Train

Virtually all trains end up at Barcelona's **Sants train station,** west of the Old City (described next). AVE trains from Madrid go only to Sants Station and the new **Sagrera Station,** far to the northeast. But many other trains also pass through other stations en route, such as **França Station** (between the El Born and Barceloneta neighborhoods), or the downtown **Passeig de Gràcia** or **Plaça de Catalunya** stations (which are also Metro stops—and  very close to most of my recommended hotels). Figure out which stations your train stops at (ask the conductor), and get off at the one most convenient to your hotel.

If departing from the downtown Passeig de Gràcia Station, where three Metro lines converge with the rail line, you might find the underground tunnels confusing. You can't access the RENFE station directly from some of the entrances. Use the northern entrances to this station (rather than the southern "Consell de Cent" entrance, which is closest to Plaça de Catalunya).

Sants Train Station

Barcelona's main station is vast and sprawling, but manageable. In the large lobby area under the upper tracks, you'll find a TI;

ATMs; a world of handy shops and eateries; and, in the side concourse, a classy, quiet Sala Club lounge for travelers with first-class reservations (TV, free drinks, study tables, and coffee bar). Sants is the only Barcelona station with luggage storage (small bag-€3.50/ day, big bag-€5/day, requires security check, daily 5:30-23:00, follow signs to *consigna*, at far end of hallway from tracks 13-14).

In the vast main hall is a very long wall of ticket windows. Figure out which one you need before you wait in line (all are labeled in English). Generally, windows 1-7 (on the left) are for regional and *media distancia* trains, such as to Sitges. Windows 8-21 handle advance tickets for long-distance *(larga distancia)* trains beyond Catalunya. The information windows are 23-26; go here first if you're not sure which window you want. Windows 27-31 sell tickets for long-distance trains leaving today. The information booths by windows 1 and 21 can help you find the right line and can provide some train schedules. Scattered nearby are two types of automated train-ticket vending machines: The red-and-gray machines sell tickets for regional and *media distancia* trains within Catalunya; the purple machines are for national RENFE trains, but these don't sell tickets—you can only use them to print out prereserved tickets (if you have a confirmation code).

Getting Downtown: To reach the center of Barcelona, take a train or the Metro. To ride the subway, follow signs for the Metro (red *M*), and hop on the L3 (green) or L5 (blue) line, both of which link to a number of useful points in town, near all of my recommended hotels. To zip downtown even faster (just 5 minutes), you can take any Rodalies de Catalunya suburban train from track 8 (R1, R3, or R4) to Plaça de Catalunya (departs at least every 10 minutes). Purchase tickets for the trains or Metro at touch-screen machines near the tracks (where you can also buy the cost-saving T10 Card, explained on page 34).

Train Connections

Unless otherwise noted, all of these trains depart from Sants Station; however, remember that some trains also stop at other stations more convenient to the downtown tourist zone: França Station, Passeig de Gràcia, or Plaça de Catalunya. Figure out if your train stops at these stations (and board there) to save yourself the trip to Sants.

From Barcelona by Train to Madrid: The AVE train has shaved hours off the journey to Madrid, making it faster than flying (when you consider that you're zipping from downtown to downtown). The train departs at least hourly. The nonstop train is a little more expensive (€130, 2.5 hours) than the slightly slower train that makes a few stops and adds about a half-hour (€110, 3 hours).

Regular reserved AVE tickets can be prepurchased (often with a discount) at www.renfe.com and picked up at the station. If you have a railpass, you'll pay only a reservation fee of €23 for first class, which includes a meal (€10 second class, buy at any train station in Spain). Passholders can't reserve online through RENFE but can make the reservation at www.raileurope.com for delivery before leaving the US ($17 in second class, $40 in first class).

For a cheaper, non-AVE option, there's a slow overnight train to Madrid (9 hours, €45, add *litera* or *couchette* for €13).

From Barcelona by Train to: Sitges (departs from both Passeig de Gràcia and Sants, 4/hour, 40 minutes, €3.60), **Montserrat** (departs from Plaça d'Espanya—*not* from Sants, hourly, 1 hour, €17.10 round-trip, includes cable car or rack train to monastery—see details on page 256), **Figueres** (hourly, 2-2.25 hours; the €14.20 *media distancia* trains are 20 minutes faster than the €10.60 *regional* trains), **Sevilla** (11/day, 5.5-6 hours; plus one overnight train, 13 hours), **Granada** (1/day, 9.5 hours via AVE and Altaria, transfer in Madrid; also 1 night train daily, 10.5 hours), **Salamanca** (8/day, 6-7.5 hours, change in Madrid from Atocha Station to Chamartín Station via Metro or *cercanías* train; also 1/day, change in Zaragoza, 9 hours), **San Sebastián** (2/day, 5.5 hours, €64), **Málaga** (3/day—two fast, 5.5 hours, €145; one slow, 12 hours, €66), **Lisbon** (no direct trains, head to Madrid and then catch night train to Lisbon, 17 hours, about €100—or fly).

From Barcelona by Train to France: To connect into France, you'll have to change trains somewhere (except for the one direct, pricey night train to Paris). Spain's tracks meet France's high-speed TGV line at the **Figueres-Vilafant** Station (2/day from Barcelona, 1.75 hours). For slower but more frequent connections, you can also change in **Cerbère** (2/day from Barcelona, 2.75 hours). Connections include **Nice** (2/day, 10 hours, change in Figueres-Vilafant and Valence; slower and cheaper connections possible with multiple changes including Cerbère), **Avignon** (2/day, 5.75 hours, change in Figueres-Vilafant and Nîmes), **Paris** (2/day, 7.5 hours, change in Figueres-Vilafant, about €140, more connections possible with multiple changes; 1 night train/day, 12.75 hours, about €140 or €50 with railpass, reservation mandatory). Train info: Tel. 902-320-320, www.renfe.com.

By Cruise Ship

Cruise ships arrive in Barcelona at three different ports (all just southwest of the Old City, beneath Montjuïc). If your trip includes cruising beyond Barcelona, consider my guidebook, *Rick Steves' Mediterranean Cruise Ports*.

Most American cruise lines put in at **Moll Adossat/Muelle**

Adosado, a long two miles from the bottom of the Ramblas. This port has four modern, airport-like terminals (lettered A through D); most have a café, shops, and TI kiosk; some have Internet access and other services. Two other terminals are far less commonly used: the **World Trade Center,** just off the southern end of the Ramblas, and **Moll de la Costa,** tucked just beneath Montjuïc (ride the free, private shuttle bus to World Trade Center; from there, it's a short walk or taxi ride to the Columbus Monument).

Getting Downtown: From any of the cruise terminals, it's easy to reach the Ramblas. **Taxis** meet each arriving ship and are waiting as you exit any of the terminal buildings. The short trip into town (i.e., to the bottom of the Ramblas) runs about €10 (the €2.10 cruise-port surcharge is legit). During high season, a ride into town can take longer and cost €10 more. For a one-way journey to other parts of town, expect to pay these fares: to the Picasso Museum or Plaça de Catalunya—€15; to the Sagrada Família—€20; and to the airport—€35-40.

You can also take a **shuttle bus** from Moll Adossat/Muelle Adosado to the Columbus Monument (at the bottom of the Ramblas), then walk or hop on public transportation to various sights. The shuttle bus departs from the parking lot in front of the terminal—follow *Public Bus* signs (*lanzadera*, #T3, a.k.a. Portbús, €3 round-trip, €2 one-way, buses leave every 20-30 minutes, timed to cruise ship arrival, tel. 932-986-000). Pay careful attention to where they drop you off if you want to catch the return bus later.

By Bus

Most buses depart from the Nord bus station at the Arc de Triomf Metro stop, but confirm when researching schedules. Destinations include **Madrid** (nearly hourly, 8 hours, €30—a fraction of the AVE train price, bus info tel. 902-260-606, Alsa bus company tel. 902-422-242), **Salamanca** (2/day, 11 hours, €56, Alsa buses), and **Cadaqués** (5/day, 2.75 hours, €24). Sarfa buses serve all the **coastal resorts** (tel. 902-302-025, www.sarfa.com). One bus departs daily for the Montserrat monastery, leaving from Carrer de Viriat near Sants train station (see page 256). For bus schedules, see www.barcelonanord.com.

DAY TRIPS from BARCELONA

*Figueres • Cadaqués •
Sitges • Montserrat*

Four fine sights are day-trip temptations from Barcelona.

Fans of Surrealism can combine a fantasy in Dalí-land by stopping at the Dalí Theater-Museum in Figueres (about two hours from Barcelona) and the Salvador Dalí House (requires reservations) in the sleepy port-town getaway of Cadaqués (pictured above, an hour from Figueres). To really relax, consider spending a day or two in Cadaqués.

For the consummate day at the beach, head 45 minutes south of Barcelona to the charming and free-spirited resort town of Sitges.

Pilgrims with hiking boots head 1.5 hours into the mountains for the most sacred spot in Catalunya: Montserrat.

Figueres

The town of Figueres (feeg-YEHR-ehs)—conveniently connected by train to Barcelona—is of sightseeing interest only for its Salvador Dalí Theater-Museum. In fact, the entire town seems Dalí-dominated.

Getting to Figueres

Figueres is an easy day trip from Barcelona, or a handy stopover en route to France. It's cheap and convenient to take a regional train to Figueres Station—they depart from Barcelona's Sants Station or from the RENFE station at Metro: Passeig de Gràcia (hourly, 2-2.25 hours; €14.20 *media distancia* trains are 20 minutes faster than €10.60 *regional* trains). High-speed trains between Barcelona and France stop instead at the newer Figueres-Vilafant Station, on

Near Barcelona

FRANCE

To Carcassonne, Avignon & Paris

Collioure
Cerbère
Portbou

Pyrenees Mountains

Figueres

Port Lligat
Cadaqués

SPAIN

Púbol

CATALUNYA

Girona

Girona-Costa Brava

Costa Brava

Vic

Roses

- - - Rail
- - - Bus

Monistrol de Montserrat

Maçanet

Tossa de Mar
Lloret de Mar
Blanes

Montserrat-Aeri

MONTSERRAT MONASTERY

Montcada

Mataró

Mediterranean Sea

Vilafranca del Penedès

El Prat de Llobregat

Barcelona

Sitges

To Tarragona, Valencia & Madrid

Costa Daurada

10 Kilometers
10 Miles

N

Barcelona
SPAIN

the other side of town. But even if you're visiting Figueres on your way to Paris, it's best to take the slower, regional train to Figueres Station in the morning, visit the museum, then go back to the same station to catch the night train to Paris. For bus connections to Cadaqués, see page 249.

Arrival in Figueres: From Figueres Station, simply follow *Museu Dalí* signs (and the crowds) for the 15-minute walk to the museum.

Sights in Figueres

▲▲▲Dalí Theater-Museum (Teatre-Museu Dalí)

This is *the* essential Dalí sight—and, if you like Dalí, one of Europe's most enjoyable museums, period. Inaugurated in 1974, the museum is a work of art in itself. Ever the entertainer and promoter, Dalí personally conceptualized, designed, decorated, and painted it to showcase his life's work. The museum fills a former theater and is the artist's mausoleum (his tomb is in the crypt

below center stage). It's also a kind of mausoleum to Dalí's creative spirit.

Dalí had his first public art showing at age 14 here in this building when it was a theater, and he was baptized in the church just across the street. The place was sentimental to him. After the theater was destroyed in the Spanish Civil War, Dalí struck a deal with the mayor: Dalí would rebuild the theater as a museum to his works, Figueres would be put on the sightseeing map...and the money's been flowing in ever since.

DAY TRIPS

Even the building's exterior—painted pink, studded with golden loaves of bread, and topped with monumental eggs and a geodesic dome—exudes Dalí's outrageous public persona.

Cost and Hours: €12; July-Sept daily 9:00-20:00; March-June and Oct Tue-Sun 9:30-18:00, closed Mon; Nov-Feb Tue-Sun 10:30-18:00, closed Mon; last entry 45 minutes before closing, tel. 972-677-500, www.salvador-dali.org. No flash photography. The free bag check has your belongings waiting for you at the exit.

Coin-Op Tip: Much of Dalí's art is movable and coin-operated—bring a few €0.20 and €1 coins.

➋ Self-Guided Tour: The museum has two parts: the theater-mausoleum and the "Dalí's Jewels" exhibit in an adjacent building. There's no logical order for a visit (that would be un-Surrealistic), and the museum can be mobbed at times. Naturally, no audioguide is available. Dalí said there are two kinds of visitors: those who don't need a description, and those who aren't worth a description. At the risk of offending Dalí, I've written this loose commentary to attach some meaning to your visit.

Stepping through or around the courtyard, go into the **theater** (with its audience of statues) and face the stage—and Dalí's unmarked crypt. You know how you can never get a cab when it's raining? Pop a coin into Dalí's personal 1941 Cadillac, and it rains inside the car. Look above, atop the tire tower: That's the boat Dalí enjoyed with his soul mate, Gala—his emotional life preserver, who kept him from going overboard. When she died, so did he (for his last seven years). Blue tears made of condoms drip below the boat.

Up on the **stage,** squint at the big digital Abraham Lincoln, and president #16 comes into focus. Approach the painting to find that Abe's facial cheeks are Gala's butt cheeks. Under the painting, a door leads to the **Treasures Room,** with the greatest collection of original Dalí oil paintings in the museum. (Many of

Salvador Dalí
(1904-1989)

When Salvador Dalí was asked, "Are you on drugs?" he replied, "I am the drug...take me."

Labeled by various critics as sick, greedy, paranoid, arrogant, and a clown, Dalí produced some of the most thought-provoking and trailblazing art of the 20th century. His erotic, violent, disjointed imagery continues to disturb and intrigue today. Born in Figueres to a well-off family, Dalí showed talent early. He was expelled from Madrid's prestigious art school—twice—but formed longtime friendships with playwright Federico García Lorca and filmmaker Luis Buñuel.

After a breakthrough art exhibit in Barcelona in 1925, Dalí moved to Paris. He hobnobbed with fellow Spaniards Pablo Picasso and Joan Miró, along with a group of artists exploring Sigmund Freud's theory that we all have a hidden part of our mind, the unconscious "id," that surfaces when we dream. Dalí became the best-known spokesman for this group of Surrealists, channeling his id to create photorealistic dream images (melting watches, burning giraffes) set in bizarre dreamscapes.

His life changed forever in 1929, when he met an older, married Russian woman named Gala who would become his wife, muse, model, manager, and emotional compass. Dalí's popularity spread to the US, where he (and Gala) weathered the WWII years.

the artworks on the walls are prints.) You'll see Cubist visions of Cadaqués and dreamy portraits of Gala. Crutches—a recurring Dalí theme—represent Gala, who kept him supported whenever a meltdown threatened.

The famous **Homage to Mae West room** is a tribute to the sultry seductress. Dalí loved her attitude. Saying things like, "Why marry and make one man unhappy, when you can stay

single and make so many so happy?" Mae West was to conventional morality what Dalí was to conventional art. Climb to the vantage point where the sofa lips, fireplace nostrils, painting eyes, and drapery hair come together to make the face of Mae West.

In his prime, Dalí's work became less Surrealist and more classical, influenced by past masters of painted realism (Velázquez, Raphael, Ingres) and by his own study of history, science, and religion. He produced large-scale paintings of historical events (such as Columbus discovering America, or the Last Supper) that were collages of realistic scenes floating in a surrealistic landscape, peppered with thought-provoking symbols.

Dalí—an extremely capable technician—mastered many media, including film. *An Andalusian Dog* (*Un Chien Andalou*, 1929, with Luis Buñuel) was a cutting-edge montage of disturbing, eyeball-slicing images. He designed Alfred Hitchcock's big-eye backdrop for the dream sequence of *Spellbound* (1945). He made jewels for the rich and clothes for Coco Chanel, wrote a novel and an autobiography, and pioneered what would come to be called "installations." He also helped develop "performance art" by showing up at an opening in a diver's suit or by playing the role he projected to the media—a super-confident, waxed-mustached artistic genius.

In later years, Dalí's over-the-top public image contrasted with his ever-growing illness, depression, and isolation. He endured the scandal of a dealer overselling "limited editions" of his work. When Gala died in 1982, Dalí retreated to his hometown, living his last days in the Torre Galatea of the Theater-Museum complex, where he died of heart failure.

Dalí's legacy as an artist includes his self-marketing persona, his exceptional ability to draw, his provocative pairing of symbols, and his sheer creative drive.

Dalí's art can be playful, but also disturbing. He was passionate about the dark side of things, but with Gala for balance, he managed never to go off the deep end. Unlike Pablo Casals (the Catalan cellist) and Pablo Picasso (another local artist), Dalí didn't go into exile under Franco's dictatorship. Pragmatically, he accepted both Franco and the Church, and was supported by the dictator. Apart from the occasional *sardana* dance (see sidebar on page 50), you won't find a hint of politics in Dalí's art.

Wander around. You can spend hours here, wondering, is it real or not real? Am I crazy, or is it you? Beethoven is painted with squid ink applied by a shoe on a stormy night. Jesus is made with candle smoke and an eraser. It's fun to see the Dalí-ization of art classics. Dalí, like so many modern artists, was inspired by the masters—especially Velázquez.

The former theater's **smoking lounge** is a highlight, displaying portraits of Gala and Dalí (with a big eye, big ear, and a dark side) bookending a Roman candle of creativity. The fascinating ceiling painting shows the feet of Gala and Dalí as they bridge earth and the heavens. Dalí's drawers are wide open and empty, indicating that he gave everything to his art.

Leaving the theater, keep your ticket and pop into the adjacent **"Dalí's Jewels"** exhibit. It shows sketches and paintings of jewelry Dalí designed, and the actual pieces jewelers made from those surreal visions: a mouth full of pearly whites, a golden finger corset, a fountain of diamonds, and the breathing heart. Explore the ambiguous perception worked into the big painting titled *Apotheosis of the Dollar.*

Cadaqués

Since the late 1800s, Cadaqués (kah-dah-KEHS) has served as a haven for intellectuals and artists alike. The fishing village's craggy coastline, sun-drenched colors, and laid-back lifestyle inspired Fauvists such as Henri Matisse and Surrealists such as René Magritte, Marcel Duchamp, and Federico García Lorca. Even Picasso, drawn to this enchanting coastal haunt, painted some of his Cubist works here.

Salvador Dalí, raised in nearby Figueres, brought international fame to this sleepy Catalan port in the 1920s. As a kid, Dalí spent summers here in the family cabin, where he was inspired by the rocky landscape that would later be the backdrop for many Surrealist canvases. In 1929, he met his future wife, Gala, in Cadaqués. Together they converted a fisherman's home in nearby Port Lligat into their semi-permanent residence, dividing their time between New York, Paris, and Cadaqués. And it was here that Dalí did his best work.

In spite of its fame, Cadaqués is mellow and feels like it's off the beaten path. If you want a peaceful beach-town escape near Barcelona, this is a good place. From the moment you descend into the town, taking in whitewashed buildings and deep blue waters, you'll be struck by the port's tranquility and beauty. Join the locals playing chess or cards at the cavernous Casino Coffee House (harborfront, with games and Internet access). Have a glass of *vino tinto* or *cremat* (a traditional rum-and-coffee drink served flambé-style) at one of the seaside cafés. Savor the lapping waves, brilliant sun, and gentle breeze. And, for sightseeing, the reason to come to Cadaqués is the Salvador Dalí House, a 20-minute walk from the town center at Port Lligat.

Getting to Cadaqués

Reaching Cadaqués is tough without a car. There are no trains and only a few buses a day.

By Car: It's a twisty drive from Figueres (figure 45-60 minutes). In Cadaqués, drivers should park in the big lot just above the city—don't try to park near the harborfront. To reach the **Salvador Dalí House,** follow signs near Cadaqués to Port Lligat (easy parking).

By Bus: Sarfa buses serve Cadaqués from **Figueres** (3/day, 1 hour, €6) and from **Barcelona** (5/day, 2.75 hours, €24). Bus info: Barcelona toll tel. 902-302-025, Cadaqués tel. 972-258-713, Figueres tel. 972-674-298, www.sarfa.com.

DAY TRIPS

Tourist Information

The TI is at Carrer Cotxe 2 (July-Sept Mon-Sat 9:00-21:00, Sun 10:00-13:00 & 17:00-20:00, shorter hours off-season, plus closed for lunch, tel. 972-258-315, www.visitcadaques.org).

Sights near Cadaqués

In Port Lligat

▲▲▲**Salvador Dalí House (Casa Museu Salvador Dalí)**—
Once Dalí's home, this house gives fans a chance to explore his

labyrinthine compound. This is the best artist's house I've toured in Europe. It shows how a home can really reflect the creative spirit of an artistic genius and his muse. The ambience, both inside and out, is perfect for a Surrealist hanging out with his creative playmate. The bay is ringed by sleepy islands. Fishing boats are jumbled on the beach. After the fishermen painted their boats, Dalí asked them to clean their brushes on his door—creating an abstract work of art he adored (which you'll see as you line up to get your ticket).

Cost and Hours: €11; mid-June-mid-Sept daily 9:30-21:00; mid-Feb-mid-June and mid-Sept-early Jan Tue-Sun 10:30-18:00, closed Mon; closed early Jan-mid-Feb. Last tour departs 50 minutes before closing. No bags of any kind are allowed in the house; the baggage check is free.

Reservations: You must reserve in advance—call, use the website, or send email with specifics on the day and time you want to visit (tel. 972-251-015, www.salvador-dali.org, pllgrups @fundaciodali.org). In summer, book a week in advance. You must arrive 30 minutes early to pick up your ticket, or they'll sell it.

Getting There: By car, follow signs to Port Lligat. Parking is free nearby. There are no buses or taxis. On foot from Cadaqués, the house is a 20-minute, one-mile walk over the hill to Port Lligat. (The path, which cuts across the isthmus, is much shorter than the road.)

Visiting the House: Only 8-10 people are allowed in (no large groups) every 10 minutes. Once inside, there are five sections, each with a guard who gives you a brief explanation in English, and then turns you loose for a few minutes. The entire visit takes 50 minutes. Before your tour, enjoy the 15-minute video that plays in the waiting lounge (with walls covered in Dalí media coverage) just across the lane from the house.

The interior is left almost precisely as it was in 1982, when Gala died and Dalí moved out. See Dalí's studio (the clever easel cranks up and down to allow the artist to paint while seated, as he did eight hours a day); the bohemian-yet-divine living room (complete with a mirror to reflect the sunrise onto their bed each morning); the phallic-shaped swimming pool, which was the scene of orgiastic parties; and the painter's study (with his favorite mustaches all lined up). Like Dalí's art, his home is offbeat, provocative, and fun.

Sleeping in Cadaqués

$$ Hotel Llané Petit, with 32 spacious rooms (half with view balconies), is a small resort-like hotel with its own little beach, a 10-minute walk south of the town center (Db-€124 mid-July-Aug, €94 in shoulder season, €74 in winter, seaview rooms-about €30 more, breakfast-€12, air-con, elevator, Dr. Bartomeus 37, tel. 972-251-020, fax 972-258-778, www.llanepetit.com, info@llanepetit

---

Sleep Code

(€1 = about $1.30, country code: 34)

S = Single, **D** = Double/Twin, **T** = Triple, **Q** = Quad, **b** = bathroom, **s** = shower only. Unless otherwise noted, credit cards are accepted and English is spoken.

To help you easily sort through these listings, I've divided the accommodations into two categories, based on the price for a standard double room with bath (during high season):

$$ Higher Priced—Most rooms €95 or more.
$ Lower Priced—Most rooms less than €95.

Prices can change without notice; verify the hotel's current rates online or by email.

.com). Reserve direct with this book for a free breakfast (not valid on weekends in high season and long weekends in shoulder season).

$ Hotel Nou Estrelles is a big concrete exercise in efficient, economic comfort. Facing the bus stop a few blocks in from the waterfront, this family-run hotel offers 15 rooms at a great value (Db-€85-90 in high season, €60-74 in shoulder season, €55 in winter, extra bed-€10-15, breakfast-€7, air-con, elevator, Carrer Sant Vicens, tel. 972-259-100, www.hotelnouestrelles.com, reservas @hotelnouestrelles.com, Emma).

$ Hostal Marina is a cheap, low-energy place, with 27 rooms and a great location a block from the harborfront main square (high season: D-€55, Db-€90; low season: D-€40, Db-€50-60; balcony rooms-€10 extra, no breakfast, no elevator, Riera 3, tel. 972-159-091).

Eating in Cadaqués

There are plenty of eateries along the beach. A lane called Carrer Miguel Rosset (across from Hotel La Residencia) also has several places worth considering. At **Casa Anita,** you'll sit with others around a big table and enjoy house specialties such as *calamares a la plancha* (grilled squid) and homemade *helado* (ice cream). Finish your meal with a glass of sweet Muscatel (Calle Miquel Rosset 16, tel. 972-258-471, Joan and family).

Sitges

Sitges (SEE-juhz) is one of Catalunya's most popular resort towns. Because the town beautifully mingles sea and light, it's long been

an artists' colony. Here you can still feel the soul of the Modernistas...in the architecture, the museums, the salty sea breeze, and the relaxed rhythm of life.

Today's Sitges is a world-renowned vacation destination among the gay community. Despite its jet-set status, the Old Town has managed to retain its charm. With a much slower pulse than Barcelona, Sitges is an enjoyable break from the big city.

If you visit during one of Sitges' two big **festivals** (St. Bartholomew on Aug 24 and St. Tecla on Sept 23), you may see teams of *castellers* competing to build human pyramids.

Getting to Sitges

Southbound **trains** depart Barcelona from the Sants and Passeig de Gràcia stations (take Rodalies train on the dark-green line R2 toward Sant Vincenç de Calders, 4/hour, 40 minutes). A direct **bus** runs to Sitges from downtown Barcelona and the airport (4/day, www.monbus.cat).

Orientation to Sitges

Tourist Information

The TI is a couple of blocks northwest of the train station (mid-June–mid-Sept Mon-Sat 10:00-20:00, Sun 10:00-14:00; mid-Sept–mid-June Mon-Sat 10:00-14:00 & 16:00-18:30, Sun 10:00-14:00, Sínia Morera 1, tel. 938-944-251, www.sitgestur.cat). Pick up the good map (with info on sights on the back) and brochures for museums that interest you. The TI can also help you find a room.

Arrival in Sitges

From the train station, exit straight ahead (past a TI kiosk—open in summer) and walk down Carrer Francesc Gumà. When it dead-ends, continue right onto Carrer de Jesús, which takes you to the town's tiny main square, Plaça del Cap de la Villa. (Keep an eye out for directional signs.) From here, turn right down Carrer Major ("Main Street"), which leads you past the old market hall (now an art gallery) and the town hall, to a beautiful terrace next to the main church. Poke into the Old Town or take the grand staircase down to the beach promenade.

Sights in Sitges

Sitges basically has two attractions: its tight-and-tiny Old Town (with a few good museums) and its long, luxurious beaches.

Old Town—Take time to explore the Old Town's narrow streets.

They're crammed with cafés, boutiques, and all the resort staples.

The focal point, on the waterfront, is the 17th-century Baroque-style **Sant Bartomeu i Santa Tecla Church.** The terrace in front of the church will help you get the lay of the land.

As an art town, Sitges has seen its share of creative people—some of whom have left their mark in the form of appealing museums. Walking along the water behind the church, you'll find two of the town's three museums, which unfortunately will likely be closed for the next couple of years. When open, the **Museu Maricel** displays the eclectic artwork of a local collector, including some Modernista works, pieces by Sitges artists, and a collection of maritime-themed works. The **Museu Cau Ferrat** bills itself as a "temple of art," as collected by local intellectual Santiago Rusiñol. In addition to paintings and drawings, there's ironwork, glass, and ceramics. Also on this square, you'll see **Palau Maricel**—a sumptuous old mansion that's sometimes open to the public for concerts in the summer (ask at TI). The third museum, which will remain open during the closure of the first two, is the **Museu Romàntic.** Offering a look at 19th-century bourgeois lifestyles in an elegant mansion, it's a few blocks up (one block west of main square: Head out of the square on the main pedestrian street, then take the first right turn, to Sant Gaudenci 1). Inside, amid gilded hallways, you'll find a collection of more than 400 dolls (€3.50; July-Sept Tue-Sat 9:30-14:00 & 16:00-19:00, Sun 10:00-15:00; Oct-June Tue-Sat 9:30-14:00 & 15:30-18:30, Sun 10:00-15:00; closed Mon year-round; tel. 938-942-969).

Beaches—Nine beaches, separated by breakwaters, extend about a mile southward from town. Stroll down the seaside promenade, which stretches from the town to the end of the beaches. Anyone can enjoy the sun, sea, and sand; or you can rent a beach chair to relax like a pro. The crowds thin out about halfway down, and the last three beaches are more intimate and cove-like. Along the way, restaurants and *chiringuitos* (beachfront bars) serve tapas, paella, and drinks.

If you walk all the way to the end, you can continue inland to enjoy the nicely landscaped **Terramar Gardens** (Jardins de Terramar; free, daily mid-June-mid-Sept 10:30-20:30, mid-Sept-mid-June 9:00-19:00).

Sleeping in Sitges

(€1 = about $1.30, country code: 34)
Because it's an in-demand resort town, hotel values are not much better here than in Barcelona (especially in summer). But if you prefer a swanky beach town to a big city, consider these options. Note that this is a party town, so expect some noise after hours (request a quiet room). I've listed peak-season prices (roughly mid-July-mid-Sept); these drop substantially off-season. The first one is on the beach, whereas the other two are old villas with colorful tile floors a few blocks into town.

$$ Hotel Celimar, with 25 small but modern rooms, occupies a classic Modernista building facing the beach (Db-€130-150, €20 extra for sea view, average price off-season-€90, check website for latest prices, air-con, elevator, free Wi-Fi, Paseo de la Ribera

20, tel. 938-110-170, fax 938-110-403, www.hotelcelimar.com, info @hotelcelimar.com).

$$ Hotel Romàntic is family-run, old-fashioned-elegant, and quirky. Its 78 rooms (including some in the annex, Hotel de la Renaixença) are nothing special, but the whole place feels classic and classy—especially the plush lounge and bar (S-€75, Sb-€85, D-€105, Db-€115, €10 extra for balcony, includes breakfast, no air-con or elevator, free Wi-Fi, Sant Isidre 33, tel. 938-948-375, www .hotelromantic.com, romantic@hotelromantic.com).

$$ El Xalet (as in "Chalet") is of a similar vintage, with a little less style and lower prices. They have 11 rooms in the main hotel and another 12 in their annex, Hotel Noucentista, up the street—both in fine old Modernista buildings (Db-€100, €25 extra for suite, includes breakfast, air-con, free Wi-Fi, Carrer Illa de Cuba 35, tel. 938-110-070, fax 938-945-579, www.elxalet.com, info@elxalet.com).

Montserrat

Montserrat—the "serrated mountain"—rockets dramatically up from the valley floor northwest of Barcelona. With its unique rock

formations, a dramatic mountaintop monastery (also called Montserrat), and spiritual connection with the Catalan people and their struggles, it's a popular day trip. This has been Catalunya's most important pilgrimage site for a thousand years. Hymns explain how the mountain was carved by little angels with golden saws. Geologists blame nature at work.

Once upon a time, there was no mountain. A river flowed here, laying down silt that hardened into sedimentary layers of hard rock. Ten million years ago, the continents shifted, and the land around the rock massif sank, exposing this series of peaks that reach upward to 4,000 feet. Over time, erosion pocked the face with caves and cut vertical grooves near the top, creating the famous serrated look.

The monastery is nestled in the jagged peaks at 2,400 feet, but it seems higher because of the way the rocky massif rises out of nowhere. The air is certainly fresher than in Barcelona. In a quick day trip, you can view the mountain from its base, ride a funicular up to the top of the world, tour the basilica and museum, touch a Black Virgin's orb, hike down to a sacred cave, and listen

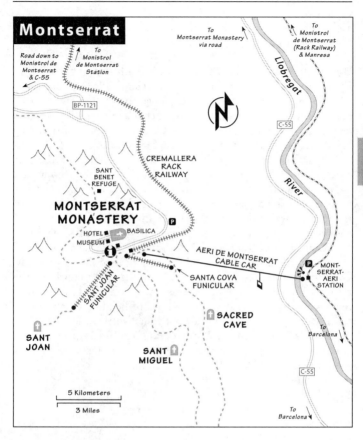

to Gregorian chants by the world's oldest boys' choir.

Montserrat's monastery is Benedictine, and its 30 monks carry on its spiritual tradition. Since 1025, the slogan *"ora et labora"* ("prayer and work") has pretty much summed up life for a monk here.

The Benedictines welcome visitors—both pilgrims and tourists—and offer this travel tip: Please remember that the most important part of your Montserrat visit is not enjoying the architecture, but rather discovering the religious, cultural, historical, social, and environmental values that together symbolically express the life of the Catalan people.

Getting to Montserrat

Barcelona is connected to the valley below Montserrat by a convenient train; from there, a cable car or rack railway (your choice) takes you up to the mountaintop. Both options are similar in cost and take about the same amount of time (hourly trains, 1.5 hours each way from downtown Barcelona to the monastery). Driving or taking the bus round out your choices.

By Train Plus Cable Car or Rack Railway

By Train: Trains leave hourly from Barcelona's Plaça d'Espanya to Montserrat. Take the Metro to Espanya, then follow signs showing a picture of a train to the FGC (Ferrocarrils de la Generalitat de Catalunya) underground station. Once there, look for train line R5 (direction: Manresa, departures at :36 past each hour).

You'll ride about an hour on the train. As you reach the base of the mountain, you have two options: Get out at Montserrat-Aeri for the cable car, or continue another few minutes to the next station—Monistrol de Montserrat (or simply "Monistrol de M.")—for the rack railway. (You'll have to make this decision when you buy your ticket in Barcelona—see "Tickets to Montserrat" sidebar.)

Cable Car or Rack Train? For the sake of scenery and fun, I enjoy the little German-built cable car more than the rack railway. Departures are more frequent (4/hour rather than hourly on the railway), but because the cable car is small, you might have to wait for a while to get on. If you are afraid of heights, take the rack train. Paying the extra €5 to ride both isn't worthwhile.

By Cable Car, at the Montserrat-Aeri Station: Departing the train, follow signs to the cable-car station (covered by your train or combo-ticket; 4/hour, 5-minute  trip, daily March-Oct 9:40-14:00 & 14:35-19:00, Nov-Feb 10:10-14:00 & 14:35-17:45—note the lunch break, www.aeri demontserrat.com). Because the cable car is smaller than the train, don't linger or you might have to wait for the next car. On the way back down, cable cars depart from the monastery every 15 minutes; make sure to give yourself enough time to catch the Barcelona-bound trains leaving at :48 past the hour (don't cut it too close, in case the cable car runs late).

By Rack Railway (Cremallera), at the Monistrol de Montserrat Station: From this station you can catch the Cremallera rack railway up to the monastery (covered by your train or combo-ticket; cheaper off-season, hourly, 20-minute trip, www .cremallerademontserrat.com). On the return trip, this train departs the monastery at :15 past the hour, allowing you to catch the Barcelona-bound train leaving Monistrol de Montserrat at :44 past the hour. The last convenient connection back to Barcelona leaves the monastery at 19:15 (Sat-Sun at 20:15). Confirm the schedule when you arrive, as specific times tend to change year to year. Note

Tickets to Montserrat

Various combo-tickets cover your journey to Montserrat, as well as some of the sights you'll visit there. All begin with the train from Barcelona's Plaça d'Espanya, and include either the cable car or rack railway—you'll have to specify one or the other when you buy the ticket (same price for either option). You can't go one way and come back the other, unless you pay extra (about €5) for the leg that's not included in your ticket.

The basic option is to buy a **train ticket** to Montserrat (€17.10 round-trip, includes the cable car or rack railway to monastery, Eurail pass not valid, tel. 932-051-515, www.fgc .es). Note that if you buy this ticket in Barcelona, then decide at Montserrat that you want to use the funiculars to go higher up the mountain or to the Sacred Cave, you can buy a €9 ticket covering both funiculars at the TI or at either funicular.

If you plan to do some sightseeing once at Montserrat, it makes sense to spend a little more on one of two combo-tickets from the train company: The €24.25 **Trans Montserrat** ticket includes your round-trip Metro ride in Barcelona to and from the train station, the train trip, the cable car or rack railway, unlimited trips on the two funiculars at Montserrat, and entry to the disappointing audiovisual presentation. The €39.95 **Tot Montserrat** ticket includes all of this, plus the good Museum of Montserrat and a self-service lunch (served daily 12:00-16:00). Both tickets are well-explained in the Barcelona TI's online shop (http://bcnshop.barcelonaturisme.com; look for them under the "Near Barcelona" tab).

If you plan to do it all, you'll save several euros with either of these combo-tickets. But during the off-season, ask the TI if one of the funiculars or the cable car is closed for maintenance; if so, the combo-ticket may not be worth it.

You can buy any of these tickets from the automated machines at Barcelona's Plaça d'Espanya Station (tourist officials are standing by in the morning to help you figure it out). To use your included round-trip Metro ride to get *to* the station, buy the ticket in advance at the Plaça de Catalunya TI in Barcelona.

that there is one intermediate stop on this line (Monistrol-Vila, at a large parking garage), but—going in either direction—you want to stay on until the end of the line.

By Car

Once drivers get out of Barcelona (Road A-2, then C-55), it's a short 30-minute drive to the base of the mountain, then a 10-minute series of switchbacks to the actual site (where you can find parking for €5/day). It may be easier to park your car down below and ride the cable car or rack railway up (cable car—€6 one-way, €9 round-trip; rack railway—€5.70 one-way, €9 round-trip, €12.30 version also includes Museum of Montserrat).

By Bus

One **bus** per day connects downtown Barcelona directly to the monastery at Montserrat (departs from Carrer de Viriat near Barcelona's Sants Station daily at 9:15, returns from the monastery to Barcelona at 18:00 June-Sept or at 17:00 Oct-May, €5 each way, 1.25-1.5-hour trip depending on traffic, operated by Autocares Julià, www.autocaresjulia.es). You can also take a four-hour **bus tour** offered by the Barcelona Guide Bureau (€45, leaves Mon-Sat at 15:00 from Plaça Catalunya; see page 39). However, since the other options are scenic, fun, and relatively easy, the only reason to take a bus is to avoid transfers.

Orientation to Montserrat

When you arrive at the base of the mountain, look up the rock face to find the cable-car line, the monastery near the top, and the tiny building midway up (marking the Sacred Cave).

However you make your way up to the Montserrat monastery, it's easy to get oriented once you arrive at the top. Everything is within a few minutes' walk of your entry point. All of the transit options—including the rack railway and cable car—converge at the big train station. Above those are both funicular stations: one up to the ridgetop, the other down to the Sacred Cave trail. Across the street is the TI, and above that (either straight up the stairs, or up the ramp around the left side) is the main square. To the right of the station, a long road leads along the cliff to the parking lot; a humble farmers' market along here sells *mel y mató*, a characteristic Catalan cheese with honey.

Crowd-Beating Tips: Arrive early or late, as tour groups mob the place midday. Crowds are less likely on weekdays and worst on Sundays.

Tourist Information

The square below the basilica houses a helpful TI, right across from the rack railway station (daily from 9:00, closes just after last train heads down—roughly 18:15, or 20:15 on weekdays in July-Aug, tel. 938-777-701, www.montserratvisita.com). Pick up the free map and get your questions answered. A good audioguide, available only at the TI, describes the general site and basilica (€6 includes book; €12 includes entrance to museum, bland audiovisual presentation, and book). If you're a hiker, buy a hiking brochure here. Trails offer spectacular views (on clear days) to the Mediterranean

The History of Montserrat

The first hermit monks built huts at Montserrat around A.D. 900. By 1025, a monastery was founded. The Montserrat Escolania, or Choir School, soon followed, and is considered to be the oldest music school in Europe (they still perform—see "Choir Concert" on page 262).

Legend has it that in medieval times, some shepherd children saw lights and heard songs coming from the mountain. They traced the sounds to a cave (now called the Sacred Cave, or Santa Cova), where they found the Black Virgin statue (La Moreneta), making the monastery a pilgrim magnet.

In 1811 Napoleon's invading French troops destroyed Montserrat's buildings, though the Black Virgin, hidden away by monks, survived. Then, in the 1830s, the Spanish royalty—tired of dealing with pesky religious orders—dissolved the monasteries and convents.

But in the 1850s, the monks returned as part of Catalunya's (and Europe's) renewed Romantic appreciation for all things medieval and nationalistic. (Montserrat's revival coincided with other traditions born out of rejuvenated Catalan pride: the much-loved FC Barcelona soccer team; Barcelona's Palace of Catalan Music; and even the birth of local sparkling wine, *cava*.) Montserrat's basilica and monastery were reconstructed and became, once more, the strongly beating spiritual and cultural heart of the Catalan people.

Then came Francisco Franco, the dictatorial leader who wanted a monolithic Spain. To him Montserrat represented Catalan rebelliousness. During Franco's long rule, from 1939 to 1975, the *sardana* dance was still illegally performed here (but with a different name), and literature was published in the outlawed Catalan language. In 1970, 300 intellectuals demonstrating for more respect for human rights in Spain were locked up in the monastery for several days by Franco's police.

But now Franco is history. The 1990s brought another phase of rebuilding (after a forest fire and rain damage), and the Montserrat community is thriving once again, unafraid to display its pride for the Catalan people, culture, and faith.

and even (on clearer days) to the Pyrenees.

The audiovisual center (upstairs from the TI) provides some cultural and historical perspective—and an entrance to their big gift shop. The lame interactive exhibition—nowhere near as exciting as the mountains and basilica outside—includes computer touch screens and a short 20-minute video in English. Learn about the mountain's history, and get a glimpse into the daily lives of the monastery's resident monks (€2, covered by Trans Montserrat and Tot Montserrat combo-tickets, same hours as TI).

Self-Guided Spin Tour

From the monastery's main square, Plaça de Santa Maria, face the main facade and take this spin tour, moving from right to left: Like a good pilgrim, face Mary, the centerpiece of the facade. Below her to the left is St. Benedict, the sixth-century monk who established the rules that came to govern Montserrat's monastery. St. George, the symbol of Catalunya, is on the right (amid victims of Spain's Civil War).

Five arches line the base of the church. The one on the far right leads pilgrims to the high point of any visit, the Black Virgin (a.k.a. La Moreneta). The center arch leads into the basilica, and the arch second from left directs you to a small votive chapel filled with articles representing prayer requests or thanks.

Left of the basilica, the delicate arches mark the old monks' cloister. Beneath that are four trees planted by the monks, hoping to harvest only their symbolism (palm = martyrdom, cypress = eternal life, olive = peace, and laurel = victory). Next to the trees are a public library and a peaceful reading room. The big archway is the private entrance to the monastery. Then comes the modern hotel and, below that, the modern, white museum. Other buildings provide cells for pilgrims. The Sant Joan funicular lifts hikers up to the trailhead (you can see the tiny building at the top). From there you can take a number of fine hikes (described later). Another funicular station descends to the Sacred Cave. And, finally, five arches separate statues of founders of the great religious orders. Step over to the arches for a commanding view (on a clear day) of the Llobregat River, meandering all the way to the Mediterranean.

Sights in Montserrat

Basilica—Although there's been a church here since the 11th century, the present structure was built in the 1850s, and the facade only dates from 1968. The decor is Neo-Romanesque, so popular with the Romantic artists of the late 19th century. The basilica itself is ringed with interesting chapels, but the focus is on the Black Virgin (La Moreneta) sitting high above the main altar.

Cost and Hours: Free, La Moreneta viewable Mon-Sat 8:00-10:30 & 12:00-18:30, Sun 19:30-20:15; church itself has longer hours and daily services (Mass at 11:00, 12:00, and 19:30; vespers at 18:45); www.abadiamontserrat.net.

Visiting the Basilica: Montserrat's top attraction is **La Moreneta,** the small wood statue of the Black Virgin, discovered in the Sacred Cave in the 12th century. Legend says she was carved by St. Luke (the Gospel writer and supposed artist), brought to Spain by St. Peter, hidden away in the cave during the Moorish invasions, and miraculously discovered by shepherd children. (Carbon dating says she's 800 years old.) While George is the patron saint of Catalunya, La Moreneta is its patroness, having been crowned as such by the pope in 1881. "Moreneta" is usually translated as "black" in English, but the Spanish name actually means "tanned." The statue was originally lighter, but darkened over the centuries from candle smoke, humidity, and the natural aging of its original varnish. Pilgrims shuffle down a long, ornate passage leading alongside the church for their few moments alone with the virgin.

Join the line of pilgrims (along the right side of the church). Though Mary is behind a protective glass case, the royal orb she cra-

dles in her hands is exposed. Pilgrims touch Mary's orb with one hand and hold their other hand up to show that they accept Jesus. Newlyweds in particular seek Mary's blessing.

Immediately after La Moreneta, turn right into the delightful Neo-Romanesque prayer **chapel,** where worshippers sit behind the Virgin and continue to pray. The ceiling, painted in the Modernista style in 1898 by Joan Llimona, shows Jesus and Mary high in heaven. The trail connecting Catalunya with heaven seems to lead through these serrated mountains. The figures depicted lower are people symbolizing Catalan history and culture.

You'll leave by walking along the **Ave Maria Path** (along the outside of the church), which thoughtfully integrates nature and the basilica. Thousands of colorful votive candles are all busy helping the devout with their prayers. Before you leave the inner courtyard and head out into the main square, pop in to the humble little room with the many votive offerings. This is where people leave personal belongings (wedding dresses, baby's baptism outfits, wax replicas of body parts in need of healing, and so on) as part of a prayer request or as thanks for divine intercession.

Museum of Montserrat—This bright, shiny, and cool collection of paintings and artifacts was mostly donated by devout Catalan Catholics. While it's nothing really earthshaking, you'll enjoy an air-conditioned wander past lots of antiquities and fine artwork. Head upstairs first to see some lesser-known works by the likes of Picasso, El Greco, Caravaggio, Monet, Renoir, Pissarro, Degas, John Singer Sargent, and some local Modernista artists. One gallery shows how artists have depicted the Black Virgin of Montserrat over the centuries in many different styles. There's even a small Egyptian section, with a sarcophagus and mummy. Down on the main floor, you'll see ecclesiastical gear, a good icon collection, and more paintings, including—at the very end—a Dalí painting, some Picasso sketches and prints, and a Miró.

Cost and Hours: €6.50, covered by Tot Montserrat combo-ticket, daily July-Aug 10:00-18:45, Sept-June 10:00-17:45, tel. 938-777-745.

Sant Joan Funicular and Hikes—This funicular climbs 820 feet above the monastery in five minutes. At the top of the funicular,

you are at the starting point of a 20-minute walk that takes you to the Sant Joan Chapel (follow sign for *Ermita de St. Joan*). Other hikes also begin at the trailhead by the funicular (get details from TI before you ascend; basic map with suggested hikes posted by upper funicular station). For a quick and easy chance to get out into nature, simply ride up and follow the most popular hike, a 45-minute mostly downhill loop through mountain scenery back to the monastery. To take this route, go left from the funicular station; the trail—marked *Monestir de Montserrat*—will first go up to a rocky crest before heading downhill.

Cost and Hours: Funicular—€5.05 one-way, €8 round-trip, covered by Trans Montserrat and Tot Montserrat combo-tickets, goes every 20 minutes, more often with demand.

Sacred Cave (Santa Cova)—The Moreneta was originally discovered in the Sacred Cave (or Sacred Grotto), a 40-minute hike down from the monastery (then another 50 minutes back up). The path (c. 1900) was designed by devoted and patriotic Modernista architects, including Gaudí and Josep Puig i Cadafalch. It's lined with Modernista statues depicting scenes from the life of Christ. While the original Black Virgin statue is now in the basilica, a replica sits in the cave. A three-minute funicular ride cuts 20 minutes off the hike. If you're here late in the afternoon, check the schedule before you head into the Sacred Cave to make sure you don't miss the final ride back down the mountain. Missing the last funicular could mean catching a train back to Barcelona later than you had planned.

Cost and Hours: Funicular—€2 one-way, €3.20 round-trip, covered by Trans Montserrat and Tot Montserrat combo-tickets, goes every 20 minutes, more often with demand.

Choir Concert—Montserrat's Escolania, or Choir School, has been training voices for centuries. Fifty young boys, who live and study in the monastery itself, make up the choir, which performs daily except Saturday. The boys sing for only 10 minutes, the basilica is jam-packed, and it's likely you'll see almost nothing. Also note that if you attend the evening performance, you'll miss the last train or cable-car ride down the mountain.

Cost and Hours: Free, Mon-Sat at 13:00, Sun at 12:00 and 18:45, choir on vacation late June-late Aug.

Sleeping in Montserrat

(€1 = about $1.30, country code: 34)
An overnight here gets you monastic peace and a total break from the modern crowds. There are ample rustic cells for pilgrim visitors, but tourists might prefer this place:

$$ Hotel Abat Cisneros, a three-star hotel with 82 rooms and all the comforts, is low-key and appropriate for a sanctuary (Sb-€43-66, Db-€76-115, price depends on season, includes breakfast, half- and full-board available, elevator, pay Internet access, free Wi-Fi, tel. 938-777-701, fax 938-777-724, www.montserrat visita.com, reserves@larsa-montserrat.com).

Eating in Montserrat

Montserrat is designed to feed hordes of pilgrims and tourists. You'll find a cafeteria along the main street (across from the train station) and more eateries (including a grocery store and bar with simple sandwiches) where the road curves on its way up to the basilica. The Hotel Abat Cisneros also has a restaurant. The best option is to pack a picnic from Barcelona, especially if you plan to hike.

BARCELONA: PAST and PRESENT

Barcelona has thrived for 2,500 years. Its location is ideal: on a gently sloping plain facing the Mediterranean, where east-west sea trade meets the natural north-south highway to northern Europe. In its day, Barcelona has been a Roman retirement colony, a maritime power, a dynamo of the Industrial Age, and a cradle for all things modern. Today it cobbles together all these elements into a one-of-a-kind culture.

Keep in mind that Catalunya's history is quite distinct from that of the rest of Spain. Catalans pride themselves on their different language and independent traditions. When the rest of Spain was riding high, Catalunya was often in the doldrums, and vice versa.

The painter Joan Miró said, "We Catalans believe that you must plant your feet firmly on the ground in order to jump high in the air." This optimistic Catalan spirit—earthy but creative—has blossomed again and again through their history. Free spirits like Picasso, Dalí, Miró, Gaudí—and even Wilfred the Hairy—have all come from this small corner of Europe.

Prehistory and Roman Origins (c. 500 B.C.-A.D. 500)

The original Iberian inhabitants settled atop Barcelona's hills overlooking the harbor, creating settlements on Montjuïc and around today's Plaça de Sant Jaume. They called their town "Barkeno." The name may (or may not) derive from the famous family of Hannibal Barca—the

Carthaginian general who passed through the area with his war elephants en route to attacking Rome, in 218 B.C.

In 19 B.C., the (future) Roman Emperor Augustus conquered Iberia. The Romans made "Hispania" their agricultural breadbasket to feed the vast Empire. In Catalunya, they planted grapes on large farming estates and shipped the wine abroad from Barcelona's busy port. Roman "Barcino"—a pleasant, sun-bathed valley with Mediterranean breezes—became a retirement colony for soldiers.

Like most Roman cities, Barcino had a forum in the center of town (today's Plaça de Sant Jaume) and a grid pattern of streets. It was a tight, 30-acre town of some 4,000 inhabitants contained within a wall (the area around today's cathedral). More broadly, the Romans brought Barcelona the Latin language (which became modern Catalan) and a connection to the wider world.

Related Sights
- Barcelona History Museum (with Roman ruins in basement)
- Temple of Augustus
- Big, sculpted BARCINO letters on Plaça Nova
- Remnants of the Roman wall (especially the towers on Plaça Nova, near the cathedral)
- Roman necropolis near the Ramblas

Medieval (500-1000)

As the Roman Empire crumbled, Barcelona made a peaceful transition, coming under the protection of Christian Visigoths from Germany who had strong Roman ties.

Christianity had entered Barcelona during Rome's last years (when martyrs such as Saint Eulàlia were persecuted). The feisty Christians built their cathedral—the core of today's cathedral—atop the Roman Temple of Jupiter.

In 711, the Moors (Muslim invaders from North Africa) swept through Spain, and Barcelona surrendered without a fight. While Moorish culture went on to dominate much of Spain for the next 700 years, its impact on Catalunya was minimal. In 801, Barcelona was liberated by Charlemagne's son, who made it part of the Frankish empire under the rule of Frankish "Counts." When Count Wilfred the Hairy (so called because he was; ruled 878-898) declared himself independent of the Franks, he launched a golden age in Barcelona.

Related Sights
- Cathedral (with its original fourth-century font)
- St. Eulàlia's tomb and silver statue in the cathedral

Glory Days: Counts of Barcelona and the Kingdom of Aragon (1000-1500)

Wilfred the Hairy's heirs sprouted and grew into powerful sea-traders who connected Catalunya to the world. When Count Ramon of Barcelona married Petronila of Aragon in 1137, it united their two realms, creating the powerful kingdom of Aragon.

King Jaume I the Conqueror (1208-1276) led Aragon's powerful army and navy in acquiring rich trading ports in the Mediterranean. He also established the Catalan Generalitat, one of Europe's first parliaments, which still governs the region today. By 1450, the Crown of Aragon ruled a mercantile empire that stretched across the Mediterranean, from eastern Spain to southern Italy to Greece. Barcelona flourished.

In 1469 came another powerful marriage: King Ferdinand II of Aragon married Isabel of Castile. This power couple—the so-called Catholic Monarchs—united the peninsula's two largest kingdoms. They drove the last Moors out of Granada, expelled the Jews, and created a unified nation-state. They sent Christopher Columbus to explore new lands under the Spanish flag. And where did Columbus come first to debrief the Catholic Monarchs upon his return? To Barcelona.

Related Sights
- The medieval legacy lives on in lots of Neo-Gothic and medieval motifs in Modernisme (especially the city symbol of St. George slaying the dragon)
- The El Born neighborhood, which flourished during this time
- Catalan Art Museum (excellent Romanesque collection)
- Columbus Monument
- Plaça del Rei and the Royal Palace, where Columbus met Ferdinand and Isabel
- The coffin of Count Ramon in the cathedral
- Generalitat building and statue of Jaume I on Plaça de Sant Jaume
- The churches of Santa Maria del Mar, Santa Maria del Pi, and the Chapel of St. Agatha (at the Royal Palace), plus the *extra muro* ("outside the walls") Church of Santa Anna
- Montserrat monastery, dating from medieval times

Decline (1500-1800)

Ironically, the glorious age of Ferdinand and Isabel also sowed the seeds of Barcelona's decline. Columbus' discoveries opened

Church Architecture

History comes to life when you visit a centuries-old church. Even if you don't know your apse from a hole in the ground, learning a few simple terms will enrich your experience. Note that not every church will have every feature. Also, a "cathedral" isn't a type of architecture, but rather a designation for a church that's a governing center for a local bishop.

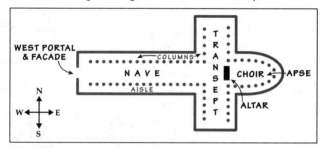

Aisles: The long, generally low-ceilinged arcades that flank the nave.

Altar: The raised area with a ceremonial table (often adorned with candles or a crucifix), where the priest prepares and serves the bread and wine for Communion.

Apse: The space beyond the altar, generally bordered with small chapels.

Barrel Vault: A continuous round-arched ceiling that resembles an extended upside-down U.

Choir: A cozy area, often screened off, located within the church nave and near the high altar, where services are sung in a more intimate setting.

Cloister: Covered hallways bordering a (usually square) open-air courtyard, traditionally where monks and nuns got fresh air.

Facade: The outer wall of the church's main (west) entrance, viewable from outside and generally highly decorated.

Groin Vault: An arched ceiling formed where two equal barrel vaults meet at right angles. Less common usage: term for a medieval jock strap.

Narthex: The area (portico or foyer) between the main entry and the nave.

Nave: The long, central section of the church (running west to east, from the entrance to the altar) where the congregation stood during the service.

Transept: The north-south part of the church, which crosses (perpendicularly) the east-west nave. In a traditional Latin cross-shaped floor plan, the transept forms the "arms" of the cross.

West Portal: The main entry to the church (on the west end, opposite the main altar).

new Atlantic trade routes that made Barcelona's Mediterranean trade-routes obsolete. Meanwhile, the center of royal power slowly shifted from Barcelona to the region midway between Aragon and Castile—the growing city of Madrid. While the rest of Spain enjoyed an unprecedented Golden Age of fabulous New World wealth and influence (producing artists such as El Greco, Velázquez, Goya, and Murillo), Barcelona became a poor and forgotten backwater.

On September 11, 1714—a date that is still marked by Catalunya's most sobering holiday—Catalan independence ended. Barcelona found itself on the losing end in the War of Spanish Succession (1701-1714), having sided against the eventual winner, the French-backed King Philip V. On September 11, Philip's forces overran the city walls and massacred those who had stood against him.

For more than a century, the Spanish crown centered in Madrid would punish the rebellious Catalans. They suppressed the Catalan language, culture, and institutions. The Generalitat was disbanded. Trade with the Americas was forbidden. For surveillance and control, the Castilians built an imposing citadel on one side of town and a fortress atop Montjuïc on the other, and ordered that nothing could be built beyond the reach of the fort's cannons. Barcelona spiraled down into a dirty, cramped city contained within its medieval wall.

Related Sights
- Monument to Catalan Independence in El Born (honoring the victims of September 11, 1714)
- Castle of Montjuïc
- Citadel Park (previously the site of the citadel)
- Barceloneta fishermen's quarter (built to house those displaced by Citadel construction)
- Betlem Church on the Ramblas (rare example of Baroque)

Industrial Revival and Cultural Renaissance (1800-1900)

In the 1800s, another revolution was brewing—the Industrial Revolution. Blessed with soft coal and rushing rivers from the Pyrenees, Barcelona harnessed the power to stoke textile mills. Having finally been given permission to trade with the Americas (1788), they imported cotton and shipped the finished cloth abroad on steamships from their busy harbor.

Workers flocked in from the countryside, drawn by good-paying jobs. Barcelona's population doubled, reaching a million, and it created a thriving middle class.

By 1850—while the rest of Spain stagnated as a fading colonial power—Catalunya was humming. In 1854, Queen Isabella II finally loosened Madrid's death-grip, allowing the growing city to tear down the medieval wall and expand northward, creating the Eixample neighborhood of modern boulevards. They used new technology to make life better for everyday citizens, bringing in modern plumbing, streetlights, and the first rail line in Spain. The city hosted a World's Fair in 1888 that renovated the city (and gave us the Columbus Monument and other urban improvements).

There was a cultural renaissance of the Catalan language and the arts. Historians divide the movement (somewhat arbitrarily) into two parts. The Renaixença (roughly 1840-1880) was a rediscovery of Catalunya's historic roots and national identity, similar to the Romantic movements sweeping all of Europe. Suddenly, people were embracing the language and traditions of their forebears. Writers wrote in Catalan, and artists revived the medieval motifs of Barcelona's 14th-century glory days. This energy flowed naturally into Modernisme (roughly 1890-1910), which continued the love affair with Catalunya's traditions while championing all things modern—things like streetcars and electric lights. The new technology was also meant to be beautiful, and Modernisme is Barcelona's version of the curvy, wistful Art Nouveau style found elsewhere in Europe. As the old city walls came down, Modernista architects like Antoni Gaudí remade the city with fanciful buildings—made of a modern concrete-and-iron substructure but decorated with colorful, playful, medieval motifs.

Related Sights

- The Eixample neighborhood, with the Block of Discord, Casa Milà, and other buildings
- Sagrada Família
- Other Gaudí and Modernista sights (see sidebar on page 146)

Turbulent 20th Century

By the turn of the 20th century, Barcelona was seething with change. Industrialization had made factory owners rich, but the working-class was still poor, living in dirty slums, and working in unsafe factories. Barcelona's Socialists fought for the right to bathroom breaks, while anarchists bombed the Liceu Opera House. The unrest culminated in the bloody riots of "Tragic Week" (1909), during which dozens of churches were vandalized and demonstrators were shot in the streets.

Barcelona developed a reputation across Spain as a breeding

PAST & PRESENT

Catalans You May Know

Catalans invented the submarine, assassinated Leon Trotsky, and founded San Diego. Here are a few names you may be familiar with.

Pablo Picasso (1881-1973)—Though he was born in Andalucía (to Spanish, not Catalan, parents) and spent his adult life in France, Picasso's formative teenage years were spent in Barcelona's Barri Gòtic.

Salvador Dalí (1904-1989)—The master Surrealist was born in Figueres, spent holidays in Cadaqués, and passed his formative years in Barcelona, where he exhibited his early works and soaked up Gaudí's dreamlike architecture.

Joan Miró (1893-1983)—Raised in the Barri Gòtic, he divided his adulthood living between Barcelona and Paris. His whimsical sculptures and ceramics adorn Barcelona.

Antoni Gaudí (1852-1926)—Resident of the Barri Gòtic (in his youth), the Eixample (in young adulthood), and Park Güell (in his twilight years). Gaudí's buildings are the iconic symbols of Barcelona's Modernista revival.

Pau (Pablo) Casals (1876-1973)—A world-class cellist who's often described as one of the best musicians ever to pick up the instrument, he retired to French Catalunya in protest against Franco.

Bacardi Rum Family—The world-famous rum company was founded in Cuba in 1814 by a man from Sitges; it's now run by his great-great-grandson.

Juan Antonio Samaranch (1920-2010)—The longtime president of the International Olympic Committee (r. 1980-2001) was born and raised in Barcelona.

Ferran Adrià (b. 1962)—This celebrity chef revolutionized cuisine with his innovations in molecular gastronomy at the (now-closed) Costa Brava restaurant El Bulli.

Antoni Tàpies (1923-2012)—Spain's best-known postwar artist is most famous for his distinctive mud-caked canvases.

Pau Gasol (b. 1980) and **Marc Gasol** (b. 1985)—Basketball-playing brothers who gained fame in the NBA (both have played for the Memphis Grizzlies; Pau now plays for the LA Lakers).

Rafael Nadal (b. 1986)—The "King of Clay," a world-ranked tennis player and frequent Grand Slam winner, is from the Catalan-speaking island of Mallorca.

ground for liberals, troublemakers, and nonconformists. In the art world, young Pablo Picasso captured the plight of society's disenfranchised (in his Blue Period), then moved to Paris and—with fellow artist Georges Braque—broke all the rules of art by pioneering Cubism. Joan Miró perplexed the masses with his childlike doodles, and Salvador Dalí shocked and astonished with his Surrealistic dreamscapes.

When Spain splintered into its bitter Civil War (1936-1939)—pitting democratic Republicans against fascist Nationalists—left-leaning Barcelona became the natural capital of the Republican side. The fascists, under General Francisco Franco (1892-1975), invited Mussolini's Italian air force to bomb Barcelona, killing a thousand citizens. When Barcelona finally fell in 1939, the war was effectively over. For the next four decades, Franco would rule Spain with an iron fist.

Catalunya was punished. The Generalitat was abolished after having been restored just a few years earlier, and the Catalan president was executed by firing squad. Franco began a program of Castilianization to assimilate the region into greater Spain. The Catalan language and traditions were suppressed. You couldn't buy a newspaper in Catalan or hear the people's language spoken on TV. You couldn't dance the *sardana*. Simultaneously, the region was flooded with poor, Castilian-speaking farmers from the rest of Spain, looking for work. The city expanded way too fast, throwing up dusty gray concrete buildings amid suburban sprawl.

But Catalunya kept the flame alive with underground newspapers and a president-in-exile living in France. Finally, Franco died in 1975, and—on September 11, 1977—millions of Catalan patriots flooded the streets to demand they get their culture back.

It ushered in a third golden age for Catalunya. The Generalitat and Catalan president returned. Catalan became the sole official language in schools. Barcelona reinvented itself, spiffing up old quarters with new buildings and expanding the Metro system. The Sagrada Família, after nearly a century of false starts, made dramatic progress. In 1992, a revived Barcelona hosted the Summer Olympic Games—for which they rebuilt Montjuïc and the waterfront—and put on a modern face for the world.

Related Sights

- Picasso Museum
- Fundació Joan Miró, plus Liceu mosaic in the Ramblas, *Woman and Bird* sculpture, and other public works by Miró
- Figueres, hometown of Salvador Dalí
- Cadaqués, a mecca for modern artists
- 1929 World Expo Fairgrounds, including Magic Fountains (at the base of Montjuïc, near Plaça d'Espanya)

- Fresh-looking Montjuïc (with Olympic Stadium) and the rejuvenated waterfront
- *Barcelona Head* sculpture by Roy Lichtenstein, on the waterfront

Catalunya Today: Feisty and Proud

Today Catalunya speeds into the future on a course that's allied with—but distinctly different from—the rest of Spain. With each visit, I seem to hear more Catalan and less Spanish spoken in the streets. With a population of 1.6 million, Barcelona is Spain's second city.

Along with the rest of Spain, Catalunya has suffered from the global economic downturn that began in 2009. Spain's real-estate bubble burst, banks stopped lending, and unemployment soared. So many young Spaniards are out of work that a new name was coined to describe them: *"generación ni-ni"* (the neither-nor generation). Under pressure from the European Union, Spain is working to dig itself out of debt.

Barcelona continues its legacy of feisty independence. Regular massive demonstrations fill Plaça de Catalunya, as the people fight to regain their cultural heritage. As if to underscore their cultural distance from greater Spain, in 2012 Barcelona outlawed the widely popular Spanish pastime of bullfighting. The Las Arenas bullring is now a shopping mall.

Related Sights
- *Sardana* dances in front of the cathedral
- The red-and-yellow flag of Catalunya flapping in the breeze

APPENDIX

Contents

Tourist Information

Spain's national tourist office **in the US** will fill brochure requests and answer your general travel questions by email (newyork .information@tourspain.es). Scan their website (www.spain.info) and Barcelona's (www.barcelonaturisme.cat) for practical information and sightseeing ideas; you can download many brochures free of charge from the national website.

In Barcelona, your best first stop is at any of its tourist information offices (see page 27). TIs are a good place to get city maps, advice on public transportation (including bus and train schedules), walking-tour information, tips on special events, and recommendations for nightlife.

Websites: In addition to the TI websites listed above, try www.barcelonaplanning.com, www.guiadelocio.com/barcelona, and www.butxaca.com. The latter two sites focus on events and are in Spanish and Catalan, respectively, but are decipherable.

Communicating

Hurdling the Language Barrier

Spain already presents the English-speaking traveler with one of the most formidable language barriers in Western Europe, and Barcelona adds its own twist to the challenge. About 75 percent of Barcelonans speak Catalan, the language unique to the Catalunya region. Though all Barcelonans speak Spanish, many locals insist on speaking Catalan first.

Many Barcelonans—especially those in the tourist trade—speak English, but still, many people don't. Locals visibly brighten when you know and use some key Catalan or Spanish words (see "Catalan Survival Phrases" on page 309 and "Spanish Survival Phrases" on page 307). Learn the key phrases. Travel with a phrase book, particularly if you want to interact with the people. You'll find that doors open more quickly and with more smiles when you can speak a few words of the language.

Telephones

Smart travelers use the telephone to reserve or reconfirm rooms, get tourist information, reserve restaurants, confirm tour times, or phone home. This section covers dialing instructions, phone cards, and types of phones (for more in-depth information, see www .ricksteves.com/phoning).

How to Dial

Calling from the US to Spain, or vice versa, is simple—once you break the code. The European calling chart in this chapter will walk you through it.

In Spain, numbers that start with 900 are toll-free; numbers that start with 901 and 902 have per-minute fees (about €0.04-0.07/ minute from a landline; more from a mobile). Note that you can't call Spain's toll-free numbers from America, nor can you count on reaching America's toll-free numbers from Spain.

Dialing Domestically Within Spain

About half of all European countries use area codes; the other half, including Spain, use a direct-dial system without area codes.

Land lines start with 9, and mobile lines start with 6. All phone numbers in Spain are nine digits (no area codes) that can be dialed direct throughout the country. For example, the phone number of one of my recommended Barcelona hotels is 933-015-151. That's exactly what you dial, whether you're calling the hotel from the Barcelona train station or from Madrid.

These instructions apply to dialing from a landline (such as a pay phone or your hotel-room phone) or a Spanish mobile phone.

If you're dialing within Spain using your US mobile phone, you may need to dial as if it's a domestic call, or you may need to dial as if you're calling from the US (see "Dialing Internationally," next). Try it one way, and if it doesn't work, try it the other way.

Dialing Internationally to or from Spain
If you want to make an international call, follow these steps:

• Dial the international access code (00 if you're calling from Europe, 011 from the US or Canada). If you're dialing from a mobile phone, you can replace the international access code with +, which works regardless of where you're calling from. (On many mobile phones, you can insert a + by pressing and holding the 0 key.)

• Dial the country code of the country you're calling (34 for Spain, or 1 for the US or Canada).

• Dial the local number, keeping in mind that calling many countries requires dropping the initial zero of the phone number. (The European calling chart lists specifics per country.)

Calling from the US to Spain: Dial 011 (the US international access code), 34 (Spain's country code), then the nine-digit number. For example, if you're calling the Barcelona hotel I mentioned above, you'd dial 011-34-933-015-151.

Calling from any European country to the US: To call my office in Edmonds, Washington, from anywhere in Europe, I dial 00 (Europe's international access code), 1 (the US country code), 425 (Edmonds' area code), and 771-8303.

Mobile Phones
Traveling with a mobile phone is handy and practical. Whether you're using a smartphone or a conventional cell phone, the basics for how to make calls and send texts are the same. For specifics on using your smartphone to get online, see the sidebar.

Roaming with Your Mobile Phone: Your US mobile phone works in Europe if it's GSM-enabled, tri-band or quad-band, and on a calling plan that includes international calls. Phones from AT&T and T-Mobile, which use the same GSM technology that Europe does, are more likely to work overseas than Verizon or Sprint phones (if you're not sure, ask your service provider). Most US providers will charge you $1.29-1.99 per minute to make or receive calls while roaming, and 20-50 cents to send or receive text messages. If you bother to sign up for an international calling plan with your provider, you'll save a few dimes per minute. Though pricey, roaming on your own phone is easy and can be a cost-effective way to keep in touch—especially on a short trip or if you won't be making many calls.

Buying and Using SIM Cards in Europe: You'll pay much

European Calling Chart

Just smile and dial, using this key:
AC = Area Code, LN = Local Number.

European Country	Calling long distance within ...	Calling from the US or Canada to ...	Calling from a European country to ...
Austria	AC + LN	011 + 43 + AC (without the initial zero) + LN	00 + 43 + AC (without the initial zero) + LN
Belgium	LN	011 + 32 + LN (without initial zero)	00 + 32 + LN (without initial zero)
Bosnia-Herzegovina	AC + LN	011 + 387 + AC (without initial zero) + LN	00 + 387 + AC (without initial zero) + LN
Britain	AC + LN	011 + 44 + AC (without initial zero) + LN	00 + 44 + AC (without initial zero) + LN
Croatia	AC + LN	011 + 385 + AC (without initial zero) + LN	00 + 385 + AC (without initial zero) + LN
Czech Republic	LN	011 + 420 + LN	00 + 420 + LN
Denmark	LN	011 + 45 + LN	00 + 45 + LN
Estonia	LN	011 + 372 + LN	00 + 372 + LN
Finland	AC + LN	011 + 358 + AC (without initial zero) + LN	999 (or other 900 number) + 358 + AC (without initial zero) + LN
France	LN	011 + 33 + LN (without initial zero)	00 + 33 + LN (without initial zero)
Germany	AC + LN	011 + 49 + AC (without initial zero) + LN	00 + 49 + AC (without initial zero) + LN
Gibraltar	LN	011 + 350 + LN	00 + 350 + LN
Greece	LN	011 + 30 + LN	00 + 30 + LN
Hungary	06 + AC + LN	011 + 36 + AC + LN	00 + 36 + AC + LN
Ireland	AC + LN	011 + 353 + AC (without initial zero) + LN	00 + 353 + AC (without initial zero) + LN

European Country	Calling long distance within ...	Calling from the US or Canada to ...	Calling from a European country to ...
Italy	LN	011 + 39 + LN	00 + 39 + LN
Montenegro	AC + LN	011 + 382 + AC (without initial zero) + LN	00 + 382 + AC (without initial zero) + LN
Morocco	LN	011 + 212 + LN (without initial zero)	00 + 212 + LN (without initial zero)
Netherlands	AC + LN	011 + 31 + AC (without initial zero) + LN	00 + 31 + AC (without initial zero) + LN
Norway	LN	011 + 47 + LN	00 + 47 + LN
Poland	LN	011 + 48 + LN	00 + 48 + LN
Portugal	LN	011 + 351 + LN	00 + 351 + LN
Slovakia	AC + LN	011 + 421 + AC (without initial zero) + LN	00 + 421 + AC (without initial zero) + LN
Slovenia	AC + LN	011 + 386 + AC (without initial zero) + LN	00 + 386 + AC (without initial zero) + LN
Spain	LN	011 + 34 + LN	00 + 34 + LN
Sweden	AC + LN	011 + 46 + AC (without initial zero) + LN	00 + 46 + AC (without initial zero) + LN
Switzerland	LN	011 + 41 + LN (without initial zero)	00 + 41 + LN (without initial zero)
Turkey	AC (if there's no initial zero, add one) + LN	011 + 90 + AC (without initial zero) + LN	00 + 90 + AC (without initial zero) + LN

- The instructions above apply whether you're calling to or from a European landline or mobile phone.

- If calling from any mobile phone, you can replace the international access code with "+" (press and hold 0 to insert it).

- The international access code is 011 if you're calling from the US or Canada.

- To call the US or Canada from Europe, dial 00, then 1 (country code for US and Canada), then the area code and number. In short, 00 + 1 + AC + LN = Hi, Mom!

APPENDIX

Smartphones and Data Roaming

I take my smartphone to Europe, using it to make phone calls (sparingly) and send texts, but also to check email, listen to audio tours, and browse the Internet. If you're clever, you can do all this without incurring huge data-roaming fees. Here's how.

Many smartphones, such as the iPhone, Android, and BlackBerry, work in Europe (though some older Verizon iPhones don't). For voice calls and text messaging, smartphones work like any mobile phone (as described under "Roaming with Your Mobile Phone," earlier)—unless you're connected to free Wi-Fi, in which case you can use Skype, Google Talk, or FaceTime to call for free (or at least very cheaply; see "Calling over the Internet," next page).

The (potentially) *really* expensive aspect of using smartphones in Europe is not voice calls or text messages, but sky-high rates for using data: checking email, browsing the Internet, streaming videos, using certain apps, and so on. If you don't proactively adjust your settings, these charges can mount up even if you're not actually using your phone—because the phone is constantly "roaming" to update your email and such. (One tip is to switch your email settings from "push" to "fetch," so you can choose when to download your emails rather than having them automatically "pushed" over the Internet to your device.)

The best solution: Disable data roaming entirely, and use your device to access the Internet only when you find free Wi-Fi (at your hotel, for example). Then you can surf the net to your heart's content, or make free (or extremely cheap) phone calls via Skype. You can manually turn off data roaming on your phone's menu (check under the "Network" settings). For added security, you can call and ask your service provider to temporarily suspend your data account entirely for the length of your trip.

Some travelers enjoy the flexibility of getting online even when they're not on free Wi-Fi. But be careful. If you simply switch on data roaming, you'll pay exorbitant rates of about $20 per megabyte (figure around 40 cents per email downloaded, or about $3 to view a typical Web page)—much more expensive than it is back home. If you know you'll be doing some data roaming, it's far more affordable to sign up for a limited international data-roaming plan through your carrier (but be very clear on your megabyte limit to avoid inflated overage charges). In general, ask your provider in advance how to avoid unwittingly roaming your way to a huge bill.

cheaper rates if you put a European SIM card in your mobile phone; to do this, your phone must be electronically "unlocked" (ask your provider about this, buy an unlocked phone before you leave, or get one in Europe—see "Other Mobile-Phone Options," next). Then, in Europe, you can buy a fingernail-size **SIM card,** which gives you a European phone number. SIM cards are sold at mobile-phone stores and some newsstand kiosks for about $5-10, and often include at least that much prepaid domestic calling time (making the card itself almost free). When you buy a SIM card, you may need to show ID, such as your passport.

Insert the SIM card in your phone (usually in a slot behind the battery or on the side), and it'll work like a European mobile phone. When purchasing a SIM card, always ask about fees for domestic and international calls, roaming charges, and how to check your credit balance and buy more time. When you're in the SIM card's home country, domestic calls average 10 to 20 cents per minute, and incoming calls are free. Rates are higher if you're roaming in another country, and you may pay more to call a toll number than you would dialing from a fixed line.

Other Mobile-Phone Options: Many travelers like to carry two phones: both their own US mobile phone (allowing them to stay reachable on their own phone number) and a second, unlocked European phone (which lets them do all their local calling at far cheaper rates). You could either bring two phones from home, or get one in Europe. If you have an old mobile phone sitting around, ask your provider for the "unlock code" so it can be used with European SIM cards. Or buy a cheap, basic phone before you go (search your favorite online shopping site for "unlocked quad-band GSM phone").

In Europe, basic phones are sold at hole-in-the-wall vendors at many airports and train stations, and at phone desks within larger department stores. Phones that are "locked" to work with a single provider start around $40; "unlocked" phones (which work with any SIM card) start around $60. Regardless of how you get your phone, remember that you'll need a SIM card to make it work.

Car-rental companies and mobile-phone companies offer the option to rent a mobile phone with a European number. While this seems convenient, hidden fees (such as high per-minute charges or expensive shipping costs) can really add up—which usually makes it a bad value. One exception is Verizon's Global Travel Program, available only to Verizon customers.

Calling over the Internet

Some things that seem too good to be true...actually are true. If you're traveling with a laptop, tablet, or smartphone, you can make calls over the Internet to another wireless device, anywhere in the world, for free. (Or you can pay a few cents to call from your computer to a telephone.) The major providers are Skype, Google Talk, and (on Apple devices) FaceTime. You can get online at a Wi-Fi hotspot and use these apps to make calls without ringing up expensive roaming charges (though call quality can be spotty on slow connections). You can make Internet calls even if you're traveling without your own mobile device: Many European Internet cafés have Skype, as well as microphones and webcams, on their terminals—just log on and chat away.

Landline Telephones

As in the US, these days most Spanish residents do the majority of their phoning on mobile phones. But you'll still encounter landlines in hotel rooms and at pay phones.

Hotel-Room Phones: Calling from your hotel room can be great for local calls and for international calls if you have an international phone card (described later). Otherwise, hotel-room phones can be an almost criminal rip-off for long-distance or international calls. Many hotels charge a fee for local and sometimes even "toll-free" numbers—always ask for the rates before you dial. Incoming calls are free, making this a cheap way for friends and family to stay in touch (provided they have a long-distance plan with good international rates—and a list of your hotels' phone numbers).

Public Pay Phones: Coin-op phones are virtually extinct in Europe. To make calls from public phones, you'll need a prepaid phone card, described next.

Types of Telephone Cards

There are two types of phone cards: insertable (for pay phones) and international (cheap for overseas calls and usable from any type of phone). The cards generally work only in the country you purchase them. If you have a live card at the end of your trip, give it to another traveler to use—most cards expire 3-6 months after the first use.

Insertable Phone Cards: These cards, called *tarjetas telefónicas,* can be used only at pay phones, for either domestic or international calls. They're sold at post offices and many newsstand kiosks. Spanish pay phones are easy to find but refuse to be rushed. After you *"inserta"* your *"tarjeta"* into the phone, wait until the digital display says *"Marque número,"* and then dial. Dial slowly and deliberately. Push the square R button to get a dial tone for a new call. The phone doesn't beep to remind you that you've left the card in, so don't forget to remove it when you're done. The cost of the call is automatically deducted from your card.

International Phone Cards: With these cards, phone calls from Spain to the US can cost less than a nickel a minute. The cards can also be used to make local calls, and they work from any type of phone, including your hotel-room phone or a mobile phone with a European SIM card. To use the card, dial a toll-free access number, then enter your scratch-to-reveal PIN code.

You can buy an international phone card, called *tarjeta telefónica con código,* at most kiosks and newsstands, but the best selection is usually at little shops catering to immigrants, who are the leading experts on calling home cheaply. You can also find them at call centers *(locutorios).* Buy a low denomination in case the card is a dud.

US Calling Cards: These cards, such as the ones offered by AT&T, Verizon, and Sprint, are a rotten value, and are being phased out. Try any of the options outlined earlier.

Metered Phones: In Spain, phones with meters are sometimes available in telephone centers *(locutorios)* and bigger post offices. You can talk all you want, then pay the bill when you leave—but be sure you know the rates before you have a lengthy conversation. Note that charges can be "per unit" rather than per minute; find out the length of a unit.

Useful Phone Numbers
Emergency Needs
Police: Tel. 091 (nationwide), tel. 092 (local)
Ambulance or Any Emergency: Tel. 112

Embassies and Consulates
US Consulate: Tel. 932-802-227, after-hours emergency tel. 915-872-200, passport services Mon-Fri 9:00-13:00, closed Sat-Sun (Passeig Reina Elisenda 23, http://barcelona.usconsulate.gov)
Canadian Consulate: Tel. 932-703-614, after-hours emergency tel. in Ottawa—call collect 613-996-8885 (Plaça de Catalunya 9, www.spain.gc.ca, click on "Contact Us," then "Consulate of Canada in Barcelona")

Travel Advisories
US Department of State: Tel. 888-407-4747, from outside US tel. 1-202-501-4444, www.travel.state.gov
Canadian Department of Foreign Affairs: Canadian tel. 800-267-6788, from outside Canada tel. 1-613-996-8885, www.voyage.gc.ca
US Centers for Disease Control and Prevention: Tel. 800-CDC-INFO (800-232-4636), www.cdc.gov/travel

APPENDIX

Directory Assistance

In Spain, dial 11811 (€0.40/min) or 11818 (€0.55/call from private numbers, free from phone booths).

Trains

Train (RENFE) Reservation and Information: Tel. 902-320-320, www.renfe.com

Airports

The following airports—El Prat de Llobregat Airport (airport code: BCN) and Girona-Costa Brava Airport (GRO)—share a customer-assistance line, tel. 902-404-704, and a website, www.aena-aeropuertos.es.

Internet Access

It's useful to get online periodically as you travel—to confirm trip plans, check train or bus schedules, get weather forecasts, catch up on email, blog or post photos from your trip, or call folks back home (explained earlier, under "Calling over the Internet").

Your Mobile Device: The majority of accommodations in Spain offer Wi-Fi, as do many cafés, making it easy for you to get online with your laptop, tablet, or smartphone. Access is often free, but sometimes there's a fee.

Some hotel rooms and Internet cafés have high-speed Internet jacks that you can plug into with an Ethernet cable. A cellular modem—which lets your device access the Internet over a mobile network—provides more extensive coverage, but is much more expensive than Wi-Fi.

Public Internet Terminals: Many accommodations offer a computer in the lobby with Internet access for guests. If you ask politely, smaller places may let you sit at their desk for a few minutes just to check your email. If your hotelier doesn't have access, ask to be directed to the nearest place to get online.

Security: Whether you're accessing the Internet with your own device or at a public terminal, using a shared network or computer comes with the potential for increased security risks. Be careful about storing personal information online, such as passport and credit-card numbers. If you're not convinced a connection is secure, avoid accessing any sites that could be vulnerable to fraud (such as online banking).

Mail

You can mail one package per day to yourself worth up to $200 duty-free from Europe to the US (mark it "personal purchases"). If you're sending a gift to someone, mark it "unsolicited gift." For details, visit www.cbp.gov and search for "Know Before You Go."

The Spanish postal service works fine, but for quick transatlantic delivery (in either direction), consider services such as DHL (www.dhl.com).

Transportation

By Car or Public Transportation?

If your trip will cover more of Spain than just Barcelona, you'll need to decide whether to rent a car or take public transportation. Cars are best for three or more traveling together (especially families with small kids), those packing heavy, and those scouring the countryside. Trains and buses are best for solo travelers, blitz tourists, and city-to-city travelers; and those who don't want to drive in Europe. Though a car gives you more freedom—enabling you to search for hotels more easily and carrying your bags for you—trains and buses zip you scenically from city to city, usually dropping you in the center, often near a TI.

Public Transportation

Public transportation in Spain is slick, modern, and efficient. The best option is to mix bus and train travel. Always verify schedules before your departure. Don't leave a station without your next day's schedule options in hand. To ask for a schedule at an information window, say, *"Horario para* (fill in names of cities), *por favor."* (The local TI will sometimes have schedules available for you to take or copy.) To study train schedules in advance, visit Germany's excellent all-Europe website, www.bahn.com, or Spain's site, www.renfe.com. Bus schedules are more difficult to track down because routes are operated by different companies; try www.movelia.es, a third-party site listing several (but not all) bus companies.

Trains

You can buy a Spain "flexi" railpass that allows travel for a given number of days over a longer period of time, but you'll pay separately ($10-35) for seat reservations on all trains. Buying individual train tickets in advance or as you go in Spain can be less expensive, and gives you better access to seat reservations (which are limited for railpass holders). Some individual ticket prices already include seat reservations when required (for instance, for fast trains).

If your trip also includes a neighboring country, consider the France-Spain, Portugal-Spain, or Italy-Spain passes (see chart in this chapter). A Eurail pass lets you travel even farther. Spain also offers a rail-and-drive pass, which gives you the ease of big-city train hops and the flexibility of a car for rural areas such as the Andalusian hill towns. These passes are sold only outside Europe. For specifics, check the railpass chart, contact your travel agent,

Buying Train Tickets

Trains can sell out, so it's smart to buy your tickets a day in advance, even for short rides. You have four options for buying train tickets: at the station, at a travel agency, online, or by phone. Since station ticket offices can get very crowded, most travelers will find it easiest to go to a travel agency, most of which charge only a nominal service fee.

At the Station: You will likely have to wait in a line to buy your ticket. First find the correct line—at bigger stations, there might be separate windows for short-distance, long-distance, advance, and "today" *(para hoy)* tickets. To avoid wasting time in the wrong line, read the signs carefully, and ask a local (or a clerk at an information window) which line you need. You might have to take a number—watch others and follow their lead.

As another option, you could buy tickets or reservations at the RENFE offices located in more than 100 city centers. These are more central and multilingual—also less crowded and confusing—than the train station.

Travel Agency: The best choice for most travelers is to buy tickets at an English-speaking travel agency. The El Corte Inglés department stores (with locations in most Spanish cities) often have handy travel agencies inside. I've recommended these and other travel agencies throughout this book. Look for a train sticker in agency windows.

Online: Although the website www.renfe.com is useful

or see my *Guide to Eurail Passes* at www.ricksteves.com/rail. Even if you have a railpass, use buses when they're more convenient and direct than the trains. Remember to reserve ahead for the fast AVE trains and overnight journeys.

RENFE (the acronym for the Spanish national train system) used to mean "Really Exasperating, and Not For Everyone," but it has moved into the 21st century. For information and reservations, dial RENFE's national number (toll tel. 902-320-320) from anywhere in Spain, or visit www.renfe.com. For tips on buying tickets, see the sidebar.

Spain categorizes trains this way:

The high-speed train called the **AVE** (AH-vay, stands for *Alta Velocidad Española*) whisks travelers between Barcelona and Madrid in three hours or less, and Barcelona and Sevilla in 5.5 hours. For decades, Spain's trains didn't fit on Europe's tracks, but AVE trains run on

for confirming schedules and prices, you cannot dependably buy tickets online unless you have a European credit card. The website rejects nearly every attempt to use a US card, but with patience and enough Spanish language skill, you might nab an online discount of up to 60 percent (available two weeks to two months ahead of travel). Another option is www.rumbo.es. This travel website (select English at the very bottom of the page) sells discounted tickets for a small service fee (about €5). Other online vendors include www.raileurope.com and www.petrabax .com (higher fees).

By Phone: You can purchase your ticket by phone with an American Express card (tel. 902-240-202), then pick it up at the station by punching your confirmation code *(localizador)* into one of the automated machines. Discounts up to 40 percent off are offered a week or more ahead by phone (and at stations).

You can also reserve tickets by phone, then buy them at the station, which you must do a few days before departure (at a ticket window, usually signed *"venta anticipada"*). You can't pay for reserved tickets at the station on your day of travel.

The Fine Print: First-class tickets cost 50 percent more than second class—often as much as a domestic flight (see "Cheap Flights" on page 238). Discounted tickets come with restrictions, such as being nonrefundable and nonchangeable. Be sure to read all the details carefully at time of purchase.

standard European-gauge rails. AVE trains can be priced differently according to their time of departure. Peak hours *(punta)* are most expensive, followed by *llano* and *valle* (quietest and cheapest times). AVE is almost entirely covered by the Eurail pass (but book ahead).

A related high-speed train, the **Alvia,** runs on AVE lines but can switch to Iberian track without stopping.

Avant trains are also high-speed—typically about as fast as AVE—but designed for shorter distances. They also tend to be cheaper than AVE, even on the same route. Railpass reservations also cost about half as much for Avant as for AVE. If you're on a tight budget, compare your options before buying.

The **Talgo** is fast, air-conditioned, and expensive, and runs on AVE rails. **Intercity** and **Electro** trains fall just behind Talgo in speed, comfort, and expense. **Rápido, Tranvía, Semidirecto,** and **Expreso** trains are generally slower. **Cercanías** are commuter trains for big-city workers and small-town tourists. **Regional** and **Correo** trains are slow, small-town milk runs. Trains get more expensive as they pick up speed, but all are cheaper per mile than their northern European counterparts. Spain loves to name trains,

Railpasses

Prices listed are for 2012 and are subject to change. For the latest prices, details, and train schedules (and easy online ordering), see my comprehensive *Guide to Eurail Passes* at www.ricksteves.com/rail.

"Saver" prices are per person for two or more people traveling together. "Youth" means under age 26. The fare for children 4–11 is half the adult individual fare or Saver fare. Kids under age 4 travel free.

SPAIN RAIL & DRIVE PASS

Any 3 rail days and 2 car days in 2 months.

Car Category	1st Class	2nd Class	Extra car day
Mini	$370	$307	$49
Compact	377	314	56
Standard	405	342	84
Intermediate auto.	443	380	123
Premium	473	410	153

Prices are per person, two traveling together. Solo travelers pay about $100 extra. Third and fourth people sharing the car buy only the railpass. Extra rail days (max 2) cost $36–$45 per day. To order Rail & Drive passes, call your travel agent or Rail Europe at 800-438-7245. *This pass is not sold by Europe Through the Back Door.*

SPAIN PASS

	1st Class	2nd Class
3 days in 2 months	$273	$219
Extra rail days (max 10)	39–46	31–36

SPAIN-PORTUGAL PASS

	Individual 1st Class	Saver 1st Class
3 days in 2 months	$311	$265
Extra rail days (max 7)	44–48	38–41

Map key:
Approximate point-to-point one-way second-class rail fares in US dollars. First class costs 50 percent more. Add up fares for your itinerary to see whether a railpass will save you money. Dashed lines are buses and ferries (not covered by passes).

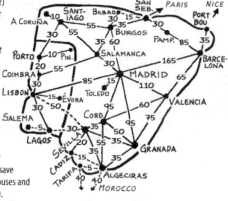

SELECTPASS

This pass covers travel in three adjacent countries. Please visit **www.ricksteves.com/rail** for four- and five-country options.

	Individual 1st Class	Saver 1st Class	Youth 2nd Class
5 days in 2 months	$447	$381	$292
6 days in 2 months	493	420	322
8 days in 2 months	583	496	380
10 days in 2 months	676	575	440

FRANCE–SPAIN PASS

	Individual 1st Class	Individual 2nd Class	Saver 1st Class	Saver 2nd Class	Youth 2nd Class
4 days in 2 months	$376	$323	$323	$275	$245
Extra rail days (max 6)	45–50	38–40	38–40	31–37	28–32

so you may encounter types of trains not listed here. The names **Euromed, Alaris, Altaria,** and **Arco** all indicate faster trains that require reservations. These can cost significantly less than AVE on some routes and yet may be just as fast. Ask about the travel time for each option when buying your tickets.

Salidas means "departures," and *llegadas* is "arrivals." On train schedules, "LMXJVSD" stands for the days of the week in Spanish, starting with Monday. A train that runs "LMXJV-D" doesn't run on Saturdays. *Laborables* can mean Monday through Friday or Monday through Saturday.

Overnight Trains: For long trips, you can usually go overnight on the train (or consider flying—domestic shuttle flights are generally less than $100). Overnight trains (and buses) are generally less expensive and slower than the daytime rides. Most overnight trains have berths and beds that you can rent (not included in the cost of your train ticket or railpass). A sleeping berth *(litera* or *couchette)* costs extra, with the price depending on the route and type of compartment. Night trains are popular, so it's smart to reserve in advance, even from home. Travelers with first-class reservations are entitled to use comfortable "Intercity" lounges in train stations in Spain's major cities.

Hotel Trains: The term Trenhotel ("Hotel Train") might as well mean fancy and expensive. At this time, international Trenhotels connect France and Portugal with Spain. All of these spendy overnight trains (known collectively as Elipsos) have names: Joan Miro (Barcelona-Paris), Luisitania (Madrid-Lisbon) and Francisco de Goya (Madrid-Paris). Full fares range from about $250 in a quad to $700 for a Gran Clase single compartment. Travelers with any railpass that covers at least one country on the route of travel can use a railpass travel day and pay about half the full fare. For more information on Spain-France Trenhotels, see www.elipsos.com; for Spain-Portugal, see www.renfe.com. Even if you can easily afford to take a Trenhotel, consider flying instead to save time (see "Cheap Flights," page 238).

To avoid the expense of an international Trenhotel, you can take a cheaper train trip that involves a transfer at the Spanish border (at Cerbère, up the coast from Barcelona, or at Irún on Madrid-Paris runs). You'll connect to a normal night train with $35 sleeping berths *(literas/couchettes)* on one leg of the trip. This plan is more time-consuming, and may take two days of a flexipass.

Buses

Spain's bus system is confusing (www.movelia.es is a good place to begin researching schedules and carriers). There are a number

Public Transportation in Iberia

of different bus companies (though usually clustered within one building), sometimes running buses to the same destinations and using the same transfer points. If you have to transfer, make sure to look for a bus with the same name/logo as the company you bought the ticket from. The larger stations have a consolidated information desk with all the schedules. In smaller stations, check the destinations and schedules posted on each office window. (If your connection requires a transfer to another company's bus in a different city, don't count on getting help from the originating clerk to figure out the onward connection.) Bus service on holidays, Saturdays, and especially Sundays can be less frequent.

If you arrive in a city by bus and plan to leave by bus, stick around the station upon your arrival to check your departure

options and buy a ticket in advance if necessary (and possible). If you're downtown, need a ticket, and the bus station isn't central, save time by asking at the tourist office about travel agencies that sell bus tickets.

You can (and most likely will be required to) stow your luggage under the bus. Your ticket comes with an assigned seat; if the bus is full, you should take that seat, but if it's uncrowded, most people just sit where they like. For longer rides, give some thought to which side of the bus will get the most sun, and sit on the opposite side, even if the bus is air-conditioned and has curtains. Your ride likely will come with a soundtrack: taped Spanish pop music, radio, or sometimes videos. If you prefer silence, bring earplugs. Buses are non-smoking.

Drivers and station personnel rarely speak English. Buses generally lack WCs, but they stop every two hours or so for a break (usually 15 minutes, but can be up to 30). Drivers announce how long the stop will be, but if in doubt, ask the driver, "How many minutes here?" *("¿Cuántos minutos aquí?"),* so you know if you have time to get out. Listen for the bus horn as a final call before departure. Bus stations have WCs (rarely with toilet paper) and cafés that offer quick and slightly overpriced food.

Taxis

Most taxis are reliable and cheap. Drivers generally respond kindly to the request, "How much is it to _____, more or less?"

("¿Cuánto cuesta a _____, más o menos?"). Spanish taxis have extra supplements (for luggage, nighttime, Sundays, train/bus-station or airport pickup, and so on). Rounding up the fare (maximum of 10 percent) is adequate for a tip. City rides cost €4-6. Keep a map in your hand so the cabbie knows

(or thinks) you know where you're going. Big cities have plenty of taxis. In many cases, couples travel by cab for little more than the cost of two bus or subway tickets.

Renting a Car

If you're renting a car in Spain, bring your driver's license. You're also required to have an International Driving Permit—an official translation of your driver's license (sold at your local AAA office for $15 plus the cost of two passport-type photos; see www.aaa.com). While that's the letter of the law, I've often rented cars in Spain without having—or being asked to show—this permit.

Rental companies require you to be at least 21 years old and to have held your license for one year. Drivers under the age of 25 may incur a young-driver surcharge, and some rental companies do not rent to anyone 75 and over. If you're considered too young or old, look into leasing (covered later), which has less stringent age restrictions.

Research car rentals before you go. It's cheaper to arrange most car rentals from the US. Call several companies and look online to compare rates, or arrange a rental through your home-town travel agent.

Most of the major US rental agencies (including National, Avis, Budget, Hertz, and Thrifty) have offices throughout Europe. Also consider the two major Europe-based agencies, Europcar and Sixt. It can be cheaper to use a consolidator, such as Auto Europe

Spain by Car: Mileage & Time

FRANCE

Santiago de Compostela — 285M·6H — Comillas

Santillana del Mar

80M·1.5H — Bilbao

St-Jean-de-Luz — 20M·.75H — San Sebastián

95M 2.5H — Potes

10M·.25H

125M 2.5H

60M 1.25H — 25M·1H

Barcelona to Cerbère (French border) 110m·2h

León — 50M 1.5H — 120M·2H

León — 150M·3H

125M·2.25H (VIA VITORIA)

Pamplona

210M·3.5H — Burgos — 150M·3H

115M 2H

220M·4H — Salamanca — 60M 1.5H — 55M 1H — Segovia

Porto — 75M·1.25H

150M·3H — 60M 1.25H — Zaragoza — 205M 3.5H — 115M·3H — Barcelona

Coimbra

185M·4H

Ávila — 70M·1.5H — Madrid

520M·9H

315M·5.5H

45M 1H — Toledo

225M·4H

220M·3.5H

Lisbon

Évora — 85M 1.5H

S P A I N

Valencia

200M·3.5H

95M·3.5H — 180M·3H

220M 2H — Córdoba

330M·5.5H

90M·2H — 155M·3H — 100M·3H — 225M 4H

Salema

Sevilla — 55M·1.5H — Arcos — 80M·2H — Ronda — 120M·2H — Granada

70M·2H

50M·1.25H

65M·1.25H

Tarifa — .5H FERRY — 70M·1.5H — Nerja

60M·1.75H

Tangier — Gibraltar

m = miles
h = hours
···· = ferry

NOTE: YOUR TIMES MAY VARY BASED ON TRAFFIC, CONSTRUCTION & ROAD CONDITIONS.

PORTUGAL — 125M·2H

APPENDIX

(www.autoeurope.com) or Europe by Car (www.ebctravel.com), which compares rates at several companies to get you the best deal. However, my readers have reported problems with consolidators ranging from misinformation to unexpected fees; because you're going through a middleman, it can be more challenging to resolve disputes that might arise with the rental agency.

Regardless of the car-rental company you choose, always read the contract carefully. The fine print can conceal a host of common add-on charges—such as one-way drop-off fees, airport surcharges, or mandatory insurance policies—that aren't included in the "total price," but can be tacked on when you pick up your car. You may need to query rental agents pointedly to find out your actual cost.

For the best rental deal, rent by the week with unlimited mileage. To save money on fuel, ask for a diesel car. I normally rent the smallest, least-expensive model with a stick shift (cheaper than an automatic). An automatic transmission adds about 50 percent to the car-rental cost over a manual transmission. Almost all rentals are manual by default, so if you need an automatic, you must request one in advance; be aware that these cars are usually larger models and not as maneuverable on narrow, winding roads.

For a three-week rental, allow roughly $900 per person (based on two people sharing a car), including insurance, tolls, fuel, and parking. For trips of this length, look into leasing (covered later); you'll save money on insurance and taxes.

You can sometimes get a GPS unit with your rental car or leased vehicle for an additional fee (around $15/day; be sure it's set to English and has all the maps you need before you drive off). Or, if you have a portable GPS device at home, consider taking it with you to Europe (buy and upload European maps before your trip). GPS apps are also available for smartphones, but downloading maps on one of these apps in Europe could lead to an exorbitant data-roaming bill (for more details, see the sidebar on page 278).

Compare pickup costs (downtown can be less expensive than the airport) and explore drop-off options. When selecting a location, don't trust the agency's description of "downtown" or "city center." In some cases, a "downtown" branch can be on the outskirts of the city—a long, costly taxi ride from the center. Before choosing, plug the addresses into a mapping website. You may find that the "train station" location is handier. Returning a car at a big-city train station or downtown agency can be tricky; get precise details on the drop-off location and hours, and allow ample time to find it. Note that rental offices usually close from midday Saturday until Monday morning.

When you pick up the rental car, check it thoroughly and make sure any damage is noted on your rental agreement. Find out how your car's lights, turn signals, wipers, and gas cap function, and know what kind of fuel the car takes. When you return the car, make sure the agent verifies its condition with you.

Car Insurance Options

When you rent a car, you are liable for a very high deductible, sometimes equal to the entire value of the car. Limit your financial risk by choosing one of these three options: Buy Collision Damage Waiver (CDW) coverage from the car-rental company, get coverage through your credit card (free, if your card automatically includes zero-deductible coverage), or buy coverage through Travel Guard.

CDW includes a very high deductible (typically $1,000-1,500). Though each rental company has its own variation, basic CDW costs $15-35 a day (figure roughly 30 percent extra) and reduces your liability, but does not eliminate it. When you pick up the car, you'll be offered the chance to "buy down" the basic deductible to zero (for an additional $10-30/day; this is sometimes called "super CDW").

If you opt for **credit-card coverage,** there's a catch. You'll technically have to decline all coverage offered by the car-rental company, which means they can place a hold on your card (which can be up to the full value of the car). In case of damage, it can be time-consuming to resolve the charges with your credit-card company. Before you decide on this option, quiz your credit-card company about how it works.

Finally, you can buy collision insurance from **Travel Guard** ($9/day plus a one-time $3 service fee covers you for up to $35,000, $250 deductible, tel. 800-826-4919, www.travelguard.com). It's valid everywhere in Europe except the Republic of Ireland, and some Italian car-rental companies refuse to honor it. Note that various states differ on which products and policies are available to their residents.

For more on car-rental insurance, see www.ricksteves.com /cdw.

Leasing

For trips of three weeks or more, consider leasing (which automatically includes zero-deductible collision and theft insurance). By technically buying and then selling back the car, you save lots of money on tax and insurance. Leasing provides you a brand-new car with unlimited mileage and a 24-hour emergency assistance program. You can lease for as little as 21 days and as long as six months. Car leases must be arranged from the US. One of many companies offering affordable lease packages is Europe by Car (US tel. 800-223-1516, www.ebctravel.com).

Driving

Driving in rural Spain is great—traffic is sparse and roads are generally good. But a car is a pain in big cities such as Barcelona.

Drive defensively. If you're involved in an accident, you will be in for a monumental headache.

Good maps are available and inexpensive throughout Spain. In smaller towns, following signs to *centro ciudad* will get you to the heart of things.

Freeways and Tolls: Spain's freeways come with tolls, but save huge amounts of time. Each toll road *(autopista de peaje)* has its own pricing structure, so tolls vary. Near some major cities, you must prepay for each stretch of road you drive; on other routes, you take a ticket where you enter the freeway, and pay when you exit. Payment can be made in cash or by credit or debit card (credit-card-only lanes are labeled *vias automáticas*).

Because road numbers can be puzzling and inconsistent, be ready to navigate by city and town names. On freeways, navigate

APPENDIX

by direction *(norte, oeste, sur, este)*. Mileage signs are in kilometers (see page 301 for conversion formula into miles).

Road Rules: Seatbelts are required by law. Children under 12 must ride in the back seat, and children up to age 3 must have a child seat. You must put on a reflective safety vest any time you get out of your car on the side of a highway or unlit road (most rental-car companies provide one—but check when you pick up the car). Those who use eyeglasses are required by law to have a spare pair in the car. It is illegal to talk on a cell phone while driving (unless using a fully hands-free system).

Drivers must turn on headlights during daylight hours if visibility is poor. Spain does not allow a right turn at a red light. For more on road rules, ask your car-rental company, or check the US State Department website (www.travel.state.gov, click on "International Travel," then specify "Spain" and "Traffic Safety and Road Conditions").

STOP AND LEARN THESE ROAD SIGNS

Speed Limit (km/hr) · Yield · No Passing · End of No Passing Zone

One Way · Intersection · Main Road · Freeway

Danger · No Entry · No Entry for Cars · All Vehicles Prohibited

Parking · No Parking · Customs · Peace

Traffic Cops: Watch for traffic radar and expect to be stopped for a routine check by the police (be sure your car-insurance form is up-to-date). Small towns come with speed traps and corruption. Tickets, especially for foreigners, are issued and paid for on the spot. Insist on a receipt *(recibo)*, so the money is less likely to end up in the cop's pocket.

Fuel: Gas and diesel prices are controlled and the same everywhere—about $6 a gallon for gas, less for diesel (gas is priced by the liter in Spain). Unleaded gas *(gasolina sin plomo)* is either *normal* or *super*. Note that diesel is called *diesel* or *gasóleo*—pay attention when filling your tank.

Theft: Choose parking places carefully. Stow valuables in the trunk during the day and leave nothing worth stealing in the car overnight. While you should avoid parking lots with twinkly asphalt, thieves break car windows anywhere, even at stoplights. If your car's a hatchback, take the trunk cover off at night so thieves can look in without breaking in. Try to make your car look locally owned by hiding the "tourist-owned" rental-company decals and putting a local newspaper in your front or back window. Parking attendants all over Spain holler, *"Nada en el coche"* ("Nothing in the car"). And they mean it. Ask your hotelier for advice on parking. In cities you can park safely but expensively in guarded lots.

Resources

Resources from Rick Steves

Rick Steves' Barcelona is one of many books in my series on European travel, which includes country guidebooks, city guidebooks (Rome, Florence, Paris, London, and others), Snapshot Guides (excerpted chapters from my country guides), Pocket Guides (full-color little books on big cities), and my budget-travel skills handbook, *Rick Steves' Europe Through the Back Door*. Most of my titles are available as ebooks. My phrase books—for Italian, French, German, Spanish, and Portuguese—are practical and budget-oriented. My other books include *Europe 101* (a crash course on art and history), *Mediterranean Cruise Ports* (how to make the most of your time in port), and *Travel as a Political Act* (a travelogue sprinkled with tips for bringing home a global perspective). A more complete list of my titles appears near the end of this book.

Video: My public television series, *Rick Steves' Europe,* covers European destinations in 100 shows, with 10 episodes on Spain (including one on Barcelona and Catalunya). To watch episodes, visit www.hulu.com/rick-steves-europe; for scripts and local airtimes, see www.ricksteves.com/tv.

Audio: My weekly public radio show, *Travel with Rick Steves,* features interviews with travel experts from around the world. All of this audio content is available for free at Rick Steves Audio Europe, an extensive online library organized by destination. Choose whatever interests you, and download it via the Rick Steves Audio Europe smartphone app, www.ricksteves.com/audioeurope, iTunes, or Google Play.

Maps

The black-and-white maps in this book, designed by David Hoerlein, are concise and simple. The maps are intended to help

Begin Your Trip at www.ricksteves.com

At ricksteves.com, you'll discover a wealth of free information on European destinations, including fresh monthly news and helpful tips from thousands of fellow travelers. You'll find my latest guidebook updates (www.ricksteves.com/update), a monthly travel e-newsletter (easy and free to sign up), my personal travel blog, and my free Rick Steves Audio Europe smartphone app (if you don't have a smartphone, you can access the same content via podcasts). You can also follow me on Facebook and Twitter.

Our **online Travel Store** offers travel bags and accessories that I've designed specially to help you travel smarter and lighter. These include my popular carry-on bags (roll-aboard and backpack versions), money belts, totes, toiletries kits, adapters, other accessories, and a wide selection of guidebooks, planning maps, and DVDs.

Choosing the right **railpass** for your trip—amid hundreds of options—can drive you nutty. We'll help you choose the best pass for your needs and ship it to you for free.

Want to travel with greater efficiency and less stress? We organize **tours** with more than three dozen itineraries and more than 500 departures reaching the best destinations in this book...and beyond. Our Spain tours include Barcelona and Madrid in 8 days, the Basque Country of Spain and France in 8 days, and Spain in 11 or 14 days. You'll enjoy great guides, a fun bunch of travel partners (with small groups of generally around 20-24), and plenty of room to spread out in a big, comfy bus. You'll find European adventures to fit every vacation length. For all the details, and to get our Tour Catalog and a free Rick Steves Tour Experience DVD (filmed on location during an actual tour), visit www.ricksteves.com or call us at 425/608-4217.

you locate recommended places and get to TIs, where you can pick up more in-depth maps of cities or regions (usually free). Better maps are available—and cheaper than in the US—throughout Spain at newsstands, bookstores, and gas stations. Before you buy a map, look at it to be sure it has the level of detail you want. Drivers will want to pick up a good, detailed map in Europe (I'd recommend a 1:200,000- or 1:300,000-scale map).

Other Guidebooks

If you're like most travelers, this book is all you need. But if you're heading beyond my recommended destinations, $40 for extra maps and books can be money well spent.

If you'll be traveling elsewhere in Spain or to neighboring countries, consider *Rick Steves' Spain, Rick Steves' Portugal,* and *Rick Steves' France.* The following books are worthwhile, though most are not updated annually; check the publication date before you buy. Lonely Planet's guide to Spain is well researched, with good maps and hotel recommendations for low- to moderate-budget travelers. The similar *Rough Guide to Spain* is hip and insightful, written by British researchers. Students and vagabonds like the highly opinionated *Let's Go: Spain & Portugal,* updated by Harvard students. *Let's Go* is best for backpackers who stay at hostels, use railpasses, and dive into the youth and nightlife scene.

The Eyewitness series has about a dozen editions covering Spain, including Barcelona, Madrid, and Sevilla/Andalucía. They're extremely popular for great, easy-to-grasp graphics and photos, but the written content in Eyewitness is relatively skimpy, and the books weigh a ton. I simply borrow them for a minute from other travelers at certain sights to make sure I'm aware of that place's highlights. Time Out travel guides provide good, detailed coverage of Barcelona, Madrid, and Andalucía, particularly on arts and entertainment.

The popular skinny Michelin Green Guides to Spain are excellent, especially if you're driving. They're known for their city and sightseeing maps, dry but concise and helpful information on major sights, and good cultural and historical background. English editions, covering most of the regions you'll want to visit, are sold in Spain.

I like Cadogan guides for their well-presented background information and coverage of cultural issues. Their recommendations suit upscale travelers. Older travelers enjoy Frommer's Spain guides, even though these, like the Fodor's guides, ignore alternatives that enable travelers to save money by dirtying their fingers in the local culture. The encyclopedic Blue Guides are dry as the plains in Spain, but just right for arty and scholarly types.

Recommended Books and Movies

Barcelona bristles with history, art, and culture. To deepen your knowledge of the city's past and present, check out some of these books and films.

Nonfiction

Dense and detailed, Robert Hughes' *Barcelona* is an opinionated journey through the city's tumultuous history, with a focus on art and architecture. *Barcelona: The Great Enchantress,* a more condensed version of his earlier book, is Hughes' love song to his favorite city.

Barcelona: A Thousand Years of the City's Past (Fernandez-Armesto) gives a historical and artistic perspective on Barcelona's culture while detailing the tensions between the city and the rest of Spain. Another rich history of Barcelona is *Homage to Barcelona* (Toibin), which includes the author's anecdotes from his time there since the 1970s.

George Orwell traveled to Barcelona where he traded his press pass for a uniform, fought against Franco's Fascists in the Spanish Civil War of 1936-1939 (and was nearly killed), and then wrote a gripping account of his experiences in *Homage to Catalonia.* The political climate during the Civil War is chronicled in *The Battle for Spain* (Beevor).

Spain has undergone incredible changes since the death of Franco in 1975 and the end of his nearly four-decade dictatorship. *The New Spaniards* (Hooper) is a survey of all aspects of modern Spain, including its politics, economy, demographics, education, religion, and popular culture.

James Michener traveled to Spain for several decades, and his tribute, *Iberia,* describes how Spain's dark history created a contradictory and passionately beautiful land.

Travelers' Tales: Spain (McCauley) offers dozens of essays about Spain and its people from numerous authors.

Penelope Casas has written many popular books on the food of Spain, including tapas, paella, and regional cooking. Her *Discovering Spain: An Uncommon Guide* blends references to history, culture, and food with travel information.

Fiction

Carmen Laforet's *Nada* details the experiences of an orphaned university student in the 1940s who discovers the haunting reality of post-Civil War Barcelona.

Ernest Hemingway's *For Whom the Bell Tolls*, a tale of idealism and harsh reality, is set against the complexity of the Spanish Civil War. That ugly period of Spanish history is also the subject of *The*

Carpenter's Pencil (Rivas), an unsentimental tale of an imprisoned revolutionary haunted by his past.

Set in the early 20th century, Josep M. de Sagarra's *Vida Privada* (Private Life) exposes dark events and scandal among Barcelona's bourgeoisie.

Themes of power, greed, and money permeate *The City of Marvels* (Mendoza), about a young man who rises from poverty in Barcelona.

The best-selling thriller, *The Shadow of the Wind* (Zafón), takes place in 1950s Barcelona; sequels include *The Angel's Game* and *The Prisoner of Heaven*.

Cathedral of the Sea (Falcones) tells the story of a humble medieval *bastaixo* who toils to build the Church of Santa Maria del Mar in El Born and gradually climbs the social ladder of medieval Barcelona.

Films

In *The Mystery of Picasso* (1956), Picasso is filmed painting from behind a transparent canvas, allowing a unique look at his creative process.

L'auberge Espagnole (2002) tells the story of the loves and lives of European students sharing an apartment in Barcelona.

In *Barcelona* (1994), two Americans in Spain try to navigate the Spanish singles scene and the ensuing culture clash.

Woody Allen's *Vicky Cristina Barcelona* (2008) stars Javier Bardem as a macho Spanish artist romancing two American women, when suddenly his stormy ex-wife (Penélope Cruz, in an Oscar-winning role) re-enters his life.

Pedro Almodóvar's piquant films about relationships in the post-Franco era have garnered piles of international awards. Spanish actors Bardem, Cruz, and Antonio Banderas have starred in his films. Almodóvar's best-known films include *Women on the Verge of a Nervous Breakdown* (1988), *All About My Mother* (1999), *Talk to Her* (2002), *Volver* (2006), and *Broken Embraces* (2009).

Salvador (2006) uses Barcelona as a backdrop for its story about the life of Salvador Puig Antich, an anarchist and bank robber executed by Franco in the 1970s.

Manuale d'Amore (2007), a love story starring Monica Bellucci, illuminates the cities of Barcelona and Rome as several couples come together across four episodes.

Holidays and Festivals

This list includes selected festivals in Barcelona, plus national holidays observed throughout Spain. Many sights and banks close on national holidays—keep this in mind when planning your itinerary. Before planning a trip around a festival, verify its dates by checking the festival's website or TI sites (www.spain.info); www.whatsonwhen.com also lists many festival dates. For more on Barcelona's festivals and feast days, see "City of Festivals" sidebar on page 33. For sports events, see www.sportsevents365.com.

Be prepared for big crowds during these holiday periods: Holy Week (Semana Santa) and Easter weekend; Labor Day; Ascension; Pentecost weekend; Assumption weekend; Spanish National Day; Constitution Day, followed closely by the Feast of the Immaculate Conception—both the previous and following weekends may be busy; and Christmas and New Year's. Look out for any local holiday that falls on a Tuesday or Thursday—the Spanish will often take Monday or Friday off as well to have a four-day weekend.

Jan 1	New Year's Day
Jan 6	Epiphany
Mid-Feb	Les Festes de Santa Eulàlia (parades, kid-friendly activities)
Holy Week	March 24-30 in 2013, April 13-19 in 2014
Easter	March 31 in 2013, April 20 in 2014
Easter Monday	April 1 in 2013, April 21 in 2014
April 23	St. George's Day
May 1	Labor Day (closures)
Ascension	May 9 in 2013, May 29 in 2014
Pentecost weekend	May 17-19 in 2013, June 6-8 in 2014
Corpus Christi	May 30 in 2013, June 19 in 2014
June-July	Grec Festival (music, arts)
June-Aug	Música als Parcs (jazz, classical music)
June 23	Festival of St. John the Baptist (bonfires, fireworks)
Mid-July	Montjuïc de Nit (music, arts)
Mid-Aug	Festes de Sant Roc (street festival)
Mid-Aug	Festa Major de Gràcia (music, dancing, food, and drink)
Aug 15	Assumption of Mary (religious festival)

APPENDIX

Aug 21-27	(major festivities on Aug 23-24) St. Bartholomew Festival, Sitges (carnival, traditional Catalan entertainments)
Sept 23	St. Tecla Festival, Sitges (fireworks, *castellers*)
Late Sept	La Mercè Festival (fireworks, parades, music)
Oct 12	Spanish National Day
Nov 1	All Saints' Day
Dec 6	Constitution Day
Dec 8	Feast of the Immaculate Conception
Dec 13	Feast of Santa Lucía
Dec 25	Christmas
Dec 31	New Year's Eve

Conversions and Climate

Numbers and Stumblers

- Europeans write a few of their numbers differently than we do. 1 = 1, 4 = 4, 7 = 7.
- In Europe, dates appear as day/month/year, so Christmas is 25/12/14.
- Commas are decimal points and decimals commas. A dollar and a half is 1,50, and there are 5.280 feet in a mile.
- When pointing, use your whole hand, palm down.
- When counting with fingers, start with your thumb. If you hold up your first finger to request one item, you'll probably get two.
- What Americans call the second floor of a building is the first floor in Europe.
- On escalators and moving sidewalks, Europeans keep the left "lane" open for passing. Keep to the right.

Metric Conversions

A kilogram is 2.2 pounds, and 1 liter is about a quart, or almost four to a gallon. A kilometer is six-tenths of a mile. I figure kilometers to miles by cutting the kilometers in half and adding back 10 percent of the original (120 km: 60 + 12 = 72 miles, 300 km: 150 + 30 = 180 miles).

1 foot = 0.3 meter	1 square yard = 0.8 square meter
1 yard = 0.9 meter	1 square mile = 2.6 square kilometers
1 mile = 1.6 kilometers	1 ounce = 28 grams
1 centimeter = 0.4 inch	1 quart = 0.95 liter
1 meter = 39.4 inches	1 kilogram = 2.2 pounds
1 kilometer = 0.62 mile	32°F = 0°C

Clothing Sizes

When shopping for clothing, use these US-to-European comparisons as general guidelines (but note that no conversion is perfect).

- Women's dresses and blouses: Add 30
  (US size 10 = European size 40)
- Men's suits and jackets: Add 10
  (US size 40 regular = European size 50)
- Men's shirts: Multiply by 2 and add about 8
  (US size 15 collar = European size 38)
- Women's shoes: Add about 30
  (US size 8 = European size 38½)
- Men's shoes: Add 32-34
  (US size 9 = European size 41; US size 11 = European size 45)

Barcelona's Climate

First line, average daily high; second line, average daily low; third line, average days without rain. For more detailed weather statistics for destinations in this book (as well as the rest of the world), check www.worldclimate.com.

J	F	M	A	M	J	J	A	S	O	N	D
55°	57°	60°	65°	71°	78°	82°	82°	77°	69°	62°	56°
43°	45°	48°	52°	57°	65°	69°	69°	66°	58°	51°	46°
26	23	23	21	23	24	27	25	23	22	24	25

Temperature Conversion: Fahrenheit and Celsius

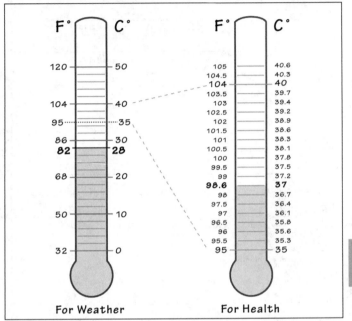

For Weather   For Health

Europe takes its temperature using the Celsius scale, while we opt for Fahrenheit. For a rough conversion from Celsius to Fahrenheit, double the number and add 30. For weather, remember that 28°C is 82°F—perfect. For health, 37°C is just right.

Hotel Reservation

To: _____   _____
        hotel   *email or fax*

From: _____   _____
          name   *email or fax*

Today's date: _____ /_____ /_____
              day   *month*   *year*

Dear Hotel _____ ,
Please make this reservation for me:

Name: _____

Total # of people: _____   # of rooms: _____   # of nights: _____

Arriving: _____ /_____ /_____   My time of arrival (24-hr clock): _____
          day *month* *year*   (I will telephone if I will be late)

Departing: ____ /____ /_____
           day *month* *year*

Room(s): Single____   Double ____   Twin ____   Triple ____   Quad____

With: Toilet _____   Shower_____   Bath _____   Sink only____

Special needs: View____   Quiet____   Cheapest ____   Ground Floor____

Please email or fax confirmation of my reservation, along with the type of
room reserved and the price. Please also inform me of your cancellation
policy. After I hear from you, I will quickly send my credit-card information
as a deposit to hold the room. Thank you.

_____
Name

_____
Address

_____
City   *State*   *Zip Code*   *Country*

*Before hoteliers can make your reservation, they want to know the informa-
tion listed above. You can use this form as the basis for your email, or you can
photocopy this page, fill in the information, and send it as a fax (also available
online at www.ricksteves.com/reservation).*

Packing Checklist

Whether you're traveling for five days or five weeks, here's what you'll need to bring. Pack light to enjoy the sweet freedom of true mobility. Happy travels!

- ❑ 5 shirts: long- and short-sleeve
- ❑ 1 sweater or lightweight fleece
- ❑ 2 pairs pants
- ❑ 1 pair shorts
- ❑ 1 swimsuit
- ❑ 5 pairs underwear and socks
- ❑ 1 pair shoes
- ❑ 1 rainproof jacket with hood
- ❑ Tie or scarf
- ❑ Money belt
- ❑ Money—your mix of:
  - ❑ Debit card (for ATM withdrawals)
  - ❑ Credit card
  - ❑ Hard cash (in easy-to-exchange $20 bills)
- ❑ Documents plus photo-copies:
  - ❑ Passport
  - ❑ Printout of airline eticket
  - ❑ Driver's license
  - ❑ Student ID and hostel card
  - ❑ Railpass/car rental voucher
  - ❑ Insurance details
- ❑ Daypack
- ❑ Electronics—your choice of:
  - ❑ Camera (and related gear)
  - ❑ Computer/mobile devices (phone, MP3 player, ereader, etc.)
  - ❑ Chargers for each of the above
  - ❑ Plug adapter
- ❑ Empty water bottle

- ❑ Wristwatch and alarm clock
- ❑ Earplugs
- ❑ Toiletries kit
  - ❑ Toiletries
  - ❑ Medicines and vitamins
  - ❑ First-aid kit
  - ❑ Glasses/contacts/sunglasses (with prescriptions)
- ❑ Sealable plastic baggies
- ❑ Laundry soap
- ❑ Clothesline
- ❑ Small towel
- ❑ Sewing kit
- ❑ Travel information (guide-books and maps)
- ❑ Address list (for sending postcards)
- ❑ Postcards and photos from home
- ❑ Notepad and pen
- ❑ Journal

If you plan to carry on your luggage, note that all liquids must be in 3.4-ounce or smaller containers and fit within a single quart-size sealable baggie. For details, see www.tsa.gov/travelers.

Spanish Survival Phrases

Spanish has a guttural sound similar to the J in Baja California. In the phonetics, the symbol for this clearing-your-throat sound is the italicized *h*.

Good day.	Buenos días.	**bway**-nohs **dee**-ahs
Do you speak English?	¿Habla Usted inglés?	**ah**-blah oo-**stehd** een-**glays**
Yes. / No.	Sí. / No.	see / noh
I (don't) understand.	(No) comprendo.	(noh) kohm-**prehn**-doh
Please.	Por favor.	por fah-**bor**
Thank you.	Gracias.	**grah**-thee-ahs
I'm sorry.	Lo siento.	loh see-**ehn**-toh
Excuse me.	Perdóneme.	pehr-**doh**-nay-may
(No) problem.	(No) problema.	(noh) proh-**blay**-mah
Good.	Bueno.	**bway**-noh
Goodbye.	Adiós.	ah-dee-**ohs**
one / two	uno / dos	**oo**-noh / dohs
three / four	tres / cuatro	trays / **kwah**-troh
five / six	cinco / seis	**theen**-koh / says
seven / eight	siete / ocho	see-**eh**-tay / **oh**-choh
nine / ten	nueve / diez	**nway**-bay / dee-**ayth**
How much is it?	¿Cuánto cuesta?	**kwahn**-toh **kway**-stah
Write it?	¿Me lo escribe?	may loh ay-**skree**-bay
Is it free?	¿Es gratis?	ays **grah**-tees
Is it included?	¿Está incluido?	ay-**stah** een-kloo-**ee**-doh
Where can I buy / find...?	¿Dónde puedo comprar / encontrar...?	**dohn**-day **pway**-doh kohm-**prar** / ayn-kohn-**trar**
I'd like / We'd like...	Quiero / Queremos...	kee-**ehr**-oh / kehr-**ay**-mohs
...a room.	...una habitación.	**oo**-nah ah-bee-tah-thee-**ohn**
...a ticket to ___.	...un billete para ___.	oon bee-**yeh**-tay **pah**-rah
Is it possible?	¿Es posible?	ays poh-**see**-blay
Where is...?	¿Dónde está...?	**dohn**-day ay-**stah**
...the train station	...la estación de trenes	lah ay-stah-thee-**ohn** day **tray**-nays
...the bus station	...la estación de autobuses	lah ay-stah-thee-**ohn** day ow-toh-**boo**-says
...the tourist information office	...la oficina de turismo	lah oh-fee-**thee**-nah day too-**rees**-moh
Where are the toilets?	¿Dónde están los servicios?	**dohn**-day ay-**stahn** lohs sehr-**bee**-thee-ohs
men	hombres, caballeros	**ohm**-brays, kah-bah-**yay**-rohs
women	mujeres, damas	moo-*heh*-rays, **dah**-mahs
left / right	izquierda / derecha	eeth-kee-**ehr**-dah / day-**ray**-chah
straight	derecho	day-**ray**-choh
When do you open / close?	¿A qué hora abren / cierran?	ah kay **oh**-rah **ah**-brehn / thee-**ay**-rahn
At what time?	¿A qué hora?	ah kay **oh**-rah
Just a moment.	Un momento.	oon moh-**mehn**-toh
now / soon / later	ahora / pronto / más tarde	ah-**oh**-rah / **prohn**-toh / mahs **tar**-day
today / tomorrow	hoy / mañana	oy / mahn-**yah**-nah

In a Spanish Restaurant

I'd like / We'd like...	Quiero / Queremos...	kee-**ehr**-oh / kehr-**ay**-mohs
...to reserve...	...reservar...	ray-sehr-**bar**
...a table for	...una mesa para	oo-nah **may**-sah **pah**-rah
one / two.	uno / dos.	**oo**-noh / dohs
Non-smoking.	No fumador.	noh foo-mah-**dohr**
Is this table free?	¿Está esta mesa libre?	ay-**stah** ay-stah **may**-sah lee-br?
The menu (in English), please.	La carta (en inglés), por favor.	lah **kar**-tah (ayn een-**glays**) por fah-**bor**
service (not) included	servicio (no) incluido	sehr-**bee**-thee-oh (noh) een-kloo-**ee**-doh
cover charge	precio de entrada	**pray**-thee-oh day ayn-**trah**-dah
to go	para llevar	**pah**-rah yay-**bar**
with / without	con / sin	kohn / seen
and / or	y / o	ee / oh
fixed-price meal (of the day)	menú (del día)	may-**noo** (dayl **dee**-ah)
specialty of the house	especialidad de la casa	ay-spay-thee-ah-lee-**dahd** day lah **kah**-sah
tourist menu	menú turístico	meh-**noo** too-**ree**-stee-koh
combination plate	plato combinado	**plah**-toh kohm-bee-**nah**-doh
appetizers	tapas	**tah**-pahs
bread	pan	pahn
cheese	queso	**kay**-soh
sandwich	bocadillo	boh-kah-**dee**-yoh
soup	sopa	**soh**-pah
salad	ensalada	ayn-sah-**lah**-dah
meat	carne	**kar**-nay
poultry	aves	**ah**-bays
fish	pescado	pay-**skah**-doh
seafood	marisco	mah-**ree**-skoh
fruit	fruta	**froo**-tah
vegetables	verduras	behr-**doo**-rahs
dessert	postres	**poh**-strays
tap water	agua del grifo	**ah**-gwah dayl **gree**-foh
mineral water	agua mineral	**ah**-gwah mee-nay-**rahl**
milk	leche	**lay**-chay
(orange) juice	zumo (de naranja)	**thoo**-moh (day nah-**rahn**-hah)
coffee	café	kah-**feh**
tea	té	tay
wine	vino	**bee**-noh
red / white	tinto / blanco	**teen**-toh / **blahn**-koh
glass / bottle	vaso / botella	**bah**-soh / boh-**tay**-yah
beer	cerveza	thehr-**bay**-thah
Cheers!	¡Salud!	sah-**lood**
More. / Another.	Más. / Otro.	mahs / **oh**-troh
The same.	El mismo.	ehl **mees**-moh
The bill, please.	La cuenta, por favor.	lah **kwayn**-tah por fah-**bor**
tip	propina	proh-**pee**-nah
Delicious!	¡Delicioso!	day-lee-thee-**oh**-soh

For many more pages of survival phrases for your trip to Spain, check out *Rick Steves' Spanish Phrase Book*

Catalan Survival Phrases

Catalan may look similar to Spanish (*castellano*), but there are important variations in pronunciation. The letter **e** is often pronounced closer to "a," and the letters **c** and **z** before vowels are pronounced as "s" (unlike the Spanish "th" sound). The letters **b**, **d**, **r**, or **t** at the end of a word are usually not pronounced (unless the final syllable is stressed). An **s** between two vowels sounds like a "z."

Hello.	**Hola.**	oh-lah
Do you speak English?	**Parla anglès?**	par-lah ahn-**glays**
Yes. / No.	**Sí. / No.**	see / noh
I (don't) understand.	**(No) entenc.**	(noh) ahn-**tehnk**
Please.	**Si us plau.**	see oos plow
Thank you (very much).	**(Moltes) Gràcies.**	(**mohl**-tahs) grah-see-ahs
You're welcome.	**De res.**	dah rehs
Excuse me.	**Perdó.**	pahr-**doh**
I'm sorry.	**Ho sento.**	oo **sehn**-too
(No) problem.	**(Cap) problema.**	(kahp) pruh-**bleh**-mah
Good.	**Bé.**	bay
Goodbye.	**Adéu.**	ah-**day**-oo
one / two	**un / dos**	oon / dohs
three / four	**tres / quatre**	trehs / **kwah**-trah
five / six	**cinc / sis**	seenk / sees
seven / eight	**set / vuit**	seht / **voo**-eet
nine / ten	**nou / deu**	**noh**-oo / **deh**-oo
hundred / thousand	**cent / mil**	sehn / meel
How much?	**Quant és?**	kwahn ehs
local currency	**euro**	**eh**-oo-roh
Write it.	**M'ho escriu?**	moh ah-**skree**-oo
Is it free?	**És gratis?**	ehs **grah**-tees
Is it included?	**Està inclós?**	ah-**stah** ihn-**klohs**
Where can I find / buy...?	**On puc trobar / comprar...?**	ohn pook troo-**bah** / koom-**prah**
I'd like...	**Voldria...**	vool-**dree**-ah
We'd like...	**Voldríem...**	vool-**dree**-ahm
...a room.	**...una habitació**	oo-nah ah-bee-tah-see-**oh**
...a ticket to ___.	**...una entrada per ___.**	oo-nah ahn-**trah**-dah pahr ___
Is it possible?	**És possible?**	ehs poo-**see**-blah
Where is...?	**On està...?**	ohn ah-**stah**
...the train station	**...l'estació del tren**	lah-stah-see-**oh** dahl trehn
...the bus station	**...l'estació d'autobus**	lah-stah-see-**oh** dow-toh-**boos**
...the tourist information office	**...l'oficina de turisme**	loo-fee-**see**-nah dah too-**reez**-mah
...the toilet	**...els serveis**	ahls sahr-**vays**
men / women	**homes / dones**	**oh**-mahs / **doh**-nahs
left / right	**esquerre / dreta**	ahs-**keh**-reh / **dreh**-tah
straight	**dret**	dreht
At what time...?	**A quina hora...?**	ah **kee**-nah **oh**-rah
...does this open / close	**...obre / tanca**	**oh**-brah / **tahn**-kah
Just a moment.	**Un moment.**	oon moo-**mehn**
now / soon / later	**ara / aviat / més tard**	**ah**-rah / ah-vee-**aht** / mehs tahrd
today / tomorrow	**avui / demà**	ah-**vwee** / dah-**mah**
Long live Catalunya!	**¡Visca Catalunya!**	**vee**-skah kah-tah-**loon**-yah

In the Restaurant

I'd like to reserve...	**Voldria reservar...**	vool-**dree**-ah rah-sahr-**vah**
We'd like to reserve...	**Voldríem reservar...**	vool-**dree**-ahm rah-sahr-**vah**
...a table for one person / two people.	**...una taula per una persona / dues persones**	**oo**-nah **tow**-lah pahr **oo**-nah pahr-**soh**-nah / doo-**ehs** pahr-**soh**-nahs
Is this table free?	**Està lliure aquesta taula?**	ah-**stah** yoo-rah ah-**kwehs**-tah **tow**-lah
Can I help you?	**El puc ajudar?**	ahl pook ah-zhoo-**dah**
The menu (in English), please.	**La carta (en anglès), si us plau.**	lah **kar**-tah (ahn ahn-**glays**) see oos plow
service (not) included	**servei (no) inclós**	sahr-**vayee** (noh) ihn-**klohs**
cover charge	**preu d'entrada**	**preh**oo dahn-**trah**-dah
"to go"	**per emportar**	pahr ahm-por-**tah**
with / without	**amb / sense**	ahm / **sehn**-sah
and / or	**i / o**	ee / oh
tapas (small plates)	**tapes**	**tah**-pahs
fixed-price meal (of the day)	**menú del dia**	mah-**noo** dahl **dee**-ah
daily special	**plat del dia**	plaht dahl **dee**-ah
tourist menu	**menú turístic**	mah-**noo** too-**ree**-steek
combination plate	**plat combinat**	plaht koom-bee-**naht**
specialty of the house	**especialitat de la casa**	ah-spah-see-ah-lee-**taht** dah lah **kah**-zah
half portion	**mitja porció**	**meet**-yah poor-see-**oh**
appetizers	**entrants**	ahn-**trahns**
bread	**pà**	pah
cheese	**formatge**	foor-**mah**-jah
sandwich	**entrepà**	ahn-trah-**pah**
soup	**sopa**	**soh**-pah
salad	**amanida**	ah-mah-**nee**-dah
meat	**carn**	karn
poultry	**aviram**	ah-vee-**rahm**
fish	**peix**	paysh
seafood	**marisc**	mah-**reesk**
fruit	**fruita**	**froo**ee-tah
vegetables	**verdures**	vahr-**doo**-rahs
dessert	**postres**	**poh**-strahs
(tap) water	**aigua (de l'aixeta)**	**eye**-wah (dah lah-**shay**-tah)
mineral water	**aigua mineral**	**eye**-wah mee-nah-**rahl**
carbonated / not carbonated	**amb gas / sense gas**	ahm gahs / **sehn**-sah gahs
milk	**llet**	yeht
(orange) juice	**suc (de taronja)**	sook (dah tah-**rohn**-zhah)
coffee	**cafè**	kah-**feh**
tea	**te**	teh
wine	**vi**	vee
red / white	**negre / blanc**	**neh**-grah / blahnk
sweet / dry / semi-dry	**dolç / sec / semi-sec**	dohls / sehk / **seh**-mee sehk
glass / bottle	**copa / ampolla**	**koh**-pah / ahm-**poy**-yah
beer	**cervesa**	sahr-**veh**-zah
Cheers!	**Salut!**	sah-**loot**
Enjoy your meal.	**Bon profit.**	bohn proo-**feet**
More. / Another.	**Més. / Un altre.**	mehs / oon **ahl**-trah
The same.	**El mateix.**	ahl mah-**taysh**
the bill	**el compte**	ahl **kohmp**-tah
tip	**propina**	proo-**pee**-nah
Delicious!	**Boníssim!**	boo-**nee**-seem

INDEX

INDEX

MAP INDEX

Audio Europe

Rick's Free Travel App

Get your FREE **Rick Steves Audio Europe**™ app to enjoy...

- Dozens of self-guided tours of Europe's top museums, sights and historic walks

- Hundreds of tracks filled with cultural insights and sightseeing tips from Rick's radio interviews

- All organized into handy geographic playlists

- For iPhone, iPad, iPod Touch, Android

With Rick whispering in your ear, Europe gets even better.

Find out more at ricksteves.com